Sartre and
his Predecessors

Sartre and his Predecessors
The Self and the Other

William Ralph Schroeder

*University of Illinois
at Urbana-Champaign*

Routledge & Kegan Paul
London, Boston, Melbourne and Henley

First published in 1984
by Routledge & Kegan Paul plc

14 Leicester Square, London WC2H 7PH,
England

9 Park Street, Boston, Mass. 02108, USA

464 St Kilda Road, Melbourne,
Victoria 3004, Australia and

Broadway House, Newtown Road,
Henley-on-Thames, Oxon RG9 1EN, England

Set in IBM Press Roman by
Cambrian Typesetters, Aldershot, Hants.
and printed in Great Britain by
The Thetford Press Ltd, Thetford,
Norfolk
Copyright © William Ralph Schroeder 1984

Library of Congress Cataloging in Publication Data

Schroeder, William Ralph.

Sartre and his predecessors.
Bibliography: p.
Includes index.
1. Sartre, Jean Paul, 1905-
2. Philosophy, Modern. I. Title.
B2430.S34S36 1984   194   84-3394

British Library CIP data available

ISBN 0-7102-0274-1 (c)

For Frithjof Bergmann

To lose oneself is to find oneself;
not to lose oneself is to remain forever lost.

Contents

Contents

Preface

Three aims govern this essay. The first is to examine Jean-Paul Sartre's discussion of the positions of certain of his predecessors on the nature of Others and their relation to oneself, and his presentation of his own theory in his *Being and Nothingness*. Sartre organizes his discussions of Husserl, Hegel, and Heidegger in such a way as to show that their positions progressively develop toward and culminate in his own; his position allegedly resolves their inadequacies. Unfortunately, this manner of presentation leads Sartre to some misleading interpretations and inadequate assessments of the contributions of his predecessors. The second aim of this essay is therefore to develop original interpretations and critical evaluations of Husserl, Hegel, and Heidegger on the above topic, correcting Sartre's oversights and misreadings, and to explore the full significance of their positions. Its third aim is then to work out an account drawing upon and doing justice to the achievements of these four philosophers.

The difference between this essay and Sartre's discussion is that I do not begin with a position to be established and thus need not distort previous theories. I examine each theory from within the perspective of its own general project. Although I do not hestitate to criticize even the most basic assumptions, I do seek to understand the importance of the differences in approach that result from them. These thinkers do not address one well-defined, commonly shared question; rather, their basic theoretical tasks determine the questions they pose and the answers they seek. Thus, their differing conclusions are often answers to different questions rather than incompatible answers to the same question. I seek to integrate the best insights of each philosopher and to fashion a new understanding of the relationships between oneself and Others.

I begin with a preliminary orientation to the theories of Husserl, Hegel, Heidegger, and Sartre. Their positions are contrasted with the Cartesian picture and with selected theories in the Anglo-American tradition. I then offer a thorough examination of the positions of Husserl (Chapter 1), Hegel (Chapter 2), and Heidegger (Chapter 3), and of Sartre's reactions to them. Sartre's own discussion determined this order of presentation. Next is an exposition and critique of Sartre's own theory (Chapter 4), which is divided into three separate sections: the phenomenological base — which explicates the modes in which the Other appears and their implications; the transcendental argument — which explores one's lived certainty of the existence of Others; and the bond between self and Other — which explores the status of the entity that both unites and separates persons: the social self. I conclude with a sketch of a full-blown alternative to the Cartesian picture that can guide further phenomenological research into intersubjectivity (Chapter 5).

My discussions of Husserl, Hegel, and Heidegger are multi-layered: first, my reading of the philosopher's position is presented; then Sartre's reading of him is described and assessed; Sartre's critique of him is then thoroughly examined; finally, my critical evaluation of the philosopher is offered. Instead of interlacing an already multi-layered text with quotations, I have provided textual justification for my assertions in the notes. Also, instead of merely citing the page, I quote the passage on which the assertion is based and, where necessary, append a brief discussion of it. This technique affords maximum ease for those who seek to simply read through the text, while offering the scholar an opportunity to assess my claims immediately because the relevant quotations are readily at hand. I hope the needs of all readers are adequately served by this approach.

Why write about the experience of Others and interpersonal relationships? There are two kinds of reasons — cultural and intellectual.

Consider some cultural facts. Personal relationships are troubled: divorces are increasing; families are breaking apart; friendships exit under great strains; temporary romances remain unfulfilling. We oscillate between a desperate effort to commit ourselves completely and an insistence on remaining islands unto ourselves. Even for those who try hardest and care most, interpersonal relationships seem only to touch the surface; at best they leave one unharmed; more often they debilitate and disorient. Although interpersonal life promises a full-course meal, for many it provides only a series of appetizers.[1]

A related fact is the lowered expectations people have for relationships. Careers take precedence; relationships are sacrificed. Injunctions to be individual, authentic, and concerned only about oneself are hawked from street corners by self-help proselytizers. One becomes convinced that one must continually oppose Others if one is to remain oneself. One trusts very few; from the rest one hopes for indifference rather than resistance. As our hopes diminish, our efforts to create radiant relationships are abandoned, and a cycle of entropy ensues. If one is fortunate, one may find one person with whom one can escape the deterioration of most social life. But in the absence of a supportive milieu, even that relationship may wither. The depth of the problem is indicated by our lack of imagination in posing solutions.

These phenomena undoubtedly have many causes: economic, technological, sociological, etc. My concern in this essay will be with the ideational or intellectual causes and presuppositions of this interpersonal ambiance. My guiding hypothesis is that a set of interrelated ideas most often associated with Cartesianism in philosophy has become accepted as "common sense" and functions as the rails along which our thoughts about Others run. This Cartesian picture underlies the sense of untranscendable distance between persons, the sense of perpetual isolation we feel, and the sense that the primordial impact of Others is oppressive. By challenging this picture, I hope to progress toward a new vision through which these conceptions can be superseded.[2]

Intellectual issues are the second motivation of this enterprise. The questions I seek to answer lie at the foundations of social science and ethics. One's conception of the nature of Others determines what can be observed and known about them and what procedures of inquiry can be most productive. One's position on the nature of interpersonal relations (e.g., are individuals basic units?) determines what social entities should be investigated. These issues are central, even if implicit, in any social scientific inquiry. Too often they are not carefully investigated before research designs are proposed or before theoretical edifices are erected. I seek to reopen these questions and commence more sustained inquiry into them. Although my conclusions will have most direct bearing on social psychology, they are also relevant to sociology, psychoanalysis, and anthropology.

In addition, the importance people give to ethics and politics depends on the adequacy with which they grasp the reality of Others and the clarity with which they understand their relationships to Others. If one does not or cannot experience the presence and personhood of Others, then ethical and political thought becomes merely academic. A thorough investigation of the problems and possibilities of one's relationships to Others can renew ethical and political theory. Too often political theory has assumed the worst about the nature of man and accepted myths about the origin of society in order to design and justify political institutions, and then those institutions have created the kind of person for which they were designed. Concrete exploration of interpersonal experience can provide a more adequate foundation for political theory.[3] Moreover, if ethics is to discover realizable ideals and to seriously address the contemporary interpersonal situation, an incisive phenomenology of interpersonal experience will be indispensable.

In our experience, Others seem so close; yet in our thinking, they remain remote. Our theories about Others follow familiar paths; on them we remain blinded, and as if looking into the sun. Our experience would guide us in different directions if only it could be seen.

A friend sits across the table; we are eating together. His presence fills the room with a characteristic color and tone; everything I do responds to those qualities. I live amidst them as I breathe air. We need hardly speak; muttered phrases constitute complex turns of thought and feeling. His style reveals his deepest secrets: I know his fundamental dissatisfaction with himself and his hesitant efforts to dance about the abyss. His care and earnestness buoy me, whether his tone is harsh or encouraging. He lives within me; I speak with his voice in conversations with different people or in ruminations at my desk on lonely nights. When he is hurt, I feel the pain; when life treats him well, I celebrate. I could not be what I am without him. I am more fully myself when I am with him than when I am alone.

Against this experience, contrast the analysis of Others that theory offers:

The Other is over there where his body is. He is separated from me by all the distance that separates our bodies. This distance becomes astronomical if I consider the space between his mind (which lies deep within his body) and mine (which lies deep within mine).

More distant than a galaxy is the Other's experience.

I am I; Others are other. I live in my body; he in his. Bodies are stable, self-contained fortresses. Since persons reside in bodies, they are enclosed, independent creatures. The person is like a little man inside the body who looks out through its eyes. The Other's body is like a cinematographic image for this little man. Although I can see the Other's body, I cannot see either his little man or what that man sees.

Persons are self-sufficient, hermetic universes.

I am myself. I begin to lose myself whenever I become like Others. Since they are not me, to be like them is not to be me. I am most myself when I am the whole source of my life. If I fall under Others' influence, I cannot be wholly myself; I get displaced. To be the person I am, I must isolate myself as much as possible and create a voice with which no one else has ever spoken.

Essentially Others oppress; struggle is needed to remain oneself.

When I speak, my words mean one thing to me and something quite different to the Other. His experience with the words differs from mine. Miraculously, we understand one another, but this depends on a mutual, unspoken agreement not to look too closely. The problem is exacerbated when we are deciphering one another's actions and gestures. Even if I look melancholy to him, I may feel ebullient. Even if he intends to offer affection when he slaps me, I may feel insulted. Outer and inner: the inner is always privileged because it is me; the outer is always something other, distinct, merely for the Other.

Talmudic machinations are needed to grasp even pedestrian words and gestures.

I live alongside Others. They have their goals; I have mine. If I am incomplete, I may be attracted to her; she may supply what I lack and vice versa. Such symbiosis makes the world revolve. Purposes may coalesce, but persons remain distinct. If someone new fills me fuller, I may detach myself from one molecule and join to make another. Persons are like atoms. My atomic structure remains intact no matter what molecule absorbs me. I remain myself with one or with another or with no one. Separations may be painful, but they do not alter what I am.

Human society is constituted by more extended associations. If purposes collide, there is struggle; if they harmonize, there is peace. My life is my own; I accept another's command only because he offers more in return than I can provide myself. I am entitled to his products only because I produce something for him. Society is a system of larger-order molecules existing in more complex symbioses; its basic units are individual persons.

Human relationships are temporary associations of self-sufficient monads whose natures are unaffected by the bonds.

Thus speaks theory.

If I now try to recall eating dinner next to my friend, only the dimmest shadows remain. I may even redescribe what I then experienced so that it conforms to these homespun reflections. Theory may proclaim that I cannot *really* know him, do not *really* commune with him, cannot *truly* be myself through him, am not *genuinely* altered by my relationship to him. With this stroke, the light of theory blinds our sight.

What is needed instead is an insistence on seeing, on quieting the chattering voice that speaks so reasonably, so that what is there can show itself.[4]

European philosophy since Hegel has struggled to move in that direction. This essay explores that itinerary.

Acknowledgments

My greatest debt is to the man to whom this essay is dedicated, my teacher and friend. His patience, encouragement, and willingness to discuss everything from the smallest detail to the most encompassing quandary were essential to the completion of this project. His ideas have continued to blaze the paths which I find most worth pursuing. Not only his thoughts but his life have inspired much that this essay teaches. Although I have tried to indicate the specific points at which his thoughts have guided my hand, he has helped me in more ways than can possibly ever be acknowledged or repaid.

Many others have helped me directly or indirectly over the many years during which various drafts of this book were being written. Deserving special mention are: Holly Smith Goldman, Richard Mann, Jack W. Meiland, Arthur Melnick, Richard Schacht, and Robert Solomon, all of whom read some or all of the manuscript and made many helpful suggestions and criticisms. Their efforts (together with those of an anonymous referee at Routledge & Kegan Paul) have facilitated many improvements in this book; for whatever flaws remain, I bear sole responsibility.

I wish to express my gratitude to the Danforth Foundation for support during my years as a graduate student and to the University of Illinois Research Board for a grant to pay for the typing, revisions, and photocopying of the final draft.

People support authors in many subtle ways. I have been fortunate in having several long-term friends whose voices often speak through my own and whose affection made the completion of this project possible. I would like to thank them all, but since I cannot mention everyone, I shall have to let these stand for all the rest: Lynne Lubin Bronner, Jennifer Church, John Coker, Roderick Ganiard, Jr, Glenn Horowitz, Ken Kress, Milena Maglic, Cary Nelson, and Arlene Wyman.

I also wish to express my gratitude to my family: Ralph, Adele, and Richard, for their continuing support and to my "second family", Mary Lou Cook and Marion Olden, for sacrificing more for me than I deserved.

Finally, I am grateful for the superb and efficient typing of several people, each of whom typed the entire book at one of its stages of completion: Laura Green, Alice Gantt, and Arletta Lynn.

Grateful acknowledgment is also made to those whose permission was required to make citations in the Notes from English translations of the major texts discussed in this essay:

Excerpts from Edmund Husserl, *Cartesian Meditations: An Introduction to Phenomenology*, trans. by Dorion Cairns (copyright © 1960 by Martinus Nijhoff Publishers BV, ISBN 90-247-0068-X (1977 edn)); reprinted by permission of Martinus Nijhoff.

Excerpts from G.W.F. Hegel, *Hegel's Phenomenology of Spirit*, trans. by A.V. Miller, with analysis and foreword by J.N. Findlay (copyright © Oxford University Press 1977); reprinted by permission of Oxford University Press.

Excerpts from Martin Heidegger, *Being and Time*, trans. by John Macquarrie and Edward Robinson (copyright © 1962 by SCM Press Ltd); reprinted by permission of Harper & Row, Publishers, Inc. and of Basil Blackwell Publisher.

Excerpts from Jean-Paul Sartre, *Being and Nothingness: An Essay on Phenomenological Ontology*, trans. and with an introduction by Hazel E. Barnes (copyright © 1956 by Philosophical Library, Inc.); reprinted by permission of Philosophical Library (via Sanford J. Greenburger Associates Inc.) and of Methuen & Co.

Introduction

The common-sense assumptions about Others described in the Preface derive from a world-view which I shall call "The Cartesian Picture." Although the components of this position have close affinities with the views of Descartes, I will not seek to establish the historical accuracy of this designation. Instead I seek to construct an "ideal type" which has been influential throughout the modern and contemporary periods. It will serve as a heuristic device for clarifying the basic positions of the philosophers to be discussed in this essay and as a benchmark for comparing European and Anglo-American theories about the nature of Others and one's relationship to them. The first task is to clarify the components of the Cartesian picture.

The Cartesian picture

The Cartesian program originates in a search for certain, indubitable propositions. Merely reliable or commonly accepted or well-confirmed propositions are insufficient; only those which *cannot* be doubted or for which doubt is unintelligible constitute genuine knowledge. This standard is extremely high, and *prima facie* it removes most empirical truths, most common sense, and even some formal truths from the realm of knowledge. Armed with this standard, the skeptic can cast aspersion on nearly everything the ordinary person accepts.

Despite this decimation of knowledge, the Cartesian discovers one realm where his standard is satisfied: the realm of one's own mental states. When one is doubting (or thinking), one cannot intelligibly doubt that one is doubting (or thinking). One's mental states are translucent; one seems to have so unmediated a relation to them that no margin for error exists. One does not have this direct, diaphanous relation to any other object of knowledge, and thus no other realm of objects is known as well as one's mental states. Moreover, nothing else has this privileged relationship to one's own states; they constitute a realm of private access which no one else can penetrate. Only this realm is truly, genuinely known.

In addition, the Cartesian takes mental states to be similar to properties

1

in that they must have an object to modify or a substance in which to inhere; they are not self-sufficient. All experiences must be modifications of individual minds; they exist only in so far as they are possessed and apprehended by an owner, a self. Consequently, the certainty of one's own mental states entails the certain existence of a self that possesses them and that remains identical through their changes. This self is taken to be within the body and 'behind' each mental act — looking out over its shoulder to see what it reveals. Since this self is a substance, it is self-sufficient and unaltered by the mental states which qualify it.

The self is typically conceived to be prior to experience and to have a special relation to its own experiences which guarantees its privileged access to them. This relation also individuates one person's act of thinking from another's and ties each mental act to one single person. This self depends on nothing else for its existence. The entire external world may be illusory, and the self would still exist as the necessary possessor of the mental acts which apprehend these illusions. Since the core of a person is his self, and since the self has this self-sufficient, hermetic character, this component of the Cartesian picture will be termed "the monad view of the self (or person)."

These then are the three basic elements of the Cartesian picture: an elevated standard of knowledge — indubitability; a privileged access to one's own mental states — the only realm that clearly satisfies the standard; and the monad view of the self.

These tenets have some important ramifications. The elevated standard of knowledge virtually silences the serious thinker because much that he had previously accepted is no longer legitimate. He becomes intimidated and cautious; the looming specters are that only immediately-present states of mind are known at a particular time and that everything else — including other people, science, nature, history, memories, and testimony — must be abandoned. If nothing beyond the self can be guaranteed by this standard, then only the self can legitimately be said to exist. Solipsism may be an inevitable result of the Cartesian picture. On the one hand, one becomes preoccupied with issues of knowledge; on the other hand, one is severed from the evidence that might resolve one's epistemic dilemmas.

This position breeds various constructivist efforts in which the philosophical task is to derive or justify one's ordinary knowledge from the small set of data that is certified by this standard. If such a derivation cannot be found for a particular type of object, it is consigned to the back wards of both epistemology *and* ontology, the latter *because* of the former. Other persons, especially their own mental states and selves, typically fall into that shadowy area since only they have access to their mental states.

Privileged access entails two other important consequences. First, a sharp distinction between mind and body is instituted because one's physiological and somatic states are not known directly. One conceives mind and body as wholly distinct spheres, each having its own elements and laws, each intersecting and interacting with the other in mysterious ways. One's bodily existence becomes supplementary and dispensable because one's mental life does not seem to require the existence of a body. The importance of that which allows one to act on the world is diminished when the status of that world becomes dubious.

In addition, the privileged access position creates a chasm between the mental state that appears to oneself and the bodily expression or behavior that appears to Others. The mental is inner, primary, superior, veridical, and essentially related to oneself; mere behavior is outer, derivative, inferior, susceptible to misinterpretation and error, and only tangentially related to oneself. Other people can apprehend only this outer 'clothing' of the true inner state. The relation of one to the other is contingent; thus, the Other apprehends only inadequate and cryptic signs of one's inner states. Many outer signs are unrelated to inner states, and many inner states do not manifest themselves in behavior. For the Other, one's outer expressions are already dubious because they are external to his mental acts, but they are doubly problematic because they are secondary and inadequate representations of one's inner states. This position creates a sense of unbridgeable distance between self and Other.[1]

The monad view of the self also has important implications. It provides the primary justification for most forms of individualism. Individual persons are regarded as atomic units from which society is constructed, and they are endowed with rights which cannot be abrogated without consent. Society is regarded as something which exacts prices from self-sufficient, independent individuals in return for providing benefits that they take to be of greater value than these sacrifices. If the individual could provide these benefits for himself, he would have no further need of society. Society and the state exist only through the consent and support of these atomic individuals.

This conception of an individual's relation to society also applies to a person's relation to other individuals. No penetrating relationship between persons is possible because each is a self-sufficient monad and because neither can genuinely know the Other. The relationships that do emerge exist only because the persons involved actively participate in and sustain them. Moreover, the theme of most relationships is struggle to retain one's individuality, for Others are seen as impingements on one's freedom. Because one determines one's life-plan by oneself, Others' main impact can only be to displace or resist it. In so far as one compromises one's own aims because of Others, they subvert one.

Not all elements of this ideal type are explicitly accepted by Descartes, but they all have an obvious affinity with his doctrines. These derivative assertions — the elimination of all that one had previously known, the divisions between mind and body and between inner state and outer expression, and the sense that other persons essentially oppose oneself — all follow naturally from the basic tenets of the Cartesian picture.

This position is the object of attack throughout this essay. Every one of the basic and derivative assertions is contested by one or more of the philosophers examined in this essay. I shall offer an introduction to their alternative positions by comparing the general strategies through which they mount this attack.

Some alternative European approaches

Many European philosophers since Hegel have overcome the difficulties created by the Cartesian picture by questioning its central tenets and by formulating alternative philosophical approaches. In this section, the positions of Husserl, Hegel, Heidegger, and Sartre will be briefly surveyed. These synopses will provide a general orientation to the territory which will later be explored in detail. Since only an overview is intended here, fine-grained amplification of and textual support for these summaries will be postponed until the appropriate chapter.

Husserl

Of all the philosophers I shall examine, Husserl remains the most wedded to the Cartesian picture. He accepts the challenge to discover absolutely certain foundations on which philosophy can erect a genuine science. In addition, he thinks occurrent mental states are directly intuited and that the self is a self-sufficient monad. However, Husserl thinks that there is a third realm of entities, in addition to mental acts and natural objects, to which our access can be adequate once certain procedures are undertaken. These procedures require neutralizing presuppositions about what exists and investigating the resulting appearances just as they appear. Once executed, these procedures reveal a realm of "senses" (noemata) through which objects are apprehended, meanings through which objects appear in particular ways. Husserl's task is to examine the relations between mental acts and their corresponding senses.

Husserl does not really address the question of Others' *existence.* Instead, he explores the processes through which certain entities come to appear as conscious beings, how the sense 'other conscious subject' becomes constituted. Husserl also eschews investigating one's *knowledge* of Others; although nothing prevents him from undertaking this enterprise, it would presuppose the completion of his actual project and would require that he develop and apply his higher-order investigations of belief and evidence. In effect, Husserl seeks to establish the *possibility* of perceiving Others as conscious beings; he elucidates the processes by which that particular sense is constituted.

4

Husserl also demonstrates the importance of that sense by showing that many other senses which operate in everyday perception *presuppose* the sense 'other conscious being'. For example, to perceive a desk as objectively present requires, according to Husserl, that one perceive it as being simultaneously perceivable by Others, and since this requirement invokes the sense 'other conscious being', that sense must already be constituted. If it could not be constituted, the character of ordinary perception would be impoverished. Husserl thus indicates a new range of difficulties that arise when the sense 'other conscious being' is rendered inoperative. A serious Cartesian would be left with only the most austere forms of experience.

Thus, despite his Cartesianism, Husserl transcends the traditional approach to Others both by stressing the foundational character of the sense 'other conscious being' and by formulating a question that seems prior to questions of both existence and knowledge: how senses are constituted. One can address Husserl's question even if Others do not in fact exist, and in order to know (to verify, establish) the existence of Others, one must first be capable of perceiving something *as* another conscious being. Even though Husserl accepts most of the tenets of the Cartesian picture, he is able to fashion an alternative problematic. Husserl's work was suggestive enough to establish some new directions, yet Cartesian enough to provoke dramatic reactions.

Hegel

Although Hegel preceded Husserl, Sartre discusses his position second because he thinks it makes important advances over Husserl's approach. Hegel genuinely supersedes the Cartesian picture. He makes no effort to prove that Others exist or to justify the knowledge one has of them; he simply assumes that other living, desiring beings exist and are apprehended. His central assertion is that only through encountering such beings can one achieve complete self-consciousness. Indeed, nearly every capacity that makes a person human (his reason, his ethical life, his self-expressive production) requires the existence of Others in order to become actualized. Others participate in the constitution of one's personhood, and vice versa. The manner in which one is related to Others determines the mode in which one exists. Thus, Hegel opposes the monad view of the self; although a primitive sense of self is possible without Others, a rich developed self requires their existence and recognition. Although human-like organisms may exist in isolation, *persons* are ontologically interlocked.

Hegel investigates the basic aim, pattern, and conditions governing interpersonal interaction by analyzing the basic event that occurs when self-conscious beings encounter one another. This investigation opens an entirely new area of inquiry for philosophy. For Hegel, the aim of interpersonal relations is recognition, and the kind of recognition one achieves is dependent on one's orientation to Others. Either one experiences an essential identity with them, or one retains a sense of separateness. If the latter, one cannot achieve recognition even though one may achieve temporary domination. If one transcends one's sense of differentiation, one can attain mutual recognition — a level of consciousness in which one experiences oneself as a member of the species. Recognition creates a supporting milieu, a larger totality that conditions one's existence. Hence, the quality of one's relationship to Others determines the kind or level of existence one can achieve.

The central implication of Hegel's position is that Cartesian self-examination, even if done thoroughly, will be insufficient to fully clarify the structures of mental life because those structures change and develop. Recognition alters the nature of one's experience. Thus, Cartesian reflection that was performed prior to recognition would fail to elucidate, and would inadequately comprehend, an entire level of experience. This is Hegel's first challenge to the assertion that immediate self-knowledge is always the most complete and adequate kind of knowledge.

His second challenge emerges from his contention that each form of conscious life breaks down and develops into another because when it seriously evaluates its experience with its own standard of adequacy, it finds itself wanting. Once this lack is apprehended, that form of consciousness disintegrates and transforms in a new one. Although each form of consciousness begins with an immediate certainty that it satisfies its standard, it gradually discovers its mistake. Consequently, most forms of consciousness fail to know themselves adequately despite their introspective capacities. For Hegel, genuine self-knowledge requires "experience," and experience involves tragedy, disillusionment, and disintegration.

Hegel offers yet a third challenge to the Cartesian privileged-access view. He contends that only through self-externalization can a self-conscious being come to understand itself. Though introspection is possible, its results are impoverished. One learns one's nature only through actions, productions, and interactions. The expression concretizes and provides content to self-consciousness. Thus, the way in which self-consciousness comes to understand itself is not in principle different from the way it understands Others. In each case, one comprehends and integrates the expressions in which self-consciousness makes itself determinate.

Hence, in addition to challenging the privileged-access view of mental states in three distinct ways, Hegel reorients the philosophical problematic of Others and mounts a powerful case for rejecting the monad view of the self.

Heidegger

Heidegger's challenge to the Cartesian picture is equally thorough, but quite different. He develops a new conception of persons in which the Cartesian difficulties are transcended. His project is ontological rather than epistemological. He seeks to clarify the nature of Being; in order to do this, he examines human being. Both are mysterious despite the fact that we exist in great proximity to them. His task is to make a more visionary apprehension of human being and Being itself possible. Far from understanding everything about ourselves, we systematically misinterpret our nature because we are governed by a theoretical tradition that has misapprehended and misread it. Only if that tradition is destroyed can our nature be revealed. Thorough revision of our typical conceptions is needed to achieve genuine self-understanding.

Heidegger has no interest in proving the existence of Others. Instead, he shows that Others are among the necessary conditions of the type of existence human beings have. He demonstrates this in three different ways. First, he claims that everything one does refers to Others in some fashion; in that sense, they are always with one. Even when one is alone, one experiences their absence and thus remains related to them. To be oriented toward Others is part of the human condition.

More importantly, he contends that one's self in the typical state is really not one's own but is an impersonal form of existence which derives from Others. His claim is not merely that Others influence one, but that, through the mediation of a generalized Other, they literally take over the function of one's self. For Heidegger, Others are present at the very core of what the Cartesian took to be most isolated and protected from them: the self.

Finally, Heidegger holds that the basic mode in which one exists is directly and symmetrically related to that of Others. He believes that there are only two basic modes of existence, authentic and inauthentic, and that one is drawn toward the authentic state in the presence of authentic Others and lulled toward the inauthentic state in the presence of inauthentic Others. This effect suggests that persons have an ontological attunement to one another.

Hence, Heidegger challenges the monad view of the self and the privileged-access view of mental states. In addition, he transforms the Cartesian task. No longer does one seek to reveal one's clear and distinct ideas; no longer does one vindicate all other knowledge by reducing it to this sphere of certainties. Instead, one tries to recover the truths that have become lost partly as a result of the errors of the Cartesian picture, and this requires a transformation of one's existence. Heidegger proposes a radically different manner of conceiving oneself and one's relation to the world. In effect, he tries to undermine the subject-object distinction and to replace it with a more accurate portrayal of the person, one which recaptures one's actual experience. On this conception, persons are enmeshed in the world and essentially related to Others.

Sartre

Sartre shares Heidegger's ontological focus and Hegel's interest in the basic aims governing encounters between persons. Yet he does accept one element of the Cartesian picture, viz., the view that mental states are translucent. Although Sartre refuses to call what issues from this immediate, ancillary self-awareness *knowledge*, he does think that a person has access to his own mental states in a way that Others in principle cannot. Sartre's most general disagreement with the Cartesian picture emerges in his contention that the mind is parasitic on the world: it could not exist if there were no world to be conscious of. Thus if consciousness exists, something other than consciousness must exist. In addition, certain kinds of consciousness require the existence of Others (e.g., shame). By appealing to these kinds of transcendental arguments, Sartre challenges the tenability of Cartesian skepticism.

Although Sartre accepts the self-translucency of mental states, he does not think this is achieved through a special procedure, e.g., Cartesian doubt or Husserlian reduction, nor does he think it implies that the theories in which our self-understanding is cast accurately capture the content of that understanding. Indeed, he thinks that much of the Cartesian picture and many of our common-sense beliefs about ourselves are false because when consciousness seeks to *know* itself, it must reflect on and *objectify* itself. In this process, the consciousness reflected on is altered; reflection makes one misunderstand one's pre-reflective nature. Because the Cartesian neglects this effect, his reflection often leads to errors and illusions. Sartre's task is to dispel these illusions and elucidate the nature of pre-reflective consciousness as it is lived. This is achieved through careful attention to lived experience and through a spontaneous process of purifying the reflective act.[2]

One of the illusions that Cartesian reflection produces is that an antecedent self owns one's mental acts. Sartre contends that there is no such self and that pre-reflective consciousness is *impersonal* — lacking any specific reference to the individual who lives it. To the extent that one experiences a sense of self, Sartre believes it derives from an awareness of a particular mode of Others: the Other-as-subject. The self thus derives from Others; they create a nature, a definition, or a character for one. The basic result of encountering other people is the experience of a determinate, continuant self: the self as seen by Others. Although this structure belongs to and defines oneself, it is also wholly dependent on and determined by Others. Sartre does not seek to prove the existence of Others because he takes the experience of the social self (*l'être-pour-autrui*) to be sufficient elucidation of the Other's lived reality. Both because Sartrean consciousness is impersonal and because Sartre takes one's sense of self to be essentially dependent on Others, he transcends the monad view of the self.

Like Hegel and Heidegger, Sartre thinks that there is an essential relation between the mode of existence of the Other and that of oneself; unlike them, Sartre believes this relation is asymmetrical. The Other's subjectivity emerges only across one's own objectivity, and the Other's objectivity is experienced as long as one retains one's own subjectivity. Sartre notes that in so far as one accepts the traditional epistemological orientation toward Others, one objectifies them; hence that type of investigation will *conceal* their subjectivity. Even if one has experienced Others' subjectivity, it will not influence one's conceptions because they are usually clarified in a frame of mind that excludes that subjectivity. Thus, the Cartesian picture cannot do justice to the experience of Others' subjectivity.

For Sartre, the essential asymmetry that defines one's relation to Others implies that conflict must be the basic theme of human interaction. The function of every concrete attitude toward Others is to gain control of the dimension of oneself that Others have created. For various reasons this effort is futile, and Sartre concludes that all human relationships inevitably *fail*. Sartre's unique contribution is an attempt to systematize the basic forms and dynamics of concrete relationships by clarifying their diverse responses to the primordial event that occurs in encounter. (Only Hegel offers a precedent for this attempt.) Sartre explores the concrete interpersonal attitudes of love and hate, desire and indifference, sadism and masochism.

Although Sartre leaves the privileged-access view of mental states unchallenged, he raises serious objections to the epistemological approach and offers an important alternative to the monad view of the self. He also explores specific kinds of relationships to Others much more thoroughly than his predecessors. He, too, introduces an alternative approach to the investigation of Others.

I have provided these introductory vignettes to indicate the kind of alternatives that European philosophers offer to the Cartesian picture. I have tried neither to clarify these points in great detail, nor to defend these interpretations, nor to offer arguments in favor of these alternatives. I am sympathetic with the directions taken by these theorists, but by no means am I uncritical of their general perspectives or their specific assertions. The purposes of this essay are: to provide that clarification and defense, to investigate those arguments, to explore those directions, and to offer that critique.

Some Anglo-American alternatives

Another perspective on the European alternatives to the Cartesian picture can be provided by contrasting them with the challenges to it posed in a different philosophical tradition. Some Anglo-American philosophers have also marshalled serious objections to the Cartesian picture. One thinks immediately of Wittgenstein and Ryle, but also of J.L. Austin. Their way of responding to the Cartesian conundrums is somewhat different; though they question the doctrine of privileged access, their efforts remain within the confines of the epistemological framework. Also, they fail to address the monad view of the self, the primary target of the European philosophers.

Wittgenstein

In the *Philosophical Investigations* and in *On Certainty*, Wittgenstein attacks the Cartesian picture's epistemological program, concept of certainty, and privileged-access doctrine. He seeks to dissolve the difficulties generated by Cartesianism and past philosophical systems. These difficulties are caused by reliance on misleading models and metaphors, overgeneralization, and misuse of language. He counsels attention to the actual uses of words, their functions, and their contexts of use.[3] Most locutions have a point and a context that render them intelligible; philosophers too easily ignore these factors when doing philosophy.[4] Wittgenstein does not seek to provide new philosophical theories; he seeks to eliminate perplexities and to prevent the emergence of new ones by recalling and exhibiting the operative grammar of everyday language-use.

Wittgenstein rejects the universal doubt that initiates the Cartesian program. The criteria for knowledge and certainty differ in different contexts; no one criterion will allay doubt in all cases.[5] More importantly, the expression of doubt emerges from a specific set of criteria which, if satisfied, would allay the doubt.[6] Wittgenstein rejects the view that certain types of propositions are essentially more basic or more indubitable than others; different assertions can be taken as fundamental from different perspectives or for different purposes, and every claim can be doubted in some situations. Once the questions that motivate doubt in a particular situation are answered, doubt should terminate; explanations and reasons must end somewhere.[7]

The implication of these general remarks for our topic is that doubting the existence or experience of Others is an empty gesture unless rooted in some specific concern that could in principle be resolved. He notes, for example, that doubting whether a specific sufferer in agony has pain is far more difficult to do than the Cartesian picture suggests.[8] Not all sources of conviction about Others' experience are cognitive;

fellow-feeling is an important source for understanding Others.[9] One does not typically infer to the existence of pain in Others on the basis of one's own pain,[10] but one can know that Others are in pain. These considerations suggest that there are adequate criteria for applying sensation terms to Others on the basis of natural expressions that exhibit or vent these sensations.

Wittgenstein's most renowned contribution to the topic has been termed "the private language argument." The argument has been given various interpretations; here I shall present one that allows useful comparison with Sartre. One specter that nourishes skepticism is the possibility that everyone might have different meanings for their words and thus that communication might be an illusion. Wittgenstein seeks to undermine this view of language; to do so, he considers the case most advantageous to the opposing position: sensations.[11] Sensations seem essentially private; hence one might plausibly think that sensation words could have private meanings. Wittgenstein seeks to show that a private language for sensations cannot be established, and in the process he rethinks the conception of sensation that derives from the Cartesian picture.

The proponent of a private language for sensations ignores both the natural expressions of sensations and the necessary preconditions for establishing meanings of terms.[12] Terms require rules of application and criteria for appropriate use in order to play a role in language.[13] These allow Others to learn the use of the terms. People (ourselves and Others) can master sensation terminology because there are such criteria, and these depend on natural contexts of and natural expressions for sensation.[14] Wittgenstein argues that efforts to establish essentially private meanings for sensation terms cannot succeed because the user could not achieve a coherent use of his own terminology.[15] He also suggests that the user cannot establish meanings for such terms because Others are essentially involved in establishing the meanings of terms; one cannot establish meanings by oneself for the same reasons one cannot give oneself a gift: Others are required to receive and acknowledge it.[16]

In the course of his discussion Wittgenstein suggests that behavioral expression is a typical component of mental states and that first-person expressions of sensations like pain are best construed as exhibitions of the sensation, rather than as descriptions or signs of it.[17] He seeks to fashion a position that lies between logical behaviorism and the view that experience and behavior are related only contingently and externally. He suggests that sensations and expressions have a necessary relation, but yet not a definitional or logical equivalence. In this respect he is similar to Hegel. Both seek to dismantle the picture of mental states that makes the privileged-access position possible.[18]

Wittgenstein also addresses the nature of the self, the referent for 'I.' In a sense, Wittgenstein denies the existence of a monadic self. For example, he contends that the word 'I' has no referent. The necessity for using 'I' in reporting mental states does not signify the existence of a self, but only indicates something about the logic of mental-state terms and the criteria for individuating mental states.[19] Wittgenstein holds that one's experiences are necessarily one's own only because that is how one talks about 'experiences.' The fact that 'I' is used to mark this organization of experiences is a consequence of the logic of their individuation. In this way Wittgenstein avoids commitment to a metaphysical self. However, this view implies that experiences are *necessarily* individuated and hence cannot be shared. Experience thus becomes a residual monadic element in Wittgenstein's position.

Wittgenstein thus transforms the Cartesian program by offering a revised version of the aims and possibilities of epistemology — introducing a complex, mutually supporting set of criteria for knowing that differentially apply in different contexts and rejecting the universal doubt that is the trump card of skepticism. In addition, he illustrates the importance of Others in constituting one's forms of life, but he does not pursue the implications of this, nor does he try to formulate an ontological analysis of the kind of social interrelatedness that language requires. Although he denies the existence of a monad *self*, he permits the monad view of persons to be defended by recourse to a monadic analysis of *experience*. Wittgenstein sought to avoid offering new positions; his main calling was therapeutic — to dispel philosophical puzzles. Yet his position has important implications which he did not develop. This unwillingness to fully pursue creative insights is characteristic of Anglo-American approaches to Others.

Ryle

In *The Concept of Mind* Gilbert Ryle mounts an explicit attack on the Cartesian picture — the metaphor of an inner theater of occult processes or the myth of the ghost in the machine.[20] His major contribution consists in providing dispositional analyses of many types of mental-state terms. Dispositions are tendencies to act in various ways; they implicate past and future behavior, and thus are not of the same logical type as discrete occurrences.[21] Mental-state terms do not refer to entities that occupy a non-physical space; they are a special way of talking about a person's behavior and expressions.[22] Since mental processes are manifest in various forms of behavior, they are accessible in essentially similar ways both to oneself and to Others. We can know Others nearly as well as we can know ourselves.[23]

Ryle thus explicates a new set of metaphors for understanding mental states. The main motive for this revision is epistemological; he thinks the Cartesian picture has misled us about the adequacy with which we typically know ourselves and the inadequacy with which we know Others. We know ourselves less well, and Others better, than the Cartesian picture suggests. One can attend to Others' mental states as well as to one's own, and one can be blind to either. One may be mistaken about the causes, location, and status of one's own mental states. Even if Others' efforts to conceal their states require hermeneutic deciphering, their characteristic, unstudied actions need not be scrutinized to be understood.[24]

The privileged-access doctrine draws support from the apparent capacity for introspection which persons possess and from the special relation they have to their own occurrent states (e.g., sensations). Ryle contends that introspection is not a special form of inner "seeing" and that most instances are fallible retrospections.[25] One summarizes one's capacities by synthesizing the actions one has performed on various relevant occasions. But this synthesis can also be done by Others if they have witnessed a sufficient number of relevant actions.[26] What the retrospector gains in greater number of occasions recalled, the observer balances off in lesser bias and ego-involvement in the results.[27] Ryle grants a special status to sensations; a person's sensations are necessarily his, but this does not mean that he can witness them directly. Sensations are preconditions for observations like letters are preconditions for forming words; just as one cannot spell letters, one cannot observe (or fail to observe) sensations. At best one can heed them and avow them. He contends that the privileged-access doctrine mistakenly overgeneralizes this status to all mental states.[28]

Ryle denies the existence of a metaphysical self; he regards it as an extraneous hypothesis which solves few problems and typically leads to an infinite regress.[29] He also objects to alternative models of the self, e.g., the committee model, that raise more difficulties than they resolve. Though he does not provide an account for all the phenomena the self is used to explain (e.g., identity over time), he does suggest an explanation for the elusiveness and mystery attributed to the self. Any effort to assess or review one's mental life cannot simultaneously review the reviewing process; to review that, an additional higher-order review is necessary, but then the higher-order reviewing escapes evaluation.[30] Thus there will always be some conscious states that cannot be reviewed or assessed, but this fact demonstrates nothing about the existence of the self.

Ryle makes no effort to explore relations between self and Other beyond epistemological ones, and his new analysis of mental states does not consider whether Others may have a deeper relationship to one's own states than the Cartesian picture suggests. Ryle's interest in Others is circumscribed by the question of whether their mental states are accessible. His critique of the Cartesian picture thus does not extend to the monad view of the self.

13

Austin

The final Anglo-American philosopher I shall consider is J.L. Austin. Austin eschews systematic philosophy. He prefers to address carefully demarcated questions and to make gradual progress on them by exploring the latent content of ordinary language. He believes that ordinary language implicitly contains many important distinctions that are not adequately captured by artificial conceptual schemes; it functions as a repository for the conceptual intuitions of many generations. Austin attends to linguistic data with the kind of care that existential phenomenologists devote to lived experience.

In his essay "Other Minds,"[31] Austin offers an explication of the ordinary use of 'know' and appends some concluding remarks about knowing other peoples' emotions. Clearly, he takes the epistemological problematic to be his central concern. Like Wittgenstein and Ryle, he does not address the *nature* of Others or their relations to oneself.

Austin astutely dismantles the Cartesian assumptions concerning knowledge and certainty. He questions both the search for absolute certainty and the privileged-access doctrine. He holds that claims to know in everyday situations presuppose specific criteria for establishing both the appropriateness of one's position to know and the adequacy of the procedures one has taken to be sure.[32] Moreover, the stringency of the requirements for knowing varies with the purposes at hand. For Austin, few knowledge claims are ever self-evident, and one can legitimately claim to know without thereby implying that one could not be wrong.[33] To say that one knows is to perform a certain type of act: to offer one's authority or word that one has fulfilled the criteria relevant to the case.[34] If some anomaly prevents one from fully satisfying all the relevant criteria, then one's claim to know is infelicitous, but not necessarily inaccurate. Austin tries to demonstrate that knowing is a human institution which allows people to have faith in one another and which exists in a context of accepted criteria and procedures for deciding whether one knows. The Cartesian neglects this when he enjoins us to adopt elevated standards for knowledge.

Austin contends that one is not always certain of one's own mental states in the way that Cartesian privileged access suggests. Often an experience one is having fails to fit the categories at one's disposal or occupies an area in which different criteria conflict.[35] Knowing one's own states (or anything else) is never a matter of directly intuiting their nature, but always a matter of adjudicating a system of categories with a set of data. In such cases the fit is often tentative, and with respect to one's own mental states, one's recognition is no more or less hesitant than in other cases; one feels one's way toward the appropriate designation. If certainty is demanded, one characteristically retreats to a more general category which will uncontroversially apply to the case at hand but will provide less information about it; e.g., one feels 'pain' rather than 'a sharp twinge.'[36] Austin notes that in the ordinary language of emotions, one does distinguish believing and knowing that one has a particular emotional state. One neither assumes that one always knows what one feels, nor that one never knows.

With respect to knowing the emotions of Others, Austin makes three helpful observations. First, some people are simply harder to know; one may require greater familiarity with them before one is willing to claim one knows what they are feeling.[37] Second, particular emotions involve both natural expressions and natural circumstances of emergence. The situation, the feeling, and the expression typically go together.[38] One becomes more able to recognize the emotions of Others as one becomes more familiar with these connections. First-hand knowledge of an emotion often facilitates one's recognition of it in Others.[39] Finally, one's knowledge of Others' emotions is not in principle different from knowledge in other contexts.[40] Questions may arise about whether the Other is deceiving one and whether one is understanding him adequately. These are questions about the complexity of what one sees and the definiteness of the boundaries of the concepts one is trying to apply to what one sees. Efforts to know can become problematic in both ways in all other contexts. Thus, knowing another's emotions may require some acquaintance with the person and with the emotion itself, but it raises no difficulties that do not also arise in other contexts of knowing.

These remarks exhibit Austin's concern for clarity and specificity in asking and answering questions. Although Austin's approach is clearly limited to epistemological concerns, he undercuts the Cartesian attempt to elevate standards of knowledge and defuses the privileged-access position by recalling our actual practices in everyday contexts. His work on other minds does not reconsider the nature of Others or their relation to us, nor does it strive for sweeping conceptual revisions, but he does make decisive contributions to the questions he addresses.

The Anglo-American tradition remains within the epistemological framework when it investigates other persons. As we have seen, the central focus in Wittgenstein, Ryle, and Austin is one's *knowledge* of other persons' mental states. Even though they reject the Cartesian search for absolute certainty and self-evident foundations, their primary concern about Others is how they are known. In addition, they challenge the privileged-access conception of mental states; each of them tries to establish some conceptual or essential link between other people's mental states and their behavioral expressions. Thus they deny the Cartesian bifurcation between an internal state and its external expression. Yet when they address the question of the self, they do not challenge the monad view *per se* even when they do reject the metaphysical ego.

A comparison of the traditions

I have offered this brief review of Wittgenstein, Ryle, and Austin in order to explore the special contribution of the European tradition to the study of Others. Even though I have explicated a limited number of figures from each tradition, some useful comparisons can be extracted from these sketches. Although there are differences of style between the traditions, these can be overdrawn and overrated; here I shall focus on differences of substance and try to indicate revealing similarities as well.

Everyone in both traditions except Husserl[41] rejects the Cartesian search for certainty, but each tradition does so in different ways. The Anglo-American tradition seeks to develop an alternative epistemology which respects our actual practices and epistemic standards; its investigation of Others remains circumscribed by the question of how their mental states are known. The European tradition seeks to reveal relations between self and Other that are more fundamental than knowledge and thus establishes a number of distinctive approaches, most of which question the status of the self as much as they interrogate Others.

This difference can explain a more notorious difference between the traditions – the piecemeal analytical approach versus the sweeping systematic approach. Largely because their questions are antecedently delimited and criteria for adequate answers are agreed upon, Anglo-American philosophers can more readily address small aspects of a question separately and in analytical detail. Since the European philosophers seek to begin anew, to raise unique questions from distinctive standpoints, the criteria for adequate answers are less well established. Hence, detailed analysis is less useful than a systematic development of the full implications of a position because the big picture is needed for an overall assessment. If a new paradigm becomes established, then details and refinements can be addressed.

Although Hegel, Heidegger, and Sartre do not completely ignore questions about knowing other people, they either elucidate kinds of knowing that differ from theoretical circumspection or explore unusual dimensions of the Other to be known. For the most part, philosophers in the Anglo-American tradition concentrate on how one can know particular mental states (or types of them) of particular people, and the situation they envision is one in which one might have some theoretical uncertainty about whether one knows those states. Heidegger and Sartre both explore more practical, familiar comportments in which one comes to know or comprehend Others. Heidegger stresses participation in common projects; Sartre stresses the experience of being looked at; each uncovers a distinctive kind of access to Others. (Although Ryle clearly saw one alternative type of knowledge – knowing how – he did not emphasize its relevance for knowing Others.) In addition,

Hegel and Heidegger explore dimensions of a *generalized Other* which is experienced in social interaction (recognition, being-with) but which is not properly identified with particular states of discrete individuals. Thus, in addition to broadening the range of questions about the relation of self and Other, the European philosophers also challenge traditional ways of formulating the questions about knowing Others.

On the other hand, Wittgenstein and his followers are not oblivious to broader questions of social interrelatedness.[42] Wittgenstein indicates the ways in which ordinary language use is rooted in forms of social life and invites a deeper exploration of the kind of social bonds presupposed by the necessity of public criteria. Wittgenstein himself did not pursue this topic, but his followers did, and they have discovered some useful insights about rule-governed behavior. This enterprise is analogous to Sartre's effort to explore the ways in which Others are presupposed by self-consciousness and to elucidate the resulting ontological relationships. The impact of Others can sometimes be found where one is least likely to look for it.

Philosophers in both traditions believe that Others' mental states and characters can be known at least as adequately as our own. This claim is defended both by casting doubt on the privileged-access doctrine and by reconceiving the relation between the 'internal' and the 'external' components of mental states. Both traditions explore the many ways in which we can be wrong or ignorant of our own mental states and character and stress the similarities in the ways we come to know ourselves and Others. We learn our aims through the ways we transform the world, and we learn our thoughts by expressing them in speech or writing. We are numb to much of our occurrent experience, and our dispositional states can only be grasped via a retrospective synthetic operation similar to the one we use to comprehend Others. Ryle's dispositional analysis of mind is not unlike Heidgegger's vision of man as a mode of being-in-the-world. Though both Ryle and Sartre believe persons have a distinctive relation to their occurrent experiences, neither is willing to call this access "knowledge."

Both Hegel and Austin seek to show a deeper connection between the expression of a mental state (the behavior) and its internal components. Behavior and the context in which it occurs specify the mental state; both the 'behavior' and the 'feeling' are indeterminate and amorphous apart from the real totality that is the expression-in-situation. We become acquainted with these totalities by direct participation. In similar ways Wittgenstein and Heidegger try to establish a tighter connection (even if not strict identity) between the internal and external aspects of a mental state; both believe that the distinction between these aspects is artificial. Though knowing Others is not like reading an open book, it is very different from trying to read a book whose print is invisible.

Many have observed that the Anglo-American tradition relies on ordinary language usage where the European tradition would rely on evidence drawn from everyday life and experience. But this difference conceals a much deeper similarity: both seek to challenge and transform common-sense assumptions by appealing to evidence of which everyone could be aware if they were sufficiently attentive. Wittgenstein appeals to ordinary use of words which theorists forget when they do philosophy. Austin appeals to the latent conceptual content of ordinary language on which we all unconsciously rely. Similarly, Sartre appeals to the data of pre-reflective experience that is concealed when we adopt a reflective, theoretical orientation to our lives, and Heidegger seeks to reveal the implicit structures that condition our everyday lives even if we are not aware of them. Both traditions thus seek conceptual and theoretical revision on the basis of a more attentive, more lucid description of what is already in principle accessible. The problem with past philosophy is that it has been blind to these deeper sources of evidence, and the effort to overcome this blindness constitutes the deepest convergence in the two traditions.[43]

Three additional differences between the traditions deserve mention. First, the central target of the European tradition is the monad view of the self; this position is largely ignored by the Anglo-American tradition because its attention remains confined to the epistemological issue. Even if the analysis of the self is addressed in the Anglo-American tradition, few have attempted to establish an essential or internal relation between self and Other. Hegel, Heidegger, and Sartre explore the many ways Others constitute and are interwoven in one's experience and personhood. Recognition, the gaze, and impersonal modes of existence all reveal dimensions of one's existence that would not exist if there were no Others; Others are not important just because they are nurturers and providers, they are literally part of one's own nature. Uncovering and exploring this kind of interconnectedness is one special contribution of the European tradition.

Second, the European tradition examines all aspects of the Other's personhood, not simply his mental states. Though "mental states" covers a wide range of capacities within the Anglo-American tradition, it does not typically include the person's participation in complex social structures and the practical engagements that derive from this. Nor does it include the structures of the Other that one makes possible in virtue of one's relationship to him, e.g., his social equilibrium. Just as the constitutive relations between self and Other are ignored by the epistemological orientation, so too are all the essentially social qualities embedded in the Other's nature.

Finally, the European tradition explores the dynamics and modes of interpersonal encounter and thus provides a richer typology of interpersonal deportments. Of special interest are the ways in which people dominate one another and the possibilities for transcending this domination. This kind of question remains unaddressed in Anglo-American theory about others, probably because it seems to cross the borderline between philosophy and science. These issues seem like factual questions rather than conceptual ones. Since Hegel, the European tradition has participated in a continuous dialogue with the social sciences; the borderline between them is taken less seriously. In addition to pressing critical questions, European philosophy both draws on and advances new developments in social science. Although the forays of European philosophy into social scientific theory can seem like crude efforts at empirical generalization, they do offer stimulating paradigms for further inquiry. By overstating their insights, they draw attention to the new phenomena they see and facilitate closer examination of them. Recently, philosophers in the Anglo-American tradition have also begun to take this borderline less seriously,[44] and they may portend greater convergence in the future.

Thus, though there are substantive differences between the traditions, there are also some important similarities. This essay seeks to render the contributions of the European tradition on intersubjectivity more accessible to those in other traditions. I shall show that the kinds of evidence and forms of argument used in the European tradition are more comprehensible than has previously been thought.

A common thread

The common thread uniting the philosophers in the European tradition is: if one looks beneath theories (Hegel), reflective experience (Sartre), traditional conceptions (Heidegger), or the natural standpoint (Husserl), one will be able to discover new and important truths about the self-Other relationship. The Cartesian picture blinds us to what is at least implicitly accessible; the general aim of any phenomenological effort is to bring these implicit realities into view. Each of these theorists uncovers some facet of Others and studies its implications. My task in this essay is to examine their efforts with the same critical acumen and incisive vision they brought to their projects.

Much of my contribution is critical. I struggle to underline the value and genuine insights of each approach, but I also patiently uncover its problems, lacunae, and inadequacies. These criticisms are not offered for their own sake. I seek to supplement and correct the conceptions of each philosopher and to lay the foundations for a more adequate theory of Others.

I try to determine how these theories supplement one another. Where they conflict, I try to decide which is most accurate. Each theory is examined on its own terms, but all are judged by the criterion of phenomenological adequacy. Gradually, a sense of the complexity of interpersonal life and the importance of phenomenological elucidation in revealing its important structures and dynamics will emerge.

If phenomenology is to prove a useful tool for philosophical investigation, it must be applied patiently, and it must build on research that has already been initiated. But new conceptions must also be offered when they seem required. This essay seeks to advance the efforts of the tradition it examines.

Chapter 1

Husserl

My initial task is to examine Sartre's predecessors, and Husserl is the first theorist Sartre discusses. Although Sartre's reading of Husserl is more accurate than his readings of Hegel and Heidegger, it is overly compact and fails to situate the general project adequately. Thus, I shall offer a more detailed interpretation which will facilitate an examination of Sartre's reading and a more thorough exploration of Husserl's position.

I begin with a general description of Husserl's version of phenomenology and continue with a careful elucidation of his discussion of the constitution of the sense 'other conscious subject.' I then turn to a brief review of Sartre's interpretation of Husserl and a discussion of his various objections. Sartre's critique of Husserl makes some insightful points; I agree with its central thrust. But since Sartre's discussion remains overly general, I will supplement his attack with some more detailed objections. In addition, I will indicate the advantages of Sartre's version of phenomenology over Husserl's. Because Husserl is the most Cartesian of the European theorists and because I think the Cartesian picture is the source of many problems in the study of Others, I will attempt to show that any view of Husserl's type — not only his own version — faces serious objections.

An introduction to Husserl

In order to understand Husserl's theory of Others, one must understand the basic assumptions of Husserlian phenomenology. This explication of these assumptions is meant to apply primarily to Husserl's position as enunciated in his *Cartesian Meditations*.[1] In that text Husserl offers an introduction to the various forms of phenomenological explication and indicates the similarities and differences between his own rigorous science and Descartes's project. The central concerns of both thinkers are epistemological; each seeks to provide a presuppositionless, indubitable discipline on which all other sciences can be grounded.[2] Husserl creates this discipline by adopting a quasi-Cartesian standpoint in which common-sense beliefs are suspended, by discovering a new field of indubitable data, and by developing an enterprise that unearths the implicit, presupposed senses which condition all experience.

21

Husserlian science

Husserl takes the defining characteristic of a science to be the fact that its truths can be repeatedly verified by any meditator with self-evident givenness.[3] Such truths do not depend on authority, testimony, or tradition; everything can be established by the individual for himself. According to Husserl, self-evident givenness can be of two sorts: adequate and apodictic. Evidence is "adequate" when what is presented in a mental act wholly fulfills one's expectations.[4] Each type of mental act is fulfilled in different ways, e.g., vaguely remembering a book title versus reciting it accurately from memory, perceiving indistinctly versus perceiving clearly; the latter term in these pairs is the fulfilled act. There are degrees of fulfillment and hence of adequacy; some acts, e.g., perception, are inherently unable to achieve complete adequacy. Evidence is "apodictic" when no possible presentation could unsettle confidence in the assertion being entertained.[5]

Each type of evidence provides a solid foundation. Husserl believes that no perceptual object is ever *adequately* evident because there are always profiles of the object included in one's expectations that are not presented as such in the act of perception. These profiles are merely "appresented"; i.e., they are suggested — presented in an extended sense — but do not truly appear in the perceived profile. Merely appresented objects are not given self-evidently and hence are not accepted as basic in Husserl's science. If they are to be admitted at all, the manner in which they are constituted must be explicated. The evidence for Others, like that for perceived objects, cannot ever be adequate or apodictic; hence Husserl's science is threatened by solipsism.[6]

Just like Descartes, Husserl believes that mental *acts* appear with complete self-evident givenness because they are wholly present to themselves. Some examples of mental acts are: thinking, believing, perceiving, imagining, desiring, and dreaming. Even if the object of such acts is not presented in a wholly fulfilled fashion, the act itself is presented with complete adequacy. Husserl advances beyond Descartes by discovering an additional realm for which the evidence is adequate: the realm of senses (*Sinne*).

Husserl defines this realm by performing a certain operation which he calls "transcendental" (or phenomenological) reduction. In lived experience one naturally takes the objects of perception to be independent of consciousness. Husserl's reduction neutralizes this assumption. One simply suspends belief in the actual existence of the world and brackets the existence-status of any object of any mental act; one regards all objects of all types of acts as mere suppositions, as possible meanings or senses, that can be used by the ego that survives this "bracketing" of the world.[7] A "sense" is an object of any mental act taken as supposed, as purely intended, or as meant. Senses, the objective correlates of mental acts, survive the suspension of the natural or common-sense standpoint; they constitute the realm of "phenomena" that is the principal theme of Husserl's investigations.[8]

The transcendental and the natural standpoints exclude one another, even though the senses uncovered in the transcendental standpoint are *used* in the natural one.[9] Senses are not literal constituents of psychic acts as such, but neither are they parts of the natural world. Senses are intermediate objects that fall between psychic acts and worldly objects (like Fregean senses) and through which acts relate themselves to objects.[10] Their non-natural, non-worldly character motivates Husserl to call the realm that encompasses them *the transcendental field*. This field is simply the set of senses that emerges through reduction. Every natural object has a number of corresponding senses, e.g., its various descriptions. Since senses, by definition, are only what is supposed by particular mental acts, the presented contents in the transcendental attitude rarely offer more or less than one expects to be there. Many senses thus appear with complete adequacy. Husserl concludes that the transcendental field is epistemologically more fundamental than the natural world.

Varieties of phenomenology

Within this transcendental field, many sorts of studies can be performed; Husserl continually enriched his phenomenology by discovering new types of investigation. I shall briefly describe five basic types: elucidative, eidetic, verificational, genetic, and static-constitutional.

Elucidative phenomenology seeks to describe the components of a sense (e.g., 'tree') or the moments of a type of mental act or the special forms of correlation between types of mental act (e.g., categorial, signitive, imaginative, perceptual, evaluative) and types of objects (e.g., thoughts, signs, images, physical objects, values). Elucidative phenomenology seeks to discern salient differences between different types of acts and senses. It also explores salient subtypes within various categories of acts and senses (e.g., factors differentiating the perception of sounds from that of sights, the perception of objects from that of states of affairs).[11]

Eidetic phenomenology seeks to uncover the essence governing a particular type of sense. It requires close examination of the sense as a type and an effort to imagine many different instances of the type, especially instances that might never be experienced. One may also imaginatively eliminate various components of the sense in order to determine whether its nature alters. These imaginative exercises locate the boundaries of the type of sense being investigated. Aspects or elements of the sense that remain constant through all the imaginative variations are those that belong to the essence of the sense.[12]

Verificational phenomenology seeks to clarify the processes and criteria through which a type of sense gets verified — is assigned the status 'actual' (versus possible) or 'veridical' (versus false or indeterminate). These designations inhere in some senses but not in others. The task is to determine the processes whereby this additional status emerges; it involves clarifying the patterns of continuous, harmonious experience which satisfy the expectations arising from the apprehension of a particular type of sense. This study of different types of verification remains within the transcendental attitude; it does not seek to reconstruct a transition to the natural attitude. Although this investigation does not directly provide justification for beliefs, its results can be reinterpreted at a higher level of epistemic analysis to yield this justification.[13]

Genetic phenomenology explores the inherent temporal order by which various types of senses get constituted. Its guiding assumption is that some senses must be constituted earlier than others.[14] For example, certain modifications of the ego (e.g., dispositional properties) may be able to emerge only after other senses have already been discerned (e.g., the occurrent states encompassed by the disposition). One might call this enterprise "diachronic" constitutional analysis because it seeks to determine the order in which senses must emerge in time.

Finally, one can investigate the constitution of senses *statically*, at a given moment of time. The general premise of this investigation is that some senses are logically more fundamental than others and thus that the derivative ones are built upon the primary ones. The derived senses require the constitution of the basic ones and are constituted through them.[15] This sort of inquiry unravels the complex layers of constitutive acts that make up a particular type of apprehension. An example from the Fifth Meditation is the assertion that the sense 'other conscious subject' is logically prior to the sense 'objective material thing.' This means that nothing can be experienced as or supposed to be objective without presupposing that it is potentially observable by other conscious beings. This is part of the sense 'objective,' and it is embedded in experiencing something as objective. Just as the sense 'other conscious being' is used to constitute the derivative sense, it too is constituted from still more basic senses and processes.

Husserl performs static-constitutional analysis in the Fifth Meditation; he tries to clarify the processes involved in constituting the sense 'other conscious being' and the ways in which that sense is used to constitute higher-order senses.[16] One might say he is trying to show both how the experience of another conscious being becomes possible (how another body comes to be supposed to be another conscious being) and then how it becomes verified as actually that (how one comes to accept the sense as fulfilled).

This sort of constitutional explication of sense needs to be distinguished from other sorts of philosophical enterprises associated with the Cartesian standpoint and the concept of constitution. First, although Husserl's enterprise is a constructive one, he is not trying to construct *justification* for beliefs, and thus he is not offering an argument. Rather, he is seeking to show how one comes to be able to experience a certain kind of object *as such*. With regard to Others, he is not providing reasons for believing Others exist, but rather is trying to construct how it becomes possible (intelligible) to apprehend something as an Other (like oneself). Belief is a special type of state that requires higher-order investigations; these presuppose the clarification of perception and apperception. Husserl's results may be used to commence a more traditional epistemological reconstruction, but he sees himself as providing something more fundamental. The issue of whether one can legitimately believe that Others exist cannot arise if one cannot even suppose something to be another conscious subject.

Second, Husserl is not trying to trace the temporal order by which a child arrives at the idea of other persons although he would certainly grant the possibility of such a study. His project is structural; it is executed at a given moment in time and seeks to clarify what senses must already be assumed in order for the sense 'other conscious being' to emerge and how those presupposed senses are combined to yield this sense. It is a synchronic rather than a diachronic study.[17] The priority he is uncovering is logical rather than temporal. However, one might use his theory to develop a set of hypotheses about the psychological genesis of the concept of 'other person.'

Finally, Husserl is not trying simply to analyze the concept 'other person,' although when he seeks to investigate essences his enterprise is very similar to conceptual analysis. Instead, Husserl seeks to disclose the preconditions and underlying components of a particular type of experience; the ways in which an experience assumes the meaning 'experience of another conscious subject.' Certain cognitions and combinatorial acts must take place in order for this experience to occur; Husserl seeks to explicate what these are and how they are related. According to Husserl, senses are *used* in the natural attitude, but they can be explicated only in the transcendental (or phenomenological) standpoint.

Husserl's enterprise can have important applications. Although Husserl does not explore these distinctions, there are differences in experiencing another person as genuinely present, as distinct from oneself, as a being with emotions, as a thinking being, as an individual, as a self-actualizing agent, and as a person worthy of inherent respect. Each of these are various modes in which the Other can appear, and some probably presuppose others. Each may represent a new level of depth in experiencing Others. Exactly what qualities and processes are involved in moving from level to level would be worth clarifying, for one might then begin to understand how interpersonal experience becomes enriched or impoverished. One might also better understand what processes are deficient in various psychological disorders, e.g., autism. Husserl himself does not develop these applications, but they indicate some useful directions for research.

Affinities with the Cartesian picture

Husserl's phenomenological enterprise has obvious affinities with the Cartesian picture that I described in the Introduction,[18] and these condition his inquiry into Others. They set its boundaries and provide its motivation.

Husserl uses elevated standards of evidence which exclude everything but one's own mental states and their sense-correlates from the realm of the self-evident. At best, Others are treated only as sense-correlates of one's own conscious processes; their existence remains bracketed or else is radically reinterpreted.

In addition, because Husserl accepts the privileged-access position, he thinks Others' conscious states can never be directly presented and hence can never be self-evident. Thus, even as sense-correlates, the constitutional status of Others is secondary; one's apprehension of Others will always be parasitic on one's own self-constitution.[19] This affinity with the Cartesian picture raises the threat of solipsism to which Husserl seeks to respond in his Fifth Meditation.

Moreover, the independence of Husserl's transcendental ego (i.e., the ego that appears in the transcendental attitude and engages in the constitutional processes) from the natural world gives it a hermetic, monadic character. Husserl's ego is threatened by an absolute isolation which it can transcend only by constituting Others out of the ongoing stream of its own conscious processes. The monadic nature of Hussel's ego tempts him to regard it as omni-productive, as the source of every sense through which it apprehends the world in the natural attitude.[20] On this view, Others do not ever condition the processes of the monadic ego; they are only quasi-reproductions of oneself.

Husserl's theory of Others

In order to understand Husserl's theory of Others, one needs to see why solipsism constitutes a problem for him and to understand what kind of solipsism he seeks to overcome. Once these preliminaries are clarified, Husserl's theory of the constitution of the sense 'other conscious being' can be elucidated. Husserl presents his theory in five basic steps. In the first, he describes an abstraction process that ensures that his constitutional analysis will not be circular. In the second, he explicates the two basic processes through which the constitution of the sense 'other conscious object' becomes possible: appresentation and pairing. In the third, he clarifies the processes by which the sense can be verified, how sense can become fulfilled. In the fourth, he demonstrates how the richness of the Other's experience becomes constituted and how one comes to apprehend self and Other as experiencing the same world. Finally, he describes how Others come to be grasped as constituting oneself and how higher-order cultural communities can be constituted.

The motivation for the theory

Solipsism takes on a special salience for Husserl in the *Cartesian Meditations* because he makes a crucial assumption: that all senses are derivable wholly from the ongoing stream of processes of the transcendental ego.[21] Although this ego is constantly developing and articulating itself through time, all strata of sense derive from the senses that exist solely within the ego; for these basic senses, the evidence is at least adequate. The enterprise of static constitutional explication would probably make no sense without this assumption; it provides the bedrock senses. This claim implies that the sense 'Other' is created out of one's own conscious life and that Others are apprehended as conscious only because one experiences oneself as conscious.[22]

These basic senses constitute the small set of pieces from which Husserl seeks to rebuild the complete structure of experience *as it is supposed* in the natural standpoint.[23] That natural standpoint provides the clue to what must be explicated and constituted.[24] The transcendental ego, its processes, and the senses that are uniquely its own provide the basic data; the task is to explicate the path from these to the higher-order, more complex senses.

Husserl believes that another's conscious life *must be* presented mediately, for any conscious process that is presented immediately *must be* one's own. If another's conscious life were adequately presented to one, he would be identical with one.[25] Husserl's worry is that the senses immediate to the transcendental ego will not be rich enough to allow the constitution of this mediately-presented sense and thus that one will be confined to a kind of logical solipsism: an inability to conceive the possibility of Others.[26] Husserl would regard this implication to be fatal to static constitutional phenomenology because the sense 'other conscious being' is used in the natural attitude; however, he would assume that *some* constitutional path *must be* discoverable for exactly the same reason.

At this point, some distinctions among types of solipsism will be helpful. There are three versions of solipsism: epistemological, metaphysical, and logical. Epistemological solipsism asserts that Others cannot be *known* to exist; since Husserl's enterprise is prior to epistemology, this version of solipsism is not his primary focus. Metaphysical solipsism asserts that Others *do not* exist; since Husserl brackets all questions of existence, this doctrine cannot be his focus. Logical solipsism asserts that Others *cannot be conceived*; the concept cannot be formed. This version is closest to Husserl's main worry: if the sense 'Others' cannot be constituted, nothing can be apprehended as another self, and one's own ego will be able to grasp only itself. Other conscious beings could not be perceived *as such*, and perhaps could not even be conceived at all.

Thus, Husserl is not trying to disprove metaphysical solipsism[27] but is seeking to show that his position does not entail logical solipsism. According to Husserl, this kind of solipsist cannot experience *any* object as objective and cannot grasp any cultural artifact as such.[28] The inability to constitute the sense 'other conscious being' would eliminate a wide variety of other senses which depend on it and seriously impoverish one's experience. If Husserl's working assumption committed him to this impoverishment, he would have to abandon it.

Although Husserl does not address epistemological solipsism, he would probably take it to be unwarranted because he regards the constitutional analysis he presents to be confirmable by any meditator. His analysis lays the essential groundwork for clarifying how Others can be known: the verification processes he explores would only need fuller development and reinterpretation at higher cognitive levels. Moreover, Husserl does not think his constitutional path is just one possible path; he takes it to be the actual path and the necessary path once one is confronted by an appropriate datum: another human-like body.[29]

The constitution of the sense 'Others'

Step 1

The first step in Husserl's explication demands a special abstractive process *within* the transcendental standpoint; one abstracts from, and thus disengages, every sense that in any way depends on or is related to the notions of 'alien' and 'other.'[30] The relevant dependency here is logical, not causal. Actual other people may have taught one to individuate and name one's mental states, but the senses inherent in those states make no reference to and do not logically depend on the *sense* 'Others.' This abstractive process yields the "*sphere of ownness.*" This step is performed in order to prevent the use of any derivative sense in the course of offering the constitution of the sense 'other conscious subject.' Failure to prevent such use would entail a failing in this type of constitutional analysis analogous to begging the question in deduction.

Husserl *assumes* that the sphere of ownness is the most fundamental; he does not establish this.

Independent criteria for determining the contents of the sphere of ownness are not provided.[31] Husserl surveys the sorts of senses that he takes to lie within it and to remain operative after the abstraction is performed: the transcendental ego and all its constituting processes, one's own animate organism and one's psychic being united with one's body, that aspect of nature which appears solely to oneself (hence lacking the sense 'perceivable by Others'), all predicates referring solely to oneself (e.g., purposes, ideals, motives), all constituted unities in so far as the unity is inseparable from the constituting act itself (e.g., imagined entities), and, finally, the distinction between self and other.[32]

Inclusion of many of these senses in the ownness sphere is puzzling, but none is more problematic than the last. By including it, Husserl is forced to distinguish what is self (immanent) and what is not-self (transcendent, other) *within* a sphere that includes only what is one's own.[33] All the sense-correlates of psychic acts that remain intact are seen as immanently *transcendent*, but the ego and its psychic acts are seen as immanently *immanent*.[34] This distinction is probably introduced to preserve the type difference between acts and senses and thus avert transcendental psychologism (i.e., the view that the transcendental sphere contains only subjective, private, mental processes), but its plausibility seems dubious. Something must be seen as not-oneself in order for there to be an immanent/transcendent distinction, and this seems to require reference to the sense 'alien' which was to be eliminated by the abstractive process. Here is one place at which Husserl's abstraction seems insufficiently radical.

Step 2

Husserl's task is to explicate the processes whereby the senses in this ownness sphere yield the sense 'other conscious subject.'[35] He describes two interrelated processes, *apperception* and *pairing*, to provide this explication.

At the outset, Husserl notes that although the Other appears to us 'in person,' the stream of conscious processes that is *presented* as such *must be* one's own. The Other's conscious life can thus only be *appresented* (apperceived), but the appresentation involved is one that can *never* be fulfilled by a presentation.[36] In ordinary perception, not every side of a material object is presented as such; those hidden from view are present 'in a fashion' however, and this fashion Husserl describes as 'appresentation.'[37] Appresented aspects are made present via associative sequences triggered by the presentation.[38] They hover between full presentation and mere signification; they are there but not *adequately* presented.[39] With perceptual objects, however, sides that are merely appresented *can* become presented; this is not true for what is appresented in the perception of Others: their conscious states.[40] In general, appresentation can only occur on the basis of a presentation; for perceived objects, the side facing us is the presented aspect; for the perception of another person, the triggering presentation is his body.[41]

The question thus becomes how the presentation of the Other's body, taken as supposed and solely as a modification of one's ownness sphere (not as an objective or publicly observable thing), can become the basis of an appresentation that accounts for its appearance as consciousness-endowed.[42] Husserl's initial answer is that there is an ongoing process of self-perception within the sphere of ownness; one continuously grasps one's ongoing mental acts as one's own. The connections of these acts with one's own bodily processes and movements are apparent; one perceives one's own organism as animated by one's conscious processes; this unity of conscious processes and bodily movement is continuously present and offers the basis on which the Other's body can receive the sense 'body animated by consciousness.' These connections exist even when one is restricted to the ownness sphere.[43]

Husserl next asserts that even though the Other's body is presented solely as a modification of the ownness sphere, its manifest similarity to one's own body can be noted. This observation is the primal act by which the two appearances become paired.[44] Pairing is not an inferential procedure, but an association that is made on the basis of apparent similarity. Pairing is analogous to the process by which a newly experienced, individual thing is apprehended as a particular type (this is a book) or a familiar one is reidentified as such (that is the book); it is a form of synthesis. Pairing is an associative-synthesis while class identification is an identity-synthesis.[45] In pairing the two appearing objects are grasped as the same; this permits all aspects of one sense to transfer to the other sense.[46]

This pairing is the basis on which the Other's body can appresent conscious states; it becomes imbued with these possibilities *by transfer* from one's own perceived animate organism. Husserl is ambiguous about what aspect of the self-perceived body is engaged in this pairing process. Either it is the body as one perceives it (e.g., when one looks at one's hand),[47] or it is the body as one imagines it would be if it were over there where the Other's body is seen.[48] I shall show below that either assumption leads to serious difficulties.

Husserl's main answer to his question is thus: the sense 'other conscious subject' is constituted through a process in which the Other's mental states are appresented on the basis of the perception of his (transcendentally and abstractively reduced) body; this appresentation is made possible through the pairing of the Other's appearing body with one's own; this pairing allows all the senses associated with one's own body (which are continuously experienced) to transfer to his body. These are the fundamental processes through which Others are perceived as conscious at a particular time.

Step 3

So far Husserl has only shown how another body that looks like one's own can be given the possible sense 'animate conscious body,' how the experience of the Other's body as 'possibly consciousness imbued' is constituted. Typically, however, Others are not perceived as possibly conscious; their sense includes the element 'actually conscious.' The sense so far constituted must thus be capable of undergoing a process of verification, which Husserl briefly describes. (At this point, he seems to shift from static-constitutional to verificational phenomenology.) Any appresented aspect of the Other has implications for future appresentations, just as one's own conscious states imply future harmonious events.[49] What manifests the harmony in the case of Others is their behavior; if, for example, the Other's possibly-animate body does not exhibit smooth and characteristic behavior sequences, it may become constituted as a pseudo-organism.[50] Husserl does not further explicate the type or degree of harmony needed for achieving the sense-status 'actual.'

These expectations are literal aspects of the sense and are appresented in the present apprehension of the Other. The future either fulfills these expectations, or it does not. Fulfillment is an ongoing process; it is never completed, at least for objects that are transcendent. At any moment a series of appresentations may explode one's anticipations and the constituted sense deriving from them; reconstitution will then have to occur. Such disconfirmation might occur if one experiences humanoid robots or ghosts or disguised Martians. Consequently, verification of a sense does not guarantee the actual existence of its referent.

The coherence of the Other's behavior does not derive primarily from oneself; one is passive with respect to it. The passivity in the verification stage and the fact that the appresented conscious states of the Other can *never* be presented account for the distinctness of the Other and form the basis of the self/Other distinction. In both of these characteristics, perception of Others is similar to apprehension and verification of one's own memories.[51] Memories never become presented as they were originally experienced, and one is largely passive with respect to their concurrence.

Step 4

Many aspects of the sense 'own animate organism' can now be transferred appresentationally to the other presented body: psycho-physical unity of consciousness and body, the possession of an ownness sphere, ongoing constitutional processes amidst continuous self-perception, etc.[52] One might wonder in what way the world in the ownness sphere and the world as appresented for the Other become identified, for in the natural attitude the world is typically perceived as the same world for both self and Others.[53] Husserl's general answer to this problem is that it simply does not arise; the world in one's ownness sphere and the appresented world for the Other are *initially* given the sense 'identical worlds'; they are not given as primordially differentiated in such a way that their sameness must be established externally.[54]

To see why this is so, two facts must be grasped. First, the relation between a presentation and its concomitant appresentations is *not* that of sign to referent; the appresentations are not absent, and they are not offered as distinct from the presentation in the way that the referent is distinct in signitive consciousness. The appresentations are given in primal unity with the presentation, and they are concomitantly 'present' — though not in the fullest sense.[55] They are present like the backs of objects are present in perception or like the immediately preceding moment of consciousness is present in succeeding acts that are constituted as a single state of mind.

Second, the Other's body as it appears in one's ownness sphere is precisely the same body as the one that is offered in the appresented sequence 'other-animated-ego-inhering-in-the-body-over-there.' The Other's orientation toward his body is appresented to me as an orientation toward the very same body as the one presented to me in the sphere of ownness.[56] The body presented to me over there and the body appresented as lived by the appresented Other are the same. His orientation toward his body is distinguished from my orientation toward my body in that my orientation is presented to me continuously while the Other's orientation is only appresented in such a way that it can never become a presented orientation.

These two facts make the explication of the world as having the sense 'identical' for both self and the appresented Other quite straightforward. Since there are not *two* distinct bodies, 'body presented in the ownness sphere' and 'body appresented as that in which the Other inheres,' the Other's body is identified as the same for me and for the appresented Other. Once this initial object in the ownness sphere (the Other's body) is constituted as the same for oneself and the appresented Other, other objects can receive an analogous addition of sense (viz., perceivable to the Other over there *as if* I were there), which is laminated onto the very same entity that is presented in my ownness sphere. This additional layer of senses consists of the set of perspectives that can be seen by Others. Again, these perspectives are *not signified* by the presentation in the ownness sphere; they are *appresented* and thus are offered in the unity of a single complex.[57] Consequently, the objects of the ownness sphere become enriched, and this enrichment emerges once the Other has been constituted. The additional perspectives are appresented as moments of the presentational core that offers itself to the sphere of ownness.[58] The identification of the core object *as presented* and *as appresented* created no special problems; it is the same type of synthesis of identification that is used in reidentifying the same object in the sphere of ownness.

More than any other step, this one indicates that Husserl is discussing the Other solely as he is for us; he does not seek to reach the Other as he is for-himself, nor does he seem to think this is necessary. Husserl's Other is reduced to the sense through which he is grasped; every other aspect of Others is suspended by the adoption of the transcendental standpoint at the outset. Husserl never returns to the natural attitude to describe the relations between the discoveries within his own standpoint and the assumptions of that one. He strives to make Others comprehensible on the basis of paradigms and associative unities drawn solely from one's own case.[59]

Husserl himself notes two problems here. He recognizes that his theory does not account for the appearance of another as disabled (e.g., blind) if one lacks that disability. In such instances Husserl thinks one constitutes the Other in the typical fashion (i.e., as like oneself), and then this sense undergoes a modification as a result of the lack of harmonious behavioral confirmation of one's typical expectations. Without an initially constituted normalcy or typicality, he thinks abnormality could never be identified as such.[60] The second problem is that animals, whose bodies do not appear as like our own, are also constituted as animate (to some extent, conscious) organisms. Husserl thinks animals are constituted as degenerate instances of conscious entities in so far as their bodily appearance and their behavior are seen as degenerate analogues of one's own body and behavior.[61]

Step 5

Since the Other is constituted as oriented toward the world toward which one orients oneself, he can be apprehended as one who can orient toward oneself as one orients toward him. He becomes constituted as one who constitutes oneself as another conscious being. With this step, one undergoes an equalization in which one constitutes oneself as a member of an open community of selves who are all oriented toward the same world and who constitute each other as so oriented.[62] One becomes capable of constituting various types of relationships among Others and constitutes Others as being capable of so constituting oneself and Others. This constituted community potentially contains everyone, for if someone can be imagined or conceived at all, they are thereby constituted as potential members of the community.[63] This equalization permits the possibility of reciprocity and mutality among members of the constituted community. The constituting ego no longer supposes itself to be a privileged subject, the sole source of the senses that constitute the world, but one among many co-constitutors of the same world.[64] With this step the major components of the perception of Others in the natural attitude have been completely constituted in the transcendental standpoint. Husserl's task is virtually complete.

Concrete cultural communities of various orders are also constituted, but these, unlike nature, are not constituted as constituted by all or as the same for all, for such communities arise and have sense through specifically social acts, i.e., acts directed only toward Others.[65] The meaning of such acts derives from patterns of behavior and sets of experiences constituted as shared by persons within the community: similar situations and events that have been lived through, similar rituals that are observed, similar phases of life and roles that each has occupied. Only by participating in the historical development of a culture can one understand this cultural stratum of meanings; thus, according to Husserl, only members of a particular culture can have adequate understanding of it.[66] Comprehension of other cultures always develops via a complicated system of analogizing apperceptions based on one's own.[67] Husserl does not develop any detailed theories of the constitution of cultural entities or of other cultures' meanings; rather he leaves these as problems to be investigated more thoroughly in other works and/or by other meditators.

Sartre's reading of Husserl and its problems

Sartre's reconstruction of Husserl renders Husserl's enterprise more ambiguous than it is; yet Sartre's view is correct in its main outlines. Sartre interprets Husserl to be attempting a refutation of solipsism by demonstrating that the sense 'objective world' cannot exist without the presupposed sense 'other subject.'[68] Thus the perception of anything as objective presupposes and confirms the reality of other people even when they may be absent from the scene.[69] Sartre notes also that one's own empirical ego, since it is an intersubjectively accessible entity, is as dependent on the existence of Others for that aspect of its sense.[70] The main implication of Husserl's view, as Sartre construes it, is that the solipsist, in so far as he not only refuses to believe in Others but also refuses to use the sense 'other conscious subject' and any derivative sense, cannot experience the world as it ordinarily is experienced; his experience must become essentially impoverished. Other people are not just one more type of object that can be affirmed or denied without serious implications; they are part of the very texture of the world as typically perceived (i.e., as objective) even when one is alone.[71]

Although the essentials of this interpretation are acceptable, some of it is misleading, and Husserl's actual project will be more adequately understood if these confusions are eliminated. The first problem is that Sartre views Husserl as presenting a *refutation* of solipsism. This construal is problematic in a number of ways. Husserl is not trying to provide evidence that demonstrates the falsity of a doctrine; he is not providing an argument in the usual sense at all; consequently, his project is wrongly conceived if viewed as a refutation. Husserl's aim is to clarify something deeper than a belief in Others; he is seeking to explicate the possibility of perceiving Others as conscious beings. Belief is a higher-order mental act that has a distinct constitution and additional modes of verification; in this sense, perception is more fundamental than belief. Moreover, he is not *justifying* the perception of Others as such but exhibiting how the emergence of the sense 'Others' is *logically* possible given his assumptions.[72]

Another way in which Sartre's construal of Husserl's position is misleading is in its implication that solipsism must be dismissed if one accepts Husserl's view. In Husserl's exposition, solipsism becomes a problem because he makes a certain assumption, viz., that *all sense* is built up from senses and processes within one's own ego. This assumption is unique to this period of Husserl's thought; it is not entailed by adopting the transcendental standpoint alone. Husserl shows only that this assumption need not commit him to transcendental solipsism, i.e., the inability to constitute anything as another ego.[73]

Husserl does indicate one path by which other egos can be constituted, but this will show that logical or transcendental solipsism is untenable only if these constitutional syntheses *must* occur given the presence of another's body. Nowhere does he *defend* this (even though he does assert it), and indeed this view is empirically inaccurate. Not only is it possible, but it often happens that in the presence of another human body one does not constitute the Other as a conscious being; one may not ever perceive his *body's* presence as actual. Moreover, Husserl shows that solipsism can be avoided only if his theory *and his initial assumption* are correct. If the initial assumption is incorrect, the whole enterprise becomes problematic, and the special version of logical solipsism that Husserl attacks becomes less viable. Finally, as Sartre eventually notes, Husserl does not refute metaphysical solipsism.[74]

A second general problem in Sartre's interpretation is that it confuses the natural and the transcendental standpoints. Sartre sometimes suggests that the actual existence of Others is what the apprehension of the world as objective presupposes.[75] But Husserl does not commit himself to this ontological claim, for he would have to abandon the transcendental standpoint to do so. He only claims that the *supposition* of other conscious subjects is presupposed by the *supposition* of the world as objective. The *sense* 'other conscious being' is presupposed, not the Other's *actual existence*. Even though Husserl believes this sense can be verified and thus that the supposition of Others' actual existence can be made intelligible on his assumptions, he cannot assert or establish actual existence while remaining in the transcendental standpoint. He can only establish what such existence in the natural attitude *means* and what constitutional processes it presupposes; he cannot establish its veridicality.

At times Sartre recognizes this fact, for it becomes the nub of one of his criticisms. Still, the two sorts of claims should be kept distinct so that one's grasp of Husserl's task does not become confused. Sartre easily falls prey to this confusion because he advocates doing phenomenological investigation *without* adopting the transcendental standpoint; hence wherever Husserl would seek "dependencies of sense," Sartre, in his own work, would seek "ontological dependencies."[76]

A third way in which Sartre's interpretation is misleading is its suggestion that Husserl thinks one's own empirical ego is dependent for its constitution on the sense 'Others.' Since Husserl never addresses the empirical ego as it exists in the natural standpoint, I shall take Sartre to mean the transcendentally reduced correlate of that ego. But for that ego Husserl asserts just the opposite: within the sphere of ownness, many of its elements remain accessible — its acts, its enmeshment in a body, its habits and traits in so far as these do not refer to Others, and its orientation in a surrounding world (solely for oneself) via ideals and values in so far as these do not refer to Others. Husserl requires much of the content of one's ego to survive abstraction to the ownness sphere in order to make the apperceptive transfer to the presented Other's body as rich as it can be.[77] Only some higher-order elements of one's ego presuppose the sense 'Others'.

Sartre's fourth misunderstanding is to assimilate Husserl and Kant.[78] Sartre takes Husserl's Other to be a Kantian-like concept through which experience is interpreted, a supplementary "category."[79] This reading involves a number of problems: First, 'other conscious being' in Husserl does not function like Kantian categories; it is a *derived* sense (not a primordial one), the *result* rather than the presupposition of a specific mental synthesis. The sense is constituted via specific procedures upon a presentation of another body like one's own. Kantian categories shape and organize experience; they *make* it be what it is, but most Husserlian senses are themselves constituted, the results of more basic synthetic activity. Second, this sense does not organize or gather together other data; higher levels of constitution become possible as a result of its constitution, but this is because new sense-strata can be appresented once the sense 'Other' is constituted. It opens new areas for synthesis, but does not provide new *forms* of synthesis. Finally, Husserl's transcendental ego has dimensions that can be experienced; for Husserl the word "transcendental" does not mean "beyond all possible experience," but designates the ego which appears when one adopts the transcendental standpoint.

Sartre's interpretative infelicities do not undermine his critique of Husserl. Nevertheless, clarifying them should prevent confusion about Husserl's actual position and facilitate an even more effective critique of it.

An evaluation of Sartre's critique of Husserl

Sartre's criticisms of Husserl are closely connected; each amplifies and develops the previous ones. Nearly all of them make correct and important points; yet some of them also contain injustices which need to be rectified. Each seeks to penetrate to the heart of the matter, and many question the value of the entire Husserlian enterprise. Although his objections are not easily separated from one another, I shall reconstruct Sartre's critique in four basic propositions.

First, while Husserl may have demonstrated the dependency of one's empirical ego on the sense 'other conscious being,' he has not provided an internal bond between transcendental egos, which are the core of persons for Husserl. Sartre contends that if one is going to posit a transcendental ego as the center of the field of consciousness, then essential connections among persons will have to be established at that level. But these are not provided by Husserl. Nor does he show how to constitute the Other's transcendental ego; his explication is limited to the Other's empirical ego.[80]

Half of this criticism is right even though Husserl would not accept its guiding assumption, viz., that an essential connection among persons must be established to avoid solipsism. By accepting the possibility of abstracting to a sphere of ownness that is wholly independent of the sense 'Others,' Husserl admits that one's own transcendental ego is logically independent of that sense. It is also logically independent of any worldly fact or entity. Husserl accepts the monadic self-sufficiency of transcendental egos and thus embraces the monad view of the person which Sartre seeks to overcome.

However, Husserl does succeed in showing how the Other is constituted as a transcendental ego. Since all aspects attaching to one's own ego within the sphere of ownness get transferred via the pairing process, the Other's transcendental ego is appresented in unity with his presented body.[81] The Other is constituted as a bodily organism animated by a transcendental ego with a field of its own which opens onto the same objects as one's own does. Husserl might even argue that in so far as one's grasp of one's own transcendental ego has been neutralized or damaged, one cannot then grasp the Other as having one; thus, there would be a kind of inner dependency between one's grasp of the Other and one's grasp of oneself. Still this would not establish a bond between self and *the Other as such*, for the Other himself is distinct from the sense 'Other' that is constituted by oneself.

Second, Sartre charges that Husserl treats the Other as a mere sense, not as a genuinely existent being beyond one's own world who can limit and alter it. In effect, the existence of the Other is never reached as long as Husserl remains in the transcendental standpoint.[82] Husserl reduces being to an infinite series of verifying acts of one's transcendental ego and thus reduces being to the knowledge one has of it or at least to the constitutional processes that account for it.[83] According to Sartre, such an analysis cannot account for the brutal thereness and insistency of being, especially of the Other's being. The weak way of putting Sartre's point is that a sense may be constituted (e.g., 'Pegasus') without referring to any actual entity, but the stronger way of putting it is that *even if* Husserl's theory is correct, the *being* of the Other has not been reached; being is more than the harmonious verification of one's own sense-constituting activity.

I agree with Sartre's claim here, but Sartre is presupposing a conception of being that is foreign to Husserl's framework, and it needs separate defense. Husserl could reply that he does not merely establish the possibility of the sense 'other conscious being'; he clarifies how this sense is verified and thus how it receives the designation 'actual.' Husserl would claim this is *all one could mean* by the reality or existence of the Other. He would claim that harmonious concurrence of the Other's behavior is the highest grade of evidence one can have for the Other since the Other's conscious processes cannot be presented directly.[84] Husserl can claim to account for the appearance of the Other as a livingly present entity because he clarifies the special character of the Other's presence; he elucidates the only manner in which the element 'actual' can attach to the sense 'Other.'

Sartre might reply in either of two ways. On the one hand, he might question this criterion of harmonious concurrence to see whether it is either sufficient or necessary for verifying the sense 'Other' in Husserl's sense. What sort of harmony? The behavior of epileptics is disjoint, but still they are perceived as existent persons. People do what one does not expect regularly, but this only reinforces one's perception of them as people. Robots may exhibit harmonious behavior, but they are not actual persons. Moreover, the precise criterion for the actuality of persons seems to depend on the sense in which one is wondering about their unreality: are they fake or artificial? dolls? mirages or ghosts? Husserl fails to see the inadequacies of his criterion.

On the other hand, Sartre might question the ontological import of a fully verified sense: is it not possible that an Other who had been continuously verified to date would suddenly prove to be non-actual (e.g., his batteries might run down)? If so, a verified sense does not establish the actuality of the being to which it refers. Husserl must accept this objection; verification in his sense only establishes the probability of the Other. Husserl grants that the evidence for the Other cannot ever be adequate, much less adpodictic, because the Other as such is never presented. Hence, for Husserl, the epistemic quality of the Other's appearance can never be as perfect as that of the self. Husserl accepts a richer concept of being (full self-evident givenness) than the one he allows to apply to Others. A more forceful position than Husserl's would show that this richer concept of being applies to Others as well.

Sartre offers such a position; he tries to elucidate the insistency of the Other's being, the way in which it qualifies, limits, and modifies one's own being. For Sartre, part of what it means to be is *not to be* constitutable by consciousness; an entity does not genuinely exist unless it need not be constituted by oneself. Although one can constitute *what it means* for another to be, one cannot constitute *his being as such*; Sartre clarifies the Other's being by elucidating its impact on oneself.

Third, Sartre objects that Husserl does not establish any access to the subjectivity of the Other as such.[85] Even if one constitutes him as a transcendental ego, one still does not reach his ongoing stream of subjective processes. He is given only as one supposes him; these suppositions may on occasion be modified, but only on the basis of complex constitutional processes in which one's expectations are disconfirmed and new unities of sense are constituted. Even then, one grasps Others only as one supposes them to be.

To this objection Husserl must plead guilty, for he does not see a way of providing any deeper access to Others than the type of constitution he offers. Indeed, Husserl assumes that if one had any stronger access to the Other, he would literally be oneself. However, this is only a restatement of the claim that Others' experience is unreachable, not a statement based on the results of careful phenomenological investigation of the data. Husserl nowhere establishes the inaccessibility of Others; yet this is one of his fundamental assumptions. Later we shall explore whether the Other's mental states might be as accessible as one's own.[86] Here, as elsewhere, Husserl's "presuppositionless" science depends on some crucial presuppositions after all.

Fourth, Sartre objects that Husserl has not dispensed with epistemological solipsism. The reality of the Other, in contrast to the self, is never presented adequately; indeed, the evidence for the Other *can never* reach the grade of that for the self. If anything, Husserl reinforces epistemological solipsism. Husserl asserts that the world cannot be perceived as it typically is without utilizing the sense 'Other.' The epistemological solipsist might willingly accept this claim and modify the typical perception of the world. He would remain within the natural-attitude correlate of the sphere of ownness and refuse to sanction the constitution of any additional strata.[87] The epistemological solipsist does not simply deny our knowledge of Others; characteristically he denies our knowledge of material objects as well; only he himself can be genuinely known. That his whole position could be shown to follow simply from a de-activation of this one sense would be a welcome, not a troublesome, result to him. Husserl seems to hope that one's naive confidence in Nature's objectivity will transfer to Others if the sense 'other conscious being' is shown to be required by it; instead, the solipsist would use the inferior epistemic status of Others to transfer that status to objective Nature.

Husserl's neglect of *epistemological* solipsism is the central problem here. Husserl thinks that his constitutional explication can be rewritten at the higher levels of belief and knowledge, but the inferior status of one's access to Others remains an obstacle to the success of this enterprise. The epistemological solipsist need only demand adequacy or apodicity as standards for knowledge; Husserl can hardly object to this demand since it justifies his entire project. For all his suspicion of the natural attitude, Husserl is too willing to accept it as the guiding clue to his transcendental explication.[88] He does not see the implications that a more serious skeptic might draw from his assumptions.

Sartre's criticisms establish two general points: (1) one cannot reduce the Other to a sense generated by one's own constitutional processes without losing his independence and his obtrusiveness, and (2) adopting the transcendental standpoint does not allow one to circumvent metaphysical or epistemological solipsism; at best, it only permits a critique of logical solipsism.

Additional objections to Husserl

My critique will begin with the specific contentions of Husserl's theory; each step will be studied for its adequacy. Although important objections can be raised at this level, my later criticisms will question Husserl's general approach: my intuition is that any constitutional analysis of the sort Husserl offers will be subject to fatal problems.

Specific objections

There are five steps in Husserl's explication: the abstraction to the sphere of ownness, the description of the appresentational-pairing process, the verification of the sense via harmonious behavior, the constitution of an intersubjective world, and the development of cultural meanings and higher-order social unities. I shall examine each step in turn.

Problems with step 1

Husserl's first step is the abstraction to the sphere of ownness.[89] This step is mandated by the sort of enterprise he wishes to engage in; the possibility of such an abstraction both justifies and necessitates his enterprise. Later I shall raise some global objections to this move and the resulting project; here I shall mention some technical, but nevertheless important, problems.

First, Husserl performs this abstractive process with some awareness that he cannot intuit the resulting realm; hence, he will not be able to offer pure descriptions of it.[90] Although one can conceive the resulting sphere of contents, one cannot experience it. One can thus only *construct* a path from this sphere to everyday experience-as-supposed. The basic contents from which constitution begins and the whole constitutional process too easily become hypothetical, and this betrays the descriptive ideal of phenomenology.

Moreover, I suggested above that Husserl offers no *independent* criteria for determining what is alien and what is own.[91] No means of verifying the contents of the sphere of ownness are provided. On occasion, Husserl tries to use the concept of 'not-alien' to demarcate this sphere, but this notion is subject to the same vagueness as 'own.' This failure exacerbates the previous problem, for since the sphere cannot be intuited as such, we are forced to simply accept the list of its contents that Husserl presents. This situation is unusual in phenomenology; one is accustomed to the possibility of verifying each claim for oneself. Husserl's abstraction thus violates his ideals of description (via self-evident intuitions) and independent verification by any meditator.

Second, a certain unseriousness pervades Husserl's enterprise because one is unable to examine this important step in any effective way. The contents allowed into the sphere of ownness determine every further step because they constitute the base on which everything is built. This base needs to be rich enough to complete the task, but not so rich as to leave no task. Husserl can arbitrarily ensure his success by simply including whatever he needs. In one sense of 'own,' one can wonder why anything in the transcendental standpoint is excluded since nothing is grasped as actual, objective, or beyond the transcendental field. In another sense of 'own,' one can wonder why anything beyond one's psychic processes themselves should be included since all correlates of such acts transcend them; in so far as they can function in many different psychic acts, the correlates are never exhausted by their acts.

Some criterion can probably be found to include all that is on Husserl's list and exclude everything else, but the reason for drawing the boundary line there at least requires some justification.[92] The problem here is analogous to that in Descartes when certain truths of reason are imported into the sphere of clear and distinct ideas without asking whether they satisfy the same criterion of indubitability that acts of consciousness do. The extra contents that Husserl needs — the immanent transcendencies (e.g., the Other's body appearing as a mere correlate of one's own act of perception) — may be subject to nagging critical doubts. Only because we have been prevented from questioning their inclusion at the outset is the enterprise allowed to proceed. If either the immediate bodily correlates of one's own conscious life or the appearing body of the Other were excluded from the sphere of ownness, no transition out of it would be possible.

Problems with step 2

Husserl's second step is his discussion of apperception and pairing. This step requires three basic conditions: the basis of the apperception — continuous self-perception related to one's own bodily movements;[93] the pairing of the presented body of the Other with one's own body;[94] and the apperception of the Other as conscious that develops from the transfer of sense from one's own sphere and is made possible by the pairing.[95] These are not meant to be temporally discrete steps, but they are logically discrete; and for the purposes of discussion they can be analyzed separately. All theories of Husserl's sort must make these claims: since the Other (in some sense) is being constituted on the basis of oneself (in some sense), there must be a source for this constitution in self-perception and an observable similarity between self and Other that grounds the basic transfer. Both requirements face important difficulties if one examines experience closely.

First, there is no continuous self-perception, much less any self-perception specifically relating mental acts to bodily movements. By "self-perception" Husserl must mean apprehension of a mental act in the course of its existence either by itself or by another mental act simultaneous with it. In order to make the current act of consciousness fully present and thus transferable, this self-perception cannot be peripheral or undifferentiated; it must 'be direct, focal, and have full grasp of the mental act it apprehends.

Such ongoing focal perception of mental acts is neither experienced nor possible. One rarely perceives or explicitly registers a mental state while living through it; it occurs in the process of intercourse with the world and the actualization of one's aims. Features of the world that bear on those aims occupy the center of one's attention. One's mental states are laminated to worldly situations; only if there is some important reason to discriminate them do they get explicit attention. In addition, not all aspects of mental states are even capable of being registered. Most mental events happen too quickly; many of one's responses are too painful to attend to; and much of the processing is too implicit to capture. Retrospective efforts to elucidate the whole of even just one mental state are often unsuccessful. Moreover, if there were an ongoing second-order act of perception of every mental state, there would have to be infinitely many of them since this second-order perception is itself a mental state to which the principle would have to apply. Finally, one can observe that introspection often alters the act of consciousness of which it is aware. It provides it with a theme and structure that is not present in the original. The emergence of explicit self-perception typically induces a displacement of the original focal object of attention; it recedes toward the horizon.

In Husserl's case, this would mean that to the extent that one was apprehending one's own awareness, one would be less able to apprehend the Other's body in the field of one's attention. If this is true, one could not apprehend the appresented Other because there would be no explicit presentation to motivate it. The reverse side of this point is that in so far as the Other's body is fully presented, his subjectivity could not be appresented because one's own psychic processes would be too implicit to be transferred through pairing. Most of our lives are absorbed in the world around us; our own mental states are rarely discriminated; at best ongoing self-perception is vague, implicit, ancillary, and impoverished.[96]

Husserl might have been misled about self-perception because of his Cartesian standpoint, a highly reflective standpoint in which one's own mental processes tend to stand out more vividly. But one experiences a correlative impoverishment of the world because of this reflectivity, and this often goes unnoticed. The theorist tends to transfer the results he obtains in the reflective standpoint to typical pre-reflective experience without realizing their large differences. Husserl makes this error in both directions: he thinks that objects of acts are still presented as they are in the natural attitude while he is reflecting and also that the self-perception that is characteristic of reflective states continues, though somewhat suppressed, in pre-reflective states. Both claims are mistaken. To the extent that the Other's body is fully presented, one's self-perception is minimal, and thus it cannot transfer; and to the extent that one's self-perception is explicit, the Other's body is not presented with any vivacity, and thus no motivation for a transfer of sense exists. Husserl does not see that our clearest perception of Others occurs when we completely forget ourselves.

The second objection to step 2 concerns whether one typically associates one's own mental acts and bodily processes in the requisite direction to make the transfer of sense possible. Presumably one needs observations of one's own body as it can be seen from the outside linked with associated mental acts — linked in such a way that the perception of the body is the center of attention (presentation) and the mental states are the peripheral articulation (appresentation), for this is the direction or vector of presentation-appresentation in Other-perception. If the *source* of apperception does not appear in this fashion, the Other's *body* cannot appropriately trigger apperceived conscious states.

Two facts are crucial. The first is that one typically grasps one's lived body *from the inside even when* one is associating mental acts with perception of one's body. More generally, the bodily dimension most characteristically experienced is the body as incarnate point of view and master instrument, not the body that can be seen in the mirror and presented as an object. In the midst of action, one rarely sees one's body at all; one simply lives through it. In addition, one rarely registers correlations between one's lived body and one's mental states. One's mental states are not distinguished from their lived-body expression; they come to completion through it. But while one is acting, one rarely experiences this organic unity from an external, third-person viewpoint.

The second fact is that one very rarely grasps one's body, *when seen as an object*, as animated. One apprehends it as if it were in a different dimension from the body one experiences from the inside. One need only look in a mirror or at one's hand to experience the mysteriousness of the connection between the experience of one's brow wrinkling and its mirror appearance or between the experience of one's fist clenched and the wrapped-up digit. The two aspects seem almost artificially related to one another.[97] Consequently, in one's own awareness the objective body does not have a primordial connection with one's mental acts, and to the extent that there is any connection at all, the relation originates in the mental acts and terminates in the animated lived-body.

Both facts undermine the parallel to Other-perception: the apperception of Others' mental states on the basis of the presentation of their bodies. In order for apperception to be possible, one would have to be presented with the Other's *lived-body*, not his object-body. But if one were presented with this, there would be no need for the entire apperceptive operation since the Other's mental process would directly accessible.

These considerations also indicate an obvious difficulty for the second aspect of the apperceptive process, the pairing of the Other's presented body with one's own. How is such pairing possible? Although one can certainly see parts of one's body externally, one does not apprehend this body as a gestalt in any complete way and could not do so without frequent scrutiny of light-reflecting media like mirrors or lakes or glass. Moreover, *within* the sphere of ownness, one's objective body may not be graspable as *one's own* since the distinction between own and alien is just emerging. One may be unable to regard one's own object-body as more intimate than the Other's body. Again, while in the midst of action or expression, one almost never *attends to* the external appearance of the body, one *uses* it; one immerses oneself in the world through it, but one does not objectify it. Thus, the way in which the presented body of the Other, which is apprehended objectively, becomes paired with one's own body is mysterious. One almost wants to say there is no basis for the pairing. If one tries to pair parts of one's own objectified body with the Other's body, one's own body will "lack life"; there will be nothing psychic to transfer. But typically one experiences nothing with which to pair the Other's presented body; thus, no pathway for the transfer of one's own psychic sense-content exists.

Though these objections seem telling, Husserl might offer the following reply: the Other's body is not paired with my own lived-body-seen-from-the-outside, but with an imaginary mnemonic projection of my body as it would appear if it were over there. Husserl's exposition is ambivalent about the object with which the Other's body is paired.[98] Even though this revised position is an entirely different theory, it also has serious difficulties.

First, our capacity to project a coherent image of our own body as if it were over there may be wholly dependent on already having constituted the Other's body as coherent, animate, and consciousness-endowed. We may be unable to form *any* coherent body-image without using the Other's animate body as a model; indeed our apprehension of the bodily coherence of the Other may be essential to our ability to coordinate our own bodily movements and to achieve the realization that we relate to the world through a cohesive, manipulable body.[99] We may thus constitute *our own* body *via* the Other's, and Husserl may have his constitutional priorities inverted. The inherently first body-apprehension may well be the Other's body, which then allows us to form the sense 'coherent body inhabited by me'; only at a much higher level of constitution would our ability to project an image of our own body alongside the Other's be possible, and at that point it would be superfluous. We may also constitute our own psychic possibilities through the Other's.

Second, even if one could project an image of one's objectified body without already presupposing apprehension of the Other as a conscious being, there is no reason to think one's conscious states would accompany the body-as-projected. Since one's own body-looked-at is not immediately related to the body one lives, one might well be able to project an image of the objectified body without reproducing any concomitant psychic processes. In this event there would be nothing accompanying the projected body to transfer to the Other's body. Thus the pairing process would provide no additional associations to be appresented with the Other's body. This inattention to one's awareness of one's body plagues both the original and the alternative version of Husserl's theory.

Third, the hypothesis that a shadow-like depiction of one's own body overlays one's apprehension of another's body in order to animate it through a transfer of sense seems implausible at best. Empirically one simply does not register a projection of one's own body on encountering the body of another; even in the highly artificial state of mind that Husserl's phenomenological explication requires, this imaginary projection is lacking. Husserl is invoking *ad hoc* hypostatizations to cover the gaps in his position.

Fourth, if Husserl hopes to use these imaginary projections of one's own body as a means of identifying the specific psychic states of the Other,[100] then he again must *presuppose* what he is hoping to constitute through this procedure. For one does not know which memory of one's body to reproduce and imaginatively project unless one has already identified the conscious state of the Other and thus unless the sense that might arise from the pairing of body presentations becomes superfluous. Husserl consistently neglects to consider the extent to which the sense 'Other' is required for the most basic conscious syntheses; for this reason he fails to see how deeply intertwined self and Other really are.

Finally, there are important ways in which self-perception and Other-perception interanimate one another through bodily apprehension and mirroring, but these can only be seen and described if one emerges from both the abstraction and the transcendental standpoint. In concrete practical life, I learn to coordinate my bodily operations by mimicking the Other's body, and as I watch the Other engaged in his tasks, a projection of my lived body participates with him. This allows me a deeper and more finely-tuned apprehension of the Other's conscious life. The Other's actions evoke immediate echoes in my lived-body. This explains why our practical responses to the Other often "comprehend" what is happening more quickly than our conscious processes. One cannot accurately describe the lived body if one adopts the transcendental standpoint; only existential phenomenology can adequately clarify the role of the body in interpersonal perception and comprehension.[101]

Problems with step 3

The third major step in Husserl's discussion concerns the verification of the sense 'other conscious being,' which transforms it from the status 'possible' to 'actual.' Husserl's "verification" is not equivalent to justifying a belief, but instead concerns the supposed "reality-status" of one's suppositions. The meaning of the world-as-supposed transforms to the degree that it continues to fulfill the expectations implicit in those suppositions. The verification of this sense occurs through harmonious behavior-sequences that are appresented as one's apprehension of the Other continues.[102] Evaluating this step is difficult because the harmony criterion is vague. In addition, Husserl never defends this criterion; again we are offered dogma instead of the ability to verify for ourselves.

In the explication of Husserl, problems about disjoint, atypical, and irrational behavior were raised; I suggested that these types of behavior by themselves would not be sufficient to disconfirm the supposition of another as a conscious subject; indeed, they might reinforce or confirm it. I also wondered whether the same criterion would apply in the case of animals, for the appropriate harmonious sequences that apply to them cannot possibly have developed on the basis of one's own case; nevertheless, animals are grasped as actual and as conscious, and this status is not assigned solely because their behavior approximates one's own. Here I shall note two deeper objections.

First, although behavioral harmony may be an adequate criterion for confirming some aspects of what becomes transferred (e.g., 'animate organisms governed psychically by an ordered set of purposes'), some aspects of what is transferred do not seem susceptible to this sort of verification (e.g., 'constituting a world of one's own,' 'existing amidst a subjective time-flow'). Some of these aspects are too general to entail any very specific behaviors or even global expressions; moreover, they refer to aspects of the Other's subjectivity which cannot *as such* be manifest in behavior since most behavior is consistent with any number of views about what sorts of processes animate it. For example, no matter how organized an animal's behavior is, Husserl would probably refuse to grant that it has a transcendental ego and the capacity to consciously adopt the transcendental standpoint. These are not just minor problems, for Husserl holds that elements of sense transfer by pairing only until they are no longer verified; at that point one must acknowledge the Other's difference. The inability to verify described above would require this cancellation of sense-transfer and would thus prevent the Other from being constituted as fully like oneself. Our experience of Others would undergo impoverishment if Husserl's verification procedures were taken seriously.

A second objection to this criterion concerns the possibility of verifying the actuality-status of the sense 'Other' *through* grasping behavioral harmonies. Which behavioral harmonies are essential? These could only be determined by identifying *typical* sequences in the behavior of actual Others, but these can be established only if one has already verified some Others as actual.[103] Providing an adequate conception of the relevant behavioral harmonies thus presupposes what it seeks to establish. Husserl's vagueness about these harmonies is not simply fortuitous; it conceals a deep difficulty in his entire approach.

Moreover, Husserl fails to acknowledge the extent to which behavioral harmony is a culture-specific, even class- and age-specific, concept. This is one reason why one cannot develop an adequate concept of harmony solely from one's own case; it would be too limited and would only verify those whose patterns of behavior were most like one's own. Husserl's procedure, if followed, would be a way of institutionalizing ethnocentricity (even egocentricity) in the very perception of Others. Another reason is that one's own case simply is not rich enough to establish a rule that would effectively delineate an appropriate type of harmony. Husserl fails to appreciate the extent to which generalizations about Others are embedded in his criterion of harmony. If all presuppositions about Others are bracketed and all senses dependent on the sense 'Others' are abstractively neutralized, then Husserl will be unable to spell out the criterion he needs to verify the actuality aspect of the sense 'other conscious being.'

Before examining the final steps in his explication, I want to consider the result of the processes Husserl has described, supposing that he could adequately answer all the criticisms so far advanced. Husserl claims that the apperception process is a kind of mirroring of oneself onto the Other. In the presence of another's body, on the basis of its similarity to one's own, all the elements typically associated with one's own body become appresented.[104] These appresented elements are not merely signified or imagined; they offer themselves and overflow the content of the presentation, but they can never become full presentations. Essentially, one's own constituted psychic life is replicated by transfer over there in unity with the body of the Other.

The central question to ask at this point is not how is this Other distinct from oneself (the fact that his conscious states can *only* be appresented establishes this difference), but to what extent is the *otherness* of the Other constituted; to what extent *can* it be constituted in this way? By "otherness" I mean neither spatial distinctness of bodies nor numerical difference of centers of consciousness, but rather qualitative difference in the stream of the Other's conscious life and its organization. Is Husserl's constituted Other simply a reproduced self, a doubled version of one's own psychic life? Isn't he necessarily this? On Husserl's analysis, one grasps the Other's psychic life through a transfer of sense from one's own case. If this were correct, the perception of another as alien, strange, superior to oneself in ability or character, or unique would seem to be impossible, at least initially. But these differences often strike one most forcefully in initial encounters.

Husserl might reply that the constituted Other is a reproduced self only in the very general sense of being someone like oneself and that his qualitative difference from oneself can be constituted through the procedures already outlined. For example, the Other's difference might emerge through one's apprehension of sufficiently distinctive behavioral harmonies. But if Husserl relies on this reply, then he must explain how the process of sense-transfer is halted at so general a level. He explicitly asserts that sense-transfer continues until some difference emerges and cancels it.[105] Husserl does not explain what these differences might be, nor does he clarify how the process is allowed to continue until everything that he wants constituted in the Other is transferred. Moreover, behavioral harmonies are unlikely to be good guides to qualitative differences in persons since similar persons may behave very differently, and different persons may behave very similarly. Finally, Husserl never explains how one becomes capable of objectively apprehending one's own behavioral harmonies so that one can compare them to the Other's patterns of behavior.

In addition, Husserl ignores the possibility that there may be significant individual differences in the constitutional patterns of particular people. Some people may more readily grasp Others as "essentially like themselves." Other people may typically grasp Others as "radically distinct from themselves." Husserl prefers to think that one story is basically correct for everyone. Although this assumption simplifies his explicative task, it may conceal central differences in conscious processing. This particular difference can have enormous ramifications at higher levels of constitution; one's fundamental attitude toward Others may be largely dependent on this variable.

A different version of the same objection concerns whether the Other's conscious life as it is for the Other can be constituted. In order to explicate the sameness of the world seen by self and Other, Husserl holds that the Other's body that appears in one's sphere of ownness is the same body as the one appresented to one as lived by the Other. But could this appresented element of the Other's body be identical with the body actually lived by the Other? Clearly not. The Other's conscious processes are not appresented to him; yet they must be appresented to oneself. One's own constitutional processes do not fill out the subjectivity of the Other as it is for him, and, on Husserl's assumptions, they cannot do so. The mirroring of self onto the Other does not sufficiently render his qualitative distinctness.

Problems with steps 4 and 5

The next steps in Husserl's explication constitute the objective natural world and the surrounding cultural world. One of Husserl's important claims is that the sense 'objective material thing' presupposes the sense 'other conscious being' — the former cannot emerge if the latter has not been constituted. Husserl explicates the objectivity of the natural world as an addition of appresentational content that derives from the possibility of an object's being seen from distinct viewpoints and thus exhibiting profiles that are potentially accessible to Others. In effect, the reduced object that is presented in the sphere of ownness is supplemented with appresentational echoes of these other profiles. Since the constitution of Others makes these echoes possible, it permits the constitution of the object's objectivity.[106]

To this explication one can object that the constitution of Others is not really necessary to this way of constituting nature as objective. Husserl frequently compares the kinds of syntheses which operate in the constitution of Others to those which operate in memory. Thus, Husserl might have considered the possibility that the other perspectives of an object might be appresented on the basis of *memory intuitions* of that object. Memories could function as the source of the other appresented profiles.[107] To be sure, an object constituted in this way would be private in the sense that nothing outside one's own actual experience would be either presented or appresented, but Husserl does no better by using the constituted Other, for the Other is only a set of transferred apperceptions based on one's own experience. The perspectives one constitutes for him are only the ones that one would see oneself if one were over there. Could one not remember what the object looked like when one was in fact over there, and could these perspectives not be appresented in the present perception? If one's memories of this object are *limited*, could one not imagine the manifold of other profiles of this kind of object on the basis of one's limited memories; would these appresentations not be as rich as anything provided by the appresented Other?

Husserl might reply that the constituted Other is necessary in order to provide the sense that other perspectives on the object are *simultaneously* possible. But if one assumes that a presented object can be identified as the same as a remembered object, there seems to be no reason why the other perspectives that arise from memory could not be seen as possibly contemporaneous. They could be associated with the presented object in the same way that profiles appresented from the Other's perspective are, and their appresentedness would guarantee that the 'object itself' (the sum of presentation and appresentations) would transcend or overflow its presently presented profile. This overflowing seems to be the essential meaning of 'objective' for Husserl.[108] Nothing in Husserl's explication of objectivity depends on the *actual* presence of Others to the object; the additional appresented profiles are those which *could be* seen by Others if they were present. Memory intuitions could just as easily provide those profiles.

Hence, the Other may be superfluous to the constitution of the objectivity of nature; at best, the constitution of Others only minimally supplements what might be achieved via memory. This is not a minor point, for Husserl's primary concern in the Fifth Meditation is to clarify the correct logical order of the various senses and syntheses that operate in one's apprehension of the world. One might wonder whether *only one* order is intrinsically possible, but if one assumes this, one should defend the ordering one proposes. Husserl is negligent on this point.

I shall complete these specific objections to Husserl's theory by noting that he is overly optimistic about the results that will occur within a particular monad when one undergoes equalization — grasping oneself under the sense 'one among many similar monads capable of being constituted by them'.[109] Husserl claims that the primary result of equalization will be a disposition toward mutuality. This assumes that the monad-self will accept its equalized status graciously. Certainly such willingness is not universal. Equally likely is a struggle to regain one's lost ascendancy, which may lead to perpetual conflict or a fight to the death.[110] Equalization can be experienced as a fall from grace — a state that the monad-self might forever strive to recover. At the very least, many additional explicative steps are needed to show how (if at all) equalization leads to mutuality. Husserl passes over the alleged ramifications of the processes he describes too quickly.

This point illustrates one important difference between Husserl and Sartre. Husserl works from within a highly reflective standpoint, and is motivated by abstract theoretical concerns. Sartre is no less rigorous than Husserl, but he seeks to carry out the phenomenological project from a standpoint that permits greater elucidation of lived experience and that has more direct applications to everyday life. These large differences between Husserl and Sartre must now be explored.

General objections

Husserl's theory of Others is determined by his first two moves: the adoption of the transcendental standpoint and the abstraction to the sphere of ownness within that standpoint. If one is seeking a full and adequate clarification of the nature of Others, these moves create severe constraints and lead the analysis in the wrong direction. I shall now explain why.

Problems with the abstraction to the sphere of ownness

Husserl believes that this step is necessary and legitimate because he assumes that the sense 'other conscious being' and its derivatives arise from senses and processes that lie within oneself. The abstraction ensures that the explication of Others will be pure, i.e., that no elements which presuppose the sense to be explicated will be used in the course of the explication. Husserl thinks he must constitute the sense 'Others' because he believes that Others' conscious states can never be presented. Husserl seems to offer an argument for this claim, but the argument is circular. Demonstrating this will indicate how Husserl's abstractive move artificially creates his entire enterprise, for if the Other's conscious states can be presented, constituting them becomes unnecessary. Far from clarifying the nature of Others, Husserl's theory presupposes, and merely elaborates, a central Cartesian dogma.

Husserl's argument is that if the Other's mental states were presented, they would be *one's own* since *any* presented mental states *must be* one's own. If the Other's states were presented to one, he would lose his distinct identity. If he is really an Other, his mental states must be appresented.[111] This assumption is deeply embedded in many conceptions of self and Other. As an argument, this position simply begs the question against someone who claims that Others' conscious states can be presented. Husserl's crucial premise, only one's own mental states *can* be presented, states his conclusion in different words.

Probably the most effective challenge to this conception has been mounted by Max Scheler in his essay "Other Minds", in *The Nature of Sympathy*.[112] Scheler makes many astute observations in this essay; no one of them alone would be sufficient to overthrow Husserl's position, but collectively they render it extremely questionable. Scheler is simply more attentive to the actual features of interpersonal experience than Husserl. Although most of Scheler's observations derive from the natural attitude, they can all be restated as claims about "experience-as-supposed" within the transcendental standpoint. Husserl might have avoided some of his deeper errors if he had devoted more attention to the interconnections between what he calls "phenomenological psychology" and transcendental phenomenology.[113]

Scheler begins by noting that not all presented mental states are experienced as one's own. Ownership is often misascribed: states emerging in oneself are often seen as Others' states, and those originating in Others can be experienced as one's own. Some states are not experienced as owned at all; they are "in the air," but their ownership is indeterminate. Scheler also suggests that some states can be literally shared, e.g., common grief.[114] These observations show at least that presented states need not be experienced as exclusively one's own, and they may show that some presented states are not one's own at all.

Scheler continues by suggesting that the *primordial level of experience*, that from which all distinctions emerge, is probably an undifferentiated stream of experiences which are not assigned to either self or Other; only gradually does the capacity to discriminate forms within this stream and to assign them to an owner become possible.[115] Children and some primitive cultures, for example, seem to experience the world in this undifferentiated fashion. They live entirely *in Others*; the collective stream of experiences flows through and unifies all its members. Thus, the monad self and the differentiated Other may both derive from a more primordial interpersonal contact, which is never absolutely lost and to which some may continue to have access.

These observations can be readily illustrated. Excitement sometimes suffuses a classroom; all experience it, but no one experiences it as uniquely his or as orginating in some specific person; it seems to flow through and emerge from everyone; each shares and apprehends it simultaneously. Similarly, one can experience one's own anger as another person's (e.g., in projection) or another's hatred as one's own.[116] Emotions are especially susceptible to being co-experienced; laughter, depression, and boredom are often experienced jointly, i.e., as shared — as one experience linking two people. In addition, two people can share the same thought; sometimes a single thought arises between two people and is only capable of being fully articulated *jointly.*[117] In certain group contexts, one is dramatically attuned to what the group is thinking and feeling, and this displaces one's own 'personal' thoughts and feelings; in such situations one seems to be approximating Scheler's primordial interpersonal contact.

If Scheler is right, he does not merely show that the Other's conscious states can be presented to oneself; he suggests that the *self itself* may be derivative — arising simultaneously with the differentiated Other. This suggests that Husserl's abstraction might have gone in the wrong direction, to the wrong source. He should have sought to abstract to Scheler's more primordial level of shared experience and to trace how the sense 'self' and the sense 'Other' and the capacity to assign some experiences to one and some to the other emerge. Even if Scheler is wrong, his position demonstrates that the kind of abstraction Husserl performs *presupposes* that persons' conscious states are never presented and that only the sense 'Others' needs to be constituted. Husserl's project is not neutral; it rests on very definite presuppositions which might well be false. At the very least, they must be defended in a non-circular fashion.

A number of other considerations supplement this critique. Scheler himself indicates that some conscious or spiritual qualities are apprehended prior to registering the Other's body as a presented object; e.g., the intrinsically first quality one perceives in Others may be whether they are friends or enemies, whether they threaten one in some way.[118] One may not even have to see a person to realize that he brings trouble; one need only overhear his movements or tone of voice. Moreover, one typically grasps the Other as engaged in some project; his body is grasped as oriented toward the achievement of certain ends, and one apprehends it through these ends. They strike one more directly than simple physical qualities like body size, shape, and hair color. These observations raise doubts about Husserl's contention that the Other's body is always the core of presentation on the basis of which all other personal qualities are appresented.

Husserl's appresentational view also assumes that a definite separation exists between expressed mental states and the bodily behaviors expressing them (the former are appresented, the latter presented), but this may be incorrect. The 'meaning' and the 'signifying expression' may at least sometimes be united in an expressive synthesis in which the meaning is inherent and immanent in the expressions themselves.[119] The Other's joy is not appresented through his smile, but concretized in it; the joy surges through the facial movements. If one is to make a distinction between presented and appresented elements, the meaning (the mental state itself) often seems to be more present than the signifying elements (the bodily behaviors). This is how interpersonal life is actually experienced if one attends to it without theoretical presuppositions. Again, Husserl's abstraction seems to be a theoretically-loaded move that betrays the best ideals of phenomenology.

In addition, to the extent that certain appearances of the Other dismantle one's orientation to the world and dissolve one's typical self-apprehension, Husserl's view that Others must be grasped through one's own constituting processes becomes difficult to defend, for these processes require one's self-apprehension and one's normal orientation to the world. If what is supposed to serve as the basis for constitution is *undercut* by the Other's appearance, then that appearance cannot have been constituted in the way Husserl prescribes. Rather, one's own experience is altered and re-constituted by the Other. This objection can be derived from Sartre's position; he shows that Others do appear in ways that have this effect, e.g., via the gaze which objectifies one.[120]

Yet this kind of objection is not limited to Sartrean examples. Others do not only limit and quash one's experience; they can enliven it and facilitate one's rising to new levels of sensitivity. Sometimes the experience of love has this effect; sometimes an insightful remark from a friend can make one able to do what previously seemed impossible. Sometimes debating with or competing against Others allows one to achieve a level of self-awareness not possible without such intervention. These examples indicate the oddness of offering a theory that holds that Others are constituted through one's own experience; in fact, Others seem to participate in the constitution of that experience.

With the abstraction to the sphere of ownness, Husserl's phenomenological investigation of Others took a wrong turn. Undoubtedly there are occasions when one comprehends Others analogically and even perceives them via appresentations based on one's own case, but these are not the typical or important cases. And, as I have shown, the abstraction rests on phenomenologically suspect assumptions. Not only are the elements of the sense 'Other' not always constituted on the basis of one's own experience, not only does the Other's body not always serve as the core of presentation in Other-perception, but the entire constitutional project may be obviated by the fact that Others' conscious states can be presented. Moreover, Husserl's project ignores the extent to which the structures of one's experience and oneself are constituted, transformed, and made possible by Others. There may be no simple, intrinsically necessary path by which the perception of another must take place. Husserl's abstractive process forecloses too many theoretical options; it prevents an examination of all the possible ways in which the constitution of the self and the constitution of Others can occur.

Problems with the transcendental standpoint

The second issue concerns the difference between transcendental and existential phenomenology: How helpful is shifting into the transcendental standpoint? Are there arguments that speak against this shift? Husserl acknowledges the possibility of performing in the natural attitude a study analogous to the one which he executes in the transcendental attitude, but he believes that transcendental phenomenology is the only path to certain and presuppositionless results. My earlier remarks raised doubts about the presuppositionless nature of his program; here some additional objections to Husserl's *epoché* will be suggested.

As soon as one decides to bracket the existential status of what one investigates, one prevents oneself from reaching the actual structures of things themselves; one restricts oneself only to senses and their configurations. Since senses seem less independent than things, one easily convinces oneself that one's own conscious processes are the source of their structure. Exclusive concentration on senses makes one miss sources of unity that exist in things as such. One is more likely to find only what one expects to find if one makes the transcendental turn. Although one's own conscious processes may be the source of some of the unity of experience, one at least does not want to eliminate other hypotheses by virtue of one's method. Husserl's adoption of the transcendental standpoint is the fateful step that led him to think that the transcendental ego and its processes are the source of all meaning and all sense. Although he need not have drawn this conclusion, it became more self-evident to him as he worked within the *epoché*. Adopting the reflective standpoint easily leads to delusions about the capacities of consciousness.

Moreover, when one brackets the more concrete forms, forces, and elements of lived *social* experience, one brackets important factors like roles, rituals, and organizing patterns of social meaning, which do not derive from the individual subject yet which provide structure to social perception. Husserl's standpoint excludes much that must be investigated if one is to achieve adequate clarification of the structures of interpersonal experience. These factors *organize* the capacities of consciousness; they are not constituted on the basis of them.

Perhaps one telling example will indicate why the transcendental standpoint is so easily misleading. Husserl's criterion for epistemic adequacy is presence — full self-evident givenness. Every Husserlian investigation revolves around this criterion. Presence seems to be a natural criterion because the transcendental attitude erases all one's practical relations to the world. Heidegger raised an important objection to Husserl's criterion, viz., that presence is a derivative mode of appearance. For Heidegger, the world is primordially organized as a series of instruments; they manifest themselves in a very different fashion than the metaphor of presence suggests. Only if this instrumental organization breaks down or is suspended does an object appear simply as present.[121] Husserl elevates to a regulatory law a mode of appearance that is secondary in lived experience; its apparent primacy is artificially created by adopting the transcendental standpoint. Others, for example, are not most manifest when they are most present, but when their practical aims are most evident. Not only does the transcendental standpoint artificially screen off entire sectors of phenomena, it suggests inadequate guidelines for investigating those it leaves intact.

If one abandons all the unity that exists prior to the reduction, one will be tempted to reconstruct it entirely within the transcendental sphere. One posits an array of constitutional processes that may not function at all in pre-reflective life. The hope of existential phenomenology is that these hypothetical processes will be superfluous: by deciphering the organization of lived experience and grasping all the structure inherent in things themselves, one will not need the supplement of the transcendental standpoint. Husserl's *epoché* conceals what needs clarification and encourages hypostatization instead of elucidating concrete, operative structures. Existential phenomenology rejects the claim that the natural attitude is based on and presupposes transcendental processes.

In addition, existential phenomenology seeks to render the structures of experience more accurately. Sartre suggests that adopting the transcendental standpoint alters the data one is trying to understand and thus makes adequate description impossible.[122] Husserl recognizes this problem, but he thinks he can circumvent it; unfortunately he neglects to say how. This problem may be one reason why Husserl continuously sought to radicalize phenomenology, to return again and again to its foundations.[123] There is no reason why imaginative variation, the central technique of eidetic phenomenology, cannot also be used in the natural attitude, nor why close attention cannot be paid to the modes and processes of appearance without the brackets.[124] The only supplement that might be needed is a way of interrupting the ordinary course of experience while maintaining the natural attitude so that the way in which that experience is structured can be observed and described. The abnormal, the eccentric, the broken, and the degenerate case can often be used to explicate the processes which operate in the normal course of lived experience.[125]

Finally, the way to break through traditional presuppositions is not to withdraw to a sphere of sanctity; no such untarnished sphere exists. Despite Husserl's effort to avoid them, his project is riddled with pre-suppositions. One can more adequately regain a new vision by examining the metaphors and models that guide current thought (and along which any thought in a sacrosanct sphere would run). In this chapter I have begun to question the Cartesian metaphors that pervade much thinking about Others and that circumscribe Husserl's entire inquiry. An examin-ation of Hegel will suggest even more important difficulties with the Cartesian picture.

Chapter 2

Hegel

The next philosopher Sartre examines is Hegel. Sartre's exposition concentrates on the Master-Slave section in the *Phenomenology of Spirit*,[1] but his criticisms also address some general issues concerning the whole of the *Phenomenology*; consequently, I shall address both topics. Sartre's interpretation of Hegel's chapter depends heavily on Alexandre Kojève's readings in his *Introduction to the Reading of Hegel*.[2] Unfortunately, Sartre's general views about Hegel lack Kojève's daring, and his specific grasp of the Master-Slave section lacks the care and sensitivity of Hegel's other recent French commentator, Jean Hyppolite.[3]

Hegel develops four or five themes in the opening pages of the Self-Consciousness chapter (which includes the Master-Slave section), and the interpretation of each of these themes interacts with that of all the others; one can provide a valid interpretation of the section only by making all these themes intelligible at once. Sartre neglects this interdependence. Because of this, he fails to do justice to the depth of Hegel's insights about the self-Other relation, most of which can only be understood if one bears in mind Hegel's remarks about the other themes: e.g., infinity (unboundedness), Life, desire, and the general aim of Self-consciousness. Thus, in order to offer a contrast to Sartre's discussion and to explore all the major insights of Hegel's text, my presentation of the Master-Slave section will both be more detailed and more extensive than Sartre's. On the other hand, my comments on general questions of interpretation concerning the *Phenomenology of Spirit* will focus exclusively on the issues Sartre raises.

Probably the most important flaw in Sartre's discussion is his assumption that only this chapter of the *Phenomenology* is relevant to Hegel's views on the self-Other relation. Actually the content of the second two-thirds of "Reason" (especially "Virtue and the Course of the World" and "Spiritual Animal Kingdom") and the whole of "Spirit" (especially "Ethical World," "Self-Divided Spirit," and "Evil and Forgiveness") should also be examined if one seeks full comprehension of Hegel's position on Others. Since I lack the space to address those sections here, my criticisms of Hegel will be more tentative and cautious than Sartre's, for I cannot ignore the limits of this investigation.

An introduction to Hegel

This exposition of Hegel will follow his order of presentation. I begin by clarifying the general aims of the *Phenomenology of Spirit*. The manner in which Consciousness develops toward Self-consciousness will then be described, and special attention will be given to elucidating the transition. Next the basic aim and *modus operandi* of Self-consciousness will be studied. The initial moment of Self-consciousness is desire; its primary object is Life; their structure and relationships will be fully examined. Hegel's discussion of Life concretizes his concept of infinity and facilitates understanding his concept of pure recognition, both of which are central in his theory of Others. I shall then explain the failure of desire; this will clarify the role Others play in the development of Self-consciousness. This introductory groundwork will provide the tools necessary for comprehending Hegel's theory of Others.

The basic aim of *The Phenomenology*

Hegel's task in the *Phenomenology of Spirit* is to exhibit the path by which anyone who thinks and lives seriously can and will eventually achieve absolute knowledge.[4] The elucidation of the content of this knowledge Hegel leaves to *The Science of Logic*; in the *Phenomenology* he simply shows how to reach the viewpoint from which the *Logic* can be written and elucidates the inadequacies of other modes of knowledge, of which there are basically five: Consciousness, Self-consciousness, Reason, Spirit, and Religion. Hegel's unique criticism of these other modes of knowledge (which are also forms of life) is that they have *internal* failings; each has its own standard by which its success is to be measured, and the actual achievement of each mode fails to satisfy *its own standard*.[5] The person who takes each stage seriously, who compares its actual results with its ideal, must eventually grasp its inadequacies. In addition, the failures of each mode of knowledge do not return the individual who lives through them to his point of origin or to a state of skeptical uncertainty. The breakdown of each mode of knowledge results in what Hegel calls an "experience": a simultaneous transformation of the individual's form of life and of the standard for evaluating it.[6] The failure leads in a specific direction toward something new; these transformations have a logic or pattern that can be explicated.[7] In general, the later stages eventually integrate the positive results from the earlier stages.

Each mode of knowing is given an ideal-typical description that is sufficiently abstract to be applicable to several different things: philosophies, historical stages in the development of the human race, psychogenetic stages in the development of persons, as well as basic modes of experience and forms of life. Most people have at one time or another lived through most of these stages of consciousness; the species as a whole has developed through all of them. Hegel encourages us to remember the stages and to comprehend their meaning by imaginatively reliving them in a particular order. To realize that each stage fails is a self-wrenching process,[8] but this agony is necessary to achieve absolute knowledge or wisdom.

Hegel's treatment of each form of life is necessarily guided by his purpose: to examine each moment's basic aim and adequacy. His principle of organization is not easily defined, but I think there are recurrent patterns in the development and structural parallels among the stages. The arrangement is neither historical nor arbitrary nor pre-determined by a fore-ordained end.[9] Clarifying its "necessity," however, would require more elaboration than suits my purposes here.

The book is a story of spiritual formation that is told from two viewpoints simultaneously. In addition to describing the experience of an idealized-individual undergoing the development, Hegel periodically inserts commentary from the viewpoint of the informed observer (i.e., himself) who has reached the endpoint of the evolution. These asides allow fuller comprehension of the story, but they are not supposed to play any role in the actual development of the individual. The sole motive of development is the comparison of the standard and the actuality of each stage.[10] The meta-observer does not intervene in the development; he merely watches the drama unfold; this is why Hegel calls his book a "phenomenology."[11]

The basic realization one achieves on reaching wisdom is that subject and object are, in a complicated and technical sense, identical. Although I cannot develop all the nuances here, the essential meaning of "identity" is that whatever is not-oneself is not experienced as foreign, but as something with which one is in harmony and in which one is expressed, because one realizes that the same principles govern and constitute both self and not-self.[12]

As the idealized-individual develops and becomes more complex, so too does the object of which he can become aware. The enrichment of each develops the other, and their patterns of development are iso-morphic. In this section, for example, Life undergoes a development which foreshadows that of Self-consciousness.[13] In general, Hegel makes a systematic effort to comprehend the relations between the individual's way of life and the kind of world he inhabits. He also thinks there are important symmetry relationships between the structure of a society *and* the structure of individual self-consciousness within it *and* the kind of thinking and artistic production typical of it.[14] The simul-taneous development of subject and object — self and world — is not unlike the analogous transformations in the standards and forms of life of consciousness.

The transition to Self-consciousness

Before clarifying the basic aim and standard of Self-consciousness, I must briefly review the final realizations and achievements of Consciousness. Throughout that first stage of *The Phenomenology*, the idealized-subject is seeking an object that will retain its self-identity and exhibit the independence and self-sufficiency that it promises as an *object* of consciousness. Against this standard, the objects of Sense-Certainty, Perception, and Understanding are measured and found wanting. None of those objects remains stable; no coherent conception of them can be formulated. All the efforts of Consciousness to find a self-sufficient object fail.[15]

At the end of this process, Consciousness realizes that its object continually divides and reconstructs itself. Moreover, Consciousness intuits that this is its own nature as well; it can then begin to see the object as an expression of its own structure. Consciousness also realizes that the theoretical constructs it develops in order to understand and explain the physical world (e.g., force) do not have an objective and independent status, but rather are the creations of consciousness itself which obey the regulative laws of its own inquiry.[16] Thus, the most developed objects of Consciousness are only its own externalizations; Consciousness begins to see itself reflected in the world.

This awareness of itself duplicated is the initial moment of Self-consciousness. Self-consciousness is thus a *result*, not a presupposition, of the development of Consciousness. Retaining self-identity in duplication or in being-other-than-itself is what Hegel means by "infinity" or unboundedness.[17] That infinity has made a very primitive appearance is not realized by the individual undergoing the development; Hegel discusses it briefly in a meta-comment offered from the narrator's viewpoint. To be infinite is not to be limited by anything – to experience nothing that is *other* than oneself – to be able to see oneself in and as everything. Hegel thinks self-conscious beings have a kind of will to infinity; they continually transcend their boundaries in order to assimilate larger regions of apparent otherness.

Two important conditions constitute the initial state of Self-consciousness: first, Self-consciousness involves a return or withdrawal of Consciousness into itself, a realization that it is duplicated yet self-identical; thus the initial focus of Self-consciousness is itself;[18] and second, although the objects of Consciousness have not disappeared, they have lost their alleged self-sufficiency; they are treated as mere appearances.[19] Because the self-identity from which Self-consciousness begins does not incorporate any of these object-appearances, it is empty and abstract. To become concrete, Self-consciousness must *show* that its object is not distinct from itself. The initial attitude of Self-consciousness toward its surroundings is thus ambivalent.[20]

On the one hand, it grasps itself as absolute, self-certain, and self-sufficient; it swashbuckles through the world. Yet on the other hand, everything other than itself is threatening to it; although objects are experienced only as appearances, their presence brutally denies the complete identity of Self-consciousness with all that is other than itself. Thus, encountering any object unsettles its fragile equilibrium. The task of Self-consciousness is to demonstrate its identity with the object, to prove its primacy by showing that what seems different is only an embodiment of itself. In every encounter, Self-consciousness loses hold of itself and then acts to recover and reestablish a sense of internal self-sufficiency. The first attempt to execute this task Hegel calls "desire."[21]

The standard of Self-consciousness

The overall aim of Self-consciousness is thus to establish through its own activity what it already implicitly knows: that what appears to be other than itself is actually only itself. It seeks to demonstrate that otherness does not really limit itself, is only itself externalized; in this way it shows that its initial sense of self-identity is the truth.[22] Self-consciousness thus *makes itself* actual; it adopts an active rather than a purely contemplative relation to the world.

Thus the difference between the standard of Consciousness, which sought *to find* an object adequate to its concept of objectivity, and the standard of Self-consciousness is that the latter requires *active intervention*; Self-consciousness transforms the object so that its identity with Self-consciousness becomes manifest. Knowledge is involved in both cases, but in the latter knowledge is achieved through altering the world rather than discovering what is there in itself. Consciousness's major realization was that the object underwent changes when scrutinized; the initial moment of Self-consciousness internalizes this self-active nature.

Self-consciousness begins with an implicit confidence in its self-identity. In its encounter with objects, it must make this certainty explicit. The standard of Self-consciousness is simply the most abstract characterization that can be given to it: consciousness of itself as other; identity of itself and its object.[23] Self-consciousness cannot remain content with appearances as they appear; it is threatened by their apparent externality and seeks to demonstrate that they are not really distinct from itself. In so doing, Self-consciousness makes itself actual and concrete.

The object of Self-consciousness: Life

The section on Life can be read in two ways. On one reading, Hegel offers an intervention, or meta-comment, from the viewpoint of the narrator. He describes the object of Self-consciousness, the living object, which undergoes a parallel development and exhibits an analogous self-relatedness.[24] On this view, Hegel explores Life's relation to species and their relation to individuals. On the other reading, Hegel is tracing a development of Self-consciousness itself, at the end of which it realizes its own embodiment and its existence as a *living being.*[25] On this view, Hegel is amplifying the nature of Self-consciousness by explicating its relation to bodily awareness. In order to act on the world, Self-consciousness must be embodied. Partly through the fact of desire and partly through the failure of desire, Self-consciousness learns of its embodiment. This realization is important for two reasons: it allows Self-consciousness to see other conscious beings as similar to itself, and it provides Self-consciousness with something to transcend when it seeks to demonstrate its own primacy in the face of another conscious being. Although both readings are illuminating, I shall concentrate on the first.

I need to examine this section because Life prefigures the development of Self-consciousness[26] and because Life provides a model for the pure concept of recognition between two self-conscious beings.[27] Hegel portrays Life as a concrete synthesis of three aspects which can be analytically distinguished but which cannot exist in isolation. The first aspect is simply the abstract quality or pulse of life that exists within all living beings. This abstract life-process articulates itself into different forms in the course of time, and when viewed at one moment these forms are the different species dispersed across the earth.[28] These distinct species or life-forms constitute the second aspect of Life. They exist for a time, actively differentiate themselves from other life-forms, yet remain bound to Life's processes until death. Even death only represents a return of the organic material to the abstract life-process. Death is not outside Life but part of its functioning.[29] Each species sustains itself by producing different kinds of individuals and by continuous reproduction; it lives on even if many of its members die.[30] The third aspect of life is the cyclic process by which the first two aspects transform into each other: Life manifests itself in new life-forms, and the various life-forms are reintegrated back into the life-process.[31] Hegel contends that each side of this cyclic process generates the other; thus to make a distinction between them is ultimately misleading.[32] The creation of new life-forms occurs through incorporating dead forms (think of the food cycle), and the supersession of old forms is at once a creation of new forms (think of reproduction or evolutionary cycles).

None of these aspects exists without the others. The life-process must embody itself in life-forms, and the life-forms must remain bound to Life's processes, and the two continuously transform into one another. The distinctness of these aspects is superseded by that special self-active, self-integrative "identity" that defines Hegelian infinity. Life itself is the synthesis of all three aspects: the self-identical, self-disruptive, self-integrative whole that motivates all transformations from within itself and that completes itself in the passage of time.[33] Although Life is a synthesis, it is not yet self-aware. Self-consciousness will discover this kind of synthesis in itself and will further actualize it through its development. Life becomes self-aware through Self-consciousness.[34]

Hegel's analysis anticipates much of later nineteenth-century biologism. It suggests that individuals are not self-contained but are only modes of the species of which they are members, experiments of that species toward the differentiation and development of its own possibilities. The species themselves have the same relation to Life as individuals do to species. Also, the living individual has the same relationship to its various organic systems and functions. Hegel's analysis can be applied at any of these levels. Nothing remains outside Life; it emerges from the inorganic and then transforms it into various environments for further differentiating itself. Once Life emerges, the inorganic becomes an essential part of the functioning of the organic. Hegel will ultimately show that the relation of Self-consciousness to Life is the same as Life's relation to the inorganic.

This discussion of Life helps clarify Self-consciousness. Life cannot be properly understood if it is seen as an abstraction divorced from all embodiments; Life actualizes itself through its species. The same is true of Self-consciousness. The first moment of Self-consciousness is a barren, unembodied, unactualized self-identity; it must undergo a corresponding amplification and self-articulation into concrete forms. Just as Life becomes actual only through its different species, Self-consciousness becomes actual only by expressing itself in manifold 'forms,' e.g., the stages of development in the *Phenomenology or* the different objects encountered by Self-consciousness in this chapter: the living object, other conscious beings, its own thoughts, and imaginatively projected reifications.[35] Desire concretizes Self-consciousness in the way that species concretize the life-process. As the process of Life supersedes the apparent independence of the life-forms, Self-consciousness must supersede the apparent independence of the objects of desire. Desire, however, fails to express the reciprocity of the life-process. Only in the experience of pure recognition will Self-consciousness achieve this reciprocity; at that point a self-dividing, self-uniting whole — Spirit — will become manifest in and through Self-consciousness.

Life provides a model for many of Hegel's other ideas in this section. Just as death is integrated into the self-development of Life, the threat of death plays a central role in the development of Self-consciousness.[36] Just as Self-consciousness elevates the life-process to a new level of completion by making it self-aware, Spirit will elevate Self-consciousness to a new level of completion in which its true nature will become manifest. Spirit is related to the mutual recognition of self-conscious individuals in just the way that Life itself is related to its three aspects. The dependence of life-forms on their environment also anticipates the dependence of Self-consciousness on its various objects.[37] Hegel's discussion of Life thus provides a clue to the interpretation of many aspects of Self-consciousness.

The second interpretation of this section takes "Life" to refer to the processes of living Self-consciousness − the body. On this reading, the development in the section concerns the way in which Self-consciousness learns its own embodiment. The section would suggest that an alternation of desire and satiation is essential to continued self-awareness; each side of this process would generate the other; satiation calls forth further desires which, in turn, produce satiation. This cyclical process would be seen as the *life* of Self-consciousness − the first concretion of its abstract sense of self-identity. Although this reading is not without interest, it does not provide the illuminating implications that the other reading does. Moreover, it does not explain why Hegel again takes up the discussion of desire after his discussion of Life; on this reading, the essence of desire has already been clarified. For these reasons I believe that the first interpretation is more adequate.

The first moment of Self-consciousness: desire

Self-consciousness begins with an implicit confidence that any object is only itself, that it is the only self-sufficient being and all else is appearance. Yet the externality of living objects threatens this sense of hegemony, and Self-consciousness must establish its implicit certainty. Desire seeks to show that the apparent object is not genuinely other, but is only itself;[38] it does so by consuming or otherwise incorporating the object.[39] Through its satisfaction, Self-consciousness makes its actuality explicit; by proving that the object is ephemeral, Self-consciousness regains its majestic stance.

There are two ways of interpreting the basic failure of desire, and both are accurate. Both interpretations show that the experience of desire results in the experience of the independence of the living object.[40] Self-consciousness is unable to fully realize its implicit self-assurance through desire. I shall examine the most general failure first.

In so far as Self-consciousness seeks to negate the object by destroying it and thus to establish its sole reality and self-sufficiency, it learns that the object is essential to the realization of itself. Two crucial facts explain why. First, Self-consciousness remains wholly implicit and unactualized if it does not express itself in desire and demolish the apparent reality of the object. Second, desire cannot establish this implicit self-awareness if there is no independent, external object to negate; it requires the object in order to actualize itself.[41]

These facts are learned through the apparent success of desire. After consuming the object, Self-consciousness is returned to the state of abstract identity; its satisfaction is ephemeral. Any new object will again directly threaten the stability of Self-consciousness. Moreover, acting on or consuming the object amounts to acknowledging its difference and distinctiveness. In the process of consuming the object, Self-consciousness proves its self-certainty and simultaneously undermines that certainty, for its actuality vanishes with the object.[42] Self-consciousness must continually incorporate living objects in order to maintain its actuality, but in acting on those objects, it implicitly grants their independence.

The only way to avoid this paradox of desire would be to find an object that would deny itself without requiring the action of Self-consciousness. If the object denies its own distinctness, Self-consciousness can see the object as itself, and it need not grant the object's independence by acting on it.[43] Also, since the object would continue to exist instead of being consumed, Self-consciousness's sense of actualization need not disintegrate. The only object which can negate itself in this fashion is another self-conscious being. Thus, an encounter with another self-conscious being is necessary to transcend the paradox of desire.[44] Although Self-consciousness exists in a primitive form (desire) without the existence of Others, it cannot achieve complete self-realization unless it encounters the Other.[45]

On the second interpretation, desire fails to actualize Self-consciousness because the desire itself disappears when the object is consumed. The experience of desire and the process of consumption, on this view, are essential to the actualization of Self-consciousness. Without its concretization in desires, Self-consciousness remains merely an abstract self-identity. Self-consciousness learns the emptiness of its initial state, and, with the disappearance of desire through consumption, Self-consciousness is returned to this emptiness. Desire represents the embodiment of Self-consciousness. Even though desires are distinct from its abstract self-identity, Self-consciousness must lose itself in them, sacrifice its empty isolation, if it is to become concrete and actual. If Self-consciousness can *accept* its embodiment in desires, its dual nature takes on a new form: living self-consciousness becomes conjoined with abstract self-identity. This duality plays an essential role in the encounter with Others, and this second interpretation offers a clue to understanding the experience of pure recognition. Both interpretations capture important aspects of Hegel's meaning.[46]

Hegel's theory of Others

Before I discuss Hegel's concept of pure recognition, I must clarify the *status* of Hegel's discussion of Others and how it differs from the

traditional epistemological approach. Although one of Hegel's statements can be interpreted as deriving the existence of other self-conscious
beings from Self-consciousness,[47] this passage is best interpreted as
explicating Self-consciousness's capacity for apprehending another
living being as potentially self-conscious and thus as having the capacity
of negating itself. The development of abstract self-identity into embodied self-consciousness makes this apprehension possible. Hegel
simply *assumes* that other *conscious* beings exist; he makes no effort to
prove their existence.[48] However, he does not believe that Others are
immediately known to be *self-conscious*. This knowledge is an *achievement*, not something present at the outset, and it is attained through
action and *struggle*, not through thought or analysis.[49]

Thus Hegel's theory differs from the traditional approach to Others
in a number of ways. Instead of seeking to prove Others' existence, he
shows how self-conscious beings become capable of grasping Others as
self-conscious. In addition, Hegel seeks to elucidate the basic *event* and
the processes that govern the encounter between primitive self-conscious
beings. Prior to Hegel, this question simply had not been asked. Hegel
clarifies what persons can become through encounter; he shows that
self-development requires interaction with Others. Social relations thus
determine one's possibilities for self-realization. Hegel investigates
knowledge of Others only in so far as it bears on the processes of
encounter; usually what can be known about Others depends on the
outcome of encounter with them. Thus, Hegel's investigation of the
governing conditions of encounter is more fundamental than the
traditional effort to justify our knowledge of Others.

The concept of pure recognition

Hegel begins his analysis of interpersonal encounter with an intervention,
a meta-comment, which describes an ideal encounter, an elucidation of
what I shall call the *concept of pure recognition*. The individual
undergoing the development of Self-consciousness does not yet experience encounter in this fashion.[50] Hegel includes this discussion for
three reasons: first, he wants to indicate the way in which infinity can
become actualized in interpersonal encounter. Each self-conscious being
becomes able to realize himself in and through the Other, and thus
Others no longer represent a boundary or limit to Self-consciousness.
This section foreshadows later developments in the text.[51] Second,
he is clarifying the conditions for satisfying the standard of Self-
consciousness.[52] Since none of the actual moments undergone by the
idealized individual (in the Self-Consciousness section) succeed in
satisfying this standard, Hegel offers an insertion to indicate the sort
of encounter that would be sufficient. Finally, because pure recognition
does concretize infinity and does satisfy the aim of Self-consciousness,

it represents an ideal for interpersonal life, one which is achieved only at the outset of "Spirit."[53]

Since Sartre's main objection to Hegel is that pure recognition is impossible, I shall try to present Hegel's exposition of it clearly and fully. Once the entire process of pure recognition is clear, the actual experience of encounter at this stage of the development of Self-consciousness (impure recognition) can then be examined.

Hegel divides the process of pure recognition into three moments, each of which is experienced by both self-conscious beings in the encounter; he emphasizes that these moments are not genuinely distinct or separable, only analytically so.[54] He then explains how the three moments are part of a dynamic unity. Through this process an emergent harmony interlaces the participants; when this fusion occurs, Spirit exists.

Self-consciousness begins in the state from which it emerged in desire: living self-consciousness. It still experiences both self-assurance and instability in the face of objects. The encounter with another self-conscious being has some similarities to and some differences from the encounter with the living things in desire. One similarity is the instability or disequilibrium created by the confrontation.[55] One difference is that another conscious being is not seen as different, for he is a living, object-negating being, too, and Self-consciousness is aware of this. In this first moment of encounter, living embodied consciousness sees itself in the Other as in a mirror reflecting itself.[56] Various interpretations of pure recognition differ in their analysis of this mirroring.

My view is that the mirroring represents an implicit realization that the Other is of the *same type* as oneself — at least in his relation to the world. Self-consciousness must make this implicit identity with the Other explicit. (A different, but equally acceptable, view is that each sees himself in the Other in so far as he sees the Other's instability before him, which mirrors his own instability before the Other. This reading also yields a sense of potentially belonging to the same type or species.) One can achieve pure recognition only by momentarily sacrificing one's abstract self-identity, one's sense of differentiation, for only if one loses that will the Other be experienced as fully *like oneself*.

This reading has much to recommend it: it stresses the development of a sense of *species* (or mediating unity) that intertwines self and Other, and it makes this section parallel with Hegel's discussion of Life.[57] Moreover, this view does not require that the Other be seen as *self-conscious* already. Since Self-consciousness learns the actuality of the Other's self-consciousness through the completion of pure recognition, no interpretation should presuppose it at the outset. Finally, this reading does not require that the initial moment of pure recognition be any different from that of impure recognition. The difference involves different ways of reacting to the loss of abstract self-identity and to an implicit sense of identity with the Other.

Self-consciousness loses its sense of abstract self-identity when it apprehends the Other as like itself. The second moment of pure recognition involves an effort at self-recovery.[58] This occurs through superseding the Other, but since the Other is its mirror reflection, it supersedes itself-as-Other simultaneously.[59] This supersession is the most difficult moment to describe. On my view, each self-conscious being *asserts himself* to be a member of the species. Each has lost his sense of himself to the Other, who almost seems more actual than himself. Self-recovery requires that each claim the same status as the Other; each *asserts* his identity with the Other; the sole actuality of the Other is denied. This assertion of identity with the Other will succeed only if the Other acknowledges his identity with the first. He must deny his sole actuality. In so doing, he accepts the identity with the first which has just been asserted. Through this process each supersedes his initial loss of self by affirming and accepting his identity with the Other. Each acknowledges the Other as part of the same species as himself. This is a vital moment, for it requires that Self-consciousness abandon its vision of itself as the sole, all-encompassing reality. If this happens, each becomes actualized through the Other's recognition, and each is confirmed in his sense of identity with the Other. The distinctness of the Other is overcome; yet his existence is preserved.

Each self-conscious being abandons his abstract self-identity, of being the primordial reality before which all else is appearance,[60] but, through this sacrifice, each achieves a richer sense of self, for each is confirmed as self-conscious by the Other. By acknowledging that the Other is the same species as himself, Self-consciousness accepts the Other's reality; yet the Other's reciprocation reestablishes his own sense of reality. Since each is confirmed by the Other, each continues to see himself as identical with the Other.

The third moment is the reciprocal return of each self-conscious being to himself, now confirmed and actualized through the recognition of the Other.[61] This self-return does not entail falling back to the initial stage of abstract self-identity, for Self-consciousness is now solidified by the recognition of the Other. Each returns with a stronger sense of his own actuality and a continuing sense of the Other's actuality and identity with himself.[62] Each lets the Other go free; neither need consume or overpower the Other because each retains an identity with the Other; the foreignness of the Other is superseded as long as pure recognition is sustained.[63] Each senses that their unity transcends their separateness; this unity is made possible by the *mutuality* involved in pure recognition.

If pure recognition is to reach completion, each must do to itself — deny its sole actuality (which is the same act as confirming its identity with the Other) — what the Other does to it (each also denies the Other's sole actuality).[64] Hence, recognition is not merely an individual action; it is not even just an event that happens to both self-conscious beings at once, but it is *done* by both at once and done with an awareness of mutuality and reciprocity. The same action affects both self and Other simultaneously because everything one does to the Other affects oneself in so far as one sees oneself in him (as similar to him).[65] If either one withholds himself, if he denies that the Other is the same species as himself by asserting his distinctness, then pure recognition will fail. (This is what happens in *impure* recognition.) Hegel adds that recognition proceeds only if each experiences the Other reciprocating its actions; if the mirror ever cracks, if at any point the Other does not act in concert with one, the recognition Self-consciousness seeks is missed, and *both lose.*[66]

Thus the acceptance of self-loss, the willingness to acknowledge oneself as part of a larger whole, is the winning of self's actualization, for one's sense of actuality is returned and confirmed. The Other becomes identical with oneself. Also, just as Self-consciousness becomes more concrete and enriched despite the paradox of desire (it becomes living self-consciousness), here too it achieves an enrichment: it becomes part of a larger social unity that provides a foundation for continued internal stability.[67] Self-consciousness comes to realize that it has an actuality for and an acceptance by the Other that concretizes its own abstract sense of reality and permanently restores its equilibrium. Hegel will eventually show that, like Life and life-forms, Spirit pulses through the mutual action of self-conscious beings, breaking itself into separate individuals (or, alternatively, spirit-forms) and then reuniting itself by overcoming their separateness.

All three of these moments occur during the encounter; they do not require distinct actions; each moment contains the others in itself. A brief example might clarify the whole process of pure recognition. Two strangers meet each other. Each experiences an uncertainty before the Other; yet each sees the Other at least potentially as like himself. He too has involvements, is embodied, and experiences a similar self-loss. Each then makes some sign that expresses his own self-consciousness, and reasserts his hold on himself; yet each acknowledges the Other's sign, and thus each participates in the Other's self-recovery. By recognizing the sign, each accepts the Other as a being like himself. Each confirms the Other, and each experiences a fullness of self as a result. Each experiences a new unity that becomes explicit through this process of mutual action.

To be recognized by the Other is to have an implicit sense of self made explicit; it also overcomes the foreignness of the stranger; no longer is he a threat to self. He continues to exist, but his self-consciousness is acknowledged. Moreover, the general foreignness of the world is reduced; as soon as one locates one 'friend' in a new setting, that setting no longer seems oppressive and alien. There are levels of this process of recognition; this example exhibits a primitive level; however, the higher capacities — intelligence, moral seriousness, social role, and individuality — also become actualized in the same fashion. Through mutual recognition each individual makes possible the full actualization of all the Others as complete human beings.[68]

The actual experience of encounter

The dynamic just described does not actually occur at this stage of the development of Self-consciousness;[69] it is achieved much later in the *Phenomenology*.[70] The self-conscious beings at this stage are unable to abandon their sense of distinctiveness; their swashbuckling selfness undermines their ability to see themselves in the Other.[71] As in pure recognition, the Other is seen as a merely living being.[72] But here Self-consciousness retains its abstract self-identity and realizes this is not apparent to the Other; the Other threatens its stability as much as the object of desire did. Self-consciousness can actualize itself only in so far as the Other acknowledges its abstract sense of self. In order to win this acknowledgement, it must *establish* its supremacy.[73]

The battle

Seeing the Other solely as a living being reflects back on Self-consciousness's vision of itself, for it realizes that its own embodiment is inadequate to express its abstract self-identity. Its self-certainty does not emerge in so far as it is merely a living, desiring being.[74] Consequently, in order to prove itself to the Other, Self-consciousness must demonstrate that it is *more* than its living embodiment.[75] To show this it must prove that it is beyond Life, wholly other than life; thus, it *risks* its life.[76] To do *this*, Self-consciousness must challenge the Other to a life and death battle; it must threaten the life of the Other, less because it seeks to destroy the Other than because it must stake its own life. In this way Self-consciousness demonstrates its abstract self-identity to the Other and itself.[77]

Since both behave similarly, they engage in a battle to the death.[78] The initial result of this battle usually is death for one or both self-conscious beings. But if the Other dies, the same problem that haunted desire again arises: the Other has disappeared; he can neither recognize the self that has proven itself beyond Life, nor can the dead body mirror Self-consciousness to itself.[79] The kind of supersession death involves is too extreme; it does not preserve and elevate as it negates, and this failure, as well as its own dependency *on Life*, is what Self-consciousness learns.[80] Self-consciousness discovers it cannot exist without its embodiment; all self-conscious beings who are still alive after the battle have learned this lesson.

But all have been thrown back to the abstract sense of self-identity that exists at the outset of "Self-Consciousness." Each must again traverse the path of desire toward the encounter with Others.[81] In the next battle, Self-consciousness will not forget the importance of Life; just before death, out of an absolute fear, one warrior will abandon the struggle, deny his claim to distinctness, and accept his dependence on Life. He will recognize the dominance and self-consciousness of the Other. The former is slave; the latter is master.[82]

The master

The master solves the problem of desire by leaving the objectivity of things and the continuous necessity to act on them to the slave; the master need only enjoy and consume the fruits of the slave's labor.[83] His commands and desires are executed without having to perform the activity himself; the slave acts as his 'body' and must deal with the independence of living things.[84] The slave's will is not his own; he follows the dictates of his master, and the master remains conscious of this through the slave's efforts to transform the world in accordance with his will.[85] Thus the master relates to the slave through the world's transformation and to the world through the slave. He sees the slave as a tool which realizes his purposes, and the slave's work and obedience continue to confirm his recognition. Hence the master appears to have achieved both the aims of desire and of recognition.[86]

There is a major problem, however, and it is fatal; it turns the master's path into a dead-end since he cannot ever achieve the aim of Self-consciousness. The problem is that he regards the slave as a mere living object, as lacking self-consciousness. Consequently, the slave lacks the capacity to recognize the master; whatever acknowledgment he offers *does not and cannot count*, for it is not offered by a self-conscious being.[87] This is further established by the fact that the master does not see a reflection or expression of himself in the slave. The slave remains *wholly other* — wholly transcended by the master — and hence cannot mirror the master to himself.[88]

This result is inescapable because the master, in further encounters, can only rewin the battle and create new slaves or lose and become a slave himself. The master is trapped in a role that cannot achieve appropriate recognition because he destroys the preconditions of recognition.

Slavery

The slave, for his part, achieves a greater actualization of his self-consciousness than at first appears.[89] To be sure, he does not achieve the recognition of the master, and the vision according to which he transforms the world is not his own. Nevertheless, he does transform the world; he can see himself reflected in the products of his work. He thus progresses beyond the paradox of desire.

One reason he achieves this success is due to the master. The master makes the slave fear absolutely for his life during the battle, and his presence is a continual reminder of that fear. This fear has an important positive function; it eliminates the slave's attachment to anything worldly, to any role, or any determinate mode of life. The slave thus recovers his own abstract self-identity, which is distinct from his life-processes and particularity.[90] Moreover, the fact that he experiences the discipline of continued service to the master, and maintains this discipline through time, provides *him* a sense of being more coherent than a merely living being.[91] His experience after the battle belies what he admits in the course of the battle. In both these ways, the slave apprehends himself as self-conscious and as being more than a merely living being.

Finally, this new self-awareness does not remain inert; it gets expressed in the work by which the slave transforms and alters the world.[92] The slave does not consume and destroy living objects as the man of desire did; rather his negation of the world is impressed upon it. He restrains the movement to destroy and expresses himself in the altered form of the still existing object. He sees himself in the world because he works in it.[93] The slave thus progresses beyond the paradox of desire; his products *remain* and provide him with a sense of identity with the world. He has not yet solved the problem of recognition, but he has learned and developed more than the master.

Results of Hegel's theory of encounter

Although Hegel's discussion can be pursued in many directions, I shall sketch four basic results. The first is that Self-consciousness realizes itself only through the recognition of Others. Pure recognition is essential to becoming a person. This does not mean that Others are required for one to exist; for Hegel, one can exist as Consciousness and even as a primitive form of Self-consciousness (desire) prior to the encounter with Others. However, to develop a human self-consciousness which transcends the life-process, a special relation to Others is required. This claim must also be distinguished from the claim that Others are necessary for one to know oneself; in this section Hegel is not primarily concerned with self-knowledge, but with the kind of person one can become and the kind of harmony with the world one can achieve.[94]

Unlike Sartre, Hegel does not attempt to explicate the certainty of the Other's existence. The second result of Hegel's treatment is to by-pass the traditional epistemological problem of solipsism and of justifying one's knowledge of Others.[95] Hegel simply takes the existence and presence of other living conscious beings for granted; he makes no effort to derive them from self. At best, he explicates the possibility of *apprehending them* as self-conscious.[96] Hegel raises different questions: what is the primordial event in social encounter? what conditions govern its results? what are its main effects? what are the possibilities for human relationships?[97]

A third result of Hegel's analysis is that self and Other develop interactively. No one can remain an isolated, withdrawn self and achieve any complexity.[98] If one tries, endless interpersonal conflict will be the result. Self and Other develop together; the manner in which one exists is intertwined with that of the other.[99] When pure recognition emerges, each becomes a moment of a larger whole which functions through them. The development of species-being eliminates the possibility of remaining an isolated, monadic self. Only by losing oneself can one find oneself.

A fourth result of Hegel's theory is the distinction between the ideal achievement of encounter and its actuality at a given stage of development. Hegel asserts the genuine possibility of achieving the ideal, but he is not a utopian. He has a sense of the adversity that must be overcome before the ideal can be achieved. Hence he preserves a realistic approach to human relationships without embracing cynicism. Some may fault Hegel for his optimism in claiming that the stages of adversity will break down and eventually yield the ideal; others will fault him for his pessimism in claiming that weathering each of the intermediary stages is necessary in order to achieve the ideal because each contributes something to its realization. This middle path, however, is Hegel's way through the apparent opposition of freedom and fate, optimism and pessimism. Interpersonal harmony is possible, but the experiences of domination, struggle, and their failures are necessary to its achievement.[100]

Sartre's reading of Hegel and its problems

On the surface, Sartre's discussion of Hegel has two distinct parts: an exposition and a series of criticisms, but its deeper structure is tripartite.[101] The first of Sartre's "criticisms" is better understood as a culmination of his exposition and an attempt to summarize the differences between his own theory of consciousness and Hegel's. That discussion functions as a transition between his interpretation and his more forceful objections. In it he takes himself to be providing a definitive refutation of Hegel's position, but closer analysis reveals that Sartre simply begs the question: he assumes, rather than establishes, the truth of his own standpoint.[102] My analysis of this transitional discussion (Sartre's challenge to Hegel) will be offered in the second half of this section; there I will show that Hegel's theory better realizes

Sartre's intent than his own position. Sartre's remaining, more cogent objections will be discussed in the following section.

In the first half of this section, I examine Sartre's synopsis of Hegel. Here the detailed exposition in the previous section will prove helpful. In contrast to my reading, Sartre's exposition is brief and cavalier; he leans heavily on traditional characterizations of Hegel. Clarifying my many disagreements with Sartre will indicate the extent to which my view challenges and revises classical formulations. Before I present a detailed assessment of Sartre's interpretation, I will offer a preliminary orientation to the problems of his approach.

Hegel's theory is the progenitor of Sartre's. Marx sometimes spoke of having inverted Hegel's theory; Sartre can best be portrayed as having chopped off its head. (Sartre's own view is Hegel's minus pure recognition.) As Nietzsche thought the slave had to transvalue the ideals of the master in order to ascend, as Freud thought the son had to symbolically kill the father in order to survive, as Harold Bloom thinks new poets must systematically misread earlier masters in order to clear a space for their own efforts, I think Sartre had to misinterpret Hegel in order to make room for his own theory.

Hegel's theory achieves many of the aims that Sartre sets for his own: it establishes an internal relation between persons, an existential grounding of the Other's subjectivity, and a way of understanding the roots of interpersonal conflict and harmony. In effect, Sartre's interpretation of Hegel denies that he achieves these latter two aims and twists his accomplishment on the first so that it is no longer recognizable. One way of understanding why this happened is to see that it leaves some tasks uncompleted and thus gives Sartre something to accomplish.

There are more specific reasons why one might expect infelicities in Sartre's reading. First, Sartre's awareness of his own solutions too easily encourages him to regard Hegel's theory as an inept anticipation of his own. He takes Hegel's central concerns to be one's objectification by Others and one's appearance for them,[103] but these processes presuppose a far more sophisticated form of self-consciousness than exists for Hegel in the Self-Consciousness section. Sartre also reads Hegel's use of terms like 'for-Others,' 'identity,' and 'self-consciousness' in ways analogous to or even identical with his own uses, but Hegel's meanings demand more subtle attention to his own contexts of use. Thus Sartre too quickly reads his own views into Hegel.

In addition, Sartre is too little concerned with the context surrounding the Master-Slave section which, as we have seen, bears heavily on its interpretation. More specifically, Sartre's desire to deny the possibility of pure recognition leads him to neglect its description almost completely. He also ignores the significance of the sections on desire and Life for the section on interpersonal encounter. Whenever Sartre reaches a difficulty in interpretation, he relies on Hegel's primer for high-school students, the *Propädeutik*,[104] rather than make the effort to puzzle out the *Phenomenology*. Even when simplifications and encapsulations are made by the author himself, they can be misleading.

Finally, Sartre's attempts to distill the essence of Hegel's position further exacerbates his tendency to err, as does his willingness to rely on traditional, 'idealist' interpretations of Hegel's basic project.[105] In combination these factors suggest a propensity for misreading; they constitute the main reasons for the mistakes I shall be elucidating.

Ironically, those aspects of Hegel that Sartre sees most accurately, he will seek to disprove most vehemently. Sartre appreciates the fact that Hegel establishes an internal relation between self-conscious beings: fully actualized self-conscious beings cannot exist without encountering and receiving adequate recognition from Others.[106] Eventually Sartre will deny this; he thinks there is a form of self-consciousness that is independent of Others; thus he tries to show that Hegel's internal relation penetrates *too deeply*. He portrays Hegel as undermining individuality by providing internal relations that are too powerful.[107] In addition, Sartre correctly sees that the outcome of pure recognition is species-consciousness, a universal self-consciousness that constitutes an ontologically irreducible dimension and that potentially includes all self-conscious beings.[108] Sartre tries to show that insurmountable obstacles prevent such a state from being achieved in practice.

Throughout this section my aim will be to explore crucial differences between Hegel's position and Sartre's and to assess their implications for the themes of this essay. I shall begin with a critique of Sartre's interpretation and continue with a discussion of his general "challenge" to Hegel.

Sartre's synopsis of Hegel

Sartre summarizes his interpretation of Hegel by clarifying the main implications of Hegel's theory of Others. The points he makes can be reduced to two: (1) Hegel establishes that one depends on Others for one's existence as a self-conscious being; one's existence amidst Others is a necessary condition for full actualization of Self-consciousness. One cannot "be complete" if there are no other people.[109] Consequently, doubting the existence of Others is senseless because one precondition for the possibility of doubting (as an act of self-consciousness) is the existence of Others;[110] (2) Hegel thus establishes an internal relation between persons that is direct, reciprocal, and deeply penetrating. No 'self' or 'transcendental ego' exists independently of Others; each person becomes himself by making himself *not-be*-Others.[111] In the course of his exposition of Hegel, Sartre elaborates a third general conclusion: (3) Hegel's view implies that the cogito cannot be the correct starting point in philosophy; the cogito is itself conditioned by Others and thus cannot be the perspective from which their existence can be questioned or their nature clarified.[112]

Although there are correct intuitions in each of these formulations, the force of Sartre's conclusions is often misguided because his interpretations are inadequate at key points. I shall indicate the problems in Sartre's reading of Hegel by reviewing each of these conclusions, correcting his errors, and indicating the implications of these revisions for an adequate understanding of Others and their relationship to oneself.

Interpersonal interdependence

Sartre is correct in saying that Hegel establishes an existential interdependence among persons. Conscious beings interact with one another to develop the self-consciousness of each. Similar processes facilitate development toward higher levels of personhood. Each individual is open to Others and requires them to become a genuine person. However, Sartre's claim that Hegel's theory answers epistemological solipsism and thus proves the existence of Others is a misleading representation of Hegel's project. Hegel simply does not address epistemological issues in the Self-Consciousness section; his interest is ontological and existential. Even efforts to unearth a transcendental argument from his remarks do them injustice; Hegel explores the existential transformations engendered by one's relations to Others. He simply *assumes* Others' existence and explores the essential processes and results of interaction.

Nowhere in the *Phenomenology* does Hegel try to prove the existence of Others or even of physical objects. At best he tries to describe how consciousness becomes capable of apprehending complex objects, the transformations which the object undergoes as a result, and the way these processes mutually condition one another. For example, one learns to apprehend Others as self-conscious through interaction (often struggle) with them, and in the process one's existence becomes essentially altered. One is introduced to an entirely new ontological dimension, universal self-consciousness or species-being. This developmental process is active and wrenching, not cognitive or theoretical. In effect, Hegel refocuses attention from the epistemological project to the basic change in oneself that occurs through encountering Others.[113] Sartre's reading of Hegel misses Hegel's effort to reorient philosophical investigation. Hegel's inquiry remains important, even if one has answers to the epistemological question, and it may even condition those answers.

Hegel cannot argue transcendentally to the existence of Others on the basis of the results of pure recognition because he presupposes the presence of another conscious being in order to begin his inquiry.[114] Nothing would interest him less than attempting to certify that the Other encountered initially is not a ghost, a robot, or an illusion.

Moreover, Hegel probably realized the bane of most transcendental arguments, viz., that their premises are infinitely harder to establish than their conclusions.[115]

Sartre himself sought to introduce this shift from the epistemological to the existential, from the clarification of reflective knowledge to the elucidation of pre-reflective, lived encounter. Sartre viciously chides Hegel for his overly epistemological focus,[116] but this focus is present only on an inadequate interpretation of Hegel. Hegel is already where Sartre seeks to be. He fully escapes the lure of the traditional enterprise while Sartre is seduced into returning to it.[117] Sartre's theory is exactly the same type as Hegel's. He seeks to clarify the basic event of encounter, the processes and structures by which it occurs, and its existential implications. Their theories are different, but they are not necessarily incompatible.

When Hegel does examine skepticism, his treatment exemplifies the same shift of emphasis, viz., he clarifies the existential implications of skepticism; he studies a skepticism that permeates one's entire way of life and clarifies why it cannot be sustained as a way of life.[118] As a mere epistemological doctrine, skepticism holds little interest for Hegel, but he shows that it too is a necessary phase in the development of Self-consciousness, just as the master-slave relation is. When he discusses solipsism, he again explores its ramifications as a form of life, and he shows why it cannot be consistently maintained if lived seriously.[119] Hegel was the first to see that *lived solipsism* may be a more important subject of inquiry than epistemological solipsism. One can read his theory of recognition (as well as Sartre's own position) as a description of the way in which the existence of Others emerges in lived experience and thus of the dissolution of *lived solipsism*.

Internal relations

Sartre is again correct in his claim that Hegel establishes an internal *relation* between self-conscious beings, but he is wrong when he characterizes this relation as *negation*.[120] Indeed Hegel shows that negation is not the sole internal relation between persons; a bond of identification opposes the urgencies of negation. This means that interpersonal harmony — mutual, beneficial development — is as important a possibility for persons as Sartrean conflict. Sartre is guided toward his misunderstanding of Hegel by his own definition of what Others *must be* — those who are *not* oneself.[121] This formula renders it virtually impossible for him to conceive any type of relationship between self and Other other than negation.

In addition, the fact that he fails to elucidate Hegel's discussion of pure recognition limits his vision, for there Hegel shows that one essential relation between self and Other is identification. From initial apprehension to final resolution, self and Other see each other as identical, and the result is an ascent to a dimension in which both participate without losing their separateness. The process does not involve apprehending an image of oneself in the Other's eyes or grasping oneself objectified by the Other, as Sartre suggests. The 'loss of oneself' simply is one's initial inability to see oneself as different from the Other; the Other participates in one's self-recovery if one does not insist on one's difference at the outset. The result of pure recognition is mutual reinforcement, mutual identification, and elevation toward species-being. Pure recognition is an internal relation; each participant is essentially altered, but the process does not involve negation.[122]

But someone might wonder whether Sartre's account applies to impure recognition. There is, after all, a passage that seems to support Sartre's reading *verbatim*.[123] Sartre's key contention is that Hegel asserts that one constitutes one's identity by actively differentiating oneself from Others. Sartre interprets this as a process of excluding Others, of neutralizing their threat to one's identity; one maintains oneself only if one continually differentiates oneself from Others and especially from their image of oneself. At this point Sartre has virtually assimilated Hegel's view to his own.

There are three problems with this reading of impure recognition. First, this type of impure recognition, even if successful, would fail to achieve the overall aim of Self-consciousness, which is to overcome the foreignness of the world — to establish that nothing is wholly other than oneself.[124] To realize oneself, on Hegel's view, is to find oneself in what is not oneself, to transcend its foreignness. Even desire, the most primitive form of Self-consciousness, incorporates its object. Were one to successfully differentiate oneself from all other persons, their foreignness, their being-other-than-oneself, would remain untouched. Thus Sartre's view of the process of impure recognition makes it unable to satisfy the aims of Self-consciousness *even if it is achieved*; hence there is something wrong with the interpretation.

Second, Sartre associates the process of impure recognition with objectification — being made into an object of Others. He believes that one differentiates oneself from the *Other's image of oneself*. For Sartre, one is reproduced through the Other's look, not by his mere presence and similarity to oneself.[125] On my view, the Other's mere appearance is what duplicates or fails to duplicate oneself. Hegel would grant that Sartre's process occurs much later in the development of the idealized-individual, but here the doubling that occurs is more primitive. The Other is seen either as another instance of the kind of entity one is (pure) or as a basically different kind of being (impure).[126] In impure recognition one grasps oneself as *more* than the Other because one retains one's sense of abstract self-identity, and this is lacking in the Other's appearance. One seeks recognition or acknowledgment of this difference from the Other. His confirmation makes one's own private intuition public. The only 'objectification' involved is a *reinforcement* of one's already existing sense of difference. This sense does not derive from the Other, nor is his image of oneself relevant because his recognition simply involves accepting one's own differentness. One need not differentiate oneself from the Other's image of one; one simply invites confirmation of a sense of difference one already has.

Third, the effort in impure recognition is *not* to negate the Other — to *make oneself* different from the Other. One already senses one's difference; one simply seeks confirmation of this sense. It constitutes the starting point and the culmination of impure recognition. Sartre's view implies that one is under threat of becoming identical with the Other, and one must *struggle* to differentiate oneself. But the only threat involved is lack of acknowledgment, which does not undermine one's sense of difference but only fails to confirm or actualize it. Even when one struggles with the Other in battle, the *aim* is not to negate the Other but simply to prove that one is beyond life. The negation of the Other in the battle is only incidental.

Thus, Sartre's reading of impure recognition would render it incapable of satisfying the aims of Self-consciousness, would involve an awareness too sophisticated for this level of Self-consciousness, and would require an active process whose result, according to Hegel, has already been achieved. For these reasons Sartre's effort to interpret even the process of impure recognition as an example of internal negation is misguided.

The *cogito*

The final conclusion Sartre draws from his interpretation of Hegel is that the *cogito* cannot be an adequate starting point for philosophy since it is conditioned by the existence of Others.[127] Sartre is thinking that reflective self-examination is a form of self-consciousness and hence must require Others on Hegel's view. This view is problematic not only because Hegel *uses* a kind of *cogito* in his own investigations, but also because the implications of Hegel's position for philosophical method are missed when presented in this way.

Hegel uses a kind of cogito throughout the *Phenomenology*.[128] First, he immerses himself in the forms of consciousness he investigates while presuming he can still provide accurate descriptions of them; this requires the kind of access utilized by the *cogito*. Second, every form of consciousness has a twofold structure: its *experience* is measured by its *standard*. This suggests that the self-reflexivity characteristic of the cogito is part of the essential structure of consciousness itself — even the primitive forms of Consciousness discussed prior to the encounter with Others. Thus, since Sartre's reading of Hegel renders Hegel inconsistent, his reading is questionable.

The central problem with this reading, however, is that it fails to capture Hegel's true contribution. The primary implication of Hegel's position is that *there are distinct, qualitatively different levels of consciousness*. Thus, the results of a reflective description may be quite different when one makes that description at different levels of the development of consciousness. There may be very few essential, ever-present structures of consciousness since it constantly develops.

The implication of this insight is that the structures and outcome of the self-Other relation may change as self-conscious beings continue to develop. No single phenomenological description will adequately explicate the structure of interpersonal relations. A whole series of descriptions will thus be required if a full comprehension of interpersonal life is to be achieved. This position challenges Sartre's methodology, for he assumes that the structures revealed in a single description will be the same for all persons at all stages of development. Hegel denies this. Even if Sartre's reflective description were *wholly* accurate at its level, Hegel would claim that it would not suffice as a complete theory.

A secondary methodological implication which results from Hegel's conception of pure recognition is that in addition to the viewpoint of the separate individuals, there is also the viewpoint of the totality (the interlocking unity they form if they achieve pure recognition). Thus a higher-order set of phenomena can become accessible to a self-conscious being. In effect, one gains an access to an emergent "group mind"; one can reflectively elucidate something beyond oneself. Sartre contests this implication in his more specific criticisms of Hegel by claiming that pure recognition cannot be achieved in practice. I shall therefore delay detailed treatment of Hegel's claim until Sartre's discussion has been examined.

Synopsis

Hence, although Sartre's reading of Hegel addresses important issues, the actual conclusions he draws are inaccurate. Hegel's theory transcends the whole epistemological orientation to intersubjectivity. Although he establishes reciprocal, internal relations among persons, they involve either identification (in pure recognition) or confirmation (in impure recognition); these relations are quite different from Sartre's internal *negation*. Finally, Hegel contends that the essential structures of interpersonal life cannot be uncovered in one descriptive effort, no matter how thorough. Analyses at different levels of a person's development will be necessary if an adequate theory of Others is to be achieved. A sensitive reading of Hegel provides an important alternative to, rather than an inept precursor of, Sartre's theory.

Sartre's challenge to Hegel: the idealism issue

Sartre's challenge to Hegel is implicit in what he takes to be the first in a series of definitive objections. He seeks a sweeping, general indictment and defends his own "realism" against what he regards as Hegel's pernicious idealism, which allegedly identifies being and knowledge and which supposedly causes Hegel to neglect ontological questions in favor of epistemological concerns.[129] In offering this criticism, Sartre continues to misread Hegel's position. Since many interpretations of Hegel are guided by this "idealist" reading, its errors must be rectified. I shall show that the concepts of realism and idealism are simply inadequate to capture the true differences between Sartre's own theory and Hegel's.

Sartre's challenge takes place in two movements. He first tries to demonstrate that Hegel is guilty of the charge of idealism; he then presents three or four basic objections to the positions he takes Hegel to hold. Each of these objections presumes the adequacy of Sartre's earlier treatment of the structures of consciousness in *Being and Nothingness.*[130] Were Hegel to join the dispute, he would certainly question that analysis. Thus, as arguments, Sartre's objections beg the question against Hegel. They are better read as an elucidation of some basic differences between himself and Hegel. Because the disputes are extremely general and range beyond the scope of this essay, I will not pursue them to their conclusions, but I will try to pose them more accurately than Sartre does.

Sartre's fundamental misunderstandings

Sartre charges that Hegel identifies being and knowledge and thus that he formulates ontological questions as epistemological ones. He adduces three pieces of evidence in support of this view: for Hegel (1) the motivation for the interaction with Others is the conversion of certainty into truth;[131] (2) one's existence-for-Others is always reduced to being an object for them; one establishes one's truth by making oneself an object for the Other;[132] (3) universal self-consciousness is reduced to one's knowing that the Other knows one as one knows oneself; this state is a mere abstraction which cannot be achieved by conscious beings.[133] Some of the problems with these allegations have already been discussed; here I shall only briefly review them.

For Hegel, the word 'truth' is never associated with the agreement of propositions with reality; its best equivalent is usually 'goal' or 'result.' Converting certainty into truth requires reaching a mode of consciousness whose experience satisfies its standard. Since few stages of consciousness succeed, the effort to achieve truth is a highway of despair.[134] It demands an active transformation of both oneself and the world; never is it merely a theoretical enterprise. Moreover, were 'truth' to be achieved, the *existence* of consciousness would be altered: it would produce harmony, wisdom, and unity with all things, not merely a handful of veridical propositions. In order to achieve 'truth,' Self-consciousness, must *make* the world reflect itself; this is hardly a 'mere' process of knowledge. The completion of Self-consciousness through pure recognition would entail an elevation of one's existence; one would apprehend oneself as part of a larger social whole which would express itself in and through one.[135] These are existential and ontological results, not merely theoretical or epistemological ones. Sartre's attempt to read Hegel's terminology in traditional ways is misleading.

Sartre's second claim asserts that Hegel reduces one's existence-for-Others to being a mere object for them. Whether one experiences pure or impure recognition, one experiences the subjectivity both of Others and of oneself; never does Hegel reduce self or Other or self-facing-Other to mere objects. Sartre's allegation applies far more to his own theory than to Hegel's. Being-an-object is neither the aim nor the origin of Hegelian encounter. Self-consciousness seeks to remove the alien character of Others; it begins by apprehending the Other as the same as (pure) or different from (impure) itself, not by apprehending an image in the Other's eyes. The outcome of pure recognition and of the slave's efforts involves an amplification, an enlargement of the Self-consciousness, a transformation of being that is not reducible to self-knowledge; a new harmony with the world is achieved. According to Hegel, the master *fails*, but he *succeeds in making himself an object for the Other*. On Sartre's reading, the master is the one who should most succeed.

Sartre's third claim is that universal self-consciousness is unachievable, it would require knowing that another knows one as one knows oneself — a matching of images. But the product of pure recognition — species being — is, on my reading, an emergent condition. It originates in and integrates the participants, but it does not annihilate their individuality.[136] Mutual confirmation of identity creates a bond between them and establishes a unifying dimension that continues to exist through their actions. Species-being does not emerge from matching of one's own self-image with another's image of oneself, but from a relation that each adopts toward the Other and that simultaneously expresses and transforms both.[137]

Sartre's basic error is to misread Hegelian identity. For some thinkers (e.g., current Identity Theorists), to show that one thing is identical to another is to reduce one to the other. Sartre interprets the 'identification' of being and knowledge to be a reduction of being to processes of knowing. For some thinkers that assertion might entail such a reduction, but certainly not for Hegel. His notion of identity is dynamic and non-reductive; neither term within the identity loses its ontological status at its appropriate level. Hegel tries to show that both being and knowing are implicated in one another; transformations of knowledge affect what is; developments in what is alter the processes of knowing. Ultimately, both transformations occur at once, and each is isomorphic with the other. Hegel's germinal idea is that both being and knowing (object and subject) develop through each other; being becomes more complex, and knowing becomes enriched. Only if one views them from a different level of analysis, does the distinctness of 'identical' terms begin to dissolve; there they are seen to function as component parts of a larger system which exists through its parts. For Hegel, the universal requires the particulars as much as the particulars are transformed by the universal. Sartre's traditional reading fails to benefit from the guidelines Hegel provides in the section on *Life*.[138] Since neither term in his "identity-claim" is reduced to the other, Hegel is neither a classical idealist nor a realist; these positions fail to represent the complexity of his theory.

When this conception of identity is applied to pure recognition, self and Other become manifestations of a species-being which emerges from them and exists through them. The distinctness of each self-conscious being is preserved, but both are incorporated into a larger system — a kind of dyad-subject — which is more than each taken separately. Sartre does offer some *arguments* against the possibility of pure recognition; these will be examined in the next section.[139]

These revisions of Sartre's interpretations of Hegel have some important implications: (1) truth is not only an epistemic term but an ontological one. Here it refers to the attainment of a harmony with Others that does not deny their separateness, a harmony that is achieved through a form of self-loss and that produces a dramatic self-recovery; (2) one can experience the Other's subjectivity without experiencing oneself as an object; *a symmetry of subjectivities* that does not entail inevitable conflict is possible; (3) Hegel establishes higher dimensions of existing than mere individuality without eliminating individuals. Species-being is literally a group subject, but it knows itself only through individuals' efforts to know it, and it acts only through their collective actions. Thus, Hegel establishes a whole new field of analysis; there is not only *this concrete Other*, but also a *We* (or Us) that emerges from a specific type of interlacing of self and Other. In short, Hegel's theory provides a richer ontology than Sartre's.

The genuine differences between Hegel and Sartre

Sartre amplifies his allegation of "idealism" with three additional assertions. *First*. The being of self-consciousness is not reducible to, but precedes and is independent of, reflective knowledge. This being is a *measure* of that knowledge; there is a structure to consciousness that

precedes and is unaltered by efforts to know it.[140] *Second.* This kernel
of self-consciousness is independent of the existence of Others and
is not transformed by encounter with them.[141] *Third.* The being
of self-consciousness is not adequately analyzed as a relation of
identity of the ego to itself; indeed there is no such self-reference in
self-consciousness; this identity presupposes the existence of a transcendental ego which is not required to understand self-consciousness.[142]
Accepting these assertions makes one a "realist"; Sartre alleges that
Hegel denies them.

Hegel's realism

I first wish to show that in many ways Hegel is a "realist" in Sartre's
sense. Hegel affirms that Self-consciousness exists prior to any effort to
know it. For example, from the most general Hegelian perspective, the
entire development of the *Phenomenology* must have occurred before
its principle and pattern can become explicit. Hegel occupies a viewpoint
from which he can survey a completed process; it has a structure that
he seeks to uncover. Reflection — the philosopher's contribution —
elucidates what could not be seen by the idealized-individual traversing
the stages, but this development *precedes* the effort of reflection.
Absolute knowledge cannot emerge without the fullest actualization of
Self-consciousness; the former depends on the latter.

Moreover, the development of Hegelian Self-consciousness presupposes a number of achievements, and this suggests that there is a
being to Consciousness and Self-consciousness that precedes any
knowledge of them (or any form of recognition). For example, the
entire development of Consciousness is presupposed before Self-
consciousness even emerges; thus a primitive type of consciousness
exists prior to any Self-consciousness at all and provides a foundation
for it. There is also a primitive form of Hegelian Self-consciousness
that precedes the encounter with Others: desire. In addition, there is
one aspect of Self-consciousness that remains unchanged by the
encounter — viz., the general aim of Self-consciousness: to make itself
explicit by bringing the world into harmony with itself. This standard
precedes and governs the encounter between self-conscious beings at
this level. Finally, there is an abstract sense of self-identity which can
be maintained in the face of Others and which can alter the course of
the interaction. Thus, Hegel can hardly be accused of reducing Self-
consciousness to knowledge, mere ideas, or the caprice of Others.

Sartre's indictment confuses recognition (pure or impure) with knowledge. Recognition is not a species of knowledge; the two phenomena
are logically independent of one another. One can recognize a particular
person without knowing anything specific about him, and one can
know a great deal about someone without recognizing him as like-
oneself. For Hegel, there are different *kinds* of existence; recognition

creates a development of Self-consciousness – an amplification of the primitive form of self-identity that exists at this stage. But this does not imply that Self-consciousness did not exist prior to recognition. Hegel clarifies the powerful contribution persons can make to one another's development.

Hegel's view does entail that even the deepest aspects of oneself can be affected and transformed by Others; no sacrosanct dimension of oneself necessarily escapes their influence. Thus, there is no transcendental ego which is impervious to the action of Others. Hegel was as uneasy with Kant's position as Sartre is with Husserl's. For Hegel, Self-consciousness exists prior to Others, but it develops through encounter.

Similarly, Sartre's charge that Hegel's Self-consciousness is only an abstract relation of self-identity and self-reference overlooks the fact that this primitive mode from which Self-consciousness begins throws the person into the world for its confirmation. Its consequences are anything but abstract; both the world and its own degree of actuality are concretized by its existential demands. Moreover, this sense of self-identity is a *genuine experience* which emerges at a certain level of development, not a mere theoretical construct. It undergoes amplification in intercourse with Others; sometimes it is deeply frustrated – as in the initial Battle and in Mastery; at other times it achieves a partial realization – as in Slavery; and on some occasions, it achieves full completion in pure recognition. When this occurs, Self-consciousness makes a major shift to a new dimension of experience in which its standard and content are entirely new. Thus in its basic nature, in its effects, and in its vulnerability. Hegelian self-identity could not be more concrete and existential.

Sartre's final charge appeals to Kierkegaard. Sartre holds that the individual has an ultimate reality that does not depend on Others or on knowledge. This appears to be the motivation for his discontent with Hegel: he fears that Hegel's species-being will swallow up the individual. I have already indicated some problems with this reading of pure recognition. Here I shall add that Hegel both agrees and disagrees with Sartre's claim. Particularity and separateness are never wholly overcome by Self-consciousness, but at this level of experience, the idealized-individual does not yet experience his *individuality*.

Indeed, throughout the development of Self-consciousness, individuality never emerges – in either self or Other. For Hegel, both the fact and the sense of individuality are very late developments in experience; they require the complete development of Reason. This is an important Hegelian contribution; one does not begin with a sense of separate, unique individuality; it emerges only through a variety of interactions with Others and the world. Once achieved, however, individuality is never wholly lost; it is superseded toward more integrated forms of social life.[143] Individuality is not antecedently given; it derives from experience and intercourse with Others. Hegel's individuality is neither merely ideal nor wholly real; once a certain level of development is achieved, it becomes actual; when that level is superseded, it is retained, but no longer can it be considered ultimate.

Is Hegel a realist? Not in the usual sense: Being can be altered by knowledge. But he is certainly not an idealist in Sartre's sense. Neither category does justice to Hegel's position. This is not surprising, for Hegel's purpose is to transcend and render inapplicable the dichotomies that plagued previous philosophy.

Sartre's Cartesianism

Even though he is innocent of most of Sartre's charges, Hegel provides a very different conception of the self-Other relation than Sartre. Their real differences can be traced to Sartre's lingering Cartesianism; summarizing them will provide a synopsis of Hegel's contributions.

I have already described Hegel's distinctive treatment of the *cogito*. Although he thinks that reflective elucidation of consciousness is possible, even for past historical forms of consciousness, he does not believe that consciousness has a single essential structure. Rather it has different forms or stages, and the relation of individual and world differs greatly in each. Separate *cogitos* are needed to clarify each stage. No single effort at self-clarification will do justice to the complexity of the life of consciousness.

Additional differences between Hegel and Sartre concern privileged access and the extent to which individual existence and social being can be integrated. Sartre insists on retaining something like an inaccessible Cartesian interiority for each person; Hegel resists this privileged access and instead insists that consciousness knows itself through its expressions, the kinds of relations it has with Others and the world. Sartre grants that Others can know everything about one that can be *known*, but he does not think they have the deepest kind of access to one's consciousness (which he calls *certainty*). Hegel contends that this "deep" access is ultimately empty; consciousness comprehends itself best by externalizing itself, and such embodiments or expressions are equally accessible to Others.

In addition, although Sartre thinks that a kind of social existence is imposed on each person by Others, it does not blend or integrate with individual existence; the two modes alternate and conflict with one another, each excluding the other. Thus Sartre falls into a dualism of being-for-itself and being-for-Others; each dimension of the person is self-contained and only externally related to the other. For Hegel on the other hand, social being makes individuality (a very late development) possible and also blends with the individual being of Self-consciousness in pure recognition. One is not just simultaneously for-oneself and for-Others; one becomes most fully for-oneself only through being for-Others. Hegel establishes a dynamic interaction between the two modes that Sartre lets fall asunder.

Hegel does not need to disprove the possibility of Sartre's position; he only needs to show that it is just one possible form of self-Other relatedness. His elucidation of pure recognition provides the crucial alternative to Sartre's vision; this is why Sartre concentrates his critique of Hegel so completely on it.

An evaluation of Sartre's critique of Hegel

Sartre does offer some challenging criticisms of Hegel. In this section my discussion of each one will divide into two stages. Initially, I shall simply assume that Sartre correctly understands Hegel and offer Hegel's best responses. The responses I shall make for Hegel will prefigure some of my own objections to Sartre's theory because in this section Sartre continues to assume his own position. Effective Hegelian replies thus become potential objections to Sartre's own view. Then I shall reformulate Sartre's criticisms so that they more directly apply to Hegel's actual theory and suggest potential Hegelian replies to these alternative formulations. I begin by presenting all of Sartre's objections; then each point can be discussed in turn.

Sartre's criticisms all seek to establish the same conclusion: Hegelian pure recognition cannot occur. Sartre uses two strategies in his discussion: first, he argues that certain processes required by pure recognition cannot occur; second, he tries to show that the end result cannot be achieved because it contradicts basic ontological facts. Sartre labels these two types of error 'epistemological optimism' and 'ontological optimism.'[144]

Sartre offers two reasons why the recognition process cannot proceed, i.e., why Hegel is epistemologically optimistic. The first is that there must be a common measure among the way one sees Others, the way one sees oneself, and the way one sees Others seeing oneself (these elements must correspond) if pure recognition is to be possible.[145] Sartre holds that no such common measure exists, i.e., that the way one knows oneself (from the interior) and the way one knows Others (from the exterior) are essentially different and incommensurate.[146] One cannot know oneself as the Other knows one, and one cannot know the Other as he knows himself.[147] Since Sartre defines pure recognition as knowing that the Other knows one as one knows oneself, he concludes that it is impossible.[148] His second reason is that it is in fact impossible both to perceive the Other as an object and simultaneously to perceive oneself as an object in the Other's eyes, for the latter entails experiencing the Other-as-subject, and the object and subject modalities of the Other exclude one another.[149] Thus, one can never apprehend oneself-as-object and the Other-as-object at once and can never experience one's identity with the Other.

Sartre's other approach is to argue for the impossibility of the interpersonal result of pure recognition – the emergent totality that integrates two separate self-conscious beings. Sartre claims that Hegel never establishes the existence of this totality and that he cannot do so.[150] The plurality of self-conscious beings is ultimate and cannot be overcome.[151] Sartre holds that one experiences a dimension of oneself that is essentially unreachable by Others, and this necessarily individuates and isolates one from everyone. Sartre asserts that Hegel is able to make this emergent totality plausible only because he adopts a third-person, observer viewpoint on the participants and because he thinks he can know them as they know themselves.[152] Whether this is possible is precisely the point at issue. Hegel allegedly forgets that he is an Other to those he describes and wrongly assumes that he can integrate the first-person and third-person viewpoints. One cannot transfer oneself into the Other's mind, and one cannot transcend one's own separation from the Other via some larger social whole.[153]

The issue between Sartre and Hegel has many ramifications. If pure recognition is possible, then harmony and mutual self-development are real possibilities in human life, and the master-slave relation can be superseded. In effect, Sartre is struggling here to defend his later conclusions, viz., that all interpersonal relations must fail and that interpersonal life is fraught with conflict. Moreover, through pure recognition Hegel seeks to establish an internal relation among persons that transcends negativity and to show how there can be social wholes that are more than merely the sum of the individuals within them. Sartre maintains an ontological individualism. This discussion will thus have important implications for these questions.

The process of recognition

Sartre's first objection is that the requisite elements in the recognition process cannot be compared because they are not commensurate and cannot all be experienced by one conscious being. This objection assumes that Hegelian recognition involves objectification, the correspondence of images, and knowledge. Although I have already indicated some problems with this reading, some further discussion of Hegelian recognition will be useful. I shall show that recognition need not involve an explicit consciousness of oneself or explicit awareness of a correspondence of self's and Other's images of self.

Recognition and self-images

A useful characterization of the process of higher-level recognition is a request or call and a correlative response or answer. One acts in a way that claims or requires a response or presumes that a certain state or position has been achieved. The response is either sensitive or insensitive to the request, and if one is appropriately answered, one experiences the Other's sensitivity and one's own self-actualization. Simply expressing the call, however indirectly, assumes that one perceives the Other as capable of response (and to that degree as similar to oneself); thus every call constitutes an implicit recognition of the Other. The call neither objectifies him nor presupposes an objectification of oneself. By calling, one makes oneself vulnerable, for there is always a possibility that an appropriate response will not be forthcoming. This opening of oneself to the Other is the loss of self involved in the first stage of recognition. In responding appropriately, the Other fulfills one's request and acknowledges one's legitimacy in making it. This acknowledgment can be offered even when one is not known as an individual. Call and response are better clarificatory metaphors than presentation of self, apprehension and confirmation of the presented self by Other, and self's apprehension of this confirmation through comparison.

Important differences between knowledge and recognition in this sense emerge when one examines situations in which the appropriate response is not given. If one meets someone unknown, there may be fear, but there is no frenzy or despair. Yet when a call is not appropriately reciprocated, one experiences a wound, a rejection, a degradation. The call leaves one open; the Other's response functions either as a restoration and completion of oneself or as a debilitation. If this response is inappropriate, one is beside oneself, lowered, or betrayed. To be or remain unknown to another has none of these effects.

Sartre might reply here that one's request or call presumes a certain vision of oneself which determines the appropriateness of the response. When that vision is not accepted by the Other, his response will be inappropriate and recognition will not occur. This initial vision of oneself is a kind of self-objectification, and thus my efforts to explicate the process of recognition without depending on objectification and the experience of correspondence fail.

This objection is mistaken because it assumes that one begins with an internal sense of the property to be recognized and then seeks acknowledgment of it. Although this can happen, it is not the primary way recognition occurs, and when it occurs in this fashion, recognition is often withheld just because of that fact. Rarely can or does one wring recognition from the Other. Usually one calls to the Other without realizing that one seeks something from him; one may even be unaware of having made the call until it is denied or refused. Sometimes the Other's recognition-yielding response occurs without any call at all; he then literally creates the quality to which he responds. Even when a prior sense of objectified self exists, there remains a risk, an entrustment of oneself to another, that is uncharacteristic of knowledge.

In addition, recognition need not be experienced as a correspondence of images. The *appropriateness* of the response is determined by the kind of call or implicit request made and the kind of relationship one has to the Other. In some situations certain *calls* can be inappropriate. There is a logic that relates calls and responses which transcends the particular images people have of one another, and this logic governs the appropriateness of responses. One can have the appropriate image of the Other and still respond inadequately, and one can respond adequately even if one has no image of the Other at all. Recognition is experienced through the adequacy of the response; it does not require separate discrimination or a comparison of a prior sense of self with the image expressed by the Other in his response. Recognition typically occurs *alongside* the substance of social life; one becomes aware of it only if it is withheld.

Another question Sartre might raise concerns the process by which one knows one is recognized. On my interpretation, this process is equivalent to the way in which one experiences the appropriateness of the Other's response. Although this kind of apprehension presumes no prior sense of oneself, one *can* experience it through the affirmation of oneself it provides. One experiences a trust maintained or a bond sustained when the response is fitting, or one discovers a part of oneself when a constitutive response occurs without any call. These results may not be discriminated or discretely experienced. Often one experiences one's being recognized in the kinds of next steps that are made possible in the interaction. One need not plumb the recesses of the Other's consciousness; the quality of his response is apparent on the surface. There is no special problem about this knowledge unless the Other is uncharacteristically idiosyncratic in his expression.

Higher levels of recognition are *essentially social* enterprises, for the logic that governs calls and responses is socially and culturally constituted. Hegelian recognition enriches oneself; like Sartre's objectification it adds a new dimension to one's existence, but this dimension is very different from the one which Sartre will elucidate. Thus, Sartre's objection presupposes that certain processes are essential to recognition that in fact are not so. Here again, the use of metaphors related to knowledge to analyze recognition leads Sartre astray.

Hegel's replies

Let us assume, for the moment, that Sartre's interpretation of Hegelian recognition is correct and inquire whether Hegel has any effective responses. Sartre charges that one cannot know oneself as the Other knows one; thus one cannot apprehend a correspondence between his knowledge of oneself and one's own. Thus the Other's view cannot be experienced as confirming one's own.

Hegel can respond that everyone has a sense of himself-objectified at higher levels of self-consciousness, and this sense *integrates* both the way in which Others see one and one's own 'private' sense of oneself. This objectified self can either be one's own impression of how Others typically see one or an ideal which one seeks to become. The Other's vision of oneself contributes to both of these objectified selves; sometimes it determines them completely. In such cases, one's objectified self is wholly identical with the way Others see one.

Among these situations, there are cases in which one has no additional private sense of oneself; one's objectified self simply is one's private sense of oneself. In those cases, the elements that Sartre views as *necessarily* distinct are identical. Thus, Hegelian recognition can occur within Sartre's framework when a person becomes identified with the objectified self he experiences through Others' judgments. Sartre might claim that this identification can never be achieved on the grounds that a private residual sense of oneself can never be lost. But this claim is belied by the phenomena; sometimes the private sense of selfness has not yet developed; sometimes it disappears; sometimes it conforms to the Other's image.

A closely related dimension of self is the self one presents to Others. It is often identical to the objectified self because one typically presents to Others what one takes them to expect, and this is grounded on how they typically see one. Hegelian recognition can also occur at Sartre's level when Others confirm the self one presents to them; if the presented self corresponds with one's sense of oneself, the three elements are again identical, and one experiences a validation from Others. Nothing in principle prevents this from happening and being apprehended. This recognition is self-reinforcing, for one tends to continue to present and see oneself in accordance with the self that Others accept once it is confirmed. The basic point in these examples is that the objectified sense of oneself mediates and synthesizes the two dimensions Sartre regards as irreconcilable (the private self and the social self).

Sartre would not accept this reply. His initial response would be that the mediating objectified sense of oneself is only a creature of reflection and that the reflective self is wholly distinct from one's immediate sense of self.[154] To this there are a number of replies. First, many people live wholly on the reflective plane, and consequently their sense of themselves in fact is dominated by their reflective self. (Sartre portrays such a character, Mathieu, in *The Age of Reason*.) Second, reflection is not so foreign to the pre-reflective level that structures which *emerge* in reflection cannot continue to haunt, or even sediment into, the pre-reflective plane. The reflective self can become that in terms of which one acts, sees oneself, and approaches the world. If one judges oneself a failure, most of one's everyday actions will unconsciously express this. Thus, Sartre's efforts to undermine the possibility of Hegelian recognition through his distinction between reflective and pre-reflective consciousness are insufficient.

Sartre's second response would be that one cannot know the Other's actual view of oneself and hence cannot ever compare it to this objectified self. Against this, Hegel would reply that there would no special problems about knowing the Other's view. His recognition is experienced through his expressions, and empty gestures are typically perceived as such. His judgment is usually evident in the way he treats one. Unresponsiveness usually indicates lack of recognition. Sartre thinks one must 'get inside the Other's mind' to truly know his view of oneself, but his opinion readily emerges in linguistic, facial, and gestural expression. To be sure, the exact degree of confirmation may be difficult to assess, but one can often determine whether or not the Other recognizes one in the sense of accepting one's presented self or confirming one's objectified self. Others' efforts to dissemble or deceive, hedge or temporize, are often obvious; and if they do not become evident immediately, they emerge eventually since a previously confirmed self will often reemerge for continued confirmation in the future. The Other must commit himself to a continuous sham and cover-up if he is to succeed in feigning recognition; usually the deception is manifest to the sensitive eye and ear. Thus, one *can know* the Other's vision of oneself; frequently he is only too anxious to make it obvious.

Sartre's third response would be that one's awareness of oneself is so intimate, so proximate, that another's view could never penetrate or approximate it. Hegel would reply that one's private sense of oneself, when it exists, is not necessarily different from one's presented self or one's objectified self. Often this private sense of self is only a fantasy, and when it has explicable content, it exists because one has made efforts to understand oneself in just the way Others do. If one seeks to understand oneself, one can only engage in the same processes from the same viewpoint that the Other uses and has. One often has the advantage of a richer source of memories, but he often has the advantage of perspective and lack of investment in the outcome. To the extent that one's intimacy with oneself has content, the Other can know that content. Both self and Other can make mistakes in attempting to know what self's nature is, but there are cases (e.g., in psychoanalysis) in which the Other can know what one is doing better than, or more fully than, one does oneself. Even if one has an immediate relation to one's own mental states, this does not provide adequate *understanding* of them, and a sensitive Other can often achieve this better than oneself. Self-understanding is anything but pellucid, and self-deception can be as pervasive as the various ways in which Others can fail to accurately know oneself.

Thus one's objectified self, the self one sees if one takes the Other's viewpoint, can integrate the self-for-itself (one's private sense of self) and the self-for-Others (what Others see). The three elements can correspond and be known to correspond. The alleged interiorities of Self and Other do not open so wide a gulf that a bridge cannot be built. The objectified self provides this bridge and makes Hegelian recognition possible even in Sartre's terms. Sartre's first argument against the possibility of pure recognition fails to establish its conclusion.

A reformulation of Sartre's objection

Sartre is trying to show that pure recognition cannot occur by demonstrating one's inability to know the Other in a way comparable to the way one knows oneself. The best way for him to attack Hegel's actual theory would be to show that one cannot come to see the Other as sufficiently like oneself to make Hegel's first stage of recognition (in which one loses one's abstract self-identity and grasps the Other as like oneself) intelligible. Hegel grants that impure recognition is the *real experience* of Self-consciousness, and he neglects to clarify exactly how the transition to pure recognition is made. Impure recognition occurs because one retains a sense of separateness, of difference. Sartre would need to show that one can never transcend this sense of separateness and must remain locked in an egocentric position. Sartre might argue either that the newly found intuition of self that emerges with Self-consciousness cannot be abandoned or that the Other can never be seen as like oneself because he is seen only externally and because one always sees oneself internally as well. Either argument might show that pure recognition cannot be achieved since the preconditions for its first moment cannot occur.

Even though Hegel does not explicitly describe the transition to pure recognition, he nevertheless does have some replies to this objection. First, the objection neglects some important facts. A Heideggerian point would be that many aspects of 'oneself' (one's actions, feelings, thoughts, ideals) are dictated by Others through group expectations and thus that in many ways one is far more deeply like Others than one may wish to acknowledge. If one experiences this fact, then one can easily achieve a kind of identification with Others — a loss of oneself as qualitatively distinct.

At higher levels of Self-consciousness, the extent to which one can experience this identification may be limited; yet recognition may still' occur. Thus when one experiences a sudden affinity or similarity of situation with another person, there can arise an immediate merging of identities, a loss of separate selfness, an apprehension of oneself as identical with this particular Other. For example, one meets someone who speaks one's own language in a foreign country, or one discovers someone at a cocktail party who shares an eccentric opinion, or one meets a person who grew up in the same neighborhood and attended the same schools as oneself. In each of these cases, a preexistent sense of separateness dissolves, and one experiences a more profound sense of similarity — an openness toward the Other that is sufficient to initiate the first stages of pure recognition.

These facts and examples show that one's interiority and one's "hold" on oneself are not nearly so tenacious as might appear in reflection. One loses one's own sense of isolation quite easily, and one experiences the interiority of another quite readily, however "impossible" this seems in theory.

Hegel could also reply that the implications of his conception of Self-consciousness differ from those suggested by this reformulated objection. Hegelian Self-consciousness *opens* one to the world and allows one to experience it as like oneself; this is what becoming self-conscious *means* for Hegel. *Not* that one finds a self apart, but that reality becomes a *mirror*, that is Hegelian Self-consciousness. Thus one's *initial* grasp of Others *should* be one of identity; to grasp oneself as separate one must retain a sense of self-differentiation which opposes the tendency of Self-consciousness to see everything (and thus the Other) as a reproduction or embodiment of itself. Thus, for Hegel, the egocentric position is not an automatic implication of the emergence of Self-consciousness; his conception is very different from Sartre's and that of many other thinkers.

In impure recognition one sees the Other as different because one sees him as *merely* living; one experiences oneself both as living and also as self-conscious, i.e., as reproduced by the world. One does not see the Other as self-conscious, and the Battle is fought to make him acknowledge this difference. Precisely one's Self-consciousness, which grasps the Other as like oneself, sets oneself off from the Other; he is not seen as seeing oneself as similar to him; he is seen as merely living. Because his likeness to oneself (in being alive) is perceived as forcefully as his difference, one struggles against him. As one learns to perceive Others in more sophisticated ways, one becomes more capable of seeing them as wholly like oneself (e.g., as also being self-conscious) and thus of experiencing complete identification with them. There is no reason in principle why pure recognition cannot be achieved.

Sartre might also claim that the original stage of pure recognition requires that one be able to see the Other's body as similar to one's own. But while one grasps one's own body mainly as an instrument, the Other's body can only be seen as an object. Since one cannot experience his body as one experiences one's own, the dynamic of pure recognition cannot begin.

Hegel could offer two basic replies to this objection. First, one does not see the Other's body *per se*; one sees his projects being pursued and desires being fulfilled *through* his body; the living expressive totality is the initial 'object' of apprehension. One sees the Other's expressed and embodied subjectivity. Similarly, one's experience of oneself in desire is not confined to private sensations; it includes one's attempt to incorporate the world and its transformation. Desire calls attention to one's embodiment and to one's dependency on the body when acting on the world. One's own embodied subjectivity is thus perfectly accessible, and this is sufficient to provide the requisite perception of similarity between self and Other.

Hegel could also add that the Other need not be seen as exactly similar to oneself; one need not, for example, see one's physical twin in order to 'lose oneself' in the requisite sense. Only the gestalt of the Other must resemble the gestalt through which one apprehends oneself. Similarly, one need not experience the Other 'from the inside' in order to apprehend him as like oneself. One's own bodily experience is not essentially interior; practical projects combine internal and external bodily apprehension. Also, because the self-conscious beings addressed by Hegel's theory are very primitive, they lack a sophisticated sense of interiority and are thus more able to see the Other's approach to the world as like their own. Self-consciousness's experience of its own embodiment is similar enough to its experience of Others' embodiment to permit the possibility of pure recognition.

Hence, Sartre's efforts to demonstrate a necessary asymmetry between self and Other fail. Hegel can reply to his objections and at least establish the initial conditions of pure recognition. One's experience of embodiment is important because it interweaves active and passive elements of experience; the apparent chasm between them constitutes the core of Sartre's second objection.

The chasm between the modes of self and Other apprehension

Sartre's second objection concerns the impossibility of achieving the final stage of pure recognition, which requires that one both recognize an Other as self-conscious and experience oneself as so recognized by the Other. Pure recognition entails that one experience oneself actively (recognizing the Other) and passively (as being recognized by the Other). Correlatively, one must experience the Other as both object and subject. But, holds Sartre, the simultaneous experience of both modes of the Other (or of self) is impossible; they exclude one another. This claim is one of the backbones of Sartre's own theory; it generates important implications for his analysis of concrete relations.

Hegel's replies

If one assumes that Sartre correctly interprets Hegel, Hegel could reply that Sartre's claim is simply false. We habitually experience ourselves both actively and passively, both as subjects and as objects. Rarely does the realization that one is seen by the Other undermine one's immersion in the project at hand; often one adjusts that project in order to take account of the Other's presence and reactions (think of seducing, lecturing, or arguing), but one adheres to one's enterprise. Although there are occasions in which one is fully displaced by another's look, they are not typical. Also, when one apprehends Others, they are grasped both in relation to one's own projects *and* as sources of their own projects. One sees another as object and as subject at once; almost every direct interaction with Others requires that one experience both dimensions. In a conversation, one is continually categorizing the Other as he speaks, and one anticipates various responses from him as one speaks; one adjusts what one says in accordance with both. Whether speaking or listening, one is both active and passive.

Hegel's special addition to this response is that in some situations one action is really twofold; it manifests both aspects which Sartre regards as exclusive. By acknowledging the Other's similarity to oneself (and thus seeing him as object), one also experiences him as a subject through that acknowledgment; when one is recognized by another, one experiences him as capable of subjectivity and as among the class of those who recognize one (and thus as an object). Recognition is a double action not only in the sense that it is done by two people at once and effects a new unity between them, but also in the sense that every active element includes a passive one and every passive element includes an active one. To recognize another is to accept one's objectivity for him; to be recognized is also to experience one's subjectivity, for that is the content of his recognition. Hegel's recognition is both active and passive at once — active through passivity, passive through activity. Sartre's objection misses this essential Hegelian point and also neglects the complexity of our everyday experience of Others.

A reformulation

Sartre might remain undaunted and try to reformulate his objection in the following fashion: one cannot experience oneself in the process of both recognizing another and being recognized by him at once; consciousness cannot direct itself outward and be receptive simultaneously; at best, the two experiences can only quickly alternate with one another.

This is an odd claim for a phenomenologist. One main contribution of phenomenology is its exposition of the active conscious processes involved in what seem to be purely passive processes (e.g., perception). What appears to be merely received is often actively structured. In volition, on the other hand, what appear to be blind active elements are constantly adjusting to the givens within which they act. The distinction between the two kinds of processes becomes less easy to make. Sartre's point is even more problematic with respect to recognition. In being recognized one experiences both the Other's subjectivity (as agent) and its content (one's own subjectivity). Recognition incorporates one into a community of subjects as it objectifies; it reinforces one's sense of self even as it dissolves one's separateness. The two modes of self and Other exist simultaneously in one process. Here Hegel's intuition is simply deeper than Sartre's.

The point can be seen even more clearly if one considers the more felicitous way of understanding Hegelian recognition: as call and response. Every call is itself an acknowledgment of the Other's capacity to respond, and every response is an acceptance of the legitimacy of the Other's call. Moreover, every response is itself a further call that requires a response, and every call is itself a response to something emanating from the Other, even if only implicitly. The call is a response to the Other's openness to respond; one does not seek recognition from rocks or trees. Hence a call responds and appeals to the Other's subjectivity even as it makes use of him like an instrument. A response seeks some sort of acceptance and acknowledgment of its appropriateness in order to discharge the responsibility implied by the call. Moreover, the response acknowledges the subjectivity implicit in the call while necessarily objectifying the Other in order to determine the best response. Thus the response originates in and addresses the Other's subjectivity even as it objectifies the call and the Other in order to orient itself appropriately.

Perception of self and Other as object and as subject interweave in each of these experiences. Whichever side one occupies, one experiences both activity and passivity, subjectivity and objectivity, recognition and being recognized. Sartre's a priori exclusivity principle cannot be maintained in the face of the experiences Hegel clarifies.

Social totalities and individuals

Sartre's third objection seeks to show that Hegel is ontologically optimistic. Hegel thinks that an emergent totality that integrates self and Other — a kind of higher-order mind — can emerge as a result of pure recognition. Sartre claims that such a higher-order mind would obliterate the individuality of its members. Since self-conscious individuals are ontologically fundamental, such a higher-order mind cannot exist. Hegel can describe it only because he assumes he is already part of it and hence that it already exists.

Sartre tries to show that Hegel adopts an illegitimate viewpoint of omniscience. Hegel, as a theoretical observer, has forgotten to consider his own relation to the idealized-individual under study. Since that is an example of a self-Other relationship, all the problems he is trying to solve recur at the level of his own inquiry. Hegel's methodology thus assumes answers to all the questions before they are even raised. Only because he assumes this access can Hegel render the idea of a higher-order mind plausible.

Hegel's response

Sartre has a genuine point here, but he also makes many errors. Although Hegel's discussion of pure recognition is a meta-level insertion and thus functions like an assumption, the description of the process of pure recognition is done both from within each conscious being in the dyad and from a third-person viewpoint that allows overall assessment. Sartre's charge that Hegel only views his principals as objects (and thus only shows a unity of already objectified subjects – objectified by him)[155] is unfair. Hegel immerses himself in his principals and tries to describe their experience as it is for them. Of course, Sartre may still ask how he knows this is their experience. Hegel can answer that he may describe at least one side of the relationship in so far as he assumes the position of one of the principals himself. He does, however, seem to take an extra, unwarranted step – adopting a viewpoint of omniscience – when he asserts that exactly the same processes are occurring in the other person in the recognition relationship. I shall pursue Sartre's objection in this form in the reformulation below.

Hegel may also note that Sartre asserts that the achievement of Hegelian totality is *impossible*. But *claiming this* transcends the bounds within which his own arguments restrict him. Sartre would have to *know* that the Other *does not* or *cannot* reciprocate efforts at pure recognition, but, by his own arguments, he cannot know whether the Other is or is not reciprocating. One simply cannot know what Others are experiencing, on Sartre's view. Hence the strongest conclusion Sartre can draw is that Hegel has *failed to establish* the possibility of pure recognition. If he were to assert more than this, he would be indulging in the same leap of faith, the same assumption of omniscience, which he attributes to Hegel.

A third, stronger response is simply that in the course of pure recognition, the range of access of consciousness extends. Since the totality exists only through the minds and actions of individuals, the "experience" of the totality as such, if it exists, is accessible to individual members; and thus an individual member, by noting the alterations and extensions of his field of consciousness, should be able to correctly determine whether and when a higher-order totality has emerged. As a member of a group, e.g., a committee, one often apprehends both the desires of the group as such (e.g., to get on to other topics, to call the question, to vote one way) and one's own desires – especially when they are opposed to or distinct from those of the group. Were there no group, the individual could perceive only his own desires, but when there is a group, he can very often apprehend *additional* desires and intentions; he can even experience his own intentions *qua member* of the group to assent to the group's will *even if* he disagrees. Thus there is a way to determine, at least in principle, whether Hegel's claim is plausible or not. Sartre could try to claim that any apprehension of group-will apart from one's own will is illusory, but this would require stronger argumentation than he provides.

A telling reformulation

There is one way to reformulate Sartre's objection to make it more conclusive. If one defends Hegel by saying that his descriptions are made from the first-person, phenomenological viewpoint (rather than the third-person, external observer viewpoint), then the legitimacy of Hegel's claim to know that exactly analogous processes are occurring in the Other is questionable. In a sense, Hegel projects himself over into the Other's mind and imagines what would happen if he were reciprocating at every point. Hegel cannot legitimately immerse himself in *both* principals at once, and if he identifies with one of them, he may be unable to know what is happening in the Other. He seems to simply *transfer* what he learns about Self-consciousness from one side of the relationship over to the other side. But Hegel can vindicate such a transfer only when pure recognition is complete. Since Hegel needs to make the transfer in the course of recognition, Sartre seems to have a legitimate point.

Henceforth, I shall call this the "transfer problem," and later I shall show that Sartre's own theory falters here as well. A different way of putting the point is that one cannot experience the totality constituted by pure recognition because one cannot experience either the Other's reciprocation of the relevant processes or his own experience of recognition. The knowledge of recognition thus seems forever one-sided.

At this point Hegel's strongest reply is that Sartre is assuming a picture of the mind (as an interior space) that his theory seeks to overcome. Hegel conceives the Other as an active, living being; his 'mind' exists in his expressions. One might expect that the processes of recognition would express themselves as well – in the way the Other responds to one's calls, in the way he accepts one's own responses, in what he expects, and in what he offers. Recognition is not a separate, discriminable experience like a particular feeling; it is a kind of social space or social foundation for a certain relation to the world – a stability, self-assurance, and self-acceptance. If the Other exhibits the traits that recognition brings into existence, then one can presume he experiences himself as recognized. When some question about his status arises, either from oneself or a third party, his loss of this supporting milieu and his consequent loss of self-assurance become quickly evident. Moreover, he would determine whether he experiences himself as recognized in ways quite similar to those one would use; he would not consult introspection because recognition is not the kind of experience that can be discriminated in this fashion. Thus, through his theory of expression, Hegel at least has some paths to pursue in seeking a resolution of the transfer problem.

Hegel could also add that vortices in one's own experience can indicate non-reciprocity in the Other. For example, gestures will suddenly fall flat, presumptions will disintegrate, and one's own sense of social orientation will waver if the Other does not respond appropriately to one's calls or one's recognition. Everything happens as if a kind of preliminary union joins two persons even before pure recognition is achieved. One's experiences provide a gauge of the continuity, depth, and development of this union. Sartre's opinion that individuality forms a kind of non-permeable, necessary boundary simply does not do justice to interpersonal experience. Although one's own experience may not be an infallible guide to what occurs in the Other, it is often accurate. Self and Other are more deeply intertwined than Sartre realizes.

Summary

Thus against the original formulations of Sartre's criticisms, Hegel is able to offer convincing replies if one allows him to explicate the concept of recognition at the more sophisticated levels of self-consciousness from which Sartre offers his critique. Hegel is able to show how pure recognition is possible even if one requires it to operate over the Sartrean experience of objectification and the social self. Moreover, even when Sartre's arguments are reformulated to address Hegel's theory more directly on the level at which it was offered, Hegel's analysis still stands. The transfer problem is the only serious objection that Sartre raises to Hegel's analysis, and Hegel's theory may contain the resources to resolve it. Although Sartre's arguments are clever and nicely put, Hegel seems to be able to respond to them effectively.

Since Sartre's major aim is to disprove the possibility of pure recognition, my efforts to reply to his objections have sought to establish its possibility and actuality. I do not think that pure recognition is a rare or difficult experience to achieve, although there are persons and forms of social life that can make its achievement difficult. I deny that individuality is annihilated or lost in the course of pure recognition. Once one is consciously a member of a constituted social whole, one acts and thinks differently than one does as a separate individual, but this does not mean that one's individuality is sacrificed. One potent point that Hegel can make against Sartre here is that individuality must be won before it can be lost, and it can be won only through many levels of recognition by Others.

Hegel not only has a more concrete, less a prioristic, approach to interpersonal experience and dynamics than Sartre, he has greater sensitivity to many of the subtle social unities and strains that exist between people. He makes the first serious philosophical effort to explore the implications of those unities. Through his theory of the necessity of expression for the actualization of Self-consciousness, through explicating various mediating structures between self and Other, and through his concept of double or ambiguous action, Hegel is able to suggest solutions to some of the problems that have troubled previous philosophical efforts to understand intersubjectivity. Any adequate theory of Others and their relation to self must build on Hegel's foundations.

Additional objections to Hegel

To offer a full-blown critique of Hegel's views on Others and the self-Other relation on the basis of this passage of the *Phenomenology* would be somewhat ludicrous. At least six times this amount of material bears on the question in that text alone. To offer such a critique would be like writing an analysis of a five-act play after having read only the first act. Nevertheless, certain kinds of critical remarks can be offered and may be useful, as long as it is realized that more could undoubtedly be said and that a great restriction of scope will be necessary. I shall not attempt to refute Hegel in ten easy pages; such an enterprise would simply be fruitless. Perhaps the best spirit in which to explore Hegel is contemplative interrogation — indicating possible trouble spots, raising doubts and uncertainties.

   Three distinct enterprises are possible. First, and most justifiably, one can examine Hegel's particular claims in this section about attitudes likes desire, fear, and mastery; questions can be raised about the strength of his criticisms and adequacy of his understanding of these attitudes. My comments presuppose the fact that Hegel's remarks about these orientations are incomplete (since he discusses them here outside of an historical context) and restricted to the level of development that an ideal-typical individual has reached early in the Self-Consciousness chapter. Second, Hegel's pure recognition, the guiding aim of interpersonal relations, can be evaluated as an ideal. Finally, the implications of Hegel's approach to relations between people can be investigated. Hegel lays the groundwork for a *way of thinking* in social theory, what one might call a functional approach, and a few general reflections on this approach may be useful.

Specific concerns

Hegel's discussion covers five major topics: desire, the battle to death, the demise of mastery, fear, and work. I shall offer some reflections on Hegel's treatment of each.

Desire

Hegel treats the attitude of desire as a pre-social one; Self-consciousness can be expressed through desire even if there are no other conscious beings in the universe. Consequently, to approach other *people* in the attitude of desire would be primitive — lacking any genuine comprehension of what another conscious being is. One might interpret the basic problem of impure recognition as a failure to transcend the attitude of desire. Desire regards the object as mere appearance, completely devoid of selfness; it thus can only manifest itself by incorporating the object — eliminating its externality, independence, and otherness completely.[156] This destructiveness is a response to the threat that encountering a living object creates. Since the desired object is not seen as a conscious being, it does not mirror oneself; one cannot lose oneself in it, and thus one cannot make the passage to pure recognition. Hence, on this view, sexual desire would be conceived as a response to a threat to one's sense of self and as a struggle to eliminate the reality of the Other by incorporating him/her bodily.

Desire fails because Self-consciousness does not become manifest to itself objectively through it; the object of desire is no longer literally there; it is consumed. Moreover, one is returned to a state in which any object will again be perceived as a threat. Desire's satisfaction, in so far as it provides a sense of reality to self, is evanescent; it exists only in so far as the object is yet to be overcome. Once satisfaction subsides, one loses one's self-manifestation.[157]

Hegel's depiction suggests that the central problem to be overcome by desire is the moment of destabilization that arises in the encounter with another; the resurgence of this loss of harmony is what eliminating the object of desire fails to overcome; the object is assimilated, but no permanent identity in otherness is achieved. Desire can, however, be lived differently; the seducer may experience each new object as a challenge, not a threat, as an opportunity to reassert self-supremacy; hence the seducer can live his desire as a kind of contest. The Other can be seen as yet another territory to annex; the seducer need not lose the achievement of previous conquests. Like the gunslinger who notches the barrel of his weapon, the seducer can maintain self-certainty while actualizing his desire. The possibility of encountering an unattainable object remains, but this need not distress him until he actually experiences it. *That* failure is quite different from the one Hegel describes, for the seducer finds self-realization in the *process* of conquest more than in its final product. Although this attitude is not without its own disharmonies and contradictions, it does represent a tentative solution to the problems of primitive desire. Hegel addresses an attitude similar to it in his chapter on "the Spiritual Animal Kingdom."[158]

I can examine Hegel's remarks more adequately if I focus on one type of desire: sexual desire. Sexual desire is somewhat more complex than Hegel's analysis suggests. Although the Other may be incorporated, self is usually *spent*. The disappearance of the Other *is mirrored* by a kind of loss of self; moreover, as self recovers itself, the Other recovers also; there is an interactive transfer of modes that Hegel thinks essential to pure recognition. Sexual desire can, of course, be possessive and refuse to spend itself; it can attempt to dominate the Other by refusing to let go (here there are definite analogies to the battle to death). In this case, one can portray sexual desire as a kind of vampirism. But sexual desire can also seek to lose itself, to spend itself completely, to achieve complete disappearance of self in the Other. In such cases, the lack characteristic of desire is radicalized and concretized. Desire need not always seek to overcome self-loss.

Sexual desire can retain its nature as desire and yet open the way toward pure recognition; hence, not all desire *qua desire* is a primitive way of orienting toward other people. It carries its own form of recognition, a recognition that remains even when desire has dissipated and one is satisfied. Even if one restricts oneself to *possessive* desire, which withholds itself and incorporates the Other, Hegel overlooks that the possessor *is possessed by* his possessions as well as possessing them. His incorporation of them is his amalgamation into them; desire can transport one beyond oneself as well as locking one within oneself. This other side of possessive desire is more adequately seen in the example of sexual desire, and it too is not without contradictions and disharmonies, but a full treatment of desire would need to include these additional perspectives.

A deeper question is whether desire is always adequately analyzed as a *lack* — something emerging from a disequilibrium and expressing a need to recover oneself. This analysis, which sees desire's source and *action* as negation, is virtually *assumed* in much of later European philosophy. The analysis of desire as lack seems obvious: desire seems to arise from emptiness; satisfaction appears to be an effort to fill oneself. Still, as the previous examples indicate, not all desire is easily comprehended under this model, and it may not adequately express the basic movement of any desire.

Desire can function as a radiation of self as much as a loss of self; it can be a medium in which self and Other gently merge. Desire, like the senses of touch and taste, offers problems for a representational theory of perception; nothing need mediate the desire and the desired. This *initial* movement can be experienced as self-emergence; a desirable objects gives one something to emerge toward and *for*. Without desires one might remain inert; they call one forth and open one to action.

One learns one's aims through them, and one attunes oneself to the world in them. In all these ways desires express content rather than lack, and the transition to satisfaction can also involve a feeling of harmony. Desire need not violate its object even if it consumes it.

Desires can be seen as integral to the process of Self-consciousness in just the way Hegel sees the division into species as essential to Life; they can create a harmony with the world through simultaneous acknowledgment of the world's actuality and self's manifestation in it. Desire allows one to grasp the world as an embodiment of self; it can eliminate the necessity to view the world as foreign, other, or mere appearance. Self can be tempered through the experience of desire; it learns that it functions as a part of an encompassing whole, and that, rather than the model of desire as lack and negation, may be the *truth* of desire — its ultimate achievement.

Hegel might respond to these considerations by stressing the primitive nature of Self-consciousness at this stage and holding that my reservations would only be intelligible for a more developed Self-consciousness. He would insist that the earliest self is experienced as absolute yet without confirmed reality; desire then becomes an effort to actualize that confirmation by eliminating the actuality of the object. But if the *aim* of Self-consciousness is to confirm its reality — to actualize its primacy — in the face of an apparently resistant world, then desire seems to *succeed* in this aim. To be sure, the object is consumed by desire, but the literal existence of the object was the source of the instability; to eliminate it is to achieve stability. Undoubtedly, new external objects of desire will be encountered, but this is a purely *contingent* fact. Perhaps Hegel would reply that in so far as Self-consciousness becomes more than abstract self-identity, it does so only in the experience of conquest and satisfaction, and it must thus endlessly continue this activity. His assertion that the crucial problem of desire is the necessity of actively negating its object supports this interpretation.

However, Hegel seems to have implicitly assumed two different standards for Self-consciousness: (1) concrete actualization *against apparent* externality and (2) finding oneself *amidst* or in harmony with *given* externality. Hegel suggests that the object of desire must not disappear if Self-consciousness is to be fully expressed. If *this* were the original standard for Self-consciousness, the attitude of *consummatory* desire would *never arise*. It arose as a means of satisfying the first standard. In effect, Hegel alters the standard (or slips in an additional one) as Self-consciousness undergoes experience. Were Self-consciousness to retain its original standard, desire would be successful since it does demonstrate the primacy of Self-consciousness.

Precisely the same objection arises for Hegel's critique of impure recognition since the master's conquest of the slave seems to yield everything that was sought by Self-consciousness (at least on the first standard); only by importing something additional, reachable only in pure recognition, is Hegel able to demonstrate a flaw in the outlook of the master. In desire and in mastery, the apparent externality of the Other is superseded. If the purpose of Self-consciousness is self-assertion, then these attitudes succeed.

Perhaps the most difficult tasks in Hegel's enterprise are to discover a standard that is truly internal to the state of mind being discussed and to retain precisely that standard when developing the internal critique. Dialectical criticism can be used as illicitly as any other critical method; errors arise when one over-generalizes the standard or leaves it ambiguous or inaccurately describes the development of experience. Although Hegel may be able to answer these objections, there do seem to be some weaknesses in his criticisms of desire, and these weaknesses may be endemic to his entire approach.

The battle to death

The second specific topic Hegel addresses is the necessity of fighting a battle to death in order to achieve recognition from another living being. One struggles because one sees oneself as distinct from the Other. His self-consciousness is not apparent to one; yet he appears similar to one in being alive; hence one must transcend Life to prove one's difference. One struggles to prove one's self-consciousness to the Other by demonstrating one is willing to risk one's life. To demonstrate the genuineness of one's risk, one challenges the Other's life.[159] Death results, and Self-consciousness thus learns that living is essential to its existence; it becomes willing to forego recognition in order to remain alive.[160]

This story has two problems. First, is the strategy of fighting this battle in any way intelligible? Why would Self-consciousness risk its newly discovered relation to life in order to achieve recognition? Might there not be some less extreme way of doing this?

Here Hegel's view may be stronger than it first appears. Through the process of desire, Self-consciousness has just learned of its enmeshment in bodily life. But in so far as one comes upon Others with a similar bodily life, one learns that this bodily existence is not *uniquely* one's own, but exists in many other conscious beings. Hence one cannot experience oneself as concretized by the life-process; one experiences only a commonness with Others, not a unique manifestation or expression of self-identity. The very encounter with other living conscious beings thus may engender a withdrawal of Self-consciousness from its attachment to Life.

Self-consciousness's reaction may be one of resentment both toward the Other and toward its own living processes, which no longer function as a unique embodiment of itself. Here may be the motive for the withdrawal of abstract Self-consciousness from its recently realized embodiment (in impure recognition). This view also explains why one decides to *risk* one's life in order to demonstrate one's self-consciousness to the Other, for one must show not just that one is more than the life process, but that one is *other* than the life process. The disassociation of Self-consciousness from its life process and the effort to challenge the life of the Other then become more plausible because they have motivated its self-loss. The challenge to the life of the Other is thus a direct attack on his apparent similarity to oneself, not merely a way of attesting to the genuineness of the risk one is taking, a motive which seems overly refined for the primitive beings which confront each other at this stage. Unfortunately, Hegel's reply to this problem suggests another one.

This second problem is serious; ultimately it questions the entire project of impure recognition. Hegel thinks the prime motive for the battle is to demonstrate that the risk of one's own life is complete, unequivocal. However, the battle will yield that conclusion only if the other living being is presumed to be capable of reciprocity, of perceiving the threat and responding in kind. For *only if the Other responds* with an equal threat to one's own life is one's risk of life complete. But this potential for reciprocity is precisely what Self-consciousness in the stage of impure recognition denies; indeed, it sees the Other as inferior — less than self-conscious — and seeks to explicitly demonstrate this inferiority (and its own superiority). The strategy of Self-consciousness thus assumes the reciprocal self-consciousness of the Other in order to demonstrate the Other's lack of self-consciousness; this project is self-stultifying.

Perhaps Hegel might reply that the Other does not initially realize his own lack of self-consciousness; making him realize this would then be the aim of the battle. But if this is the battle's motive, the original self-conscious being must *apprehend* the Other's sense of self-certainty. This is to grasp the Other as self-conscious, which contradicts the initial condition of impure recognition.

These reflections introduce my most general question about the battle: if the Other does not initially appear as self-conscious, is there any sense in engaging him in a struggle to obtain confirmation by recognition? Can a being who does not appear to be self-conscious even seem capable of recognition? And if the Other is not capable of recognizing Self-consciousness, the motive for the battle disappears. On the other hand, if the Other *is* seen as self-conscious, then the original self-conscious being can identify himself with the Other in the initial moment of encounter, and the dynamic of *pure recognition* becomes possible. Hegel would need to explain more fully why pure recognition does not ensue. Hegel seems to be in a dilemma at this point.

107

Mastery

The master succeeds in dominating the slave and experiences a sense of recognition as long as the slave executes his commands.[161] The master satisfies his desires without confronting the externality of the world; this he leaves to the slave to transform into something usable. The only problem is that the slave's recognition *loses* its significance because the slave loses his status; he becomes a mere thing — an extension of the master that cannot provide genuine recognition. The master cannot see himself in the slave; he thus remains only partially realized.[162]

Hegel's discussion of the master is fraught with problems similar to those mentioned in the discussion of desire: when he criticizes the attitude, he seems to import standards that were not there at the outset. Moreover, his discussion of the master seems insufficient; one wants a deeper internal contradiction to demonstrate the necessity of the *breakdown* of the master's orientation. At best, Hegel shows that mastery is a dead end, but he does not demonstrate its transformation into anything else; the attitude may eventually atrophy, but it does not develop into something new. Marx may have been right not to trust the forces of the dialectic to overthrow the masters; a more active revolt may be necessary.

I shall begin this discussion with some preliminary questions. Hegel claims that the slave finds himself embodied through his work, but if the slave is able to see himself in those products, so too should the master, for his commands direct the slave's activity, and his designs are what the new world reflects. The master need not work; yet the objective world is transformed according to his will and thus expresses and reflects himself. The slave's success should only *increase* the self-certainty of the master. This appears to be a salient oversight on Hegel's part, for the master can achieve actualization of Self-consciousness along with the slave; indeed, *since* the demand for and plan of the work is not the slave's own, one wonders whether *he can* achieve any adequate sense of self-manifestation in it. Moreover, the master does achieve the continuous reinforcement of self that comes from the slave's obedience. This may not be mutual recognition, but it is the kind of acknowledgment of superiority that Self-consciousness sought to attain at the outset of impure recognition.

In addition, one may doubt the seriousness of the difficulty Hegel presents to the master. If the slave's recognition is inadequate, why can he not seek recognition from other established masters? Perhaps masters can reach territorial settlements, recognize each other, and use their stables of slaves to make themselves manifest to each other. This seems to be what happened in feudalism. Moreover, once the master's dominance is recognized by a significant number of slaves, what would make him seek to dominate *everyone*? *That* form of recognition would be achieved. Indeed, the slave and his work provide a kind of extension or solidification to the master's self-consciousness which can be apprehended and acknowledged by other masters without having their own sphere of dominance questioned. Thus, the *masters* might be more adequately prepared for the achievement of pure recognition, a development Hegel did not choose to pursue.

Given these considerations, one can open a deeper question: does the master fail *on his own terms*? Does Hegel's critique succeed only because it imports the standard for *pure recognition*, viz., mutuality? At the outset of the battle, Self-consciousness experiences itself as primary and seeks to force the Other to recognize this primacy. The master seems to accomplish this aim. How could the master expect reciprocal recognition if he is seeking to confirm his dominance and his difference from the Other? The ideal of pure recognition may be known *by Hegel* to be the ultimate achievement of Self-consciousness, but he cannot utilize this knowledge in the description of the experience of the idealized individual living through the experience. If he does, he violates the basic tenet of his phenomenology and abandons his effort to provide *internal* criticisms of each moment of consciousness.

Hegel argues that the master's self-consciousness is not manifest in the slave, who is subordinate and thing-like; yet the slave does acknowledge the master's superiority in his obedience and his work. The master may not see himself embodied *in* the slave, but he does see himself manifested *through* the slave; the world made by the slave reflects the master's self-consciousness. One might say that the slave becomes an extension of the master's *life* while the *objective world* becomes the arena of his self-consciousness; thus the master is able to discover *both* aspects of himself outside himself and realizes himself as a living as well as a self-conscious being. Moreover, there is even a basis for the master's *recognizing* the slave – *qua* extension of himself, for the slave may actualize the master's plans to a greater or lesser degree of perfection, and this can be the basis for a recognition appropriate to the slave. These reflections suggest that the master may achieve a far more successful mode of life than Hegel acknowledges and that something more powerful will be needed to undermine the master's way of life, something like Nietzsche's famous transvaluation of the master's values by the slave.

Fear

Hegel's remarks on fear suggest its importance in facilitating the rebirth of the slave's self-consciousness. Hegel claims that absolute fear for one's life shakes one's foundations, obliterates all one's attachments to particular products, roles, or experiences, and facilitates the development of *pure* self-consciousness — a sense of difference from any incarnation. Fear makes this pure self-consciousness vividly present;

through it the slave comes to see himself as distinct from the master's vision and from his own immersion in the processes of life.[163] This analysis of fear has been developed by the existentialist tradition under the rubric of anxiety (*Angst*) or dread. The position is that this experience enlivens one, allows a truer sense of oneself to emerge. *Angst* effects a separation from the process and demands of everyday life and opens up the possibility of self-determination and authentic action.

Against this view of fear a number of objections can be raised. I agree that the main effect of fear is a disassociation from any action or role, a *withdrawal*, a distancing of oneself from any situation in which one finds oneself. Hegel believes that this provides a new sense of self, a universality above any particularity, a self-awareness distinct from anything one does, any characteristic one has, any habit or talent in which one expresses oneself. I disagree with Hegel's characterization of this newfound sense of "self" and with his claim that it has positive value. The strongest point is simply that the newfound "self" cannot be actualized; it cannot manifest itself in any way, for any concrete expression of it will be particular and thus will fail to express its universal nature.[164] The universality achieved by this withdrawal is *empty* of all content; nothing positive — no new dimension of self — is discovered in *fear*; one only learns that one has the capacity to withdraw from or disown every action and quality one has.[165]

Although this is a fact and one might even call this fact a realization of Self-consciousness, characterizing this as an achievement — especially as an inauguration of a new life of the self — is misleading because this self can *never* find expression; indeed, *it poisons all self-expression.* It makes impossible precisely what the whole stage of Self-consciousness is trying to realize: the possibility of finding oneself in and as the Other and of achieving harmony with the world. The "universal" self-consciousness that emerges in fear separates one *absolutely* from everything in the world and anything that might provide positive content to oneself. Thus this "completion" of Self-consciousness immediately becomes its incapacity to ever identify itself with anything.

This general point suggests a number of specific problems with Hegel's conception of fear. First, Hegel asserts that fear makes possible an identification with the products of one's work; the slave becomes capable of grasping his own actualization in laboring because the master inculcates great fear. To me this is unintelligible; if the slave's fear locks him into this "universal" self-consciousness, then apprehending himself in the working process or its products will be impossible, for they are particular, concrete manifestations. To find himself in work would be to *lose* his "universal" self-consciousness.

Hegel could reply that the slave has been identified with — and sees himself as a mere appendage of — the life process, and fear makes possible a distinction between himself and this process. But how valuable is an *absolute separation* from one's life and one's world; perhaps such a separation will make it *forever impossible* to achieve any harmony with the world. Especially if one maintains the attitude of "universal" self-consciousness, no such unification will be possible; it creates perpetual alienation from the world, from Others, and from everything that one can be said to be. Hence if one is forced to act (as the slave is), one is likely to undergo a division within oneself and experience the being who works or acts as a false self.

Second, the general aim of this stage of Self-consciousness is the achievement of recognition, but fear may throw one so far back within oneself that one will never be able to lose one's sense of differentiation or separation from Others. Hence one might be forever unable to find oneself in Others, a capacity that pure recognition *requires*. The achievement of "universal" self-consciousness will provide one a permanent sense of one's separateness from Others because one will never be able to apprehend the Other as "universally" self-conscious since this condition cannot be expressed. Thus, no matter how similar he is to one *qua* species or even *qua* particular situation in life, one will never be able to see oneself wholly embodied in him and to lose oneself sufficiently to enable the dynamic of pure recognition to begin. In addition, one's actions come to be experienced as manifestations of a false self (as described above); then even if one's actions and works were recognized by Others, this recognition would only confirm a self that was already experienced as false. In such circumstances, recognition, far from confirming oneself or making possible the realization of self, will only deepen one's sense of isolation and helplessness.

No doubt someone will object that fear at least allows the slave to dissociate himself from a debilitating role and to see himself as capable of other expressions. Were Hegel's fear partial, leaving intact some elements of oneself, this objection might be acceptable. But the fear Hegel praises is total; it severs all one's particular embodiments from one's abstract sense of self. This empty selfness leaves one no basis for self-reconstruction and parenthesizes all future efforts at self-expression. Even if the slave sought expression in a different sphere of existence (as the Stoic does in thought), the effect of fear would be no less debilitating. Unless some sphere of potential self-identity is preserved, fear is more likely to permanently prevent the actualization of Self-consciousness in Hegel's sense.

For these reasons I am skeptical about the positive value of fear. In general, an atmosphere of fear will be detrimental to any effort to achieve harmony with the world. Fear, when experienced as a sense of challenge, i.e., when not threatening one's very existence, may be productive, but even in that case, one must *already* have some sense of oneself and one's abilities in order to effectively confront the fear and the challenge.

Hegel generalizes his remarks on fear and contends that war is socially productive since it facilitates a shaking of the elements of civil society from an exclusive focus on particular concerns and re-animates their sense of attachment to the State. One can imagine this view making the decisions of government leaders much easier, and one can imagine it used to vindicate the "liberation" of individuals from their subcultures or their cultures (e.g., in colonization). Such institutional actions can only destroy the individual's ability to identify with anything. He is made helpless; he may even embrace the State as a last resort, but no self-embodiment, no genuine cultural ethos, can emerge from such a last ditch embrace. Even if it could, what sort of harmony or unity of self and Other would exist? Essentially one's self has been *destroyed*, and, *at best*, another has been provided; the tactic only serves to return the individual to his point of origin — now perhaps less able to express himself in the new situation since he realizes that his identity can be so easily manipulated.

Work

Hegel thinks that work is forced upon one by servitude to another; one would have no reason to delay the assimilative process of desire if the Other were not standing over one. Instead of *consuming* the living object, the worker *transforms* it; his desire becomes formative, he shapes the raw material in accord with 'his' will. Thus although the worker's desire seems frustrated because the object is not consumed, in fact, a richer realization of self is achieved because the world comes to manifest himself. The solidity and permanence of the product can function as a means for achieving a sense of permanent self-expression. Also the worker can experience himself in his living body since it makes this transformation possible. Work thus seems to effect the transform-ation of a subservient slave into a self-actualizing self-conscious being.[166]

Although this view of work has also had great influence on thinkers like Marx and on all subsequent attitudes toward the laboring process, a number of specific objections can be raised against it in the context of its function in the development of Self-consciousness. First, how the worker sees himself realized in the products of work is difficult to understand, given that the command to work, the type of work, and the goals and means of working are forced upon the slave by the master. Beyond this, the slave's product is confiscated and used to satisfy the master's desires. Only the process of transformation is contributed by the slave, and thus one would expect him to achieve only the *concept* of self-embodiment through formative activity, not an actual concretization of self. Even if the results of the laboring process were experienced as self-actualizations, would not the slave be even more debilitated when those products were consumed or used by the master? At best, the slave's labor can only *suggest* an *ideal* of self-realization — the life of an artisan: designing, planning, actualizing, and using the objects of his laboring process.

One also wonders whether *any* type of laboring activity will provide even this ideal of self-realization. If the labor process is divided, and one makes only a small contribution to the final product, one will not be able to see oneself in the whole. Or if one's labor is generalized and repetitive, tilling the soil or harvesting the crop, one will also be unable to experience oneself embodied because such labor only facilitates a natural process; it does not fashion a product. Hence, one can wonder whether any slave labor is capable even of providing *the concept* of self-embodiment.

Moreover, the permanent presence of fear exacerbates these difficulties. The slave finds himself in work by fleeing from fear, by avoiding the severe dissociation with which fear threatens him and frenetically embracing the process and products of labor. This identification is unlikely to be complete since the shadow of fear will continue to haunt him, and the "universal" self-consciousness created by fear will be attenuated by this effort to escape. Hence, work under fear can only be a compromise that loses the possible benefits of either extreme; one loses one's abstract sense of self apart from one's work, and one never can find oneself fully embodied in one's work.

Still another factor that will affect the extent to which one can find oneself embodied in one's work is its *quality* and perhaps even whether it is appreciated by those who are significant. If the products one makes are shabby or if one's efforts are regarded with indifference by those who matter (the master, in this case), then one is unlikely to achieve any self-embodiment in work. Hence many factors other than the simple fact of participating in a transformative process affect whether the worker will be able to find himself realized by his work.

A final difficulty is that although work, under the best of circumstances, may resolve the dilemmas of desire (the disappearance of one's self-objectification), it does not achieve any of the aims of recognition; indeed the self-embodiment it achieves, however complete it may be, is wholly non-social. But since Others are on the scene, the aims of Self-consciousness must extend to include them as well. Since the slave may achieve restricted and minimal realization through productive activity, one might expect the withdrawal from the social sphere that in fact constitutes the next stage of Self-consciousness: Stoicism. Hegel postpones the necessity of addressing the problems that work creates for the achievement of the aims of Self-consciousness and recognition. Since one's own products are not produced by Others, Others can only apprehend them as foreign; thus Others can only find *themselves* embodied in them through supplementary activities, e.g., criticism and evaluation. Whether these products create an obstacle to achieving pure recognition is also left unaddressed.

For each of these specific topics, I have tried to offer salient reservations, indicate possible problems, and suggest alternative ways of understanding the phenomenon. None of these remarks is intended to "refute" Hegel; my efforts throughout this section have sought to provide the kind of commentary appropriate to Hegel's style of philosophizing. One needs both to consider his analyses within the perspective of the section in which they appear and to reflect on their more general significance. I have tried to suggest useful additions to Hegel's fruitful beginnings.

General criticisms

More general problems can also be raised. Two of these will be explored: the first concerns the adequacy of pure recognition as an ideal for interpersonal relations; the second concerns the general functional approach through which Hegel analyzes social encounter in this section.

Pure recognition

I shall explore three kinds of questions about pure recognition. The first concerns its possibility: To what extent can Others initially be seen as identical with oneself? The second addresses some inherent problems of achieving it among many individuals; close attention will be given to understanding the third person's relationship to an already mutually recognizing dyad. The third examines whether pure recognition is the most that can be achieved in interpersonal life; is this ideal worthy of governing all personal encounters? This question will be explored both from within Hegel's basic assumptions and independently of them. Since the exposition of pure recognition is quite involved and not easily summarized, the reader is asked to review the exposition offered earlier in this chapter before considering the following critique.[167]

The first question is analogous to the one which created problems for Husserl: why is the Other initially seen as a duplication of oneself, in whom one can lose oneself? Hegel claims that the Other is seen as a living being, a being which mirrors oneself *qua* living being, and thus one with whom one can immediately identify oneself. But the Other's body does not appear as one's own body typically appears when *lived*. Hegel does realize that one cannot grasp the Other as self-conscious by analogy through one's own self-consciousness. One must initially lose one's self-consciousness and then regain both it and the Other's at a higher level. Yet even if one abandons one's abstract self-identity, how does one apprehend the Other's behavior as a living process, a process similar enough to one's own life-process to motivate identification? Although the Other can be observed to satisfy his desires through consuming, this does not differentiate him from any of the other animals. Why does one not seek pure recognition from *every* living being if consumption is the motivating similarity? Moreover, if the Other *is* seen as self-conscious, even just potentially, how is this apprehended? If it is his bodily similarity, how is this apprehended and how rich a similarity is needed? Hegel need not account for the existence of Others if that is not his central concern, but he should provide a further clarification of why Others appear as they do to this primitive form of Self-consciousness. Although I will not press this issue here, it is a possible lacuna in Hegel's analysis.

The second question concerns what Sartre calls the problem of the Third. Suppose two living beings achieve pure recognition; what happens when they, either separately or as a dyad, confront a Third person? Presumably the dialectic of pure recognition reoccurs, but does it transpire *differently* because they have already achieved recognition? Is it *more difficult* for them to lose themselves in order to recover themselves through recognition of the Third, or is it easier? Does the presence of the Third alter the relationship between those who have already achieved recognition? Does their relationship unravel or threaten to? If one person within the dyad seeks to acknowledge the Third, but the Other does not, does this alter their recognition of one another? If there is a breakdown of pure recognition as a result of the Third, then this considerably alters the standard governing the interpersonal dialectic of Self-consciousness, for pure recognition would then have to occur among *everyone* (and virtually simultaneously) in order to remain a stable achievement. Is such a massive social transformation feasible?

Perhaps I can do more than simply raise questions. The achievement of pure recognition creates a new sense of self that is reinforced by the Other. To the extent that one remains in continuous contact with the reinforcing agent, one should be more easily able to lose oneself with a Third because one will be continuously aware of the interactive flow of recognition and thus more able to enter this dynamic with Thirds. If one loses contact with the reinforcing partner, the new sense of self may become ossified into a fortress to be defended, and one may be unwilling to relinquish one's achieved sense of self to recognize the Third.

This position stands in sharp contrast to Sartre's; he thinks that the Third will be more disorienting if he is encountered while the recognizers are proximate to one another. This difference reflects the difference between Hegel and Sartre on what is happening in interpersonal encounters. For Hegel, the process is more dynamic and mutual, and the result of the process is quite distinct from the result Sartre sees. Hegel's pure recognition creates an energy in which both individuals participate and which becomes a dimension of what they both are. Sartre's looking-looked-at relation is asymmetrical; the Other imposes a structure on one which he does not share; he dominates one by defining one. Sartrean onlookers can sustain uneasy compromises if each adopts a complimentary attitude, and this collusion can be disturbed by the presence of Thirds; hence Sartrean onlookers tend to withdraw from social life in order to maintain their collusion. Hegelian recognizers, however, do not collude; they create something new between them which is ongoing and mutual; hence they seem more capable of incorporating the Third.

Still there is a difficulty: potential division within an existing dyad when the Third enters. If only one moves to include the Third, the Other may lose contact with the emergent medium between them altogether and may thus lose that dimension of himself constituted by the recognition; this could lead to potential resentment, jealousy, and a sense of abandonment and isolation. The problem will always exist because the mediating totality does not function independently; it unites individuals but does not create a new entity that has consciousness and intentions of its own. It operates only through the self-consciousness of individuals that comprise it, and they must respond individually to the presence of the Third.

The problem of the Third has yet another dimension. The original aim of Self-consciousness is to apprehend all otherness in dynamic identity with itself, to eliminate the foreignness of the world and discover itself embodied in it. If pure recognition obtains only between particular sets of persons, however, then the criterion of Self-consciousness will not be satisfied until all Others have been included; those not included would continue to be foreign. The problem for the Third is that at the outset he will apprehend himself as unrecognized and yet realize that the Others recognize each other; hence here is a *factual* basis for him to regard himself as different, separated, and excluded from the constituted dyad. Hence the difficulty of increasing the range of pure recognition may lie in the Third himself; *he* may be unable to lose himself – to see himself as fundamentally like the Others – in order to recover himself by being recognized. The problem thus may not be in the dyad's unwillingness to incorporate him, but in his willingness or inability to see himself as incorporable.

If this problem has any substance, then there may be a conflict between the achievement of pure recognition and the satisfaction of the criterion of Self-consciousness. In short, *even if* one achieves pure recognition, that very success may render the aim of Self-consciousness unachievable since one may be unable to extend the scope of pure recognition to all self-conscious beings. The problem is significant because the process of pure recognition is a mutual action; it requires the participation of both parties. If the position of the Third is such that he cannot participate in the initial phases of recognition, then the efforts of those in the dyad to include him may not succeed.

A third question concerns the extent to which pure recognition is an adequate ideal, a standard toward which one hopes all interpersonal relationships will eventually be guided.[168] This question can take two forms: to what extent does pure recognition embody Hegelian infinity, which is the ultimate model for all other Hegelian standards? is the unity achieved in pure recognition the deepest unity one can discover in interpersonal relationships? The first questions the ideality of pure recognition within Hegel's framework; the second appeals to other frames of reference. I think these questions should be raised because Hegel does present pure recognition as an ultimate aim of Self-consciousness and because clarifying the highest possibilities for inter-personal relationships is one underlying aim of this essay.

With respect to the first form of this question, one should note that pure recognition occurs only because each sees the Other reciprocating appropriately. If either party refuses this reciprocity, the process of pure recognition ceases. This makes pure recognition seem like scratching the Other's back only if he is willing to scratch one's own. To what extent is this simply mutual masturbation rather than a true embodi-ment of Hegelian infinity? Is there a genuine apprehension of an emerging interpersonal unity, or is there simply an awareness of a lack in oneself that can be filled if one makes a few perfunctory gestures? Is each fantasizing that more is present in the actions of the Other than the Other is truly offering? If so, is this embodiment of infinity not false? If the recognition experienced is not really offered or is offered only for an ulterior motive, to what extent is the recognition genuine, stable, and lasting?

The point here is that recognition proceeds only if a central condition obtains, and this suggests that there is a kind of *limit* or *boundary* on the actualization of pure recognition, and this implies that pure recog-nition does not embody unboundedness or unlimitedness (infinity). Although Hegel includes this mutuality condition, it plays no essential role in the dynamic. If the motive for offering recognition were pure, i.e., based solely on one's apprehension of the Other as oneself, one would continuously be able to see oneself in the action of the Other, and recognition could proceed to completion. Hegel may have compro-mised his description to achieve greater "realism," i.e., conformity to what many social theorists regard as man's inevitable motivation (self-interest and its variants), but he seems to have missed the fact that this makes his ideal relationship an inadequate expression of infinity in interpersonal experience.

A second important feature of recognition is that the Other is returned to himself at the end of the recognition process. Although I interpreted this self-return as an elevation of self to a higher level rather than a return to the point of origin, there remains the danger that this returning of the Other to himself will simply let the Other go. Were this to occur, pure recognition would not fulfill the requirements of Hegelian infinity. This point raises the question of how lasting the achievements of pure recognition are apart from any problematic circumstances. Do the persons meet, acknowledge one another, then separate essentially unchanged (like medieval knights), or does this meeting transform each by creating a mediation between them? One wants to think that pure recognition is transformative, but the final moment in which the Other is returned to himself then becomes puzzling. Perhaps this question only shows that my interpretation of pure recognition is incomplete, but it may show that there are unresolved tensions in Hegel's description. It illustrates the difficulty of trying to offer a theory which allows genuine unification and interpenetration of persons without denying the differentiation that separate embodiment seems to entail.

A final issue concerns the extent to which the mediating totality that emerges from pure recognition takes on a character of its own in the way that the process of Life does. Earlier I noted that it did not have its own agency in the way Hegelian Life does. However, it does have a reality distinct from the two individuals involved, because the effect of a mutually recognizing dyad on a Third is different from an encounter among three separate individuals. Can this totality ever *divide* self-conscious beings from one another? Can it split a person off from himself? If so, then pure recognition offers only an incomplete concretization of Hegelian infinity.

Because a self-oriented motivation, an abandonment of the Other, and a potential divisiveness accompany pure recognition, its adequacy as an ideal within Hegel's own framework can be questioned. In addition, one wonders whether pure recognition is the most that self-conscious beings can achieve in relationships. Certainly deeper devotions, more powerful effects, more complete restorations, and more fulfilling unities between people seem possible: love, inspiration, forgiveness, friendship.

Hegel may object that he did not intend to explicate the ideal governing all relationships, but even in other chapters dealing with interpersonal relationships, the search for pure recognition remains predominant. They seem to be measured in comparison with it, and they seem to be progressively moving toward its actualization, as one would expect on my interpretation. Hence the possible reply that Hegel's elucidation falls too early in the book to play such a pivotal role is misleading, for its explication takes place from the point of view of the *retrospective theorist*, not from that of the ideal-typical individual.

Perhaps Hegel sought to explicate an ideal that was at least attainable, or more likely, that could realistically be achieved by large numbers of people. If this were the case, he could grant that closer personal relationships are of course possible but retain pure recognition as the minimum ideal for interpersonal relations. It may offer a truly universal unity even if it lacks the intensity and intimacy of love. Hegel's ideal allows a genuine species-consciousness to *emerge*; since love between all persons may be impossible, Hegel may justifiably claim that his is the more adequate social aim.

One question remains: do these additional ideal relationships conflict with the achievement of pure recognition? If these other ideals are important to achieve, at least in one's relationships with some few people, their compatibility with the minimal ideal becomes an important concern. Will one who is in love be moved by the achievement of pure recognition with a stranger? Will he be capable of identifying with the Other sufficiently to permit the dynamic of pure recognition to occur? Will the veneration one feels for a special mentor permit one to grasp an average person as self-conscious as well, or will all Others fall short in comparison with him? Will the sense of acknowledgment have the same significance once one has experienced passionate love or friendship? Perhaps these more intense interpersonal ideals do conflict with the universal achievement of pure recognition.

And if this were the case, perhaps Hegel's point would be that the quality of life that would emerge from a culture which had universal recognition — but which lacked any of these more intense ideals — would after all be richer, saner, and more sensible. Even if this incompatibility exists, perhaps the value of universal pure recognition would outweigh that of the other ideals (even if achieved) *if* they necessitate the consignment of most everyday relationships to impure recognition. This issue at least needs some discussion. Hegel did not often grant the incompatibility of what appear to be opposites or contraries. His instinct would probably be to search for a synthesis, and perhaps one should read the section on Spirit as an effort to provide such a combination of interpersonal and social ideals.[169]

Hegel's general approach to relationships

I will conclude these reflections on Hegel with a discussion of his general approach to the study of interpersonal relationships. For Hegel, Self-consciousness seeks to satisfy a certain standard — to experience itself in and as otherness, to exist in harmony with the world. Pure recognition is the concretization of this goal in interpersonal relationships, at least at this stage of development (at any other stage, the same telos-aim structure exists, although the particular aim may be different — more complex or more specific).

Thus Hegel's general approach is to elucidate the inherent aim in relationships and to determine whether the actual experience in a particular relationship can satisfy that aim. The aim gives the relationship a unique dynamic or an inner logic. If the relationship cannot achieve its aim, a dialectical transformation of both the standard and the possibilities of concrete experience occurs. Sartre adopts this theoretical approach in his theory of possible responses to the look; each response seeks to satisfy the same function or aim. I wish to raise some questions about this approach as a means of effectively illuminating human encounter.

Perhaps the most important difficulty is the likelihood that human relations do not possess one simple, overarching aim or function. Different types of relationships seem to have different functions, and different instances of a single type of relationship may be lived with different aims and expectations. Different individuals may adopt different aims during the course of the same relationship, and one may have many irreducible aims. Is pure recognition the fundamental motivation, the basic aim or function, underlying all relationships? Could *any* hypothetical aim play this role? How might one attempt to verify this kind of functional hypothesis?

To be sure, any relationship can be *interpreted* to have such an aim, but how illuminating will this be? The theorist seeks an aim that will provide some organization and coherence, but one that will also answer new questions and point toward phenomena as yet unseen. Even if there were one function which all relationships did satisfy, how much would that one aim explain about any particular relationship? Would it distort or clarify one's comprehension? Moreover, as one examines possible counter-examples, will one attempt to incorporate them by moving to an ever more general formulation of that aim, and if so, will that aim not become less and less informative about the particular relationship? In addition, even if one has a middle-level aim that encompasses a large number of relationships, for many of those cases which it "covers," it may only have perfunctory clarificatory power; other aims might explain far more about these particular cases than the one which also applies to other cases; does one rely on one's original hypothesis to elucidate these cases?

A different, "stock" answer to counter-examples is that the problematic cases can be rendered more intelligible when seen as surface manifestations of the underlying aim. Evaluating such assertions is difficult because the criteria of intelligibility are rarely neutrally defined; they are integrally connected to the kind of interpretation or organization the hypothetical aim provides. Moreover, historical facts, even if one could discover them (this is difficult), about the basic function of the primal social act (supposing there ever were individuals without a social context, which is improbable) would be superfluous to the discussion since the basic function of social relationships may change with the development of history or differ in diverse cultural contexts. At least Hegel does not try to provide his analysis with a quasi-historical justification, and at least he allows for the possibility of different aims in different contexts, but the question remains: exactly how much clarification of human relationships is provided by this approach?

Perhaps these concerns can be made more concrete by applying them to an example taken from Hegel's Master-Slave chapter. Hegel tries to clarify the master's orientation through his hypothetical aim, recognition. This approach helps us understand the master only if the effort to dominate *is* an effort to win recognition. Although recognition may have been a peripheral theme, the slave-owners of the pre-Civil War United States primarily sought cheap labor. Contemporary sadists either seem curious about the effects of unusually harsh actions or seem to be trying to pass beyond the limits of their own humanity. In these instances, recognition does not add much illumination, at least on the face of it.

Moreover, if recognition were an underlying aim, one would expect mastery to break down if it were not achieved. But if the tortured person constantly scorns the sadist, this only increases his curiosity; it does not make him give up his efforts to dominate. In addition, if the posited aim is achieved, one would expect the relationship to cease or alter, but when the servant class recognizes the "rights" of their masters to dominate them, no transformation occurs; the relationship continues much as before. The recognition offered may even become more and more perfunctory and ceremonial without significantly affecting the status of the institution. Thus positing recognition as a basic aim for this particular relationship does not offer much insight; it does not coordinate the simplest observations about mastery and leads to few new ones.

In response to these kinds of considerations, a Hegelian could retreat to claim that he is elucidating *one form* of mastery or an ideal-type of the master-slave relationship that should not be compared to the historical exemplifications of this relationship. But this is only to define a type into existence; it leaves open the question of the extent to which the type is exemplified; it postpones and relocates the questions rather than resolves them.

Hence, Hegel's general approach to the study of relationships is not without problems. But these problems must also be seen in the context of those of the alternatives. At least the functional approach does provide a *potentially* informative way to organize *at least some* areas of human interaction; it is not restricted to merely juxtaposing ideal types, which seems even less informative about the salient dimensions and factors affecting interpersonal life. Although the functional approach seems overly reductivist and oversimplifying, at least some logic or pattern is provided. One is led to further questions; one understands what it would be to improve hypotheses in the area; one can develop a conception of higher-order (inclusive or integrative) aims or functions that is at least intelligible. One is not left with a series of randomly associated notes and observations; further work using the method might offer a deeper synthesis. Moreover this approach can be related to other investigations profitably, as Sartre discovered. As one explores the phenomenology of encounter and dynamics of interaction more fully, one can modify one's conceptions of the dominant aim and function.

Hence, although there are serious problems with this approach, it does not lack intellectual value and a mechanism for self-correction. The extent to which this approach is ultimately productive will depend not only on the imaginativeness of its practitioners, but also on the effectiveness of the efforts of those who seek to provide alternatives to it.

Thus, both at the most general level — in his basic method and in the basic ideal of pure recognition — and at the particular level — in his discussion of desire, fear, the master, work, and the battle, Hegel's theories have some flaws. I have tried to offer the kind of criticism that seems germane to Hegel's investigations and to isolate some specific problems for further research. Hegel's insights are rich and perceptive; they merit further development.

As a whole, Hegel's position offers a significant alternative to the Cartesian picture of persons. Not only does Hegel abandon the entire Cartesian problematic and substitute a more vital and more fruitful one, he directly attacks two of its central assertions: the monad view of the self and the privileged-access conception of mental states. Hegel shows how persons are ontologically interrelated and interdependent. He also shows that mind comes to realization only through its expressions; the self comes to know itself in much the way that Others come to know it.

Chapter 3

Heidegger

Sartre completes his survey of his predecessors with a discussion of Heidegger's conception of being-with in *Being and Time.* Since Sartre himself offers no explication of Heidegger's general project yet presupposes an understanding of it and since my position is that no adequate comprehension of a philosopher's theory of Others is possible without a sense of the project which determines his formulation of the problem, I shall first attempt to clarify this general project. My expectation is that such a clarification will obviate some misunderstandings of Heidegger's theory and perhaps also suggest some deeper objections than Sartre sees. This exposition will be limited to the general project that Heidegger presents in *Being and Time* and will elucidate only those issues essential to an understanding of Heidegger's theory of Others.

An introduction to Heidegger

Heidegger's aim is to resurrect and explore the question of Being and its meaning.[1] About his concept of "meaning" I shall have nothing to say since it does not bear on his discussion of being-with. Many philosophers have thought the question of Being either meaningless, impossible to answer, or not worth answering. Heidegger disagrees. But he believes that this antagonism to his question must be accounted for and that it indicates something important about Being: not just that it is *not easily* understood, but that it *resists* understanding.[2] The source of this resistance will be discussed below.

Being and understanding

Being — that toward which Heidegger is trying to direct attention — is not itself an entity but governs every entity and is manifest whenever anyone experiences an entity.[3] Moreover, it cannot be examined in itself, apart from entities; one can clarify it only through clarifying one's understanding of entities.[4] Thus, one clarifies Being through clarifying entities — including the entity that does the clarifying[5] — in a special fashion. One might think of Heidegger's Being as the *process* in and through which entities appear, their becoming manifest.

123

Whenever one confronts an entity (of any type, in any mode), one has an *implicit* comprehension of the being of that entity, for Being is manifest through it, conditions *what* it is, and thus conditions our style of access to it.[6] Not only does one have an implicit comprehension of the being of *what one confronts*, but one has an implicit comprehension of the being of one's *confronting* itself. People have an implicit comprehension of their own being, but this too exists only in so far as they confront something in some fashion. Heidegger's aim is to make these *implicit* comprehensions *explicit.*[7] The basic assumptions of the enterprise are that people have this implicit comprehension and that it can be made explicit.

Previous efforts have been made to clarify this understanding, notably in Greece prior to Plato, but Heidegger believes these efforts were deficient. Worse, they have been translated and promulgated throughout the tradition of Western philosophy in a way that has further concealed these already deficient insights.[8] Hence, not only is our implicit understanding of Being not immediately apparent, easily missed or discounted, it also lies buried beneath the shrouds of misinterpretation. Heidegger's task thus includes breaking through these misreadings and bringing to the foreground what has remained in the background.[9]

Heidegger offers two reasons for the original deficiency in attempts to understand Being; since these factors disturb *every* effort to clarify Being, they help explain the resistance of Being to our understanding. One reason for the deficiency is that Being has been sought, approached, or thought about as if it were an entity, only more encompassing. Such an approach is misleading because Being is not itself an entity even though it conditions every entity.[10] A second reason for this deficiency is that in so far as man has attempted to understand his own being, he has done so on the basis of his understanding of non-human entities. He perpetually interprets his own being in terms of what is not himself;[11] to Heidegger this indicates an essential feature of human beings – to be-in-a-world. Their immersion is so complete that they interpret themselves on the model of the things around which they dwell.[12]

In so far as people *understand* themselves inadequately, they *live* inadequately, for Heidegger believes that the manner in which one understands oneself and the manner in which one lives are directly related.[13] One cannot alter one without altering the other. Reading Heidegger can be a wrenching experience since part of his task is to challenge one's way of life so that one can more fully and lucidly understand oneself and, through this, Being itself. Conversely, the richer understanding of one's existence he provides allows one to live more vibrantly.

Being is thus inherently resistant to human understanding. Moreover, traditional efforts to clarify one's implicit understanding have exacerbated the difficulties. The tradition of Western philosophy has understood "Being" to mean "presence."[14] An entity is thought to exist in so far as it can become present, and man exists in so far as he can become present to himself. The state of mind in which such presence is most manifest is called "knowledge." According to Heidegger, presence does not adequately capture the being of entities or of people, and, consequently, presence cannot yield an adequate comprehension of Being itself. In addition, theoretical knowledge is not the only state of mind to which the being of entities appears; it also appears in states of mind characteristic of everyday life.[15] This traditional interpretation of Being and traditional bias toward theoretical knowledge compromise most efforts to clarify Being.

Perhaps one can see why a discussion of the tradition's comprehension of Being is important if one sees how it structures philosophical investigation of Others. Because of the tradition's orientation, one raises the question of Other's being only in situations in which they are present to one and in which one faces them in an attitude of theoretical knowing. Specifically, one wonders while facing their bodily *presence* how one can *know* the *presence* of their personhood. This context has conditioned most philosophical attempts to clarify the being of Others. If there is something fundamentally wrong with this governing context and if a new context can be provided, then the question of the Other's being might appear in a wholly new light.

In order to make one's implicit comprehension of Being more accessible, the tradition must be challenged; its precise errors must be exhibited. But this questioning must be supplemented by an effort to better understand human being and the being of entities as they appear in everyday life. This can be done through efforts to recover and reanimate this implicit comprehension and to reconceptualize experience on the basis of this recovery. This recovery is facilitated by efforts to illuminate the primal experiences of Being, which can be made accessible[16] but which keep getting betrayed when one tries to capture them theoretically. Heidegger uses both linguistic and phenomenological techniques to make this implicit understanding of Being manifest. He also criticizes traditional formulations of ontological problems and traditional answers to them in order to increase one's receptivity to these techniques.

Heidegger thinks his general project is important for two reasons. First, he thinks one's understanding of Being functions as a model to guide one's understanding of every entity.[17] If there is such a model governing all inquiry and if it is faulty, then rectifying the flaws, or at least reconsidering its adequacy, will have important implications. All the specific regions of Being would have to be reexamined. If, for example, a different model should guide thinking about the being of Others and if their existence should be clarified in attitudes of mind other than theoretical knowing, then questions about their nature and their relation to oneself may require reformulation. This is what Heidegger concludes.

Second, human beings have a special concern with the question of Being because they are inherently concerned about their own existence; how and what he or she is, is an issue for any person.[18] If one's understanding of Being is faulty, one's understanding of one's own being will be faulty, and the way one lives will be affected by this. Raising the question of Being anew may make possible a change in how people live.

Dasein and its existentials

One cannot clarify Being except through clarifying some entity. The entity Heidegger chooses to examine in *Being and Time* is *Dasein* (man).[19] Man has an understanding of his own being even when he inquires into Being; hence he has a clue to answering the question.[20] In addition, man's being makes inquiry into Being possible because he is *open* to Being; he has primordial access to it; thus man's special form of being is a condition of possibility for the inquiry; for this reason it is a sensible point of departure.[21] Heidegger is primarily interested in Being; he investigates man's being only to clarify Being; hence he does not seek to explore man's being exhaustively. He seeks to clarify the structures of human beings that will most facilitate the clarification of Being and which function as conditions of possibility for inquiring into Being.[22]

At the same time as he investigates human beings, he seeks to ground his investigation. His task has an object-level (clarifying man – *Dasein*) and a meta-level (clarifying the conditions that make this clarification possible).[23] Some commentators have stressed one of these tasks to the exclusion of the other;[24] Heidegger's explicit statements suggest an emphasis on the meta-level,[25] but his actual results suggest an emphasis on the object-level.[26] These two levels of inquiry interact: in addressing one level, Heidegger also clarifies the other, for what grounds all inquiry is man's implicit understanding of Being; yet the structure of man's being is what makes that implicit understanding possible. Moreover, the structures that condition inquiry also condition every other mode of existing. Hence the two levels of the inquiry amplify each other.[27]

Heidegger clarifies the being of man and the conditions of possibility for that clarification by elucidating what he calls "existentials."[28] Being-with (*Mitsein*) and the impersonal mode of selfness (*Das Man*) – the primary subjects of this chapter – are existentials. They are part of a structurally integrated whole: being-in-the-world.[29] In order to understand what Heidegger is saying about the relation of self and Other, one must know what an existential is. Heidegger explicitly contrasts existentials to "categories."[30] Presumably he has Kant in mind; Kant's categories are the constitutive forms of the being of physical objects. Existentials, this contrast would suggest, are the constitutive forms of *being human*.

I shall interpret this to mean the following: (1) existentials constitute the essence (i.e., at least the necessary conditions) of being human, the structures without which an entity could not be a human being;[31] (2) existentials exist in every way of being human; one cannot exist in any state without all the constitutive forms of being human applying (this is *not* to say that one is explicitly conscious of them);[32] (3) existentials make possible man's unique kind of being, viz., the capacity to have an implicit comprehension of Being (and the propensity to misinterpret it) and to be always concerned about his own being in some fashion.[33] The first and second elements of my interpretation relate more to the 'object level' of Heidegger's inquiry (the being of man) while the third relates more to the meta-level (the conditions of clarifying man's being).

Existentials are *not* the forms through which "man's mind must see itself" because they are not forms of *understanding* and thus do not concern only the mind; they are forms of *existing* (a *broader* idea), and they govern the emergence or the happening of man's being.[34] Some forms of 'understanding' (not primarily theoretical ones) are among the existentials, but there are other kinds of existentials too. Moreover, existentials govern the totality of human existing, not just his understanding of himself. Heidegger is not just trying to clarify man's essence, although he does do that; he is trying to clarify the deepest structures of human existence, and this is what gives his enterprise its quasi-Kantian flavor.

This reading of "existential" can be amplified with an example that Heidegger discusses: worldhood. Worldhood is the contextual background of instrumental uses in which the use of any particular instrument appears.[35] Just as words presuppose a context of other words to gain their sense, instruments presuppose a context of other instruments to gain their function. For Heidegger, instrumental-use is the basic mode of existing of any entity within the world. On my reading, worldhood itself is an existential of human being[36] because one cannot exist in any mode without there being some instrumental context correlative to that mode, because any entity which did not exist within such a context would not be human, and because this context makes possible a person's having a particular arrangement of tools or instruments around him; indeed, it necessitates that there be such an arrangement.[37] Worldhood provides a special access to the being of entities; this access has been concealed by the philosophical tradition which remains obsessed with a derivative and limited instance of this fundamental instrumentality — pure presence.

Heidegger seeks to supersede the subject-object distinction by revising the conception of each side of the distinction.[38] Instead of understanding things as independent presences, he conceives them primarily as instruments; this is their basic way of manifesting themselves in everyday life. Instead of conceiving man's primary relation to things as theoretical cognition or even as mere perception, he conceives it as care.[39] Man's being is more accurately revealed in his involvements, purposes, and possibilities; around these the instruments of the world are organized. Theoretical cognition is only one form this involvement can take. The two reinterpretations interlock: man's cares throw him into the world, and the instrumentally organized world is already prepared for that insertion. There is no basic separation between man and world when they are adequately understood.

One's practical orientation to the world has its own kind of vision, understanding, and intelligibility, which Heidegger clarifies. Heidegger's crucial philosophical move against the tradition is to demonstrate that its ways of conceptualizing man and things are mere special cases, atypical modes, of his more basic forms.[40] One does sometimes merely perceive an object that appears distinct and independent (merely present), but this is only a degenerate instance of an instrumental relation to it, and it arises primarily when the more typical instrumental comportment breaks down.[41] When the pen runs out of ink, then its mere presence becomes manifest; while it writes, one barely sees it at all. Heidegger's position thus subsumes traditional conceptions, but also supersedes them.

Existentials constitute the essence and conditioning forms of being human. Although they are a priori structures of a human being (*Dasein*), fully understanding them requires a reconceptualization of both things and persons. Although they can be elucidated separately, they do not exist apart from one another; they exist as a totality; no one of them is more basic than the others.[42] Heidegger initially clarifies the existentials exhibited in everyday life. His discussion of being-with occurs in the course of that clarification. Although being-with is an a priori structure of being human, this does not mean that it will lack implications for understanding the being of Others.

One might wonder how Heidegger justifies his claims about the existentials. His exposition is not heavily laden with arguments, but he does try to show that traditional conceptions can be subsumed under his view as special cases. He also attempts to make one's implicit comprehension of one's own being explicit. He does this by drawing attention to experience as it is actually lived in everyday life and then describing the conditions of possibility of that experience. The sympathetic reader should be initially open to his descriptions and then determine whether they clarify the general features of experience more accurately than current conceptions do. One can also further investigate the kinds of evidence he marshals (folk uses of words, existential uses of words, primordial experiences) to see whether other examples point in different directions. Although Heidegger's insights are often initially persuasive, he rarely attends to the full range of examples and evidence that bear on them.

Heidegger distinguishes two modes in which humans can exist. They can be translated as "authentic" and "inauthentic"; Heidegger says he intends no ethical overtones. He means simply the difference between being oneself and not being oneself.[43] The adequacy of one's understanding of Being depends partly on one's mode of existing; one way to achieve a clearer understanding of one's own being is to *be oneself*. One major tendency in Heidegger's thinking about Others (*qua* Crowd) is to conceive them as typically opposed to authenticity. This direction in Heidegger's thought is only a *tendency*; he does allow that being-with still exists when one exists authentically; he thinks that relationships among authentic people are possible, and he thinks some specific relations to Others facilitate authenticity. On the other hand, Heidegger thinks the "Crowd" often lulls one to inauthentic existence and, worse, it takes over and occupies the very role of the 'self'; one is often dominated by an impersonal "public" (*Das Man*).

Some implications

What are the implications of these introductory remarks for Heidegger's theory of Others? First, one should expect Heidegger to raise questions about the traditional formulation of the question of Others and the assumptions that guide it. More specifically, he questions two assumptions: that one is present to oneself while Others are never presented as such and that there is a difference between 'oneself' and Others even in the inauthentic mode of existing.[44]

Second, although Heidegger's inquiry may have implications for understanding the being of Others, that is *not* the primary focus of his investigation. He is clarifying the existentials of human beings; one of these is being-with Others. This means that all one's concrete relations to Others are conditioned by this a priori, essential structure of one's existence.[45] Heidegger does not directly address the existence of Others or their essential nature; he examines one's basic relatedness or comportment toward Others.

Third, one would expect Heidegger's conception of Others to be importantly related to Worldhood.[46] Others partly establish these instrumental contexts and are typically situated within them. In addition, one uses instruments to fashion something that is destined for Others; this is one of one's primordial relations to Others, according to Heidegger.

Fourth, in line with his effort to transcend the subject-object distinction, one should expect Heidegger to clarify an essential connectedness between self and Other which would be prior to and condition any experience of self apart from Others or of the Other as distinct from self. One should expect him to demonstrate the priority of this relationship by showing that experiences in which a concrete relationship to another is lacking are only special instances, perhaps limiting cases, of this primary relatedness.

Heidegger's theory of Others

I can now proceed to elucidate Heidegger's views about the fundamental relation of self and Other. These can be reduced to five basic propositions. I shall begin by simply presenting them; then I shall clarify each one more fully and explore its philosophical implications.

The basic position

Heidegger first asserts, against Husserl and the Cartesian tradition, that no self is present in everyday, pre-theoretical experience.[47]

This assertion clears the way for his second claim: Others are not experienced as distinct from (other than) oneself in any significant sense, but rather are typically experienced as similar to, even interchangeable with, oneself.[48] More generally, one's basic experience of other persons is *not* that they are present, self-subsistent beings whose minds are hidden, but rather that they are *engaged*, accessible beings who share the same instruments and gathering places and function much like oneself.

Third, Others condition one's concerns and aims even if no particular other person is physically present. Human beings exist always-related to Others; Others are a part of the texture of the "world," in Heidegger's special sense.[49]

Fourth, *who* one is, the *mode* in which one exists, typically is the impersonal mode of selfness (*Das Man*); the Crowd functions as the very soul of one's life, articulating its possibilities and limits.[50] Heidegger amplifies this claim into his famous epigram: "Everyone is the other, and no one is himself."[51] Here he quite literally means *not* just that the self is *other* (i.e., alienated from itself), *but* that Others *constitute* the self. Most of us live an impersonal, unindividuated existence governed by the Crowd.

Finally, he holds that the quality of one's self-awareness and self-knowledge depends on the mode of 'selfness' one lives; one does *not* always know oneself immediately, and one *may not* know oneself at all.[52]

The defense, details, and significance of these claims still need exposition. Before offering this more detailed explication, I wish to suggest one way in which these claims can be integrated.

Although this picture is nowhere explicitly affirmed by Heidegger, one need only ask how these propositions fit together in order to see it clearly. Heidegger describes two existentials in the sections concerning Others: being-with and the impersonal mode of selfness. These two structures *can* (but *not* always must) be related in the following fashion: *because* one exists *with* Others, one also exists in an impersonal mode; they are so completely *with* one that they are *within* one.[53] This explains why there is no self experienced in everyday life and why Others are experienced as like-oneself, as undifferentiated from oneself. One is like them to such an extent that each could *be* oneself.

Moreover, the fact that one always exists with Others threatens one with the ever present possibility of invasion by them even if one has, for a time, achieved an authentic individuatedness; hence, *because* of Others, one has a perpetual tendency to *lose* oneself, to fall away from being oneself.[54] Confirmation that this is Heidegger's assessment of the predominant (but not exclusive) role of Others in everyday life can be found in his contention that Others obfuscate one's ability to understand: they turn discourse into idle talk, and they disorient one's possibilities with layers of ambiguity.[55] Others are often *opposed* to the achievement of authenticity, and thus they *prevent* one from achieving adequate comprehension of one's own being and hence of *Being itself*. Although there are other tendencies in Heidegger's thinking about Others, this picture offers an easy synthesis of his position, and he seems, on occasion, to be mesmerized by it.

The specific propositions

The first proposition

Heidegger begins by claiming that there is no experience of the self in everyday life. He supports this by challenging the various linguistic and experiential motivations that lead one to postulate the self. His basic experiential defense is that everyday life is lived in the midst of demands to be met, tasks to be performed, functions to be fulfilled; these occur without any concomitant sense of self giving the orders or witnessing the events. Against Husserl, who believes that the self is the omnipresent source of all meaning, Heidegger notes that the self is only experienced in highly reflective states of mind, such as the one Husserl adopts in making his reductions.[56]

In addition, Heidegger demonstrates that the philosophical conception of self that is modeled on the notion of substance — a self-subsistent substrate remaining identical through various changes of state — is inadequate.[57] At best, this model falsifies human existence (portraying it as like things); at worst, it inaccurately depicts the way worldly entities exist. The only way to adequately conceptualize human selfness is to understand the basic structures of human existence, which is Heidegger's project in *Being and Time*. These structures reveal a more dispersed, engaged, and active being than the traditional conception allows. Thus, according to Heidegger, the tradition which asserts the continuous existence of a thing-like self is mistaken, for both conceptual and experiential reasons.

One reason why the self is thought to be like a substance is that one's spatial location can always be designated as 'here.' Heidegger offers an unusual reply to this position. Instead of claiming that spatial locations characterize only a person's body, not his mind or self, he reanalyzes spatiality itself and shows that pre-theoretical, everyday spatiality has a different structure than the space of geometric co-ordinates. Space is a system of interdependent instrumental axes. The 'here' that defines the 'place' of the self can only be identified in terms of a series of 'theres' — locations of instruments needed for some task.[58] Instead of offering a unique location for the self, the 'here' indicates a nexus of changing purposes. Not only is the primordial 'here' not identical across time, it cannot support the conception of an isolated monad self since the 'here' cannot even be identified except in a more encompassing instrumental context. Although Heidegger's analysis of existential spatiality is more elaborate, this description is sufficient to indicate his method of rethinking the considerations that have traditionally been used to support the substance-conception of the self.

The second proposition

Since much of Heidegger's critique is directed against the view that presence defines the primary mode in which entities exist, he begins his discussion of Others by criticizing the application of this view to them. When one thinks about Others in a theoretical fashion, one imagines oneself as an unseen spectator, facing entities which appear like images on a cinema screen; one follows their movements and watches their expressions, but their selves — their inner mental lives — are hidden from one, the subject of hypothesis. This picture suggests that Others' existence is shadowy because they are not wholly present, and it demonstrates that theorizing about Others arises in a special mode of interpersonal experience — detached observation. In this mode all of one's practical concerns are bracketed so that one can better attend to what *presents* itself.

Heidegger's elucidation of the pre-theoretical experience of Others is offered as a direct contrast to this underlying picture. He makes two central points. First, Others are always initially found engaged with the world, amidst their own purposes and tasks.[59] Even if they are just standing around, this itself is experienced as a kind of purposiveness they have at the time.[60] In short, one does not primarily see the Other's body which hides his mind; one apprehends 'what he is about,' 'what he is up to.' For Heidegger, this is a direct and lucid experience of the Other's existence since his existence *is* his being-in-the-world. Second, Others are not experienced as distinct from oneself but as like-oneself, engaged in tasks like oneself, enmeshed in concerns very like one's own, sharing the same world with one. Heidegger's second proposition is thus that Others are not typically distinguished from oneself; one experiences them as replicas of oneself, not as alien creatures.

Some important implications follow from this: (1) one cannot define Others as those who are *not-oneself*, as Sartre does, because that definition violates one's everyday experience of Others. Even though such abstract formulas sound innocuous, they easily disorient one's philosophical comprehension; (2) one no longer needs to locate the essence of Others in their 'inner being.' Others' tasks are not 'expressed' by bodily movements; one cannot even see 'bodily movement' except through special theoretical concentration. One can only see tasks being performed: shoppers, sellers, craftsmen, travelers, clerks. Apprehending Others' purposes requires no special sight or inference; they are perceived primordially. To see mere 'behavior' requires a distortion of everyday experience. On Heidegger's view, the existence of Others suddenly becomes palpable and unmysterious; one no longer feels trapped on this side of a yawning chasm that cannot be bridged.

The third proposition

Heidegger's third proposition elucidates the existential being-with. Even if Others are not physically present to one, references to them are interwoven into one's world.[61] The materials one works on are made by Others; the tasks one performs are taught by Others; the product one makes is destined for Others; the functional uses of things come to them collectively – *everyone* understands what things are for; one's own understanding is only a specification of this common sense. One's existence is always articulated in a world, and one can be in a world (in Heidegger's sense) only with-Others.[62] This relatedness to persons is a priori; it precedes all empirical relationships to Others and makes them possible;[63] concrete relations specify this basic relatedness. Anyone who lacked this basic relatedness to Others would not be human, would lack the mode of existence characteristic of human beings.[64]

The basic character of being-with is solicitude: being oriented toward and caring for Others.[65] Although solicitude has deficient forms, e.g., indifference, these presuppose, rather than disprove, the fact of being-with, for only in so far as one is with Others already (in so far as their concerns are manifest to one) can one be indifferent to them.[66] Even the experience of being alone presupposes the more basic relatedness of being-with because loneliness is an experienced lack of something that can be and has been present, and being-with constitutes this background relatedness.[67] These are the kinds of arguments with which Heidegger establishes the necessity of being-with. His strategy is to subsume apparent counter-examples as special cases of the basic structure or to show that they presuppose it.

Some philosophers have tried to demonstrate the existence of Others through a process of sympathetic understanding; allegedly if one can "feel with" another person, one can be assured that he is a genuine subject. Heidegger objects that sympathetic understanding is only another specification of being-with. One's ability to open oneself to or close oneself off from Others presupposes this ontological structure: one is already with Others if one is able to attend to their concerns or if one is able to become hardened to them.[68] Heidegger wants to say that all efforts to *demonstrate* the subjectivity of Others achieve much less than is already there in pre-theoretical experience and presuppose the basic relatedness he calls being-with.

Solicitude has two generic forms: deficient and non-deficient. Some deficient forms were discussed above. Among the non-deficient forms, there are two general types, positive and negative: authentic and inauthentic.[69] *In inauthentic solicitude*, one displaces a person from his own concerns by taking over his life, directing it for him, taking over his tasks or executing them for him; in this fashion one facilitates the loss of being-oneself for both the Other and oneself.[70] *In authentic solicitude*, one frees a person for his own concerns; one opens up his possibilities for him; he learns that he has unique possibilities that differ from those of the Crowd; in this mode one "leaps ahead" of the Other and opens up his world.[71]

No special effort is needed to embody authentic solicitude. In so far as one exists authentically, as one's own self distinct from the Crowd, one facilitates this possibility for all Others in the vicinity; this is a form of authentic solicitude. The Crowd functions only if its members do not realize the existence of possibilities other than those it dictates. The authentic person undermines this mystique and at least extends the opportunity to Others to become themselves. Hence becoming authentic triggers further authenticity,[72] and those who live inauthentically reinforce one another in their acceptance of the Crowd. Thus one's mode of existence, being-oneself or not-being-oneself, tends to be symmetrical with that of the neighboring Others. This is one important contrast between Heidegger's theory and Sartre's.[73]

The fourth proposition

Heidegger's fourth proposition is initially the most difficult to understand, but it is based on a very common set of observations. Clarifying these first will make his abstract assertion easier to comprehend. The idea of the Crowd plays a major role in nineteenth-century social theory, from Kierkegaard to Nietzsche. Heidegger describes this phenomenon with lucidity, and he explains how the Crowd (*Das Man*) dominates one most of the time. This domination is so complete because it is concealed;[74] one does not realize that one's thoughts, feelings, beliefs, and ideals are Crowd-clichés shared by everyone. One's thoughts appear to be one's own, but in fact they follow dominant trends in the media, one's class, or one's peer-group.[75]

More importantly, one's actions are in complete conformity with everything the Crowd expects even when one seems to be choosing for oneself.[76] Often one lacks the sense that one's actions originate with oneself; one does what is required by circumstances. Since no one seems to *do* the act, no one accepts responsibility for it.[77] If one looks for particular people who motivated one to act in a particular way, no one emerges. The Crowd is *diffused*; it is not an individual, but emerges through many individuals.[78] It is not even an ethos uniting its members; it is too hidden, and most of its members would explicitly deny allegiance to it even though they are dominated by it. The Crowd levels out extremes, forces behavior to conform to a mean, and silences all serious discourse.[79]

Much of this description is unoriginal except for the claim that no appropriate ontological analysis of the Crowd exists. Every category through which one tries to understand it (e.g., genus-species, concept-exemplar, whole-part, substance-property) is inadequate because such categories apply only to self-subsistent, present entities. But the Crowd functions through absence rather than presence and exists in a diffused state.[80] Heidegger himself makes no effort to offer an ontological analysis of the Crowd.

He does offer an explanation for its domination. According to his third proposition, Others are always with one. In so far as one is with Others, one's inveterate tendency is to be concerned about how one compares with them. As soon as this happens one becomes determined by their norms, rules, aims, and actions; one begins to live as they do, although this happens covertly.[81] Examples of this phenomenon exist in any academic field. As soon as one becomes concerned with one's status in the profession *vis-à-vis* one's colleagues, one begins to accept their criteria of evaluation, their agenda for inquiry, their intellectual tasks and aims. This tacit acceptance circumscribes one's own commitments, and these constitute the core of one's intellectual life. The usual illustration is the business corporation, but the phenomenon is no less present in other spheres of life.

The theoretical innovation implicit in these observations is that 'selfness' has *modalities*. If one lives, thinks, judges, feels, and apprehends one's possibilities as the Crowd does, then one lives an impersonal mode of selfness; one lacks individuation.[82] If all one's actions are, in effect, actions of the Crowd, then one's self *is* the Crowd-self or an impersonal self. To be oneself is only *one modality* of existence.[83] The self of everyday life is predominantly an impersonal self (*Das Man*).[84]

Moreover, authentic selfness is, according to Heidegger, *not* a wholly distinct type, but a *variant* or form of the impersonal mode of selfness.[85] Thus the impersonal self is the *existential*; it conditions all other modes of selfness.[86] This suggests that sociality is inescapable; even authentic individuals define themselves in terms of what is common or typical; though they achieve a distinctive kind of existence, they never transcend their immersion in social life and their being-with Others. In addition, one never wholly escapes the impersonal mode; the Crowd always surrounds one — ready to lull one to sleep — even when one achieves some measure of authenticity.

Heidegger's fourth proposition thus asserts that *who one is*, is wholly dependent on one's relatedness to Others; there is no selfness apart from this relatedness, and typically the self one lives is impersonal — absorbed in this relatedness.[87]

The fifth proposition

Heidegger's fifth proposition asserts that the quality of one's self-knowledge, including one's tacit comprehension of one's existence, depends on this social relatedness as well.[88] One misunderstands oneself most when one exists impersonally, for one's existence is then most hidden from one. In this state one interprets human nature on the model of external objects, and one then invents a series of structures (e.g., the 'self') in order to vindicate these interpretations.[89] One falsely believes these postulated structures are ever-present when in fact the central question of one's existence is concealed by one's absorption in the impersonal mode of selfness.[90] Since this mode is the existential, Heidegger's position implies that there is an *essential tendency* to fail to comprehend one's existence adequately, to know oneself truly. One's own being, and correlatively human being and Being itself, elude understanding because one exists inauthentically.

Heidegger makes the same point in a different way: only by seeing through the subtle fog inherent in the impersonal mode of existence can authentic selfness ever arise.[91] One understands oneself differently as soon as one achieves a different mode of existence. What one *can do* remains invisible in the everyday existence dominated by the Crowd; when one's essential possibilities become visible, the transition to authentic existence is taking place. Hence because of the close connection between one's mode of existence and one's self understanding, one's self-understanding is as deeply conditioned by one's relatedness to Others as one's existence.

Synopsis

To summarize: Heidegger seeks to clarify the nature and meaning of Being, that which conditions all existing entities, and to which humans have an essential relation in so far as their own being is an issue for them throughout their lives. He attacks one basic model that has governed the Western tradition's thinking about Being – the model of presence.[92] Humans are not present to themselves; their existence is essentially situated in the world amidst Others. One's world is organized instrumentally, and Others establish these instrumental relations. Heidegger seeks to illuminate Being by clarifying human being (*Dasein*); his focus in this inquiry is *not* on the being of Others; he explores them only because the conditioning structures of one's existence, the existentials, implicate Others. This occurs in two ways.

First, one necessarily exists *with Others* – oriented toward and concerned for them – even if they are absent, and they are not differentiated from oneself at the most basic level of experience. Heidegger seeks to transcend the subject-object distinction in part by asserting this essential relatedness to Others. He challenges the traditional priority of the self and its knowledge of itself.

Second, he holds that there are *modes* of selfness, and the one we typically live is the impersonal mode of selfness, in which we are not ourselves but are dominated by a hidden, elusive Crowd. This mode of selfness is an existential; one can thus never ultimately transcend it; authentic selfness is only a modification or variant of the impersonal mode. Moreover, the quality of one's self-understanding (and one's consequent understanding of Being itself) is conditioned by one's mode of selfness; one's failure to grasp oneself adequately arises from an immersion in the Crowd.

Sartre's reading of Heidegger and its problems

Sartre's interpretation of Heidegger is the most accurate of his readings of his predecessors. Although I have some disagreements, in general I think Sartre reads Heidegger carefully and raises important questions about his views. My discussions of Sartre's interpretation and critique will be closely interlocked since many of his objections follow from his interpretation of Heidegger's general project. In this section, I shall describe the central disagreements between Sartre and Heidegger in order to more effectively clarify Sartre's critique.

Sartre on Heidegger's basic approach

In his exposition of Heidegger's general approach, Sartre makes three basic points. *First*, he notes that Heidegger refuses to adopt the viewpoint of an external observer who studies an independent system of relationships. Instead, Heidegger seeks to make explicit one's implicit pre-theoretical comprehension of one's own existence.[93] This project is comparable to Sartre's own efforts to elucidate the data of pure reflection, to depict the structures of human existence that operate in lived experience. Both projects depend on the fact that human beings are reflexively related to themselves, but Sartre and Heidegger characterize this reflexivity differently. Sartre describes it in terms of the presence of consciousness to itself, which can be adequately recovered if reflection undergoes a purification. Heidegger wishes to avoid the Cartesian overtones of this description, but he acknowledges this reflexivity when he asserts that one's existence is always at issue or in question, at least implicitly. Both thinkers seek to make explicit what anyone can apprehend on his own if he overcomes theoretical biases and recaptures experience as it is actually lived.

There are, however, important differences. For example, Sartre's efforts lack the meta-level Kantian element of Heidegger's enterprise — the stress on elucidating the *conditions* of inquiry in addition to its results. Both theorists seek to illuminate essential structures of any person, but Heidegger also seeks to elucidate the conditions of possibility for any inquiry. Sartre takes this to be the *primary* aim of Heidegger's work; it constitutes the central target of his attack because he thinks that investigating such conditions of possibility encumbers, rather than facilitates, the clarification of the relatedness of Others to oneself.

Second, Sartre stresses that Heidegger establishes a relationship of being between persons, rather than one of knowing. Sartre concentrates on being-with; he treats Heidegger's second existential, the impersonal mode of selfness, as a mere amplification of being-with. He notes that being-with is an ontological relationship and is a priori.[94] Sartre's basic disagreement with Heidegger lies in how this essential relatedness to Others (being-with) is to be understood.

Sartre portrays Heidegger's existentials as similar to Kantian categories — constituting and shaping the field they govern.[95] In contrast, Sartre thinks that Others can only be apprehended a posteriori; Others essentially transform one *after* one experiences them in a certain way. They do not function like conditioning features of any possible way of life, structuring any possible experience. Sartre thinks the Other reached by Heidegger's being-with can only be an abstraction which lacks any relationship to concrete other people encountered in everyday life.[96]

I have granted the Kantian dimension of Heidegger's work; some passages in *Being and Time* have an unmistakably Kantian tone. Nevertheless, I disagree with Sartre's effort to read Heidegger's existentials in exact analogy with Kant's concepts. Heidegger's existentials are necessary conditions of being human, exist in every form of life, and condition any empirical orientation. Sartre can agree with the first two elements of this analysis. Our disagreement arises over the interpretation of the third element. Sartre does not grasp the relationship between Heidegger's meta-level inquiry and his object-level inquiry with sufficient clarity.

For Heidegger, the forms of everyday life are not *shaped* or *organized* by the existentials but *exhibit* them because those forms are simply variations on the existentials. Thus, any relation to Others — whether it be isolation, indifference, empathy, or hatred — is a variant of being-with, and any mode of selfness — whether it be tradition-directedness, other-directedness, inner-directedness, or autonomy — is a variant of the impersonal mode of selfness. This is the sense in which existentials 'condition' actual concrete life; they are its most widely applicable features. Concrete modes of existence are only modifications of them. They are the deepest, most pervasive, most common structures of being human.

They are a priori because *any* inquiry presupposes the existentials; inquiry is a form of life and hence is subsumed within their range of application. Heidegger's inquiry has a meta-level; he seeks to ground his investigation while he pursues it, and many of his uses of Kantian terms simply call attention to that fact. Sartre believes that Heidegger's existentials define and structure the field over which they apply.[97] On my reading, however, the existentials simply *apply* in all ways of life or are presupposed by them. Heidegger's existentials do not *make* us be what we are; they simply describe the most general features of our lives. The important question is whether Heidegger's existentials are *illuminating*: whether he has subsumed their possible empirical modifications emptily and abstractly or informatively.

Another way in which Sartre's interpretation is insensitive emerges in his failure to acknowledge the degree to which Heidegger's inquiry is ontology (the object-level) as well as fundamental ontology (the meta-level). The ontological aspect of Heidegger's essay consists in his clarification of the nature of being human. Heidegger's analysis of persons can also transform one's understanding of other regions of being (e.g., tools, Others, art). He does not only discuss human beings even though they are his primary concern; along the way he takes initial steps toward more adequately understanding other kinds of entities. His primary insights about other people are that they exist engaged in the world like oneself, use the same world that one uses, and are not typically differentiated from oneself. They are with one and in the world as much as one is with them and in the world. I have stressed that Heidegger's investigation cannot be read as an exhaustive treatment of Others' existence, but it does represent some first steps in that direction.

Third. To some extent, Sartre realizes that the central issue is whether Heidegger's claims are illuminating, and Sartre thinks they most definitely are not. They offer mere definitions — arbitrarily interrelated terms — that fail to illuminate concrete experience.[98] Although I acknowledge that Heidegger's supporting arguments are sparse and understand the impression that he offers only arbitrary definitions, I cannot agree that he offers no support for his views.

Heidegger supports his contentions in three different ways. First, he shows how his theories resolve or obviate problems that more traditional positions cannot resolve. Second, he tries to demonstrate, rather than merely assert, that potential counter-examples to his claims can be subsumed as variants of his existentials. Heidegger's efforts to defend his existentials in this way are simply missed by Sartre. Finally, Heidegger's assertions are ultimately descriptive; he offers a phenomenological explication of the basic structures of human being; one can only evaluate his claims by carefully examining various ways of life to determine how pervasive Heidegger's existentials actually are. One must also try to imagine ways of life that might lack them. Sartre's own theory cannot be defended in any other way. *Arguments* cannot be the *only* defense of Heidegger's propositions; one must also struggle to recover a pre-theoretical vision of what existing is actually like and what factors are invariant and fundamental.

Sartre on Heidegger's specific claims

I have one other basic disagreement with Sartre's reading of Heidegger, and to make this point, I must review Sartre's presentation of Heidegger's more specific contentions. In addition, I shall indicate how Sartre's own position differs from Heidegger's; this may facilitate a better understanding of Heidegger as well as Sartre. Sartre's exposition concentrates on Heidegger's second, third, and fourth propositions.

Sartre notes that Heidegger's basic self-Other relation is being-with rather than being-for.[99] In effect, Heidegger does not take face-to-face encounter to be the appropriate paradigm for investigating relations between persons; instead of a *me* confronting a *you* in potential opposition, Heidegger sees a *we*.[100] People exist essentially related to one another as interdependent co-users of the same instruments; they experience a shared world.[101] Others are grasped as engaged in their pursuits just as one grasps oneself in the process of achieving one's own ends.

Sartre portrays being-with as a relation that connects distinct entities. In addition, Sartre notes that inauthentic selfness is a condition in which people are interchangeable; one member of the Crowd is like another.[102] This existence-in-common is perhaps best represented by a group engaged in a cooperative enterprise.[103] Sartre believes that being-with entails existing inauthentically; one lives the impersonal mode of selfness *because* one exists perpetually with Others. Thus, Sartre reads the two existentials as two aspects of one relation to Others which has two basic modes: authentic and inauthentic.[104]

Finally, Sartre notes that the modalities in which self and Other exist are symmetrical on Heidegger's view; one exists inauthentically when those around one do, but one is moved toward authenticity when one encounters Others who live authentically.[105]

Sartre's differences from Heidegger

Sartre's own theories contrast sharply with Heidegger's. Sartre holds that the basic relation between persons is being-for rather than being-with; for him persons exist in potential opposition rather than in joint solidarity. Sartre thinks one cannot discover an ontological bond between persons unless one examines face-to-face relationships.

Sartre also does not believe Others are adequately conceptualized when they are taken to be undifferentiated, interchangeable terms. This view ignores the *defining* feature of Others, i.e., *not-being-oneself*. The essential relation between persons must be a form of negation, not a primordial unity or lack of differentiation.

Finally, Sartre thinks that the relation between self and Other must be asymmetrical: if self exists in one modality (subject), then the Other must exist in the opposite modality (object); for Sartre, this asymmetry entails perpetual instability in human relations.

At this point, I am simply explicating these differences without comment; I do not even admit that these theories are necessarily opposed to one another. I wish only to provide a clearer grasp of Heidegger's position by indicating Sartre's alternatives to it and to explain the underlying direction of Sartre's critique by making his position explicit.

Problems with Sartre's reading

My disagreements with Sartre's interpretation of Heidegger's specific claims are that it portrays him as engaged in a task which he explicitly avoids and that it couches the basic result of his theory in a framework that he would not accept. Heidegger is *not* primarily interested in the being of other people; he is trying to articulate the essential structures of being human which also constitute the preconditions for any inquiry. Being-with is an existential for any person; it applies to other people as well as to oneself, but it is not meant to establish the existence of other persons.

Whether other people actually exist is not a question that Heidegger is trying to address. To admit this may be to admit Sartre's basic criticism, viz., that Heidegger does not effectively resolve the traditional problem.[106] However, Heidegger is trying to bypass the traditional problem, to *break through* it, to shatter the framework that generates it. Sartre portrays Heidegger as claiming that there is a *relation* that binds *separate* persons together: being-with.[107] But Heidegger is trying to undermine the ontology that treats persons as separate entities which must be provided with ontological *bonds*. He also tries to undermine the subject-object distinction by denying that people are enclosed subjectivities. The self does not exist in isolation from Others; in the typical state Others constitute one's self.

In every act one performs or word one speaks, Others penetrate one; they are constantly with one even though they may not be present in the vicinity. Others are with one whether one experiences oneself as distinct or not. There is no inside from which one must escape; there is no separate self which must be joined to other equally separate selves. The ontology Sartre presupposes in presenting Heidegger's theory prevents him from capturing its critical, revolutionary force. Heidegger's stance on the existence of Others is difficult to assess; instead of trying to answer the question, he tries to show that it is based on inaccurate assumptions. The issue is whether his allegations are correct.

Sartre does realize some of the implications of Heidegger's theory despite the infelicities of his presentation. He underlines that the basic implication of Heidegger's position is that the traditional problem is a false problem because it assumes conditions that do not exist in the typical state.[108] One might question the being of Others if one exists authentically, but one's question will not be epistemological; rather one will be questioning their way of life as impersonal, inauthentic selves. One cannot help questioning Others in this way if one exists authentically.

If there is no prior sense of self in terms of which the existence of Others can be doubted, then the traditional approach has been superseded. Heidegger even stands it on its head, for *the* question is how one can become one's own self, not whether there are Others. One is necessarily *with* Others; to be oneself is a contingent achievement.

Although Sartre acknowledges these implications, his presentation of Heidegger's specific claims is offered in metaphors that presuppose the view Heidegger is trying to deny. Whether Heidegger's theory *succeeds* in avoiding the dilemmas he sought to avoid, whether he provides *sufficient reasons* to make his position convincing remain, as yet, open issues.

An evaluation of Sartre's critique of Heidegger

Sartre's critique of Heidegger is penetrating; not only does he present important objections to Heidegger's specific propositions, he also raises deep questions about his entire enterprise. However, such sweeping criticisms need careful examination because they may beg the question and may attempt to evaluate a theory with criteria it seeks to undermine. My tasks in this discussion will be to determine whether Heidegger's theoretical innovations solve philosophical problems rather than merely relocate them, to advance the larger inquiry of this essay toward foundational questions, and to assess the real adequacy of Heidegger's ideas. Some of Sartre's objections are stronger than others; I shall pursue Heidegger's replies in order to ensure that the issues between them are not oversimplified or ignored.

A summary of Sartre's objections

Sartre presents five main objections. *First*, Sartre asks for the justification of the claim that being-with is the most basic relation between people.[109] He also wonders why being-with is a necessary condition of being human — what justifies claiming this fundamental status for this admittedly interesting empirical state?[110] Sartre asks these questions rhetorically; he implies that Heidegger has no response.

Second, Sartre wonders how being-with establishes the existence of Others. If one makes the Other's being a function of one's own being, or of its a priori structures, has one not simply fallen back into solipsism? And if the claim is that these descriptions elucidate only the "subjective appearance" of the Other, of what philosophical interest is it?[111]

Third, if the essential relation to Others is being-with, to what extent does the 'Other' whom one is with remain *differentiated* from oneself; if no differentiation exists, on what basis does Heidegger claim to reach *other* persons at all? Yet if Heidegger can differentiate Others from oneself, what prevents this difference from becoming an *opposition* which would destroy the solidarity that "being-with" connotes?[112]

Fourth, although Others may be apprehended as in the world — engaged in practical pursuits — and thus as existing in the same way as ourselves, what guarantees the identity of the worlds in which we are enmeshed?[113] Being-with should at least integrate self and Other into the same world; yet can one grasp the Other's world as the same as one's own? If this identity cannot be guaranteed, has Heidegger advanced beyond the monad view of the self?

Fifth, even if there is a fundamental comportment toward Others inherent in all forms of existing, does this account for the concrete relations of friendship or antagonism one has with specific people? Is the Other *with whom one is* related to the concrete Others one encounters, or is this Other merely an abstract structure that lacks connection to everyday interpersonal life?[114]

The basic target of Sartre's critique is Heidegger's attempt to establish an a priori, essential relation between self and Other. Sartre thinks this kind of relation can only reach an abstract Other – an entity that is inadequately differentiated from one's own existence. This relation will thus be uninformative about actual experience and ineffective in answering the important questions. Sartre himself seeks an essential relation between self and Other, but he believes this relationship cannot be an a priori structure. It must be a posteriori; one can only *encounter* Others; one cannot *constitute* them.[115] Others' existence can only be a *fact*, never a *necessity*.[116] This relation to Others cannot be a condition for one's experience; it can only be a result of it.

What does this difference amount to? Sartre's key assumption is that other people are *distinct* from oneself; this means that their existence cannot be a function of one's own. Sartre thinks that the Other posited by Heidegger's theory can only be an amorphous, satellite-like structure, an appendage of one's own life. The relation of this structure to concrete living Others must be tenuous; hence Sartre concludes that Heidegger's theory only seems to supersede the monad view of the self; in reality *Dasein* is as isolated as a Cartesian ego.

Discussion of Sartre's objections

On the central issue that divides them, I think both Heidegger and Sartre see something important. With Heidegger, I think that some structures do condition our encounters with Others; not all essential relations between people emerge out of the immediate face-to-face situation. With Sartre, I believe that these general conditioning structures do result from interactions with Others; they are often habituated forms of experiencing and interacting with Others which have developed from past encounters. Heidegger often talks as if his existentials do not ultimately derive from encounter with concrete Others at all; he seems to think that they are innate, necessary features of human existence (like Chomsky's universal grammar). This way of conceiving the existentials is inadequate although the insights they suggest reveal important features of interpersonal life. Heidegger and Sartre ultimately address different aspects of social life. Sartre's structures emerge in the particular encounter of the moment; Heidegger's structures exist prior to and condition these encounters even if they are sometimes transformed and developed by them. A full analysis of interpersonal life must elucidate both kinds of structures.

In this section I will explore Sartre's view that Heidegger has misconstrued the nature of the existentials. In my own critique, I shall more thoroughly examine the insightfulness of Heidegger's existentials and the adequacy of his defense for them.

Sartre's first objection

Sartre's first objection is the least accurate; he claims that Heidegger fails to justify his assertion that being-with is an existential of human being. The kinds of justifications Heidegger gives can be better understood if the meaning of being-with and Sartre's objections to this notion are further examined. Being-with involves a basic reference to or orientedness toward other people; it is specified by concrete attitudes to Others. Being-with ensures that Others are always grasped as engaged in the world and as similar to oneself in this respect. Considering some possible objections will provide further clarification.

Let us begin with Sartre's own disagreement; he says that the basic relation to Others is really being-for: one always apprehends a social dimension of oneself through the look of Others. Heidegger's response is that this notion of being-for is only one of many forms of being-with.[117] It indicates a particular way of being oriented toward Others, of referring one's enterprises to them, of being involved with them. Being-with is this general orientedness, this opening out toward Others which permits one to apprehend their subjectivity in Sartre's sense.

Sartre might respond that Others' projects can conflict with one's own; he would claim that the *solidarity* implied by being-with no longer exists in this case. Heidegger might reply that conflict is *one way* in which Others are apprehended as engaged and one way of living one's fundamental comportment toward them. Even if one tries to withdraw from the conflict into solitude, this is only another orientation toward Others, a different way of being-with them. Heidegger is *not* claiming that one will always feel comradeship with Others. Camaraderie is one concrete specification of Being-with. Any particular relation will only be an instance or form of this basic reference-toward-Others.[118]

The standard philosophical criticism at this point is that postulating these general structures is at best redundant and superfluous and at worst meaningless and theoretically confusing. The less extreme form of this objection holds that nothing informative is added by asserting that people typically exist-with Others. In the midst of a particular relationship, to learn that one is instantiating a more general relatedness simply adds nothing and clarifies nothing. The more extreme form of this objection holds that to extend the claim that one is essentially related to Others to cases in which one typically does not experience any such relation empties the claim of what little content it may have and thus makes it meaningless. Because the claim denies nothing, it asserts nothing. The common feature of both objections is the assertion that being-with is a kind of contentless blank, an empty metaphor, which contributes nothing to one's understanding of concrete relationships.

Heidegger would remain unmoved by these remarks because he thinks his conception of being-with does have content and is informative.

For example, it indicates an active relation rather than a passive one. This is the force of his statement that the basic form of being-with is *solicitude.*[119] To be with Others is to be oriented toward or concerned for them, not simply to be open or receptive to their initiatives. In addition, one's engagements *refer to* Others in manifold ways. For example, while one writes in one's study alone, the text one composes is destined for an audience; the pen one uses was manufactured by Others; usually one is engaged in a discourse whose rules are prescribed with varying degrees of explicitness by Others. Even if one struggles to write with one's own voice, to break all conventions, one's project is to overthrow traditional forms that exist because of Others and are currently sustained by them. Thus, even when no Others are in the vicinity, one's actions are oriented to them in various ways.

Even if one is chopping wood for one's own fire while living as a hermit in the backwoods, one's project is part of a general struggle to live on one's own, to remain independent of Others; this self-conscious separation from Others governs one's everyday life. The hermit is as much with-Others in Heidegger's sense as the political organizer.[120] To turn away from Others is only a different way of embodying one's basic relatedness to them.

Hence "being-with" has content, and it has implications for our apprehension of Others. They are given as engaged in endeavors; in this way they are not differentiated from us. Even if one perceives someone as an enemy or a member of an out-group, this attitude acknowledges that Others exist in-the-world as one does and in the same world as one does. If one has visitors who simply sit around and occupy one's time with trivia, one interprets this as an engagement rather than a lack of all engagements. One may apprehend them as resting between tasks, as tarrying, as delaying the onset of their own tasks, or simply as having the task of wasting one's own time.

To be with Others thus implies a very general form in which Others are apprehended. This fact supports the major reorientation Heidegger is trying to effect — from a conception of human being governed by presence to one governed by instrumentality, solicitude, and care. A person is never simply there, enigmatic like a sphinx, with an interior that must be deciphered. If Others appear that way, this is regarded as a practical engagement they have. Being-with is the form one's general interest and enmeshment in the world takes in the interpersonal field. It implies that one is never metaphysically isolated from Others, never without some orientation to them.

These clarificatory remarks indicate the kinds of justifications Heidegger gives for his position. They are of three types: subsumption of counter-examples, descriptive elucidation, and challenges to the tradition. First, Heidegger explicitly addresses a wide variety of apparent counter-examples in order to show that they can all be subsumed by being-with. The hermit case illustrates this strategy. Being-with is the most general, deepest form of interpersonal orientation.

Second, Heidegger offers descriptive elucidation of social experience in everyday life. These descriptions reveal typically unseen but universally accessible features of our experience. They suggest the supporting data for and implications of Heidegger's general claims. The observation that we always grasp Others as engaged in projects exemplifies this defense. Such an apprehension would be expected if we indeed always do exist-with Others.

Finally, Heidegger tries to revise the concepts, assumptions, and questions central to the philosophical tradition. In this way he recasts one's theoretical approach to Others and makes one more receptive to his general claims. If one grants that one does not always exist authentically, then one will have less metaphysical resistance to his claim that being-with is a necessary condition of being human because one will have less confidence in the omnipresence of the self.

Thus Heidegger offers many distinctive kinds of justification for his propositions. Sartre simply misconstrues the logical structure of Heidegger's discussion. In my own criticisms of Heidegger, I shall explore the adequacy of each of these kinds of justification and the specific propositions supported by them.

Sartre's second objection

Sartre's second criticism of Heidegger is his most telling point; in order to provide a forceful reply, I shall have to marshal all of Heidegger's resources. Sartre charges that because being-with is an a priori existential, it cannot provide any *bridge* to other persons; it does not establish, justify, guarantee, or in any way elucidate the existence of *concrete other people*. If being-with is an a priori, necessary structure of being human, then it exists in any person *even if* no other persons exist. Being-with, however informative it is about one's own existence, asserts nothing about other people. Moreover, Sartre contends, if the existence of Others were constituted solely through being-with, then their existence would be wholly dependent on oneself, and this would simply be metaphysical solipsism in disguise. If, however, Heidegger retreats by claiming that he is only explicating how Others *must appear* to us, then he is not addressing the correct problem, viz., what Others are in themselves, and, again, has not really escaped solipsism.

Sartre elevates this charge to apply to Heidegger's conception of "transcendence" generally. Sartre claims that Heidegger's "transcendence" never permits one to encounter a world beyond one's own construction because it *defines* man's existence and is a priori.[121] Here Sartre stresses the Kantian or meta-level dimension of Heidegger's position; he conceives Heidegger's existentials as essential features that define any person in any possible world and that structure his experience irrespective of the character of his surroundings. He also stresses the fact that existentials are structures of *one's own* existence; he thus wonders whether the existence of Others has even been addressed. If it has not, then despite the appearance of a solution, this nettlesome issue has in fact been ignored – not superseded.

In this objection, Sartre is raising a number of important questions about Heidegger's existentials: what is their ultimate foundation? do any interesting object-level implications emerge from Heidegger's meta-level claims? how does one know that the existentials revealed by an analysis of 'one's own' existence apply to Others? Each of these questions will be considered further as I discuss Heidegger's replies. I think this objection uncovers a deep problem in Heidegger's position.

Sartre claims that being-with Others does not guarantee the real existence of concrete other people because it is essentially a fact about oneself, and this fact neither entails nor presupposes anything about concrete other persons.[122] Although the 'with' suggests the real existence of Others, this suggestion is undermined by the kind of structure that being-with is, viz., an existential, a necessary condition of being human. If it is really necessary and operative in every form of life, and if it is a priori and, consequently, *independent* of the contingent, idiosyncratic features of particular environments, then it should exist even in children brought up by animals, or in people who live in a society of androids, or in those who are born on abandoned islands or planets. Hence, the fact that one always exists in some orientation toward "Others" does not imply anything about the humanity or even the real existence of those to whom one is "oriented."

Heidegger's initial replies

Heidegger has a number of replies to this formulation of Sartre's criticism. His first reply would be that even if the surroundings contain only animals or androids, then a person in that situation will exist *with* such beings; a relation of solicitude will exist between him and them, and they will function as the locus for his impersonal or Crowd-self. On this view, Heidegger's claim is that humans will necessarily develop in active relatedness toward whatever entities are the environment. This would be a significant concession, for it would grant Sartre's basic contention that existentials are self-contained structures that will relate the person to whatever is around him. The reply accepts that being-with does not entail a relatedness to other *persons*.

Sartre could press the point further and suggest that the *with-relation* might even exist between a person and the objects of his own fantasies, and if this is possible, then nothing about the actual existence of anything other than oneself is established by the presence of this existential. Various forms of paranoia suggest the possibility that some persons' primary orientation is toward such fantasized objects. If this is Heidegger's only reply, then Sartre does show that the existence of other persons is not established or addressed by being-with.

A better line of reply for Heidegger would be to claim that people exist-with Others *because of* Others' real existence. In short, he could argue that being-with exists only because there are entities to which one is related, and the strongest version of this reply would hold that only other persons can make possible this kind of with-relatedness. Even if Heidegger could not establish this strong version, he might be able to show that *something* other than the oneself exists because one typically abandons oneself to it. Heidegger might then claim that the precise analysis of this *something other* is a task for regional ontology, not for the fundamental ontology of *Being and Time*.

This reply grants that being-with is not an innate, self-contained structure and that it *requires or presupposes* the actual existence of other persons. The existence of being-with would then entail the existence of other persons or at least something other than oneself. Heidegger himself makes no effort to provide this kind of argument or support for the existentials. At the very least, one can conclude that Sartre demonstrates the need for this kind of supplementary argument.

One might pursue this reply by exploring whether such a link to actual Others *could* plausibly be developed within Heidegger's theory. To do this, one needs to examine Heidegger's grounds for asserting that being-with and the impersonal self are existentials. His basic insight seems to be a sociological one: all humans develop within a culture and become socialized. Men cannot survive without such a culture, and every culture engages in a socialization process. This socialization is the source both of the socially embedded meanings that govern the use of instruments and of the dominance of the Crowd in the impersonal mode of selfness. Existing in a culture creates solicitude toward Others. These very general facts thus would constitute the ground of Heidegger's claim that being-with and the impersonal mode of selfness are necessary conditions of being human. They would be created by the conditions of human development.

Using such general facts, Heidegger might develop an argument which would show that being-with requires the real existence of other persons and that it would be highly deficient in cases where a human being developed among a group of animals, for example. He might also plausibly argue that it would not exist at all if the individual developed in total isolation, and presumably he might then claim that such an individual would not be fully human.

Some additional difficulties

There are some major difficulties with such sociological efforts to ground being-with and to relate it to the real existence of Others. These problems amplify Sartre's objection and indicate why he offers a theory of an entirely different type than Heidegger's. The fact that human beings develop in a society of Others like themselves is a *contingent* fact, even though a general one. If Heidegger grounds his existentials on that fact, he would in effect be grounding an ontological claim (necessary) on an ontical one (contingent), and this *order* of justification could never be acceptable to Heidegger, for the ontical always depends on and is conditioned by the ontological. Thus, not only could he not accept *this* effort to ground his existential-ontological claim, *any* effort to ground the claim on similar general facts must be unacceptable.

To the extent that an existential *can* be grounded, it is thereby *conditioned* by what grounds it, but, for Heidegger, existentials are the fundamental structures that condition everything else; they ground all inquiry and are allegedly embodied in one form or another in every way of being human. Existentials thus must condition every way of relating to persons; they cannot then arise from (or exist because of) one form of that relatedness (e.g., socialization processes). In addition, what is produced by contingent facts cannot exist a priori; it is an a posteriori result of those facts. But Heidegger insists that being-with is a priori; thus it cannot be grounded or defended in this fashion. Consequently, a sociological relation between the existence of Others and being-with cannot be established without abandoning Heidegger's view that being-with is an existential.

This is a different version of Sartre's point. Given the basic framework of Heidegger's theory, one's relatedness toward Others *cannot* require or presuppose the existence of Others, but, as Sartre shows, neither can it *establish* that existence. Hence, Heidegger's theory does not and cannot address the traditional problem. Indeed, *anything* that functions like an a priori condition similar to one of Heidegger's existentials will be unable to provide an explication of the existence of Others. One kind of theory that might succeed would elucidate a structure that exists a posteriori — is *imposed* on one — and that provides an essential link between self and Other in that it exists only because of Others and yet is a genuine structure of oneself. These are the conditions Sartre's theory seeks to fulfill.

Further Heideggerian replies

Two replies might still be useful to Heidegger at this point. The first one holds that Heidegger simply never meant to address the traditional problem; to discuss the being of Others would be to do *regional ontology*, a task he never meant to undertake. At best, his theory — an analysis of the deep structures of one's own existence — has some implications for that topic. The second reply asserts that the traditional problem has been displaced; one cannot effectively raise it inside Heidegger's perspective. Thus, the first reply implies that Sartre is unfairly criticizing

Heidegger for failing to succeed in a task he never adopted, and the second reply implies that Sartre is trying to raise a question that has been rendered untenable by Heidegger's theory. If Heidegger adopts the first reply alone, he would be granting Sartre's point and admitting that his apparent efforts to address the existence of Others are deceptive. Even if Heidegger claims that his position merely has implications for the existence of Others, Sartre has a powerful reply. For Heidegger's theory can have such implications for either of two reasons: *either* the being of Others is constituted by one's own being-with them *or* the being of Others is simply another application of Heidegger's analysis of human beings. The existence of Others would thus be addressed either because it would be conditioned by one's own or because they too are human beings and the essential structures of being human also apply to them.

In the few remarks that Heidegger does offer about Others, he asserts that they exist in the world as one does and that they exist with one (with reference to one) as one does with them (with reference to them). One can interpret Sartre to be raising the question of how these claims *are known*. In effect, he seeks to place Heidegger on the horns of a dilemma: implications about Others follow (or are known) either because one's own existence conditions theirs in some way *or* because they are instances of humanity like oneself. But on either interpretation, there are serious difficulties.

If the way Others exist is known because it is conditioned by one's own existence, then their existence is a *function* of one's own existentials; their nature is in some way constituted by the conditions of one's own. Sartre suggests that this simply makes the Other a satellite-like extension of oneself, and this view thus becomes a form of solipsism, for the Other would not be distinct from oneself.

There is a stronger argument in Sartre's favor, however. The particular aspects of Others that Heidegger mentions are expressions of *their* existentials. But if Others' existentials are a priori, necessary structures, they cannot be conditioned by contingent facts (like our existence). Hence our existentials cannot condition them for the same reason that Heidegger cannot allow our existentials to result from interactions with them: a priori, necessary features of human being cannot be conditioned by contingent a posteriori events. Hence the reason we know these aspects of Others cannot be because their existence is conditioned by our own. The first horn of Sartre's dilemma is not an acceptable solution for Heidegger.

This leaves the second horn of the dilemma, which is clearly the one Heidegger adopts in the text: one understands something about Others because they too are human; the existentials also apply to them.[123] Sartre's question at this point becomes: how does one know there are Others in whom the a priori structures of *one's own* being are also

151

instantiated? Although other bodies are apparently engaged in purposive activities, does this assure that the existential worldhood applies to them? Although they appear to adjust their actions to the demands of Others, does this assure that they exist-*with* (with reference to) them? What justifies the claim that the existentials apply to anyone beyond oneself? Heidegger simply *transfers* his analysis of human being to other human bodies, but he provides no justification for this; in effect, he assumes, rather than demonstrates or explicates, the existence of other persons. He may have shown what other humans must be like *if* there are any, but he has not established the 'if' clause.

Heidegger might reply that the humanity of another's body can be directly apprehended through its purposiveness, its reference to Others, etc. But this will not distinguish other people from animals, and the subtleties that distinguish human purposiveness and sociality from those of animals are not likely to be directly apprehensible. One would need to grasp the life-world of the other entity to know whether its experience is informed by Heidegger's existentials; yet this life-world is not directly apprehensible. Heidegger seems to have no adequate reply to the second horn of Sartre's dilemma.

The conclusion of this argument is that Heidegger cannot defend the implication he wants his theory to have for the existence of Others. His position thus neither directly nor indirectly addresses the question Sartre is pressing. The plea that Heidegger did not intend to address the existence of Others is *lame* given the absence of any clear path by which he might do so. Thus, the ultimate burden of Heidegger's defense against Sartre falls on his claim to have *displaced* this traditional question.

Heidegger's main point against the traditional approach is that it presupposes an independent self whose existence is certain and in terms of which the existence of Others can be questioned. Heidegger claims that one does not experience such a self in the typical state; it is governed by the demands, values, and codes of the anonymous Crowd. Thus, Others inhabit the center of one's life in the impersonal mode of selfness. Quite literally, Heidegger means that one is *not-oneself*, that Others *are* one's self. This seems to demonstrate the necessary existence of Others if there is anything that satisfies his description of being human. The question concerning the existence of Others is thus unintelligible because if questioning occurs, there is a human being who questions, and there must therefore be Others.

One can challenge the inference Heidegger draws from the impersonal mode of selfness. One can exist as an impersonal self even if there are no other persons. For example, one may continue to exist impersonally even if Others have all been destroyed by nuclear catastrophe. Or a "wild child" may exist impersonally with respect to the pack of animals that reared him. Thus the actual existence of other persons is not presupposed by the impersonal mode of existence.

Moreover, one can question the extent to which the "Others" who govern one's impersonal self are related to concrete actual Others and their demands; they may be wholly unrelated, for Heidegger neglects to clarify the connection. These "Others" are probably the *perceived demands* of an imagined-fantasized synthesis of many concrete Others. Thus, these "Others" who dominate one are in part a function of one's interpretive and selective processes; they are, in effect, a projected appendage of oneself, and their relation to actual Others may be quite tenuous.

Finally, the impersonal self, like being-with, cannot be grounded in the contingent facts of social life without compromising the a priori nature of the existentials. Heidegger cannot derive the impersonal self from the real existence of Others or a surrounding culture.

For these reasons, one can still sensibly ask whether Others exist even if one exists in the impersonal mode of selfness, and the answer is in no way obvious. Either the traditional approach does not presume a self-contained independent self, or Heidegger's existentials are only a different kind of self-containment. Heidegger's challenge to the tradition is less successful than he thinks.

Thus neither of Heidegger's final replies effectively rescue him from the thrust of Sartre's second criticism. I have tried to reconstruct his position as favorably as possible and have found no way to adequately respond to Sartre's second objection. Only if Heidegger modifies his conception of the existentials — allowing them to be conditioned by contingent facts — could he develop an effective response.[124]

Sartre's third objection

In this objection, Sartre examines the "Other" that is the real terminus of Heidegger's existentials: the "Other" whom one is-with and the "Other" who dominates one in the impersonal mode of selfness. Sartre wonders whether this "Other" is ontologically differentiated from oneself or whether he is ultimately identical with one. Is there only a single being of which all "individuals" are modifications and which renders the individuality and differentiatedness of each person illusory? How is the "Other" whom one exists-with distinct from oneself? Since Sartre shares Heidegger's first-person viewpoint, I shall examine Heidegger's replies from within that perspective.

Heidegger's replies

Heidegger offers two different answers to this question. The clearest distinction between "oneself" and "the Other" can be drawn in the authentic mode of existence; for the inauthentic mode, a very different answer is required.

When one exists authentically, one has a hold of oneself; one exists resolutely in the face of one's finitude, heeding the call of conscience to structure one's possibilities oneself. In this mode, one exists truly as oneself; one has risen above the impersonal mode of selfness. The "Other" in the impersonal mode of selfness is thus what one transcends, and the difference between oneself and this Other is reducible to the difference between the authentic and inauthentic mode of existence. There is thus no danger of an inability to distinguish oneself from "the Other" even though this distinction amounts to a difference between modes of selfness. Moreover, concrete Others appear as distinct individuals when one exists authentically; the typical relation one has to them is leaping-ahead – opening their authentic possibilities for them. One's more explicit sense of one's own possibilities underlines their difference from oneself.

Yet Heidegger's central claim is that to be a differentiated individual is not the typical way in which persons exist. Even in the authentic state, one never wholly escapes the appeal and influence of the Crowd. In the inauthentic state, Others (the Crowd) lie at the core of oneself, governing everything one is and does. Heidegger's *point* is that precisely in this mode the Crowd *is* oneself; they constitute one's selfness, and there is no difference between 'who one is' and the Crowd. Thus, in the inauthentic mode, what Sartre seeks cannot be given because it does not exist. One's 'identity' is dominated by the Crowd. In effect, one can interpret Heidegger as seeking to overcome the view that persons are isolated selves – ultimately distinct from each other – whose relationships to each other are only overlaid on this isolated monadic condition.

A reformulation of Sartre's point

Sartre, however, understands this implication of Heidegger's position, and at this point the thrust of his objection can be more lucidly presented. Sartre uses the fact that the impersonal self is an a priori, necessary condition of being human to demonstrate that Heidegger does not really transcend the monad view of persons. There are two crucial questions: what is the relation of the Crowd governing one's impersonal self to concrete other people? what is the relation between the Crowd embedded in one's own existence and the Crowd embedded in one's neighbor's existence?

Sartre's first point is that because the Crowd is an a priori condition of one's existence, it cannot result from or react to external influences, for it exists irrespective of such influences. But this means that the impersonal mode of selfness is not altered or affected by the concrete Others one experiences. With arguments similar to those discussed in the previous section, Sartre can show that Heidegger cannot permit any contingent, concrete relatedness between other people and the Crowd that dominates one's life.

Sartre's second point again takes the form of a dilemma. *Either*: the Crowd is *numerically identical* for all persons, and in that case, there really is no basis for differentiating them; there would be one being manifest in many different locations, and this would vindicate Sartre's charge of monism. *Or*: the Crowd that dominates one's own existence is *different* from that which dominates everyone else's, and in that case, "the Crowd" is as individuated an entity as persons are, and it does not then provide a basis for overcoming the monad view of persons. It would simply function as an additional structure which, for the most part, dominates one's life, but which provides no relation to anything outside oneself. Either analysis of the Crowd is problematic, and the reason for these difficulties is Heidegger's claim that the Crowd is an a priori and necessary feature of one's life. If it were a posteriori and contingent, then it could *arise and develop*; it could interact with, be affected by, and modify the concrete Others with whom one comes in contact.

Heidegger sees an important fact, but the theoretical structure in which he situates it prevents adequate understanding of it. The Crowd is a developing totality that organizes the implicit and explicit demands of many persons; each person contributes to it even while being dominated by it. Moreover, the various ways in which persons can deflect or dispel the impact of the Crowd also require investigation; Heidegger invests it with an almost mystical power. Only if these kinds of questions are addressed (and if the claim that the impersonal self is an existential must be reconceived to enable such questions to be intelligibly asked, then it *must* be reconceived) will Heidegger's theory be able to achieve its aims — to discern the intertwining relationships between people that underlie and condition any effort to achieve differentiated individuality and to overthrow the Cartesian picture.

Similar questions about the Crowd can be raised from the third-person point of view. In any given society, there will be many subcultures; this means that there will be different "Crowds" and that they (in addition to the individuals who are governed by them) will have some relation to one another. Moreover, different "Crowds" will have different degrees of organic unity. These relations must be explored. From the first-person viewpoint, the Crowd may condition one's experience of and relation to Others, but from a third-person viewpoint, the Crowd is conditioned by the way people interact; it emerges from individuals and groups in interaction. The unique ontological nature of the Crowd also needs further study. Hegel's dialectical relationships will probably provide a more adequate framework for comprehending the Crowd than Heidegger's existentials.

Heidegger may attempt to brush aside the kinds of investigations

I am encouraging as merely ontical enterprises without significance for the basic ontological questions he is exploring. This reply would miss the thrust of Sartre's second and third objections. Sartre's point is that precisely because Heidegger insists on finding existentials, *because* he seeks a priori, necessary conditions, he is unable to answer these crucial objections, and he loses the philosophical benefits that his position initially seems to provide.

Heidegger does show, against Sartre, that persons need not be regarded as *necessarily* distinct from one another in all modes of existing. One cannot assume that there is an unavoidable differentiation between self and Other because there are forms of life in which that distinction is reduced to nothing. A theory of Others must be able to account for different kinds of differentiation in different forms of life. Heidegger does point the way toward one promising way to overcome the monad view of the self, a view which Sartre himself is anxious to refute.

Sartre's fourth objection

Sartre's fourth criticism is offered between parentheses, but it nevertheless appears to be a serious one. Heidegger claims that Others exist in the world just as one does and, consequently, that their projects haunt the instrumental relations that furrow one's world; this is one way in which they are essentially *with* one. Sartre wonders how Heidegger can justify this claim.

The rationale for this question may need further clarification. The "world" for Heidegger is *not* the totality of existing objects; clearly self and Other exist among the same totality of objects. Rather the "world" is the instrumental organization which a person discerns in his environment; Worldhood is the existential which make the emergence of such an organization possible and necessary. The instrumental assignments are not secondary meanings overlaid on already existing things, but they define the fundamental manner of existing for worldly entities. Because persons' purposes differ, their instrumental organizations may differ, and each person might be said to exist in a different world.

Although these worlds may not be private, they may be unique to each person; Sartre's question concerns the extent to which "worlds" are subjective, and thus the extent to which persons are enmeshed in the same world. If this mutual enmeshment cannot be demonstrated, then Heidegger's theory will imply a monadic analysis of persons; it will have failed to establish a fundamental bond between people.

Heidegger's replies

Sartre does not portray Heidegger's position fairly enough in this objection. Even if the specific arrangements that each person establishes among the instruments that constitute the world differ (Heidegger would grant that they do), there is nevertheless a common background of instrumental functions, assignments, and references from which these specific organizations are drawn. Only this common background, which constitutes everyone's horizon, could be stable enough to function as an alternative conception of the *being* of entities, and this is what Heidegger seeks to provide with his conception of instrumentality.

Moreover, since many different persons can share this common background of use-assignments, different persons can exist *in* the *same* world. The relationship between each person's idiosyncratic way of organizing things and the common world is analogous to that between a dialect of a language and the language itself.[125] Although the analogy to language helps one to comprehend Heidegger's position on the structure of "the world," in *Being and Time* these instrumental relations constitute the *foundation* of *language* – a more primordial kind of 'meaning' from which linguistic meaning is derived.

There are situations in which one experiences not-being-of-fhe-same-world as another person, viz., when one is a foreigner in a different culture. Heidegger does not discuss whether there is a common background of instrumental significance governing use-assignments in all possible cultures. That is the correct formulation of the problem of identity of worlds or worldhood, *if* there is such a problem for Heidegger. If people exist in the same culture, then their common background of instrumental assignments is sufficient to establish that they exist in the same world.

Sartre might pursue his objection by asking how one *can know* another shares this common background of instrumental references. Without entering into all the revisions Heidegger offers of the analysis of knowing, one can present a reasonable reply to this question. One knows that the Other exists in the same world because one perceives that he uses things in the same way as one uses them. One realizes another inhabits the same world by seeing that he typically uses the implements around him in a way that is familiar and plausible. How someone uses something is more accessible than how a person 'sees' something, and this is one advantage of conceiving the existence of a person as being-in-the-world.

Sartre's fifth objection

Sartre's fifth criticism is closely related to the second. In the second, he argues that Heidegger does not and cannot address the existence of other persons; in the fifth objection, he argues that Heidegger's existentials do not elucidate *concrete* other persons and do not illuminate concrete interpersonal relationships. Heidegger's ontological claims provide no greater understanding of ontical, merely contingent, interpersonal affairs like friendship or fellowship. The operative word in this objection is *concrete*. What does Sartre mean here?

Sartre seeks a way of illuminating *any* face-to-face interpersonal situation and a way of understanding the relationship of self to Other in such situations. He wants a theory which will provide an understanding of how the existence of distinct persons is interlocked and an analysis of the fundamental structures that emerge from one's *interactions* with other people.

Because Heidegger attends only to being-with and the impersonal self and because these structures exist even when no face-to-face situation exists, they do not provide any *special* understanding of such situations. Again, Sartre's complaint concerns the fact that existentials are a priori, necessary, and unrelated to concrete other people. I shall try to avoid covering ground that has already been covered in previous objections; I have granted that Sartre has a point. I wish to investigate whether Heidegger can provide some understanding of concrete Others.

Heidegger's replies
Heidegger's first reply to this objection carries substantial weight. Sartre emphasizes *face-to-face situations* in clarifying his notion of concreteness; this suggests a bias toward *presence*. Sartre seems to assume that concrete relations exist only when Others are present before one's eyes. Heidegger might note that this bias toward presence explains Sartre's emphasis on *vision*; an important feature of face-to-face relations is that each can *see* the Other. These are Sartre's biases in formulating the objection; Heidegger does not share them.

Although he thinks there is a 'sight' related to being-with, it is not perception or observation; he calls it 'considerateness' and 'forbearance,' each of which has deficient modes. For Heidegger, the dominant elements in a face-to-face situation are not the mutual presence of each to the Other but the intuitive grasp of what each is about and the peripheral attunement to and care for this. Heidegger draws attention to the often uncanny and minute sensitivity people have to Others' aims and needs in concrete situations.

Heidegger could thus reply with some justice that his existentials do have useful implications for understanding concrete Others. He can argue that Sartre misses these because he imports his own biases into the formulation of the task. Heidegger tries to clarify our experience of concrete Others through descriptive elucidations of the mutual attunement of self and Other and the embeddedness of sociality in instrumentality.

Moreover, Heidegger can reply that the fact that his existentials function even when one is not face-to-face with Others does not imply that they have no special illuminating power when Others are in the vicinity. He contends that solicitude is the basic mode of relatedness with Others whether they are present or absent. In hundreds of subtle ways one adjusts to them, refers to them, and responds to their calls. He does not pursue these details because ontical study – an examination of the empirical modifications and forms of his basic structures – is beyond the scope of his investigation. He tries to clarify the interpersonal structures that are *always* operative, and these do apply to face-to-face situations even if additional factors sometimes operate in them too.

Synopsis

My overall verdict on Sartre's dialogue with Heidegger is mixed. First, Sartre badly misjudges the logical structure of Heidegger's theory; Heidegger offers a number of types of justification for his position. Second, Sartre does uncover some deep weaknesses in Heidegger's theory: it is inherently unable to establish the existence of Others, and the existentials it identifies cannot be related to actual, concrete Others without being reconceived. Third, against Sartre, I think that Heidegger can provide some answers and that his theory does illuminate some aspects of concrete interpersonal life. Although his theory is not fully developed in this direction, there is nothing in principle that prevents it from being pursued in this way. Heidegger is a phenomenologist of no less penetration than Sartre. That being-with and the impersonal self are salient structures of interpersonal life cannot be denied; they may have to be recast, but their importance remains.

Additional objections to Heidegger

In the previous section I argued that Sartre's first objection to Heidegger (that he did not attempt to defend his position, that he offers only a series of definitions) is mistaken. I showed that Heidegger offers three different kinds of defense: subsumption of possible counter-examples, descriptive elucidation, and challenges to traditional conceptions that support alternative positions. I now wish to examine the adequacy of these kinds of defense; it is one thing to argue for a proposition; it is another for the arguments to succeed. I shall indicate some inherent limitations in Heidegger's strategies, and these lessons should be useful for any attempt to develop a theory of intersubjectivity. Since most of Heidegger's specific propositions exemplify one of these strategies of defense, I shall also offer specific critical comments on them in the course of the discussion. I shall conclude the chapter with an appreciation of Heidegger's contributions.

Heidegger's strategies of defense

Subsumption

Heidegger's most potent justification is the claim that alleged exceptional cases presuppose or are forms of the basic structures they supposedly call into question. Thus, being-alone is said to be a form of being-with; indifference, a deficient kind of solicitude; being-against, a type of being-with; and a theoretical surmise made at a distance, a form of practical engagement.[126] These points are meant to demonstrate the universal applicability of being-with. Are they successful? Do they demonstrate that being-with is an existential of human beings?

I do not think they do. But before I explain why, I want to indicate a general problem with this kind of argument. There are many ways of incorporating phenomena into classifications; a new classification often sufficiently reorients one's perceptions to make inclusion of borderline cases plausible. One too easily stretches both the case and the new classification scheme. I have tried to show that Heidegger's position meaningfully subsumes many different forms of life. But the claim that one comportment is prior to or more basic than another is always difficult to evaluate.

To illustrate this, one might simply invert Heidegger's claim: could all concrete instances of being-with be conceived as species or forms of a more primordial being-alone? One easy way in which they can be interpreted in this fashion is simply as *reactions to* this aloneness. One might even offer this as an *explanation* of why solicitude is a general property of human existence; the intolerability of this primordial isolation could make each person reach toward Others to escape it. But the *reactive* character of this solicitude might weaken this theory; it would not show that being-with is a form or species of being-alone, only that it is one response to it. One might, however, argue that concrete being-with is just a way of embodying a more fundamental isolation which is never really transcended, for one often does experience a sense of isolation even in one's most intimate encounters or most fulfilling social transactions. The theory would then be that aloneness is one's basic metaphysical condition; no matter how strongly one might struggle against it, one would never overcome it. All concrete attitudes would simply be different ways of bearing it. In a similar fashion, one might try to demonstrate that all versions of solicitude are really variants or forms of indifference.

I do *not* think these alternatives are correct, but I offer them in order to show how one can stretch classifications and conceptions of priority in such a way that nearly anything can be interpreted as prior to most anything else from *some* perspective. Hence, one cannot place much confidence in the simple assertion of priority. The issue becomes not just in what sense being-with is prior, but *how illuminating* is the claim of priority?

I now want to show why I think Heidegger's being-with is not as encompassing as he claims it to be. There is a form of life that cannot be subsumed under being-with. This form of life I term "lived solipsism"; the lived solipsist does not refer to and is not oriented toward Others.

The lived solipsist does not acknowledge other bodies as centers of consciousness; he sees only an organization of instruments expressing his own ends. He lives his relation to other people much as one lives one's relation to one's own body; he lives amidst Others without any cognizance of them, without expecting any resistance from them, and without acknowledging any distinctness to them. The lived solipsist is anything but a hermit; Others are all around him, but they "mean nothing" to him. His way of life lacks *any* awareness of other sources of purposiveness or other states of mind than his own. Lived solipsism is not egoism since egoism usually entails choosing one's own good *over* the good of Others; the lived solipsist does not even grasp that there are Others to select against. He is narcissistic, but he may not have a developed sense of self. He does *not* view Others as robots; he experiences them like tools in his workshop, but these tools lack any reference to Others. Nothing comes from other people; nothing is owed to them; nothing he does is destined for them.

Some people do live in this fashion; indeed, I would claim that lived solipsism is a permanent possibility for everyone, a state into which people intermittently fall. The proliferation of interest in narcissism may indicate that lived solipsism is becoming more pervasive. It involves a *blindness* toward other people. It is the *zero degree* both of sensitivity to the personhood of Others and of relatedness to them.

Heidegger cannot subsume this form of life under his conception of being-with without stripping it of all content. If even lived solipsism is a species of being-with, then it truly is a meaningless expression, and the assertion that we are necessarily *with*-Others says nothing. If lived solipsism exists, then being-with is not a necessary feature of being human. I think that for every claim of priority that Heidegger offers, a crucial exceptional case that really indicates a limit to the truth of his claim can be found.

Heidegger has at least two replies to my objection; the second one is quite important. The first questions whether the lived solipsist is a human being. Perhaps he exists *beneath* the level of *human* being; he may be less than human in so far as he is not open to and has no access to the humanity of other persons. Perhaps being-with is still a necessary condition of *human* being. This reply appeals to a loaded concept of "human being." Clearly, human creatures can live like solipsists. This reply makes Heidegger's claim stipulatively analytic; it excludes counter-examples from being "human," and this renders the claim uninteresting. It would then really be a mere definition, as Sartre claimed.

Far more compelling is a second line of reply. It simply grants this one exceptional form of being human and sets it aside with the question: so what? Does it alter the fundamental insight in Heidegger's theory? Since lived solipsism plays an important role throughout this essay, I shall take some care to respond to this objection both in the context of Heidegger's theory and in the context of my general approach to the problem of Others. The objection demands an account of the intellectual significance of lived solipsism. I shall first discuss its wider import and then demonstrate its applications to Heidegger's position. There are four major reasons for its importance.

First, focusing on lived, rather than epistemological, solipsism more adequately locates the worry that underlies this topic. The lived solipsist may well 'have the concept' of another person; he may even 'have a belief' that other people exist, but that belief does not turn any wheels; it engages nothing in his way of life. Moreover, proofs and arguments are not going to change the lived solipsist. Much of the philosophical machinery that has been developed to attack skepticism is simply irrelevant to what *I* regard as the main problem in this area: explicating the lived experience of the reality of Others and its implications. Indeed, the value of existential phenomenology and Heidegger's ontological inquiry lies in the fact that they at least address this problem.

Moreover, to acknowledge lived solipsism is to acknowledge that there are asocial ways of being human. The major implication of this is *not* that individuality is basic and sociality must be created (I disagree with this view), but rather that sociality can be *lost*. It has degrees and types and patterns of development and disintegration, and each of these must be studied. I am suggesting that lived solipsism should function for an existential phenomenology of intersubjectivity in a way that the state of nature did for eighteenth-century social theory, except that lived solipsism is *not* a fictional construct and that the ways of making the transition to sociality are legion. The manner in which the transition occurs defines the basic *tenor* of the sociality that is achieved. Lived solipsism is a limit-phenomenon; studying it should facilitate fuller clarification of the various ways of being social.

Second, to acknowledge lived solipsism as a way of being human is to refuse to arbitrarily exclude certain forms of life from the realm of the acceptable or discussible. To sever the lived solipsistic frame of mind from the human is to try to eliminate people's awareness of it in themselves and to try to construct a concept of being human that includes only what they wish to see. Perhaps lived solipsism is less pervasive than I think, but one does not achieve greater understanding of the ways of being human by avoiding them. Solipsism in its lived form is not a self-conscious withdrawal from Others, nor is it an angry rebellion against Others; both of these would still be forms of being-with. Lived solipsism is a *loss* of contact, an *absence* of relatedness, a *deadness* toward people. In similar ways, one can become dead to one's body, to temporality, to ideals, to emotions, or to the intellect; there are equally important limit-phenomena to be investigated in those areas as well.

Third, lived solipsism demonstrates that even the most minimal form of sociality can be *lost*; one cannot be complacent about the threads interweaving self and Other in everyday life. Social existence requires lived sociality; modern social structures may undermine their own support. The lived solipsist exists within a constituted social order, but he provides it with no life blood. Lived sociality is an *achievement*, not a *natural* condition of man. It is not necessarily a willed or self-conscious achievement, but it is not an a priori given which can only assume different specific forms. By understanding lived solipsism and the ways in which the transition to lived sociality can occur, one can better assess the gains and losses of sociality. With Hegel, I think that sociality facilitates some of the most important human excellences, but with Heidegger, I recognize that it also contains some potential for debilitation.

Fourth, elucidating lived solipsism helps one to understand Heidegger's being-with more adequately. It also helps explain why seeking general, all-encompassing conditions is *not* the most effective theoretical approach. Lived solipsism demonstrates that there is a way of being human that lies outside the bounds of being-with, even when that concept is defined broadly. In order to demonstrate that men *necessarily* exist with Others, Heidegger had to incorporate, and simply conjoin (rather than integrate), many *different* ways of orienting and/or referring to Others; he uses "being-with" as an umbrella term to refer to all of them collectively. This strategy allows each apparent counter-example to be subsumed under at least *one* of these forms of relatedness. It can then be viewed as a species of being-with, and it will fail as a counter-example.

Some of the *different* forms of relatedness that are conjoined in the concept of being-with are: existing-for-the-sake-of-Others, using-the-products-of-Others, existing-in-expectation-of-Others, existing-in-community-with-Others, and sharing-the-same-codes-as-Others. If any *one* of these forms of relatedness to Others defined being-with, then discovering ways of life that *lacked* it would be easy, for *each* of these forms can exist in the absence of the others. Only by conjoining them all under one umbrella term could Heidegger have hoped to arrive at a generally applicable structure. But if even this amalgamated concept fails to subsume all forms of life, then the motivation for collecting these various forms of relatedness under one concept disappears.

One can then distinguish the various forms of relatedness that

Heidegger explores and clarify their boundaries and their degree of applicability, and this more detailed investigation will yield *deeper* understanding of the interpersonal field. Of course, one will not have located an a priori, necessary condition of being human, but lived solipsism discredits the plausibility of that task; it may not be achievable. One will be clarifying the many diverse structures operative in social life and their relations to one another. One will also discover the central differences in the ways persons can exist socially, and one may also determine which general types of social structure are most effectively supported by the different modes of social relatedness.

This approach provides the basis for a conception of intra-social contradiction in a culture, for if the dominant forms of relatedness in a social order are incompatible with the kind of social structures that exist, then the micro- and macro-levels of social life will exist in contradiction with one another, and one can expect deep strains and eventual transformations in the social system. Once one acknowledges a zero degree of general sociality (lived solipsism), one can begin to identify the zero degrees of the various forms and aspects of sociality. If one inverts Heidegger's search for general structures, then one will achieve a richer, more differentiated, and more finely-tuned comprehension of interpersonal life.

For these reasons, lived solipsism is a philosophically important phenomenon which seriously challenges Heidegger's project. Heidegger's defense of the claim that being-with is an existential had a chance of success only because he conjoins very different modes of social relatedness.

Similar remarks apply to Heidegger's other existential: the impersonal mode of selfness. It too is not one single feature or dimension; rather it consists of a number of dimensions in which Others play a formative role. Some examples are: the various grammars that organize the systems of signs (including spoken and written language); the institutions which establish the basic issues any person must face and which condition his approach to those issues: religious, economic, political institutions, and the family; general norms of conduct; and the dominant metaphors, rules, programs, and criteria of evaluation that govern the processes of thinking. One's actions, thoughts, aspirations, and internal divisions are largely functions of the interpersonal and cultural milieu in which one lives. This is not to say that the *outcome* of these processes is fixed, but the rails that guide these processes derive from Others, and they condition whatever emerges.

These dimensions of the self operate whether Others are present or absent, and although they are subject to modification by individuals, in some form they do constitute one's core. But they are very different from one another, and the conditioning role they have is obscured by attempting to discuss them under one rubric. The importance of these structures and the extent to which they are related to Others can best be determined if each is treated separately. Deeper understanding of each can be achieved by examining them separately.

These dimensions of the impersonal self are not exactly existentials in Heidegger's sense. They are not a priori; they emerge via social interaction. In order to save Heidegger's valuable insights, one must modify the theoretical edifice in which they are organized. Most social structures of the self are a posteriori in the sense that they derive from interpersonal interaction as a person matures. The existence of Others is implicated in the presence of these dimensions; they would not exist in this form if Others did not exist. In addition, these dimensions do not operate automatically; a person may be able to influence or modify their operation. These dimensions derive from a long series of interactions over periods of time; they gradually become embedded structures that are presupposed by particular interactions. If one alters Heidegger's conception of an existential to incorporate these properties, one revises his overall enterprise, but one may also be able to make more effective use of his insights.

Lived solipsism is not necessarily a counter-example to the universality of the impersonal mode of selfness. The lived solipsist can still exist impersonally in Heidegger's sense; he may still be guided by norms and cultural meanings, use language, etc. But he will lack any explicit awareness of the connection between these factors and other people; he will experience them as natural givens of the environment. As I am interpreting the impersonal self, a human being would have to develop alone on a deserted island to avoid it. Only then would the few constant features of his world be wholly unrelated to Others, and only then would the minimal degree of consciousness he would achieve have no socially constituted general structures in the background. He would still lack a personal existence (perhaps he would even be incapable of it), but he would not exist as a Crowd-self in Heidegger's sense. Heidegger might respond that such a creature would not really be human, and this reply may have greater force against this example.

The general implications of these remarks are that Heidegger successfully subsumes counter-examples only at the expense of genuine clarification of intersubjective life. The existentials he defines are amalgamated notions that consist of many different elements that lack any important relation to one another. If there are ways of being human to which even these broadly defined structures do not apply, then the supposed benefit of this amalgamation is not received. The more important task then becomes to examine each specific component of his structures and to clarify its relations to the others.

Descriptive elucidation

Heidegger also uses descriptive elucidations as direct and indirect evidence for assertions. They provide direct evidence when they exhibit the pervasiveness of the existential in everyday experience. Examples of such direct descriptive support are the observations that any use of a tool implicitly presupposes a reference to Others — for its origin, aim, function, or construction — and that the typical appearance of persons is to be engaged in their own pursuits, to be-in-the-world.[127] They also provide indirect evidence by suggesting problems for other views. Examples of such indirect support are the claims that no self is apprehended by the agent in the course of executing his everyday affairs and that Others are grasped *not* as opposed and distinct from oneself, but rather as undifferentiated from oneself.[128] After discussing some of the general problems in defending claims like Heidegger's descriptively, I shall briefly discuss some of his examples to determine their effectiveness.

Descriptive elucidation is often difficult to assess; the crucial questions are: how deep is the description? how extensive is the field over which it applies? how unambiguously does it support one theory over others? Just as facts can often be made consistent with the most diverse theories, so descriptions can often be made to support divergent philosophical frameworks. Moreover, even when a point implicit in a description is suggestive, it may indicate only a marginal phenomenon rather than a central one.

Genuinely deep insights suggest numerous supporting observations and are sufficiently powerful to raise doubts about entrenched theories with which they cannot be made compatible. Also, to be illuminating a description must be concrete and fresh. It should suggest new ways of comprehending a range of phenomena, and it should command assent without seeming obvious. General, familiar, or surface observations are typically unhelpful. Depth, suggestiveness, and incisiveness are thus important criteria for evaluating descriptive elucidations.

Two other general points about descriptive evidence should be noted. Existentials are supposed to be necessary conditions of being human. Descriptive insights alone can never *establish* such claims. One would need, in addition, some procedure for examining *possible* cases as well as the actual cases one has experienced (i.e., something like Husserl's imaginative variation or "eidetic reduction"). Heidegger does not utilize such a procedure to support his claims. One must interpret them as a challenge to discover exceptional cases. Heidegger seems to believe that a carefully elucidated single phenomenon can provide richer and deeper insight than the more mechanical procedures of formal thought. Indeed, his descriptions do evoke new comprehension; with remarkably few sentences, he creates an effective reorientation of perspective. Still, establishing an initial change of perspective is far from demonstrating the presence of a necessary condition.

A second general point concerning descriptive insights is that they almost always operate only within *implicit* limits; for example, none of Heidegger's existentials function when one is sleeping. In addition, incisive descriptions too easily suggest supporting examples; more difficult to locate, especially when under the initial spell of the new perspective, are the recalcitrant phenomena. One often needs to break the spell of the description in order to see potential counter-examples. These remarks indicate some inherent weaknesses of descriptive evidence.

Heidegger uses descriptions to provide indirect support to his position by raising difficulties for alternative positions. The first of these is the proposition that no self inhabits everyday activity. This claim is exceptionally difficult to evaluate because of the many meanings of "self." Surely, in some senses of the word, e.g., explicit object of self-consciousness, Heidegger is right. Typically one lives in a first-order unreflected experience rather than in the second-order reflection required for explicit self-consciousness. But there are senses in which one typically experiences a "self" in the course of everyday life without reflecting; for example, the project in which one is involved is typically apprehended as belonging to an organization of projects that has an ongoing continuity in time, and these projects provide a sense of self.

More importantly, some people will simply deny the alleged description. Because they antecedently believe in the existence of a self, they may experience it directly whenever they make a decision. They will describe the experience of making a decision as "themselves choosing" and stare mutely if one denies the accuracy of their description. They might acknowledge that the direct experience of themselves recedes while they are executing their decisions, but they would insist that it reemerges with each decision. Heidegger and his opponents can come to an impasse here quickly because descriptions need not be accepted at face value; they can be interpreted differently or denied.

Heidegger's general point in this proposition, however, may be that people are *outwardly oriented* in the course of daily life; the *project at hand* absorbs one's attention, *not* the fact that it is *oneself* performing it or expressed in it. Here again, there is something correct about this insight, but there are also difficulties. For while performing many actions in the presence of Others, one senses how the act appears to them, and this ancillary sense of oneself draws one's attention inward. In this sense, one *can* have a sense of self in the course of an action even on the revised interpretation.

Finally, Heidegger's real point may be that the origin and direction of one's actions do not typically arise from one's own self, but from the impersonal mode of selfness. This observation is true enough, but the possibility of authentic selfness restricts its application.[129] Moreover, when one experiences oneself authentically in one's actions, there is a very definite sense of one's self expressed. This kind of experience supports those who claim that there is a self in everyday experience.

Not unpredictably, therefore, there are interpretations under which Heidegger's claim has some truth, but for each one, there are important restrictions. The ambiguity of the proposition further limits its usefulness. Descriptive elucidations are often insufficient to overthrow theoretical commitments because they can be reinterpreted in terms of those commitments and because many different descriptions of a phenomenon can seem legitimate.

A second descriptive proposition Heidegger offers is: Others are typically apprehended as undifferentiated from oneself. Again, the precise meaning of this statement is unclear; presumably Others are not grasped as identical to oneself (numerically identical), but they are also not grasped as explicitly distinct. They are apprehended as *like* oneself in that they exist in the same situation or condition or are the same sort of creature; they are not, according to his view, grasped as existing in a distinct mode (e.g., as objects vis-à-vis one's own subjectivity or as subjects vis-à-vis one's own objectivity). This insight is important, for one need only try to imagine various sorts of counterexamples to it to see that *any* apprehension of another as differentiated only arises on the basis of an experienced similarity of condition. Heidegger underlines this experience of background similarity.

On the other hand, Heidegger ignores the many senses in which Others are experienced as distinct from oneself: as having distinct bodies, distinct projects, distinct characters, distinct origins, etc. Whether Heidegger's similarity of condition is the primordial experience of Others is open to debate. In addition, Heidegger neglects the dynamic implicit in this apprehension: one seeks to reaffirm one's difference when one experiences a sense of identity with Others (and vice versa). Thus, the experiences of one's identity with and one's difference from Others may require one another and engender one another (à la Hegel); neither may be more basic than the other.

Heidegger may thus be able to use his descriptive evidence to challenge the position that Others must *always* be experienced as (or *defined* as) absolutely differentiated from oneself, but as support for the claim that lack of differentiation is the basic experience of Others, its force is limited.

Similar results emerge from a discussion of Heidegger's descriptive elucidations when they are used as direct support for the necessity of being-with. The fact that references to Others are imbedded in the very apprehension of a cultural artifact does not prevent the possibility of experiencing a world of instruments that lacks such social assignments. One can imagine a "wild child," conscious enough to have purposes and clever enough to alight upon material means of satisfying them on his own, who is able to apprehend an instrumental organization of the world that is shared by no creature in his experience and which refers to no other person, either for its origin or its meaning.

Heidegger's discussion of *Dasein*-with suggests that the primary way in which we apprehend Others is as engaged in projects like we are. This claim is meant to alter our comprehension of Others and to convince us that our contact with Others is far more direct than the Cartesian picture allows. By rethinking the nature of human existence, Heidegger reconceives the existence of other persons, and this descriptive elucidation of how they are typically apprehended is meant to support the new conceptualization. There are some important exceptions to this description, however.

One is that one sometimes apprehends another's gaze in a way that completely obliterates one's contact with the Other's body and his engagements; it throws one into a state of self-consciousness so severe that it *eliminates* one's perception of Others. In addition, one can simply *use* Others like one uses tools in the workshop, e.g., the way a captain or coach uses his players. Here Others are not grasped in the midst of their own pursuits, but those pursuits are organized around one's own projects. Finally, one's own concerns can be so absorbing that one simply fails to apprehend Others at all even though they are present. These examples show that Others are not always grasped as engaged in projects; they imply that there are different modalities of apprehending Others. They range from bare registration to full-loss. No single all self-encompassing form of apprehending Others exists. Heidegger's descriptions simply exhibit one important form.

Descriptive elucidations can suggest a reorientation of perspective, but they rarely provide compelling evidence for the change. They are especially weak against entrenched beliefs, for the beliefs condition the way experience will be described. At best, descriptive evidence can raise doubts about universal claims (e.g., Heidegger convincingly refutes the claim that one *always* experiences a self), but rarely does it unambiguously establish a general theory. It is subject to interpretative dispute, qualified by other theoretical considerations, and limited by the fact that other descriptions may be equally legitimate.

Challenging traditional conceptions

Heidegger offers three arguments that challenge traditional conceptions of self and Other. The first is that knowledge is a concrete way of being oriented to other people; it is an instance or form of being-with, and hence it cannot disprove that one *is-with* Others.[130] In general, one might wonder whether these kinds of claims (x presupposes y) advance one's understanding of the topics they address. Consider the fact that not-being-able-to-know-another would *also* exemplify being-with him; it is an orientation that sometimes arises in the course of experiencing a particular Other. However, if being-with is exhibited in either case, either when one can know another or when one cannot, then it cannot provide much understanding of what knowing another person involves. The being-with structure is *thin* in that it does not clarify or provide much insight into the phenomena that "presuppose" it.

In addition, being-with does not help answer the serious questions about knowing other people. Many factors affect the extent to which another can be known: his willingness to reveal himself to one's inquiries, the interferences created by his self-image, the faithfulness of his behavior to his ideals, the difficulty of making his many aspects cohere, the expectations created by one's own relationships with him. Each of these factors suggest special problems that arise primarily in knowing *other people*, but the assertion that one is already with them, that knowing is *a form* of being-with them, provides no suggestions for answering them. Even if it is true, Heidegger's claim is unhelpful.

Heidegger's second criticism attacks the traditional attempt to establish the existence of Others through analogy with one's relationship to oneself. Heidegger asserts that the fundamental relation of a person to himself — that his existence is an issue for him — is simply different from his fundamental relation to Others, solicitude.[131] He concludes that no effort to comprehend Others through analogizing processes can succeed. This argument, however, is too weak. In order to show that analogizing processes *cannot* be called upon to illuminate Others, one must show that no important similarity in self-self and self-Other relations *can* be established, not merely that the major forms of these relations are distinct. Moreover, even if they are *distinct*, this does not establish that they are *so different* from one another that no analogy can usefully be drawn. Perhaps one's own being-at-issue (care-for-oneself) is analogous to referring to or caring for Others; Heidegger's treatment of the call of conscience suggests such a possibility.[132] Perhaps not only one's own being, but also that of Others, are issues for one, and perhaps each is at issue in equally pressing ways; the interconnectedness of the modes of existing of self and Other suggests that such a position would not be alien to Heidegger's thought.

Hence, not only is Heidegger's argument too weak to establish its conclusion, there are also elements within his position that suggest that his conclusion is inaccurate. Sometimes Heidegger draws conclusions that his evidence does not support.

Heidegger's third challenge to the tradition concerns its starting point. The skeptic doubts the being of Others, but Heidegger thinks one's own being is *most* in question. The serious task is to affirm that one is an authentic self. Through the impersonal mode of selfness, Others deeply penetrate oneself;[133] in need of demonstration is the fact that *one is one's own self.* Thus Heidegger reverses the terms of the traditional problem. One's own existence is not an indubitable given from which that of Others can be called into question; the haunting reality of Others is so pervasive that one's existence as one's own self is cast into doubt. Only by starting from a contrived theoretical position can the traditional approach to Others get under way. Since that position is pre-empted by Heidegger's analysis, the traditional question allegedly dissolves.

This conclusion is tempting, but one must be careful. Perhaps there are *different* questions; instead of displacing the traditional issue, Heidegger may have discovered a new one. The crucial question is whether the impersonal mode of selfness requires the actual or acknowledged existence of Others, for if it does *not*, then the traditional question is independent of Heidegger's position and is not really displaced by it.

Even if authentic selfness is only a modification of the impersonal self, one nevertheless has a more vivacious and articulate sense of self in that state; perhaps the traditional question with all its presuppositions — including the more vivid awareness of self — *applies*, takes root, when one exists in this state. The traditional question would then simply arise at a different point; Heidegger must show that being one's own self does not reintroduce the traditional problematic.

In addition, a "wild child" brought up by wolves might exist as an impersonal self, dominated by herd-requirements. If one presumes that this child has had no contact with humans, then existing as an impersonal self may not presuppose the existence of other persons, only of other quasi-conscious creatures.

Also, even if one supposes that Heidegger dissolves the traditional question, the fact that there are two basic modes of existing (authentic/ inauthentic) raises the question of how one determines which mode of existence another person has. There may thus still be a problem about one's knowledge of *how* he exists *even if* there is no problem about the fact *that* he exists.

One thus cannot conclude that Heidegger successfully eliminates the traditional question. Again, the connection between his attack on the tradition and his own theory is weak. This third type of defense also fails to establish his general position. Heidegger's critique of the tradition provides a fuller *understanding* of his own position, but it does not offer the convincing defense he needs.

Synopsis

Although Heidegger presents some intriguing propositions, his defense of them leaves much to be desired. His subsumption arguments are not always successful, and even when they are plausible, their success comes at a high price; Heidegger papers over the differences between the elements conjoined in his existentials. Though his descriptive elucidations can have real impact on receptive people, they do not convincingly establish the adequacy of his position. Even his challenges to the tradition are not as compelling as they should be. Suitably reinterpreted, Heidegger's theory contains important contributions, but the arguments he offers need to be tightened and supplemented.

Heidegger's contributions

Although I have so far been critical of much of Heidegger's theory, I do not wish to slight the value of his contributions to an adequate phenomenology of intersubjectivity. These must now be noted, and their implications clarified. Heidegger offers four contributions of enduring interest.

First. If one reformulates the *kind* of relatedness Heidegger discovers and details how the existentials derive from interactions with Others, then Heidegger's structures will be significant discoveries. Although they may no longer be existentials in his sense, they will illuminate many forms of social life. They are not universal, necessary features of being human, nor do they exist a priori. One can be human and lack these structures, and they emerge in the course of long-term interaction with Others and are shaped by the kind of interaction that takes place. Heidegger's structures differ from Sartre's and Hegel's in that they do not emerge suddenly through a particular experience, and they often constitute the background on which a particular interaction occurs, but they are compatible with these other kinds of essentially social bonds.

Second. Heidegger's descriptions of everyday life are more illuminating than those that would derive from the traditional epistemological approach to Others. In addition, his results alter the basic approaches that govern efforts to know Others. Being-with is a more general form of relatedness than knowing, and Heidegger's analysis of the former transforms what is involved in the latter. Not only does he show that knowing objects is a different process – a more practical process – than theoretical contemplation, he notes that one's perception of and attunement to Others is distinct from one's relation to objects. One's typical relatedness to Others involves solicitude, foresight, and forebearance. For Heidegger, to elucidate how one knows people when one sits with them in cafes, shops with them in markets, works alongside them, or plays games with them will be far more illuminating than to stare at them interrogatively in search of some certification of their conscious states. Unfortunately, Heidegger does not pursue his very brief remarks about *knowing* Others; he merely points in the direction of a new theory rather than working out the important details that might have effected the transformation from one paradigm to another.

Third. Heidegger takes advantage of the "flaw" to which Sartre objected – that his Other remains abstract, generalized, and unrelated to concrete other persons in the environment. The *positive* side of Heidegger's theory is his realization that there are abstract mediations which sometimes suffuse or dominate our interactions with Others. Thus, to apprehend the *concrete* Other before one is often an *achievement.* To perceive Others is not initially or always to grasp them as differentiated, unique beings; even when one does succeed in grasping them this way, one's perception is often filtered (e.g., by stereotypes, expectations, projections). Thus, Heidegger's analysis opens an important new question that is distinct from the question of self's relation to concrete Others, viz., the relation of a person to Others in general, to the community as such, and the various modalities such relatedness can take. There is thus an ontological question concerning the generalized Other as well as one concerning concrete Others, and the two questions may require different answers. Heidegger suggests that there are more phenomena in the interpersonal field to clarify than concrete Others.

Fourth. Heidegger shows that persons do not necessarily exist as individuals. Whether individuality is valuable is uncertain, but Heidegger shows that it is not a *necessary* feature, and may not even be the *typical* feature, of being human. To exist as an individual, personal self is an achievement, and thus individual separateness cannot be the point of departure in an investigation of the relation between self and Other. I agree that pre-personal existence, the impersonal mode of selfness, often dominates one's life. The fact that one's bodily organism is self-contained and distinct from other bodily organisms does not entail that individual, self-contained, independent persons necessarily are correlated to those bodily organisms. The ontology of persons has too long suffered from the analogy to physical objects and from Cartesian dualism; that ontology has to be refurbished, and new grounds on which to develop it more accurately must be found. Heidegger makes a significant contribution to this task.

Chapter 4

Sartre

An introduction to Sartre

Before I explain the central tenets of Sartre's theory of Others, I shall clarify some of the aims and conclusions of the earlier sections of *Being and Nothingness.*

The aims and conclusions of *Being and Nothingness*

Sartre subtitles his major treatise "an essay on phenomenological ontology." The book is an ontological inquiry in so far as it elucidates the various types of entities there are, clarifies the differences in their modes of existence, and exhibits their relationships to one another. Sartre's project is phenomenological in so far as he elucidates the central structures of lived experience. Sartre's essay is an unusual combination of abstract conceptual reasoning and sensitivity to philosophically illuminating concrete experiences.

Like Heidegger, Sartre believes that the nature of lived experience is systematically concealed. Much philosophical theory, and especially Husserlian phenomenology, issues primarily from a reflective standpoint. Reflection alters and veils the real characteristics of pre-reflective experience. Sartre seeks to recover the realities of lived experience by purifying the reflective act and carefully describing the results.[1] Sartre's phenomenology is rigorous and rooted in description, but he refuses to adopt the transcendental standpoint that is the hallmark of Husserl's enterprise.[2]

The basic distinction Sartre discovers is that between material objects (being-in-itself) and conscious being (being-for-itself).[3] In order to describe the relationships between these two sorts of Being, he presents a full analysis of the modes of consciousness and the structures through which conscious beings relate to their surroundings. Sartre offers an exhaustive analysis of the nature of persons in the course of his discussion. One of his essential points about consciousness is that it is inherently empty; its content is provided by what is not-it. Consciousness cannot exist by itself; it exists only because it is *conscious* of something in some mode, and its own nature is exhausted in a pure apprehension of its object.[4]

Prior to his analysis of Others in *Being and Nothingness*, Sartre elucidates the basic characteristics of all conscious acts (to be intentional or directed and to be simultaneously non-directedly or non-thetically conscious of themselves),[5] some basic types of consciousness (perception, reflection, bad faith),[6] the basic relation between conscious and non-conscious beings (negation or nihilation),[7] the structures through which the world is apprehended and organized by a conscious being (possibilities, value, the circuit of selfness, facticity, and transcendence),[8] and the manner in which temporality and the psychic self are experienced.[9]

Sartre includes a discussion of other conscious beings in this study for three reasons. First, the Other-*as-subject* is a unique, ontologically irreducible entity. Second, by becoming conscious of the Other-as-subject, a new *dimension of oneself emerges sui generis* — one's *being-for-Others (l'être-pour-autrui)*, which I will henceforth call "the social self." Sartre's study of the structures of consciousness and types of entities would be incomplete without an analysis of Others and of their relationship to oneself. Third, Others provide a special means by which conscious beings seek to achieve their basic aim — to become self-sufficient and yet retain an absolute freedom.

In order to comprehend how Others do this, a brief excursus into Sartre's central thesis about this basic aim is needed. Sartre's central theme is that while people (conscious beings) are indeed distinct from material objects (non-conscious beings), the distinguishing feature is a curse rather than a blessing.[10] Material objects are complete, self-sufficient, full, and inert; they need not sustain themselves to remain what they are; they simply are what they are.[11] Conscious beings have exactly the opposite status; they are never complete, never self-sufficient, always empty and self-transcending; hence, they must constantly sustain what they have been in order to continue being it. To achieve or retain identity is a *task*, a project. At any point, persons can break from their past and define themselves anew.[12] Conscious beings are also insufficient in that they constantly project goals in order to embody ideals, but ideals require a continuing commitment in order to be sustained. Thus, conscious beings can never simply be what they seek to be; they must continually make-themselves-be-it.

According to Sartre, the *basic goal* which encompasses all of a person's specific goals is to attain self-sufficiency (like material objects) without sacrificing consciousness.[13] If people could succeed, they would be God-like, for God, if He existed, would be a self-moving creative plenitude — losing Himself only to recover Himself. Unfortunately, persons cannot achieve this basic goal; their self-recovery can never be complete.[14]

Instead of accepting the usual division between mind and body, Sartre substitutes an alternative double-aspect theory of persons. Each person has elements of facticity (which is that aspect of people that *resembles* inert material objects, e.g., the past, the body-as-object, a social definition) and elements of transcendence (which represents the aspect of consciousness proper, e.g., future possibilities, values, the body-subject). People possess both aspects at once at every moment.[15] Although their essential aspect is transcendence, they always bear a burden of facticity; they exist in a specific situation (body, place, historical moment) which is not wholly their own creation. People exist without foundation or a pre-given plan; thus, they must provide themselves a foundation and implement their own plans.

People sometimes deceive themselves into believing that they have provided themselves a foundation; they do this by interpreting their transcendent aspects as elements of facticity or vice versa.[16] Other people offer a whole new arena in which this sort of self-deception may occur, for Others create one of the dimensions of one's facticity: one's being-for-Others (*l'être-pour-autrui* or "the social self"). The social self exists because of Others, but it genuinely qualifies oneself. One cannot alter it by oneself, and once it is experienced, one cannot escape it. If one could control this dimension of oneself, one could provide oneself with a foundation, for one would be a self-created *object*. Since this dimension is essentially dependent on Others, the attempt to control it entails an attempt to control them. For Sartre, this theme informs all concrete relations with Others.

The aims of Sartre's theory of Others

Sartre's theory of Others is complex and original; he offers nothing less than a theoretical clarification of a dimension of other people that no previous philosopher had seen, one which largely explains one's primitive resistance to solipsism. This dimension is the Other-as-subject, and it explains one's resistance to solipsism via its effects; it creates a new dimension for one – the social self.

Sartre's conception of the Other-as-subject overshadows anything that traditional philosophy had meant by "the subjectivity of Others." Sartre shows that the conception that Others' subjectivity is hidden, i.e., that it is somehow inside their bodies and at best signified by their behavior, accurately characterizes only one dimension of the Other – the Other-as-object. It completely fails to capture his subjectivity. That subjectivity is best expressed in his power to constitute a dimension of oneself and to prevent the realization of one's own aims. It is manifest in the capacity, which any other person has, to make an object of oneself either by looking at and categorizing one or by resisting one's own projects. To be objectified by the Other is to be totalized, defined, judged, limited – incorporated into a system of ends that one has not chosen – and at the mercy of an alien consciousness.

This objectified self is an aspect of oneself that haunts one and, according to Sartre, conditions all one's relationships with Others. One experiences it most markedly when one feels oneself under the gaze of another person. One's experience of the social self is disorienting; it displaces one's own hold on the world. Quite literally, one loses one's own subjectivity and becomes an object. Thus, the Other's subjectivity effects a radical transformation of one's existence, a change of modality: from subject to object.

Sartre claims he is not seeking to *prove* the existence of Others; he is best interpreted as explicating the lived reality of Others by investigating the implications of essentially-social states of consciousness, e.g., shame and fear.[17] I think Sartre is offering a kind of transcendental argument. He does assert that the Other-as-subject is a necessary condition for the emergence of the social self, and he defends the ontological independence of the Other-as-subject by demonstrating that the social self cannot be derived either from oneself alone or from the Other-as-object. Sartre concludes that the social self is not reducible to any other source or structure.[18]

As a transition from his discussion of Husserl, Hegel, and Heidegger to his own theory, Sartre summarizes the outlines of his position by suggesting four conditions for the solution to the problem of Others: (1) one must find a way of elucidating one's *certainty* of the Other's existence, a certainty that is more basic than one's knowledge of them;[19] (2) this can be done by discovering an internal or essential relation between self and Others — a structure that transforms one but which cannot exist without Others (the social self);[20] (3) this relation will bond one to a dimension of Others that had rarely been previously acknowledged (the Other-as-subject);[21] (4) these will all become manifest once one shifts from the objectifying, third-person point of view characteristic of knowledge to the first-person point of view characteristic of phenomenological elucidation.[22]

The divisions and strategy of the exposition

Sartre elaborates his position in three distinct stages, and I shall follow his pattern in this exposition and critique. Initially, he presents a phenomenological elucidation of experiencing Others. He first analyzes the experience of the Other-as-object and then turns to the Other-as-subject; these descriptions provide the foundation for the rest of his theory.[23] He follows this elucidation with a preliminary version of his theory, which I shall reduce to five key claims. In them he clarifies the basic relation of the Other-as-subject to the social self, defends some important claims about the social self, he marshals evidence for the central proposition of his theory of interpersonal experience: the exclusivity claim. This claim asserts that one cannot both look at (i.e., objectify) the Other and simultaneously be looked at (i.e., be objectified) by him; one exists in either one mode or the other at any given time.[24]

Sartre continues his exposition by presenting a more abstract discussion of the nature of the Other-as-subject.[25] The core of this discussion consists of an argument that the Other-as-subject is a necessary condition for the social self. In response to some potential objections, he clarifies the status and boundaries of the Other-as-subject. Even if it is concrete rather than abstract, it cannot be individuated or known like most objects. Sartre's response to these objections forces one to completely rethink his position.

Sartre completes his theory of Others with an abstract characterization of the bond between oneself and the Other-as-subject: the social self.[26] He demarcates its relation to the person it qualifies and to the Other who creates it; in doing so Sartre clarifies the basic relation between self and Other — internal negation. He also defends two additional contentions, which I shall call "the exhaustivity claim" and "the asymmetry claim": viz., that these two modes of existing (subject and object; looking and being looked at) represent the only possible modes of experiencing Others and that, whenever the self is in one of the modes (e.g., looking), the Other is in the opposite mode (e.g., being looked at).

Sartre offers a distinctive approach in each of these three movements of his presentation. The second one (the transcendental argument) will be most familiar to philosophers, and my critical approach can therefore be more straightforward — to question the truth of the premises and the adequacy of Sartre's replies to objections. The first one (the phenomenological base) is the most concrete and descriptive; there the task is to consider alternative descriptions and possibilities that raise doubts about the general conclusions Sartre seeks to extract from his descriptions. The third one (the ontology of the social self) remains theoretical, but it addresses ontological issues in an unusual fashion. There the task will be to develop alternative ontologies on the basis of my earlier, alternative descriptions and to question the legitimacy of the general implications Sartre draws from his discussion. Thus, my critical approaches will be tailored to Sartre's distinctive task in each movement of his theory.

Although I am dividing this examination of Sartre's theory into three separate sections, *within* each section, I shall initially offer a full exposition of Sartre's position and *only then* provide criticisms. This method will allow the reader to formulate his own assessment of Sartre's theory before reading mine. In addition, this method of separating the analysis and critique of each phase will allow a more balanced reading of Sartre's position. If one is presented with Sartre's theory all at once, one easily becomes overwhelmed. His descriptions seems so insightful that his theory commands conviction too quickly. Later, one reacts strongly against one's former uncritical assent and then tends to reject aspects of the position that are more defensible than they seem. Consequently, a piecemeal presentation and discussion has the advantage of opening alternative possibilities early so that one can remain continuously critical, and it also prevents too cursory a rejection of Sartre's views because his replies can be examined immediately after the objections have been presented. The disadvantage of this method of presentation is that later developments in the theory may rectify earlier infelicities and thus obviate earlier criticisms. To minimize this disadvantage, I will try to incorporate, or at least indicate, later complexities while explicating earlier parts of the theory, or else I shall postpone discussion of a difficult point until everything relevant to it has been clarified.

An initial Sartrean objection

Before beginning the exposition, I feel obligated to mention one major interpretive bias of this chapter. Many of my criticisms offer *supplements* to Sartre's theory: I often claim that his views are *incomplete* rather than incorrect, and I attempt to rectify his oversights in order to develop a theory that has wider application. Some of these criticisms directly invalidate Sartre's position *if* one interprets it as clarifying essential, invariant structures of interpersonal experience. Very often Sartre gives the impression that this is what he intends and that, in effect, there is nothing more to say about interpersonal experience (and relationships). In general, my objections show that his claim to have presented an exhaustive theory (or even *the* essential structures) of interpersonal experience is incorrect.

This means that Sartre might seek to sidestep the central thrust of my criticisms by holding that he is presenting only the philosophically important aspects of interpersonal experience and is thus deliberately oversimplifying to underline facts that are crucial to his inquiry. He might thus contend that although some complexities have been passed over, they add nothing of philosophical interest and do not controvert the central claims of his position.

My stance with respect to this reply will be to show that, in all important cases, my objections do have important philosophical implications; they do not exhibit mere details or oversights, but are elements of experience that cannot be neglected if one is to present an adequate theory of Others and their relationship to oneself. Moreover, I simply deny that Sartre intends to present *some* aspects of experience that have special philosophical importance. Sartre draws sweeping conclusions about the *necessary failure* of all *possible* human relationships on the basis of his theory of interpersonal experience; consequently, one must interpret his claims to be about the *necessary* features of interpersonal experience. To the extent that important exceptions to those

179

claims exist, the large conclusions he derives from them must be correspondingly restricted.

To further defend himself against my objections, Sartre might draw on a footnote to his theory of concrete relationships among people.[27] This footnote suggests that the theory that grounds his conclusions is not universally valid, but is only valid at this historical moment or in this culture or under some similar qualification. My response here is that my emendations demonstrate some important alternative modes of interpersonal experience (in this era and culture) and indicate the boundaries that circumscribe Sartre's 'type' of interpersonal orientation. Hence, neither of Sartre's very general replies will undermine the force of my objections.

On the other hand, I do not deny the value of Sartre's central theoretical insights. I think that *no serious philosophical work can be done on intersubjectivity without taking account of Sartre's contribution.* I will, however, struggle to assess its true significance and attempt to retain only what is genuinely accurate in his analysis.

The phenomenological base

The Other-as-object

Sartre begins by describing the mode of existence of the Other that is most familiar: the Other-as-object. Consider a Sunday afternoon in a public park. Sartre notes that one ordinarily perceives objects as instruments; the world perfectly mirrors one's immediate purposes. Thus, if the park appears as a palette of colors, a symphony of natural harmonies, and a feast of exquisite smells, then one's purposes are aesthetic. If, however, one is determining which parcel of land to purchase from the city in order to develop a new subdivision, then the qualities dominating one's attention will be the lay of the land, its relation to surrounding commercial development, the ease of excavation, and the firmness of the ground.

If one suddenly apprehends another person, a significant change in one's perception occurs. Sartre notes that the previous organization of the world is momentarily shattered; a *new* organization and a new set of properties are suddenly superimposed on it.[28] One may, for example, react with fear; the Other's menace will then appear on the face of the world as a set of sticks and stones that may become weapons. The space between oneself and the tree beside which the man is passing no longer appears as the perfect distance for appreciating the scenery, but as the minimum distance that must be traversed to attack one. Moreover, the world's objects turn different faces to the other person: a nicely shaped stone may suddenly appear as a potential missile.[29] A new set of properties, meanings, and relations emerge as a result of seeing the Other. These relations are the correlates of *his potential* purposes. These new elements that Others introduce into one's perception of the world may be evanescent or only peripherally present; the Other may be absorbed in a book or lost in contemplation – oblivious to everything around him. Nevertheless, the innocence of one's solitary perception is compromised. Even if the quaking and superimposition that Others typically create is minimal, the mere suggestion of it is unsettling.[30]

One can clarify this transformation by contrasting it with the perception of an obstacle: one is ready to take a trip, but the car will not start. Either one calls a serviceman and prepares for a delay, or one travels by other means, or one abandons one's plans. The instrumental organization of the world simply alters in response to one's change of purpose; one remains at its center despite its recalcitrance. When one apprehends Others, one is momentarily deposed: an alternative center challenges one's hegemony. In Sartre's example, the Other remains *objectified*. This means that the displacement he creates is *fixed*; his purposes are registered but circumscribed. One recovers and integrates his organization of the world into one's own.[31] In short, as long as one still *looks at* the other person, his purposes are subsumed under one's own. There is a whisper of something more overwhelming, but the whisper dies away. However, this momentary quaking, the super-imposition and quasi-displacement, can be used as a clue with which to elucidate the Other-as-subject.[32]

There are problems with this analysis: one can imagine many kinds of cases in which one experiences persons as objects and no displace-ment or potential reorganization of one's world occurs. One case occurs when one is completely preoccupied with one's own concerns and barely registers the presence of other people. If one is running to catch a bus, one may remain oblivious to the purposes of Others even though one perceives them. Another case occurs when one encounters persons in role-governed relationships. Often the roles of Others com-plement one's own, e.g., teacher to student, salesperson to buyer, bureaucrat to citizen. The other person's organization of the world is *already incorporated* into one's own via the rules that govern the relationship; consequently, no quaking or alteration of one's own instrumental organization occurs. Only if Others emerge from their roles (and hence if they appear as *more* than mere objects) does one's own organization become compromised. A third case occurs when the person one encounters is *familiar* (e.g., a lover, friend, or family member). In such cases that person's habitual instrumental ordering may dovetail with one's own. Very often some part of one's world is already structured for them and with them; hence their organization is not experienced as distinct from one's own. Finally, one can experi-ence Others as potential *extensions* of one's own purposes. In such situations the Other's instrumental organization is assimilated to one's own; he is perceived as a satellite.

Naturally, in each of these cases, the Sartrean effect *can* occur: the bystander may trip one; the Other's role may be that of an executioner; the familiar person may betray one; and the satellite may refuse to stay in orbit. But these possibilities do not alter the fact that Sartre's condition does not occur in all types of encounters in which Others are objectified. Indeed, it primarily characterizes only one specific type: strangers who are perceived as having purposes that are not complementary to one's own. Sartre's objectified Other conceals an element of subjectivity, but in actual experience, Others can really be experienced as mere objects.

The Other-as-subject

Sartre's phenomenological investigation of the Other-as-subject can now be examined. He elucidates this experience by contrasting it with a pre-reflective consciousness that is absorbed in a project. Sartre's keyhole example is justly famous and recounted by all his expositors; for variety, I shall offer a different case which will exemplify all the important points.

The central example

F., an adolescent, has secretly stolen into his older sister's room and is engrossed in her personal diary. Five features of F.'s situation should be noted.

First, in the center of F.'s attention are the sentences in the diary, their meaning, and the images they evoke. F., immersed in his reading, neither defines what he is doing nor experiences any qualities that might be applied to his project. Sartre characterizes this fact by saying that F. does not *know* he is reading his sister's diary but simply *is* the process of reading.[33] F. has no self-awareness except the temporal organization and the peripheral self-registration of the reading process. He has no awareness that *he* is reading the diary.[34] A woman's adventures are simply unfolding.

In addition, the situation exhibits a particular organization which manifests F.'s purposes like a mirror. The demand that pages be turned, the relative absence of everything in the room but the diary, and the savory taste that flavors the air, express his project and organize his possibilities.[35]

Also, F.'s action is performed with a naive innocence that precedes the experience of good and evil. As long as he remains immersed, no judgment can qualify the event, and no divided consciousness or bad conscience can infect his action.[36]

Moreover, F. does not perceive himself as located, either spatially or temporally. His time is the internal time of the reading; it is no particular time of day or date. His space is the space of the pages and the imaginary scenes they evoke. His future is the set of pages yet to be turned, the privileged events yet to be plundered. His past is the set of budding sexual experiences that provide him a frame of reference to comprehend what he reads. His present is only his presence to the diary, his collusion with its self-revelation.[37]

Finally, F. is master of the situation. At any point he can decide he has had enough and abandon the diary. Only when this free flow, these open possibilities, and this lack of definition disappear, will F. realize his then-past mastery.[38]

Suddenly, outside, a floorboard creaks, the doorknob turns, and briskly in walks F.'s sister. Caught in the act! Now, only the social self exists. F. experiences only what she sees.

The basic transformations

Sartre elucidates the transformative power of the Other-as-subject and the burdensomeness of the resultant social self by noting the changes in F.'s experiences.

The first change is that F. experiences an overwhelming consciousness of self even though he remains on the pre-reflective level of awareness. His act has undergone a coagulation; it now has a unity, a character, a name. F. experiences himself as a defined person: intruder, spy, traitor. The accusation leaps from her eyes and surround him like a cocoon. This solidification of himself is his experience of the social self.[39] His existence now has a new dimension. Sartre thinks that only the Other-as-subject can motivate this transformation. Although the social self is created by Others, one nevertheless accepts it as an incarnation of oneself. F. becomes the embodiment of his sister's vision; even if he does not share it, he does not treat it as a delusion or an error. Through essentially social emotions such as shame, fear, and pride, the social self is continually reawakened.[40]

Sartre holds that one cannot ultimately control the social self, for although one can try to influence the Other's judgment, the Other is free to see one in whatever way he wishes. His power is grasped through one's own impotence. Moreover, one is ultimately blind to the content of the social self, for although the Other may communicate his judgment in deeds or words, to the degree to which Others can lie, dissemble, fail to know their own minds precisely, or fail to express themselves accurately, one cannot be sure of the content of one's social self. Its existence is certain and intrusive, even if its nature is hidden. It is like a shadow thrown by one's own actions in the light of the Other's look;

whenever one experiences the shadow, one experiences the Other-as-subject.[41]

The second change in F.'s experience is a loss of perceptual and instrumental contact with the world. While he experiences the social self, the diary before him disappears.[42] His original project loses its impetus; the world no longer offers a set of possible options. He now exists in a different mode: mere objectivity. F. barely sees his sister, for the look itself cannot literally be looked-at. One can look into another's eyes, but they do not reveal the Other's subjectivity. When one experiences the social self, the Other's *eyes* are hidden; one is overwhelmed by the Other's *look*.[43]

The third change is a loss of innocence; to experience the Other-as-subject is to fall from grace. Moral judgments about oneself now become possible because they have something to qualify. F. may be marked as evil in his sister's eyes, and this stigma will haunt him. Even when the Other's judgments are positive, they are no less haunting and no more reassuring, for at any moment the Other's assessment may change for reasons unrelated to anything one has done. Once one experiences the Other's subjectivity, one's acts will always have a public, external side which will be experienced with greater or lesser lucidity.

This transformation displaces one's subjectivity but never renders it unrecoverable. Though one can be mesmerized by the social self, one cannot be coincident with it. F. begins to recover himself when he begins to escape his sister's definition; he may experience its validity, but not its finality. While the social self occupies the forefront of one's attention, one's future seems closed.[44] In fact, it remains open, and one's awareness of this eventually returns. As one recovers one's own viewpoint, one's awareness of the Other-as-subject fades. Living consists in a perpetual alternation between these two viewpoints. Both are elements of one's existence, but each displaces the experience of the other. For Sartre, they exclude each other.[45]

The fourth change locates F. in objective time and space. F. now experiences himself *in his sister's room*, which is off limits, *holding his sister's diary*, which is strictly forbidden. He no longer organizes distances among things; distances become objective measures between his body and objects seen by his sister. Her space becomes his own. He can date his sister's contempt because his own time flow has stopped. Sartre believes this experience of Others is the origin of our conception of public or universal time and space.[46]

The fifth change summarizes all the rest: F. loses control of the situation; he finds himself enslaved by the Other-as-subject.[47] Every expression of his mastery — free flow of time, his own instrumental organization, a sense of possibilities — is eliminated. F. is entrapped in his nature. The social self is like a blank slate that the Other-as-subject fills in and like a cage created and sustained by the Other-as-subject.

The philosophical import of the example

Sartre's description lays a foundation for achieving his three theoretical goals: to offer an alternative response to the traditional problem of other minds; to reconceptualize the ontology of persons; and to elucidate the aim that governs all interpersonal relationships.

With respect to the traditional problem of other minds, Sartre advances two novel assertions. *First*, he seeks to elucidate one's lived certainty, rather than one's knowledge, of the existence of Others.[48] For Sartre, one does not *know* even *one's own* existence; knowledge is too meagre or distant a relation to capture one's comprehension of oneself. The simultaneous ancillary awareness that each moment of consciousness has of itself provides a *lived certainty* of one's existence. A thorough inventory of one's experiences provides a similar certainty of the existence of Others. Everyone has had experiences like the one just elucidated, but not everyone grasps their philosophical import.[49] To experience the social self is to experience the subjectivity of Others. One discovers their reality across the alteration of oneself they create. Although one can abstractly doubt one's own existence, that doubt is rendered impotent by a full clarification of consciousness; similarly, although one can abstractly doubt the existence of Others, that doubt is neutralized by a full elucidation of the experience of the social self.[50] Sartre seeks to reveal a relation to Others that is more intimate and more penetrating than knowledge.

Second, Sartre criticizes the traditional project of *knowing* Others because it conceals the phenomenon to be clarified. For Sartre, the effort to know objectifies what it addresses, but to objectify Others is to conceal their subjectivity. As long as one's attention is directed to the Other's expressions with the hope of finding sufficient signs of his consciousness, one cannot experience the Other's subjectivity. Only if one shifts one's attention to the transformations of one's own experience, can the subjectivity of Others be apprehended.[51] Only when one's experience is confined to the Other-as-object, does one need to *infer* the existence of another consciousness; once the Other-as-subject appears, his reality is only too pressing.

With respect to the ontology of persons, Sartre seeks to show that each person is ontologically dependent on Others; no one is complete in himself. One dimension of oneself, the social self, is created and controlled by Others, and vice versa.[52] Each person lives in an additional dimension because of Others, and each creates an additional dimension for Others.

With respect to personal relations, Sartre tries to establish that the social self constitutes the problem which relationships seek to solve. Because the experience of the social self is so disorienting, one perpetually struggles to control it. Only two strategies are available: one can constantly objectify Others and thereby seek to prevent the emergence of one's social self, or one can induce the Other to see one exactly as one wishes to be seen and thereby control his subjectivity even as one submits to it. Sartre believes that all concrete relationships can be reduced to these two strategies and that, since they seek to control what cannot ultimately be controlled, they will all fail.[53]

The first series of claims

This first movement of Sartre's theory can be summarized in five propositions:

Claim 1   The experience of the Other-as-subject is materially equivalent to the experience of the Other's look directed at one.[54]

Claim 2   The experience of the Other's look directed at one is materially equivalent to the experience of the emergence and/or continuance of the social self.[55]

Claim 3   The experience of the emergence and/or continuance of the social self is materially equivalent to the experience of the five changes described above.[56]

Claim 4   The experience of the Other-as-subject and that of the Other-as-object are exclusive.[57]

Claim 5   The content of one's social self is ultimately unknown to one.[58]

I shall demonstrate that each of these claims has serious difficulties.

The first three claims form a unit. Although Sartre probably did not regard them as distinct assertions, one discovers their differences through analysis. Their present formulation requires a brief comment. I have used the notion of material equivalence to relate kinds of experiences rather than statements because Sartre's own formulations are cast in the material mode. This version could be transposed into the formal mode without difficulty, but since Sartre's inquiry is phenomenological, I have retained his manner of expression. Moreover, the notion of material equivalence is neither too weak nor too strong for his purposes. It leaves open the issue of how the equivalences should be interpreted: as conceptual or as empirical or in some other fashion. I shall address this issue in greater detail when I discuss Sartre's transcendental argument. My criticisms will stand regardless of how one interprets these connections. If Sartre means to be defining technical terms, then the objections will demonstrate the limits of the empirical application of that terminology. If he means to elucidate empirically necessary and sufficient conditions, then the objections offer counter-examples and thus define the limits of his theory.

Claim 1

Claim 1 asserts that the experience of the Other-as-subject is materially equivalent to the experience of the Other's look directed at one. The relevant questions are: are there additional ways of experiencing the transforming power of the Other's subjectivity, and does the experience of the Other's look always imply an experience of his subjectivity? Consider the second question.

There are, of course, countless cases in which Others in fact are observing and judging one and yet one does not experience the Other-as-subject in Sartre's sense, simply because one does not realize they are doing so. However, these cases do *not* provide counter-examples to the claim as stated, for it asserts that the *experience* of the Other's look is sufficient for the experience of the Other-as-subject, and in the alleged counter-example, that experience does not occur.

In order to forestall all such counter-examples, I have cast all of Sartre's claims in terms referring to how the world is experienced rather than to how it is. This interpretation permits Sartre's assertions the greatest chance of accuracy. However, circumventing such counter-examples incurs a price: a potential gap is opened between one's experience of the Other and his actual existence, a gap that must be bridged by careful argument and/or elucidation.[59]

Some initial problems The Other-as-subject neutralizes one's organization of the world and imposes a definition on one. However, one can experience the Other's look and fail to experience him as a subject in this sense. One may intentionally design one's actions to be seen and interpreted by the Other. If he follows one's lead, one experiences him as an object in one's control rather than a subject, despite the fact that one experiences oneself looked-at and defined by him. One can respond to the phenomenon Sartre describes by *presenting* oneself to Others. Since these exhibitions become part of the way one organizes the world, the Other's capacity to look becomes reintegrated into one's purposes even though one may continuously experience the transformation he engenders.

Sartre's first reply to this objection would be to grant such cases[60] but to hold that one can never completely control the Other. To try to influence his appraisal by posturing is dangerous since he may see through one's veneer; one cannot be sure he will be captivated. One's attempts to determine whether one's act is convincing often cause one's demise.[61] Moreover, one's sense of the Other's threatening subjectivity is inescapable; one must continue to perform because of this. But even if one does sense this subjectivity in the background, one still does not experience the Other-as-subject in Sartre's sense (even though one *is* experiencing the Other's look) because, as long as the Other cooperates,

Sartre

one's world is not transformed and one's 'nature' is not imposed. Although the Other's look still traces one's outline, it draws according to one's own promptings. The Other becomes a controlled, mesmerized subject.

Sartre's second reply would be that in such circumstances the Other has become an *objectified-subject*, which is only a form of the Other-as-object. For example, if F. were to look back at his sister's look and constitute her as 'the one who sees me as evil,' then she would be an objectified subject for F. Her look would lack power: it would be a property of her-nature-for-him. Another example occurs when one observes another person objectifying a Third. Even though he may dominate the Third, he is still an object for oneself. Since the power of his gaze does not extend to oneself, he is an objectified-subject. Sartre's claims about the Other-as-subject cannot be refuted by examples which appeal to the objectified-subject because this is a mode of the Other-as-object.

But the *mesmerized* subject described above is not an objectified-subject since his look *still operates*; one's identity is constituted by it. When another is objectified, this capacity to define one is neutralized; his look loses its force. The look of a mesmerized subject has force, but it derives primarily from oneself rather than the Other. One experiences oneself objectified, but this objective nature is projected and sought by oneself.

Sartre might also reply that one *is* experiencing the Other-as-subject *just because* one continues to experience the social self. But this is precisely what the example questions. The fact that one experiences the social self indicates that one is experiencing a Sartrean *look*, but the fact that the whole structure is integrated into one's own purposes indicates that one is *not* experiencing the Sartrean subject. In such cases the Other is experienced neither as a subject nor an object in Sartre's sense, but in a third modality – *mesmerized* subjectivity – which lies between the two and is not reducible to *objectified* subjectivity.

Consider now the other direction of the equivalence in Claim 1. Is the experience of the Other's look necessary for the experience of the Other-as-subject? Can transforming subjectivity be discovered in experiences which have very different implications than Sartre's look?

Although Others obviously exhibit different kinds of subjectivity, not all such manifestations will constitute problems for Sartre. Too many critics have missed this point. They insist that Others can express subjectivity through love or concern, and they believe they have refuted Sartre. They neglect to show that their alternative modes of subjectivity have the transformative power and philosophical import of Sartre's Other-as-subject. To do this, one must show that when such alleged additional modes of subjectivity are experienced, they essentially alter – create new modes or structures of – one's experience.[62]

188

Alternative modes of the Other's subjectivity   At least three additional modes of the Other's subjectivity fulfill this condition. Heidegger's theory can help elucidate the first. Heidegger claims that one experiences a challenge to become authentic in the presence of an authentic person. The authentic Other serves as an example; in his presence, one evaluates one's life differently, and one's sense of what is possible broadens. The authentic Other transmits a more serious, intense relation to ideals. Through his challenge, one's former ideals become enlivened, and new ones emerge. To be sure, one must be accessible to his challenge, but his way of life is stimulating in itself. Here the Other's subjectivity is his radiance, his capacity to inspire, and the transformation he effects is the strengthening of one's will.

Sartre might question the frequency of this experience, but that would miss the point. One could question the frequency of his paradigmatic look as well, if one stressed its most extreme form. The essential requirement is the *transformation of one's mode of existence* – one's possibilities and one's relation to the world. The authentic Other has this effect; he calls one's life into question. Although one may fail to apprehend this effect, a similar blindness can veil the power of Sartre's look. When they are experienced, both modes of the Other's subjectivity have influential transformative effects. The frequency of the paradigmatic experience is less important than the pervasiveness of the alteration involved.

A second additional mode of the Other's subjectivity is Hegelian recognition. In a face-to-face situation, recognition sustains one's reality and value. For Hegel, an encounter with another creates a disequilibrium. Who and what one is fall into brackets; one loses oneself. If one receives the Other's recognition, this sense of oneself is returned, and one's sense of self is expanded in the process. If one is never recognized, one may experience a disintegration of self. Mutual recognition elevates each and unites both; each discovers himself in and through the Other.[63] In mutual recognition, one can transcend Sartre's level of perpetually conflicting personal relationships and achieve genuine harmony.

A third dimension of the Other's subjectivity emerges in the experiences of co-feeling and emotional infection in which one loses one's individuality. Different degrees of fusion into a larger whole are possible. At an exciting sports event one only senses an ancillary union with other spectators; at a moving concert the fusion may be greater, but if one is a co-participant in the game or the musical ensemble, one's fusion with other participants can be complete. One's awareness of a distinct individuality simply fades, and one is incorporated into a larger whole which functions as a unit. Here the Other-as-subject is the collective subjectivity. The union can be so complete that experiences seem like universals – instantiated everywhere at once – or like eddies in a single common stream. Thus, the implications of this mode of subjectivity are again quite distinct from those of Sartre's look.

None of these additional modes of the Other's subjectivity emerge through the Other's capacity to look, and none of their effects resemble those of the Sartrean Other-as-subject. Each requires further analysis and description to be established as an alternative to Sartre's conception. At the end of this chapter I shall use Sartre's own method of elucidation to document a richer vision of the Other's subjectivity than he was able to achieve.[64]

Claim 2

Claim 2 asserts that the experience of the Other's look directed at one is materially equivalent to the experience of the social self. One side of this equivalence asserts that the experience of the Other's look is sufficient for the experience of the social self. This assertion has a number of difficulties.

Another's face can express many kinds of looks; for example, he can look angrily, intently, doubtfully, devotedly, or even blankly. These looks communicate without words; often one responds more to them than to explicit behavior or testimony; yet only in rare cases do they motivate the experience of the social self. Sartre would discount such examples by indicating that they are *objectified looks* which simply lack the power to engender the social self. The alleged counter-examples fail because they do not address the Sartrean look. This reply is adequate for *some* of these cases; often another's look lacks operative effect; it only expresses his state of mind.

In other cases, however, another's look can have the power to transform one even though it does not produce the experience of the social self. Such looks can embody demands, exclamations, imperatives, invocations, or invitations. Like tentacles, the Other's spirit can envelop one through his look, and one responds subliminally and semi-automatically: one swoons, defers, obeys, withdraws, or melts. There is the blatant appeal of the television-commercial starlet as she smiles suggestively, and there is the boss's demand for silence in his folded arms, screwed-up eyes, and impatient swiveling.

In these looks, the Other's intentions are even *more pressing* than in Sartre's gaze, but *they do not operate through the social self.* Sartre's look paralyzes and displaces one's subjectivity, but in these looks, the Other insinuates his intentions into one's responses; one's subjectivity is retained, but it conforms to the Other's command. Thus, there are looks which are even more potent than Sartre's and which do not operate through the mediation of the social self.

In addition, not all looks that are experienced as *seeking* to effect a judgment, definition, or evaluation of oneself *succeed* in so doing, and such looks do not evoke the experience of the social self, even though one experiences them as efforts to objectify. For example, one can remain indifferent; one may experience the Other as judging one's actions, but the judgment may have no effect because one does not care. One remains impervious to the Other's assessments even though one does experience his look and his judgment.

Also, one may seek a lucid assessment from the Other and then experience his look as rash, insensitive, inattentive, or overly short-sighted. In such cases, the Other's judgment is modelled like a new coat, studied in the mirror, and rejected for lack of fit. A potential social self emerges and hovers over the scene, but it leaves one unaltered and falls away. Although there are cases in which one cognitively rejects another's definition and yet experiences the social self, the cases to which I am referring are different. One grasps the intent, but it misses. Although Sartre might claim that anything the Other sees is part of one's social self *whether or not* one accepts it, this overlooks the real phenomenological differences between the experience of those looks which penetrate and those which do not.

Yet another problem arises because Sartre fails to consider the impact of antecedent circumstances on the effect of the look. According to Sartre, the experience of the social self is like an imprisonment; it limits what was an open space. But *if* that space is *already* closed, the Sartrean look can have a *liberating* effect. It may transvalue old judg-ments or undermine habitual self-images, and thus it may reopen the future. For example, through the influence of her boyfriend, A. may come to believe she is 'too masculine.' She becomes resigned to this definition; it becomes a "nature" over which she has no control. A sensitive friend may reveal A.'s feminine nature, and though the friend's look may seek to brand A.'s character, its effect may be to free A. of her former burden. A. may find her future suddenly open; the Other's look can help her *recover* her subjectivity. Sometimes new looks simply undercut the accumulated effects of previous looks.

Each of these objections shows that another's potent look does not always motivate the experience of the Sartrean social self. What about the other direction of the equivalence in Claim 2? Does one always experience the Other's look directed at one whenever one experiences the social self?

Sartre himself raises a question about this assertion. Because he responds to it in depth later in his discussion, I shall postpone detailed treatment of it until then.[65] Here I shall mention it only in passing. The obvious problem is that a sudden eruption of the social self can occur without anyone else being present. For example, if one is walking through Central Park late at night and hears a rustling in the bushes, one will suddenly experience oneself in danger. Apprehensively one stops and cowers. But no one is there. Or consider a dancer struggling to perform a complex movement which, despite intense effort, she

191

cannot attain. Suddenly she breaks down in tears — ashamed of her clumsiness — despite the fact that she is rehearsing alone.

In both cases, the social self emerges; yet in both, *the Other's look seems to be lacking.* Can it inhere in the wind or the darkness of an empty auditorium? Eventually Sartre will answer yes to this question,[66] and this answer will create serious difficulties for his claim that the Other-as-subject is a transcendent entity.

Claim 3

Claim 3 asserts that the social self is experienced if and only if the conjunction of the five basic characteristics — a self-definition, an alienation, a loss of perceptual-instrumental contact, a location in objective space-time, and loss of control over the situation — are also experienced. This claim is more difficult to criticize because Sartre seems simply to be defining what he means rather than explicating a phenomenon. Nevertheless, a brief critique will demonstrate the experiential restrictions of this definition.

Two variables condition the effect of experiencing the social self: one's own self-image and the Other's intentions. If the Other's judgment confirms one's self-image, then the experience of the social self is not nearly so disorienting. Although one's self-image probably derives from past judgments of Others, it still functions as a buffer against the transformation Sartre describes. The Other's intentions may also function in this way. His presence may be overwhelming unless he deliberately withholds his judgments. One may still experience the Sartrean transformation, but the Other's initiative can influence its severity. The Other-as-subject does not have an unmediated relation to the social self; he must penetrate protective layers before the full effect is experienced.

Another social theorist, Erving Goffman, explores a dimension of social self that is related to Sartre's but is more encompassing.[67] One's experience of Others is a function of social definition and social perception. Consider the simple act of a greeting. Its precise meaning depends on the frame through which it is interpreted. A greeting can be an initial expression of mood, a polite convention, an invitation, an act of forgiveness, an attempt to offer support, or all of these at once. The frame that is selected depends on a complex process in which both people integrate their presentations for and interpretations of one another. Ongoing presentations and interpretations build on and react to former ones; the memory of prior events and the way individuals respond to them condition one's response to Others' actions and evaluations of oneself. Sartre's phenomenological explorations of the social self neglect to address these social interpretative factors that affect one's experience of the social self.

Another difficulty with Sartre's basic point in Claim 3, which illustrates one of the difficulties in social theory generally, is that among at least a large subset of people, entire patterns of response have altered precisely in reaction to the kind of insight Sartre had. Thus now, many years after his theory's publication, the phenomenon he describes is less pronounced among that subset of people. People who have been influenced by third-force or humanistic psychology or psychotherapy learn to particularize, restrict, and individualize their perceptions of people as they express them. So instead of saying: "You're really an awful pain," such a person will say: "Right now, I see what you are doing as being a real bother to me." Here the locus of responsibility for the judgment as well as the sequence of behavior over which the judgment ranges are made explicit, and the judgment itself is confined to a particular time; this carries the implication that it can and probably will change. This way of offering evaluations of Others emerged once the deleterious effects Sartre described became more widely understood.

Although this way of talking does not eliminate the experience of the social self in Sartre's sense, the way it is experienced and the general *effect* of experiencing it is altered. One no longer feels totalized and displaced; one is given room to respond, and even if one accepts the judgment, one has a sense of its limitations. Thus some of the most distressing aspects of the phenomenon Sartre described are being eliminated among this set of people, at least partly because of Sartre's observations. In social theory, over time, people's actions can undermine the truth of a theory.

Sartre's lack of subtlety can sometimes have important implications. One of the stronger conclusions he draws from his theory, against any form of Marxism that looks to the gradual elimination of alienation, is the assertion that the alienation *endemic* to the experience of the social self is part of man's essential interpersonal condition and *cannot* be overcome.[68] Given the general phenomenon Sartre elucidates, "alienation" can have at least three distinct meanings: (1) a sense of disparity between what the Other sees or may see and one's self-image; (2) an experienced incompatibility between a particular person's assessment and the sedimented summation of views that one takes to be one's typical social self; (3) a complete abdication to the Other's projects, point of view, judgments, and demands — a complete loss of any sense of one's own agency. The first of these is Sartre's primary meaning for "alienation," but the others frequently accompany the experience of the social self and might be thought to be essential to it.

However, none of these experiences *necessarily* accompanies the social self. One may be *liberated* from encrusted stances toward one's life by the Other's look, and the Other's judgment may be experienced as identical with those one typically experiences and also with one's own view of oneself. One can thus receive *confirmation* through the experience of the social self, as well as disorientation. Finally, the Other's active viewpoint can be identical to one's own in the case of, for example, working on a common project together – political organizing or group farming. Or one may use the Other's view of oneself to mold a group fusion among people (e.g., an orchestra conductor, a teacher). In each of these cases, the Sartrean alienation is overcome; there may always be the possibility of its reapprehension, but it is not a necessary feature of interpersonal life.

Sartre might reply here that his political point is that this alienation cannot *ultimately* be overcome – not that it cannot for a time be avoided. The possibility that some people will objectify Others cannot be eliminated. Since the social self is a necessary bond between two conscious beings, improving political, economic, or social conditions will not eliminate it. Although Sartre is partially correct in this reply, he still has not shown that the experience of the social self is always alienating. One can learn to find an appropriate response to the Other's judgments and to the intersection of his aims with one's own without experiencing Sartrean alienation. In addition, one can learn to judge Others in order to facilitate their development, and social justice can maximize interpersonal harmony. Although one can never eliminate the *possibility* of Sartrean alienation, improving social conditions can significantly reduce its destructiveness.

Hence Claim 3 must be amended. Not only are there additional factors affecting one's experience of the social self, there are many ways in which its destructiveness can be minimized. In order to achieve a complete and adequate phenomenology of interpersonal experience, these complexities must be made explicit.

Claim 4

Claim 4 is one of the important premises in the argument which concludes that struggle in interpersonal life is *unavoidable.* It asserts that the experience of the Other-as-object and the experience of the Other-as-subject (and correlatively self-as-subject and self-as-object) are *exclusive*; one can apprehend the other person either in one mode *or* the other, *never both at once.* Sartre presents some clever arguments for this view; they depend on two assumptions: (1) certain analogous experiences or properties seem to exclude one another; and (2) all states of consciousness are simple.

The first argument examines *perception.* When one perceives another, one objectifies him; one apprehends his body, his eyes, etc. But when one experiences the Other-as-subject, one does not actually *perceive* him at all; indeed, one's perceptual grasp of the world is virtually eliminated.[69] The two experiences are so distinct and so incompatible that they allegedly cannot occur at once. Sartre also draws upon the different experiences of distance in the two modes of experiencing

Others. When one perceives or looks at (objectifies) another, he appears at a given distance from one; this distance is related to the projects in which one is engaged and the salience of the Other to them. In the experience of the Other-as-subject, no distance at all is experienced; he appears immediately present: his look pierces one like the noonday sun. Again, these seem to be incompatible qualities.

Sartre's underlying view of consciousness supports these observations. He holds that regardless of the complexity of the object or the subject's non-thetic concomitants, one can exist in only one thetic mode at a given time. For example, he believes one must either be perceiving or imagining, never both at once.[70] Since the experience of the Other-as-subject is a distinct thetic mode of consciousness, Sartre concludes that it must exclude all other thetic modes, especially the one in which Others are objectified.

This claim must now be carefully examined. One should note that the notion of simultaneity cannot bear the weight of this claim alone; if there are examples that indicate that the two experiences occur at once, the reply that the person quickly oscillates back and forth between them will be a weak one − adopted *ad hoc* to save the theory. One must also realize that this claim probably can be *made* true if one is willing to limit the experience of the Other-as-subject to its most extreme forms. *Perhaps, at its extreme*, that experience does exclude apprehending the Other-as-object, though my examples will contest this. But this defense involves two problems.

First, it would make the experience of the Other-as-subject unusually rare and thus eliminate its broader significance. It would become a marginal phenomenon − perhaps philosophically interesting − with minimal significance for a general theory of interpersonal experience. But Sartre does seek to ground a more general theory of relationships on this claim; hence, to defend the claim in this way undermines its purpose. Second, it would lessen the social self's explanatory power. Sartre's observations do seem to illuminate interpersonal experience: the social self supports the concept of social role, for only through the social self can a fixed set of expectations be formalized and accepted. However, once one realizes how pervasive the social self is, one must acknowledge that it occurs in various hybrid states − intermingled with fantasy or perception (even the perception of the Other-as-object) − and with much less intensity than Sartre describes.

At one point, Sartre adopts a more reasonable view. He allows that the experience of the social self may be compatible with retaining one's own subjectivity;[71] on this view, the social self could arise even if the Other is experienced as an object. But this denies the exclusivity claim.[72]

Some crucial examples   Let us begin evaluating the exclusivity claim by imagining the hero of a Western movie. The hero has his gun on the outlaw, and the heroine seems safe; the outlaw is experienced as an object. Suddenly the outlaw's accomplice speaks from the shadows, his gun trained on the hero. Trapped! The hero now experiences the Other-as-subject from the viewpoint of the accomplice. But he retains his experience of the outlaw as object; his gun is still aimed at him, and though his instrumental organization is disoriented by the unexpected event, he may still choose to try to kill the outlaw and take his chances with the accomplice. Although the two experiences, subject and object, relate to different people, the exclusivity claim should still hold. In this case, the more the hero experiences the accomplice *as subject*, the more he will seek to maintain the experience of the outlaw *as object* since that is his only hope.

But *is* the hero paralyzed? Quite the contrary; he continues to examine the situation for ways to integrate the unseen gun trained upon him into his own aims; he seeks ways to trick the accomplice or obstruct his vision. Although he is uneasy, cautious, and clearly conscious of his own vulnerability, he nevertheless continues to explore the situation for a way out. In short, here, to the extent that the hero experiences the accomplice as subject, he *also* experiences him as object; he seeks ways to use the accomplice's apparent advantage against him.[73]

The case is similar for the soldier on guard duty who hears a suspicious rustling noise. He experiences the Other-as-subject all around him and his vulnerability is oppressive, but just because of that unease, he intensifies his watchfulness and prepares himself for any surprise. Experiencing the Other-as-subject *reinvigorates* his perceptual and instrumental contact with the world, which may have become slackened by inattention or boredom.

These observations seem generalizable. Anyone playing competitive sports will experience the opponent both as object and as subject, and usually both at the same time. The quarterback versus the defensive backs; the batter versus the pitcher; the boxer versus his adversary; one tennis player versus another. In all these cases the subjectivity of the Other, potential and actual, is experienced only to better apprehend his objectivity and vice versa. For example, much of the time one is cataloging the Other's tendencies even when one is defeated on a point, and one is constantly trying to apprehend one's own tendencies from the Other's viewpoint in order to escape them.

Sartre might reply that in all these experiences the alleged Other-as-subject is really only an objectified subject — a look that has become incorporated into one's own world-organization. But this reply is mistaken. One does experience the Other's subjectivity in these examples. The social self can be continuously experienced in the course of one's efforts to transcend it. One *loses* the point or the game primarily when one *loses* contact with the *subjectivity* of the Other. As with competitive games, so too with the social "games" of everyday life; one attends to the various 'moves' open to the Other, both to understand those he adopts and to grasp the way in which one's own position (or face or status) might be altered by those he might make.

The perpetual presence of the Other-as-subject is quite real; yet it occurs *simultaneously* with the Other-as-object in most cases. The two modes isolated by Sartre are not exclusive alternatives; they are end points on a continuum, and most interpersonal experience falls in the middle area. One typically experiences the Other neither as pure object nor as pure subject, but as an amalgam of both.

This experience of simultaneity can perhaps be most clearly demonstrated in a case in which the Other is not present as such but in which one's own mirror image becomes an embodiment of the Other-as-subject. If one stares at a mirror close up for long enough, the bizarre experience of having one's consciousness appear on the other side — in the image's look — occurs. One appears to be seeing oneself in the process of seeing. To be sure, one's own experience undergoes some modification as this occurs, but one nevertheless maintains the objectifying perceptual experience of the mirror image. Indeed, as one experiences the mirror image's borrowed subjectivity more forcefully, one *looks at* it all the harder — only to discover that its force *increases*. It seems to absorb and project back all the energy one transmits. This example clearly indicates a simultaneous experience of looking and being-looked-at in the strong sense.

Another experience that has this character is sexual intercourse; here too there can be some oscillation between subjectivity and objectivity, but mutuality and the simultaneous experience of the Other-as-subject and the Other-as-object can also be achieved. Sartre might reply that the Other cannot be experienced as a transcending subject if she or he is experienced as embodied, but my point is that in sexual mutuality, both persons are wholly embodied, yet neither loses their subjectivity. Both consciousnesses exist *between* the two Sartrean modes, and the Sartrean dialectic of conflict is, at least for the moment, overcome.[74]

Some additional examples derive from the experience of social roles. Some roles define their occupants either as subjects or objects. The roles of employer, preacher, and king are ones in which their occupants are invariably experienced as subjects. The *roles themselves* transcend the complementary roles (employee, supplicant, citizen); so the direct presence of such role-occupants nearly always generates the experience of the Other-as-subject. However, one may be surprised when one sees them in the flesh, for they have an object side as well, and one often experiences this simultaneously with their role-subjectivity. Thus, in the face of one's king one imagines oneself a gnat; yet one *nevertheless* may experience his frailty and his imperfections. The same simultaneity occurs in the reverse situation of subordinate roles. The role of waitress or servant is, by definition, a subservient role, and in so far as one experiences people in that role, they are invariably apprehended as objects. However, there are moments when these role-objects assert their subjectivity, and one suddenly experiences oneself looked-at by them — *even as* one continues to experience them as objects. Neither experience disappears; both exist at once.

More general considerations These counter-examples can be given further theoretical support if one sees why the first reason in defense of Sartre's position, the apparent incompatibility of the properties of each experience, is inadequate. One problem is that the two properties do not belong to the same object; hence, for example, one can experience the *distance* of the Other-as-object *and* the absolute *presence* of the Other-as-subject since these are experienced as quite distinct entities. Indeed, the Other-as-subject is not located *in* one's world at all; he is not part of one's instrumentally organized world, but exists beyond it. This is Sartre's own position. Since incompatible properties *can* belong to two *distinct* entities in the same field of experience, the incompatibility does not establish the exclusivity claim.

The stronger reason why the incompatibility argument fails, however, is that the transformations involved in experiencing the Other's subjectivity are not total; they are best represented as *graded* changes. The Other-as-subject is *absolutely* present only rarely; in most cases there are many intervening layers of protective coating that his look only partly penetrates. Some of these layers are due to previous attributions of the Other-as-subject; some are due to one's own self-image; some are due to other factors. The point is that the Other-as-subject *can* be experienced even if it is *less* than absolutely present, and these lesser grades of presentness allow a more lively contact with the world — including the Other-as-object. These graded transformations suggest that the two modes of the Other can gradually shade into one another; this is why they can be experienced at once. In effect, the same person can be apprehended as half-subject and half-object, and both modes are clearly apprehended. The largest proportion of interpersonal experience exists in this gray zone; only rarely do the Sartrean extremes emerge. My claim thus becomes that *most* interpersonal experience violates the exclusivity claim.

Still another respect in which Sartre operates on simplistic presuppositions is revealed in his obliviousness to the possibility of higher-order experiences, those built on an already constituted Other-as-subject or Other-as-object. One can experience the Other as looking while simultaneously experiencing his previous look as looked-at; one can even anticipate the new look. These higher-order complexities are suggested by the social role and the sports examples.

Finally, there seem to be situations where the entire continuum spanning the apparently incompatible extremes is transcended, and one reaches a wholly new level of experience. In such circumstances, the Other is experienced as neither distant nor absolutely present, but in unity with one; he is experienced neither as perceived nor perceiving, but as co-experiencing.[75]

The basic explanation for the inadequacy of Sartre's exclusivity claim, however, is the mistaken assumption he makes about the simplicity of acts of consciousness. Either the experience of the Other-as-subject is *not* a new *mode* of consciousness, or else one *can* experience two 'modes' simultaneously. Probably the latter is correct, for the basic analogy that Sartre uses to support his contention about the modalities of consciousness also seems to fail. Perception and imagination do not necessarily exclude one another; one does not shift wholly out of perception while one is daydreaming except in rare cases; in addition, one often finds passing images suffusing one's perceptual experience (not merely perceptual protensions, but literally imagined representations). A new acquaintance may remind one of an old friend, and both faces may hover together — one is perceived while the other is imagined (this is distinct from seeing the friend's face *in* the face of the Other).

The central point here is that the modalities of consciousness are not so exclusive of one another as Sartre believes. Often one modality of consciousness is maintained more or less autonomously while another modality is superimposed over it. One's attention may be absorbed in both modalities, or it may be divided between them, and then one experiences a half-version of each mode. Both modalities may achieve full attention, and both may reinforce one another. For example, surreal perception (consider a fog or a blinding blizzard) can reinforce one's simultaneous imagination of things in it.

Claim 5

Claim 5 asserts that one cannot *know* the content of the social self.[76] Here Sartre underlines "knowledge." The claim can be interpreted in two ways, and Sartre seems to accept both. The first interpretation is that one cannot know the content of the social self *while experiencing it*. The ground for this assertion is as follows: when one experiences the social self, one experiences the Other-as-subject, and by the exclusivity principle (Claim 4), one cannot then be experiencing the Other-as-object. But to know anything requires that one is able to objectify it, and to objectify the Other would be to experience the Other-as-object; hence the effort to know the Other's judgments excludes the experience of the social self.[77] Even if one accepts this argument, critics will charge that the Other does often communicate his judgments and that one can thus learn the content of the social self.

The second interpretation is that the nature of the social self and/or the failures inherent in communication make *adequate* knowledge of the content of the social self impossible. Two reasons can be given for this. First, the content can change at any moment since Others are perpetually free to revise how they see one; hence, perfect knowledge of the social self at any one time, supposing that it could be attained, would not provide any certainty about its content at any future time. Second, even at a given time, one cannot know the content of the social self since the Other's actual judgment is essentially hidden from oneself by the separation between two conscious beings; neither can have any immediate consciousness of the *content* of the Other's vision.

Here an objector might contend that communication can still produce knowledge. Sartre would respond in two ways. First, any communication would only provide *probable* understanding – not certain knowledge – of the content of the social self, and this probability is reduced by the following factors: inattention, bias, imprecision, deceit, and misrepresentation. Second, there are strong reasons why these factors often operate, for to report the results of what one sees presupposes a reflective act which translates vision into language. But in this reflective act, the Other's assessment may become partly objectified; it may undergo a change, and hence the original judgment may become inaccessible to the Other himself. Thus, communication does not provide reliable knowledge of the content of the social self.

Response to the experiential interpretation   The experiential reading of this claim depends on the exclusivity claim (Claim 4), and thus, since that claim has been shown to be inadequate, that interpretation will not be acceptable. More direct criticisms of this reading of Claim 5 can be given, however.

My contention is that, in many cases, one does not only apprehend the presence of the social self, one also apprehends its content – the specific qualities that the Other sees. Although this apprehension is not always fully explicit, it can be brought to clarity, and it can be used as a basis for asserting that there is a tacit or pre-reflective comprehension of the social self most of the time. In my earlier example, F. clearly realizes his sister's judgment, and *if* the book he is reading *is not* her diary, he will experience the social self constituted by her to be mistaken. Indeed, precisely because one does have this tacit comprehension of the Other's judgments, one does not always experience the social self constituted by the Other as what one is.

One often apprehends the typical Other's totalization of one's activities even when alone; one may even adopt the Other's viewpoint oneself, and in this way one can learn what he is likely to see. One reason one can have this tacit comprehension is that the social self is *co-constituted*: on the basis of one's own actions, the Other formulates his totalization and assessment. One can always adopt his viewpoint and grasp what he is probably seeing in one's actions. There is thus a kind of knowledge that *does not need* to objectify the Other or his assessments; this tacit knowledge, which Sartre would call pre-reflective comprehension, often operates when one experiences the Other-as-subject. The Other's reactions and the way in which the look is experienced provide a fund of intuitive data with which this pre-reflective comprehension can operate; it is not mere hypothesizing or imagination. Is this tacit knowledge merely probable? Often the Other's expressions reveal more than he is willing to admit, and some reactions are so clear that to say one's comprehension of them is merely probable is misleading. Their content is as certain as the look itself.

Response to the theoretical interpretation My response to the theoretical reading of this claim is two-pronged. First, the most Sartre can claim on this reading is that the social self cannot be *completely* known. That the social self will have additional content in the future; that new Others will modify it, and that uncertainties surround all communication, collectively make *complete* knowledge of it impossible. I grant this point. One cannot know the future changes in the Other's assessment, nor can one always grasp how well new looks will cohere with old ones. Sartre should note, however, that this creates a problem for the theory of the social self, for its nature then becomes extremely open-ended, and therefore any claim made about it will be difficult to verify.

Second, I suggested above that the Other-as-subject is neither so hidden nor so overpowering that one can have no comprehension of the content of his look. Indeed, when one asks Others to communicate their vision, quite often one seeks to confirm these pre-reflective intuitions. They are not *always* confirmed, but they sometimes are. Even when they are not, this does not always settle the matter, for the Other may lack the moral strength to communicate his assessment in a truthful way. This can often be recognized. Sometimes the Other can be so ironic or vague that little can be concluded from his communicative efforts. Difficult it may be, but not impossible. One can clarify vagueness, unravel levels of irony, and demand greater attentiveness, and very often one can grasp whether the Other is fulfilling these requests. Hence the Other's reports can be clarified, and this may lead to the confirmation of one's intuitions.

Hence, though this reading of Claim 5 makes a conclusive point, it does not eliminate the possibility of knowing one's present social self. One can admit that the Other's assessment may sometimes be unknown, and that sometimes no amount of communication will be sufficient to clarify it. I also admit that the Other's future assessments cannot be known. This is all Sartre establishes.

Synopsis

This discussion has shown that in so far as he seeks to lay the foundations for a complete and adequate theory of interpersonal experience, Sartre's theory is flawed. But he seeks to achieve two other aims — an explication of the lived reality of the Other's existence and clarification of the ontological interrelatedness of self and Other. Sartre addresses these topics in the next two movements of his exposition. So far I have shown that phenomenological elucidation can contribute to philosophical understanding but that its results are revealing only when it incorporates a wide range of examples and is sensitive to all the elements in a region of experience. Sartre's work may be faulted on this score, but it is not yet clear how serious the fault is, for if his other two purposes are adequately served by his description, then the experiential limits of his theory may be less significant. The most one could then conclude would be that one must be careful when generalizing from this theory. It might still provide sufficient basis for the philosophical breakthroughs he seeks.

The transcendental argument

Sartre next investigates the *existence* of the Other-as-subject. I shall reconstruct his position as a transcendental argument. Sartre insists he is *not* offering a *proof*; this disclaimer has invited many alternative interpretations of his project. His position does contain an *argument* as well as some replies to some obvious objections and some further defense of important premises. Not all of the argument is explicit, but the direction of his remarks is clear.

In clarifying Sartre's conception of the Other-as-subject, one must tread a delicate path through a number of tensions and oppositions, and one cannot ignore the implications of his replies to objections for his position. Although Sartre does provide interesting replies, they may lead him into still greater difficulties. Before presenting objections to his argument, I shall offer as careful and sympathetic a reconstruction of it as possible.

The status of the argument

The first interpretive task is to determine Sartre's project. On one side, he claims that he is not giving a *proof* for the existence of Others.[78] Yet he does offer an argument and replies to objections; so he seems to be seeking to *establish* something. Sartre does not think it possible to *disprove* solipsism or to show that believing solipsism is *unintelligible*. A person may believe that he himself does not exist as long as the belief remains abstract and makes no contact with actual experience. Sartre's claim is that anyone who believes solipsism must also believe it in this same abstract, indifferent-to-experience fashion, for Sartre thinks there are pre-theoretical, pre-cognitive intuitions which permit one to apprehend the existence both of one's conscious life and of the Other-as-subject.[79] The certainty one has of their existence is not *epistemic*, it does not engage belief or knowledge; it even *excludes* them in their technical sense.[80] Sartre thinks that there is a level of experience that precedes or lies underneath belief, that it can be described, and that the description of this fundamental, pre-reflective experience will reveal the Other's existence and provide an explanation why solipsism is not taken seriously by ordinary people.[81]

Ultimately, Sartre wants to claim that an essential relation can obtain between an experience undergone by oneself and the actual existence of Others.[82] His phenomenological description elucidates the way in which the Other is revealed; by itself, however, this is not sufficient. Sartre needs more than merely an explication of an experience. He needs a demonstration that *the experience cannot exist if Others do not exist.*[83] He must show that the crucial experience cannot arise in any other fashion. In this way he can vindicate one's intuition that Others exist. The transcendental argument establishes the philosophical centrality of the experience by making its ontological implications explicit.

This *lived certainty* of Others' existence cannot be proven or rationally reconstructed; it does not lend itself to belief or knowledge because believing and knowing, for Sartre, are *objectifying* states of mind, and if one objectifies the Other, the experience on the basis of which one's lived certainty arises disappears.[84] So the very effort to provide a philosophical reconstruction conceals the lived certainty one can have at the pre-reflective level. Hence Sartre does not provide a proof for the Other's existence in the traditional sense, but he argues that the Other's existence is a precondition for the possibility of an experience people all undergo. I shall show that although his arguments are *not conclusive*, they are strong and important, and the approach Sartre discovers is novel and worth developing.

This interpretation implies that a number of ways of comprehending Sartre's argument are wrong or inadequate. By examining these inadequacies, I hope to clarify my interpretation somewhat further. I shall begin by noting the general difficulty that many Anglo-American philosophers have in interpreting Sartre at this point. Sartre's crucial claim is that the *existence* of the Other-as-subject is *a necessary condition* for the experience of the social self.[85] Traditionally philosophers approach such claims with a preconceived notion of what *could be* being claimed; the operative distinction is empirical/conceptual. Either the necessary condition is an empirical one, and the relation involved eventually must be seen as a causal one (e.g., oxygen is necessary for life), or the necessary condition is a logical one, which means that either a definition is being stipulated or a deeper — but nevertheless *conceptual* — bond is being uncovered.

The major difficulty is that Sartre is not stipulating a definition, nor describing a necessary antecedent cause, nor examining relations among concepts. If he were stipulating a definition or analyzing concepts, the question of Others' *existence* would not be addressed, for he would still have to demonstrate that the concepts involved have referents, and Sartre nowhere makes an effort to do this. Moreover, Sartre is not claiming the Other-as-subject is causally necessary to the existence of the social self, for he is in general opposed to using the concept of causation in understanding ontological connections, and the relation between the Other-as-subject and the social self is deeper and tighter than typical causal relations. If there were only a causal relation between them, self and Other would only be externally related, and this would reintroduce the possibility of adopting the monad view of persons that Sartre struggles to overcome.

Sartre seems to believe that there is a kind of necessary condition that lies between the conceptual and the causal; 'ontological' would be a convenient label. There is thus a kind of essential or necessary relation that exists between *entities themselves*, not merely the concepts used to capture them. This kind of relation obtains between these entities *because they are the kinds of things they are*; given that such entities exist, the relation *must* obtain between them.

To clarify this reading I shall briefly review some alternative interpretations of Sartre's argument. Arthur Danto, in a recent book, offers two interpretations, neither of which is satisfactory. He claims that Sartre is asserting that a necessary relation holds between the concept of shame and the concept of Others.[86] The very idea of shame would thus presuppose the idea of Others. To interpret Sartre as explicating concepts is to view him as if he were Husserl; Husserl examines the constitution and essential relations of "senses" (which are close to Anglo-American "concepts"), but Sartre refuses to replicate Husserl's enterprise because it fails to have ontological import. As Danto himself admits, one can always ask whether anything corresponds to the concepts, and this is precisely what Sartre asks of Husserl. One would hardly expect Sartre to repeat the mistakes of a theorist he has criticized, and everything in Sartre's text suggests he is talking about *entities*, not concepts.

Danto's correlated, but perhaps somewhat different, view is that Sartre is exhibiting a necessary connection between one person's states of consciousness — between the *experience* of shame and the *belief* in the Other's existence.[87] However, this view too, as Danto realizes, would not establish the existence of Others, for even if the belief in Others is

essential to shame, one can always wonder whether the belief is justified
— whether something corresponding to it exists. Thus Sartre, if this
interpretation were correct, would simply be confused; he would not be
establishing what he claims to establish; he would not even be addressing
the appropriate entity. But Sartre clearly does not think shame arises
from a *belief* in Others; indeed, he says the social self *cannot* be derived
from any aspect of oneself, including one's beliefs, i.e., he explicitly
denies what Danto's interpretation would have him assert.[88] Even if
Sartre's argument fails, the interpreter should allow Sartre to offer an
argument for his actual conclusion.

Marjorie Grene, in another recent book, contrasts Sartre's view with
Descartes's move from clear and distinct ideas to the existence of God
in the *Meditations*.[89] Although Sartre does compare his project to
Descartes's and even refers to his proof of God, his primary reference
is to the *cogito* rather than to this strategy, which Grene characterizes
as "moving from one self-contained intuition to another." Grene's
reading is more adequate; at least she acknowledges that Sartre is
trying to reach the existence of the other subject, but it still has infelicities. Grene does not further clarify what sort of move this is; what is
the logical or essential link between such intuitions? How *can* they be
linked in this way? Moreover, Grene's view implies that one can have
an intuition of the Other-as-subject; presumably this means that the
Other appears to one with some kind of evidence.[90] But Sartre denies
this: one does not ever perceive or intuit the Other-as-subject; he is
not explicitly or evidentially *known* at all.[91] The result of Sartre's
discussion is not an intuition, but an experiential realization that the
Other does exist.

Sartre does *not* defend an inference; he explicates the preconditions
of an experience. The Other-as-subject is not exactly there to be seen;
when he is present, one's attention is absorbed by one's social self. He
can be comprehended pre-theoretically, and in concrete experience one
apprehends the meaning of his existence because it has important
implications: he establishes a structure to which one must constantly
react. Sartre holds that people have a continuous lived comprehension
of their own existence (this is his reinterpretation of Descartes's *cogito*),
and he simply tries to show that they have a similar lived comprehension
of the Other's existence *via* transformations in their own existence.

These features of Sartre's position give it a Kantian flavor, but there
are significant differences between Kant's argument for a necessarily
presupposed set of concepts and Sartre's argument. The main difference
is that the Other, for Sartre, is not a *concept* used to *organize* one's
experience, but a transcendent *condition* of that experience which
undermines the structure it has for oneself alone.[92] The Other is not a
pre-conscious structure that functions as a form of synthesis and
operates without one's awareness. The pre-theoretical grasp of Others

Sartre describes does not entail that the Other lies deep within, implicitly organizing one's experience. The kind of 'presupposition' involved in Sartre's discussion is thus distinct from Kant's. Sartre's Other is *beyond* one's own experience, but his existence necessitates a radical modification of one's own existence, and this is directly apprehended.[93] His argument seeks to show that this modification could not occur without the existence of Others; this is the sense in which their existence is presupposed.

Moreover, Sartre is not demonstrating that the Other's *existence* is *necessary*; rather he claims it is only contingent.[94] This means that Sartre does not establish that Others exist in all possible worlds, but only in worlds in which beings like us exist and undergo the structural modification that we do undergo.[95] This pre-theoretical comprehension of Others would be *unavailable* to anyone who had never experienced the social self.

An exposition of the argument, its defense, and Sartre's replies to objections

I can now sketch the actual structure of Sartre's argument. First I shall present the argument and Sartre's defense of it; then I shall consider the objections Sartre anticipates and the replies he makes to them. Many of the premises in these arguments are explicitly asserted, but some of them have been supplied to make the arguments valid. The "minor argument" constitutes Sartre's defense for his "major premise."

The major argument (implicit)[96]

1 *Basic experience explicated*: One has experienced oneself transformed into an object (the social self).
2 *The major premise*: If one has experienced the social self, then a transcendent Other-as-subject exists.
   Therefore:
3 A transcendent Other-as-subject exists.

Before presenting the minor argument, one should note a few facts about this one. The conclusion does not assert that the Other-as-subject is *known*, only that he exists. Indeed, what differentiates this argument from a proof is that it does not validate one's knowledge; it elucidates one's lived certainty that Others exist. This claim is epistemologically interesting because one typically takes certainty to be a result of, or mode of, knowledge. Sartre here opposes knowledge and certainty. If one has one, one cannot have the other. To *know* something is to objectify it; the existence of the objects of such consciousness can only be probable, never certain, according to Sartre.[97] If one has *certainty*, one has a direct, pre-reflective experience of that about which one is certain. One can *explicate* this certainty, but it cannot be the subject of proof or demonstration.

Henceforth Sartre splits the two dimensions of the Other apart: only the Other-as-*object* can be *known* (with probability), while only the Other-as-*subject* can be apprehended with *certainty*. Like the *experience* of these modes of the Other, which he claims exclude one another, the two dimensions themselves are exclusive; they are disjoint — related only by contingent, external connections.[98]

The minor argument

1 If one has experienced oneself transformed into an object (the social self), then something exists which is making this transformation possible. (Implicit.)
2 The something which is making the transformation possible must be either oneself, a physical object or event, or a transcendent Other-as-subject. (Implicit.)
3 A physical object or event cannot make this transformation possible.
4 By oneself, one cannot make this transformation possible.[99]
   Therefore:
5 A transcendent Other-as-subject is making this transformation possible. (From 2, 3, 4 by elimination.)
   Therefore:
6 If one has experienced the social self, then a transcendent Other-as-subject exists. (From 1, 5, by substitution.)

The crucial premises in this argument are numbers 3 and 4. Sartre arrives at Premise 2 by admitting only two basic forms of being besides Others and being-for-Others: being-in-itself (physical objects and events) and being-for-itself (consciousness, oneself). Someone might want to claim that animals can motivate the change. Sartre can grant this because it amounts only to accepting that the physical presence of an animal can become the embodiment of the Other-as-subject. Sartre is seeking to elucidate the Other-as-subject; whether this subjectivity is embodied in a person or in something else is not important to him. He simply notes that other persons are the characteristic entities which embody it.

I have deliberately stated Premise 1 vaguely to leave *open* the question of *how* this transformation is made possible, i.e., via what sort of relation. Previously I claimed that the relationship is not causal; neither is it logical or conceptual in the strict sense. As I explicate Sartre's understanding of the Other-as-subject more thoroughly, this relationship will become clearer.

Sartre's defense of key premises

In support of Premise 3, Sartre offers one central consideration. Physical objects and events can create resistance or difficulties, but this does not generate the kind of transformation involved in the experience of the social self.[100] To experience the social self is to have one's purposes *neutralized*, to be made into an object. Experiencing an obstacle or a resistant event at best motivates one to *change* one's purposes; often it is only the occasion for developing more inventive means to achieve what one sought originally. In changing one's purposes one retains one's own organization of the world and one's perspective on it; no disintegration occurs; no foreign self emerges. One can be forced to alter one's aims through prohibition, counter-purposes, etc., but they emanate only from conscious beings, not from physical objects or events.[101]

I owe my inclusion of Premise 3 to the reconstruction of the argument that Phyllis Morris offers in her book *Sartre's Concept of a Person*; I had not seen that physical objects also had to be excluded.[102] However, Morris grasps the nub of the issue only obliquely; she contends that physical objects cannot intend other entities as objects; in general, her reconstruction is cast in terms of 'intend another as object' phrases. Although Sartre accepts the truth of this view and ultimately he wants to say that physical objects cannot be subjects, what he means by "subject" is this ability to *transform* one's world, to displace one from one's position, and to provide one a new dimension of being. Animals do frequently intend one as an object, but they do not always motivate this transformation. People can also intend one as an object (i.e., be aware of one), and they can be experienced as doing this without instantiating the Other-as-subject. If his look is objectified, the Other will not appear as a subject. Hence, the *essence* of the Other's subjectivity is *not* to *intend* one as an object but to *make* one experience oneself as an object. Morris also portrays the relation between the Other and the social self as a causal one, which I shall show, is *inaccurate*.

The most important premise is the fourth, for if only conscious beings can effect this transformation, then Sartre must show conclusively that one cannot generate it by oneself. Sartre realizes this is the crucial premise to defend; so he offers three different types of considerations in its support: empirical, a priori, and *reductio*. These considerations carry the same message, but they do it in different ways.

The empirical consideration simply directs one's attention to the *locus* of the transformation: one *experiences* the source of the shift as outside oneself; the social self is imposed; it arrives from the outside.[103] One can try to attribute qualities to oneself in reflection, but this effort is essentially ineffectual, according to Sartre. They become mere postulates; even if they summarize one's past accurately, they are not experienced as qualifying or limiting one's future.[104] *The Other can* close the future off to one; at least, he can be experienced as doing so. To the extent that one can experience oneself as having an unchangeable nature at all, it is only as an object for another subject. Thus, the source of the transformation is experienced as beyond oneself, not within oneself.

Sartre offers two a priori considerations in defense of Premise 4. The first holds that the social self is a limit on and totalization of consciousness and that such a limit *cannot* be imposed by consciousness on itself.[105] The freedom of consciousness perpetually threatens and potentially overthrows any boundaries it might try to create for itself. Always threatening its own plans is its ever-present possibility of changing them. Threatening its promises, its self-imposed rules, and its commitments, are the freedoms to abandon, to default, and to ignore. Consciousness never remains confined within the artificial limits it imposes on itself; those limits only operate as long as consciousness sustains them.

The social self does not need one's support; it exists regardless of whether one wants it. If the Other is going to rape one, one can struggle or argue, but one cannot prevent their purposes from cutting across one's own; one cannot abandon the self-embodiment that makes rape possible. One can clothe oneself, deface oneself, or make oneself repulsive, but the Other may choose to rape one none the less. The uses the Other makes of one are limits; they continue to exist as long as the Other sustains them. The case is similar with character-trait ascriptions. If the Other sees one as ugly, one can do little either to sustain or overthrow this judgment. One can argue, cut one's hair, or have plastic surgery; the Other may still insist on seeing ugliness. One need not do anything to sustain their judgments, and they may sustain them despite what one does. The social self thus represents a limit that ultimately is beyond one's control.[106]

The second a priori consideration holds that the social self is an objectification of oneself and that no consciousness can objectify itself in this fashion.[107] As mentioned before, reflection may struggle to achieve this, but its results are not convincing, nor do they effect any transformation of what one is. The psychic self, the object of reflection, can only exist on the reflective plane of consciousness; as soon as one returns to the pre-reflective level, the psychic self disappears. The social self, however, exists on the pre-reflective level and exists despite one's efforts to ignore it.

Here, however, Sartre has an ever stronger point. He claims that the very *ability* to reflect is wholly dependent on already having experienced oneself as an object for another subject. Reflection is only a degraded effort to achieve the distance on oneself that one experiences through Others, and it could not be attempted if one had not already experienced the social self. Why so? The primary reason Sartre offers is that there would be no motivation for taking the reflective standpoint. One would simply live one's own purposes, never taking them as objects of second-level acts of consciousness. The emergence of the social self provides the possibility of experiencing oneself as an object; reflection arises as an effort to mimic the viewpoint of the Other.[108] It provides the model for reflection to imitate.

Phyllis Morris adds a secondary, related reason: the Other provides one a vision of oneself as an object; reflection would not know what to seek if one had not already experienced the social self.[109] This means that any experience of oneself objectified is possible only because of the Other-as-subject. Thus, for both these reasons, the self cannot effect this transformation; and even to the extent that the self weakly approximates it, that ability is wholly dependent on the experience of the social self.

Sartre offers a third kind of consideration; it can be represented as a *reductio ad absurdum* argument. Suppose the transformation of oneself were effected by oneself; then the social self would be an object within the world that one had created. This would mean that the social self could be an object of knowledge and that it would function within some set of purposes one had. But neither of these implications is correct. Sartre contends that the social self cannot be *known* by oneself (Claim 5).[110] Moreover, the social self does not function instrumentally for oneself; rather it reduces one to an instrument for the Other.[111] Consequently, the initial assumption — that self could objectify itself — must be wrong.

To the person who objects that the Other-as-subject is only imagined, Sartre would respond by taking the allegation seriously. Imagination is a specific type of mental act, it has a describable structure and specific properties; it alters the perceptual act in specific ways. It excludes perception, and the object imagined is not posited as existing. The Other-as-subject cannot be a mere object of imagination because its reality is too pressing and present. Nothing is more different than being made a fool of and imagining oneself to be a fool. Although the social self is not strictly perceived, its reality is apprehended across the limits and alterations of one's own projects.

Sartre's replies to objections

Like any good philosopher, Sartre does not rest assured with a straightforward defense of his position. He also anticipates the stronger objections that might be raised by critics and tries to reply to them. Strangely, many of Sartre's commentators raise the same objections and believe they have thereby defeated the argument. Too few seriously consider

Sartre's replies and their implications. The implications are far-reaching and require a revision of one's understanding of the Other-as-subject.

The first objection asks whether the Other is *only inferred* on the basis of the existence of the social self: whether the Other is posited (like nuclear particles are inferred as the best explanation of phenomena otherwise inexplicable, e.g., streaks in cloud chambers), or is just something indicated or signified by the various events in one's own experience (like a road sign signifies the town it names), or is merely an *ad hoc* concept — postulated to handle certain puzzling phenomena.[112] If any of these were correct, the existence of the Other-as-subject would become *hypothetical.*

Sartre's replies depend on two observations: first, the social self would have to appear without the Other-as-subject in order for the Other to be merely inferred from it; second, one would have to be able to apprehend the social self's content, apprehend its qualities, in order to derive a concept of the Other from it by postulation or hypothesis. The social self's content would have to be accessible *first* in order that the concept of Other could be constituted.

Sartre's essential point here is that the Other-as-subject is not an achievement of cognition — via belief, inference, postulation, or signification; rather, he is the *necessary condition* for the existence of the social self.[113] One difference between a necessary condition and an inferred or constructed object is that a condition must always appear with what it is a condition for and an inferred entity need not (e.g., the inference may not be made). In a sense, Sartre is relying on the considerations supporting Premise 4 and is suggesting that the objector has not fully understood his position, but he spells out his replies carefully to demonstrate that the preconditions of the objection are not fulfilled.

Sartre notes that the social self is not wholly identical with oneself; it is experienced as foreign even if one accepts it as oneself and takes responsibility for it.[114] It is not the same as what one is for oneself alone; indeed, its emergence for the most part displaces what one is for oneself. Moreover, the social self never arises from oneself or by itself, never without the motivation of the Other-as-subject who is in the background when one experiences it.[115] The social self does not arise first so that the Other can later be deduced, posited, constructed, or constituted; when the social self arises, the Other-as-subject is already there.

Sartre continues by noting that the social self is not even perceived objectively. One does not apprehend its content at all; all that happens is that one finds oneself defined or neutralized by purposes not one's own. What these purposes are and how one fits into them can only be guessed, never known.[116] Hence the data from which the Other would have to be inferred are ethereal and lack the determinateness necessary to be able to make inferences or to constitute concepts. The Other is the *precondition* of the social self, not its *meaning*.

The most common epistemological retort to Sartre's argument is that it does not establish that the Other exists, only that people *believe* in the existence of Others. This objection is exactly analogous to the previous one, and it commits a frequent error in assessing phenomenological claims. The objector fails to be serious about his position. Belief is a specific type of mental state; it builds on prior states; it is necessarily second-order since it affirms or asserts a state of affairs which must first be registered. (Husserl developed an entire doxology or phenomenology of belief.) Sartre claims that the *preconditions* for having a *belief* in the Other-as-subject do not obtain here. The social self is not accessible to one in a determinate fashion; so a belief cannot arise on the basis of it. Moreover, since belief always *objectifies* the state of affairs or entity it affirms and since the Other-as-subject *cannot be objectified*, he could no longer be experienced if one believed in him. Thus the preconditions of belief are lacking, and if belief arose, it would eliminate what it sought to grasp. The objector is simply not examining the phenomena very carefully; to summarize one's experience of the Other-as-subject by saying that one believes in the Other's existence simply ignores the data. No belief (or inference or hypothesis) is involved here. There is a stark, radically transforming, experience; Sartre is simply explicating the preconditions of that experience.

The second objection Sartre considers is also a common and important one; his response to it is clever and subtle. He claims that the Other is a necessary condition for the experience of the social self; yet there seem to be obvious counter-examples to this position, viz., countless situations in which one experiences the social self and assumes the Other's presence, but when one turns, no one is there. This absence of the Other seems to establish that he is *not* a necessary condition for the experience of the social self.[117]

To this Sartre offers a complex set of replies: he encourages us to examine the phenomenon more closely; he reemphasizes a distinction that has been central throughout; and he further elucidates what the Other-as-subject is. But his strongest move is to claim that the experience of the absent Other presupposes a more primordial presence of the Other. I shall examine these replies in turn.

Is the Other-as-subject truly absent when one realizes that a human body is not there? Sartre first notes that the absence of the Other's body often makes us experience the *presence* of the Other-as-subject and our own objectivity *more forcefully*.[118] Had the floorboards creaked outside F.'s door, he might have apprehended his sister's subjectivity and abandoned his reading even if it was only a 'false alarm.' Even if he tried to ignore the precipitating event, his objectivity would be far closer to the foreground than before; it may haunt him.

In addition, Sartre emphasizes the distinction between the Other-as-subject and the Other-as-object. The example demonstrates only that the Other-as-object is not in the vicinity, *not* that the Other-as-subject is not present.[119] Even in the best of circumstances, the Other-as-object is never more than probable. Since he offers this response, Sartre discusses the relation between the Other-as-subject and the Other-as-object more fully. He concludes that the Other-as-subject, though concrete and livingly present, is nevertheless not denumerable; it is pre-numerical and thus does not individuate along the same lines or in the same fashion as the Other-as-object. The Other-as-subject does not individuate at all: it is neither one nor many. It is like a universal function which becomes embodied in any number of events – the most common of which is the bodily presence of another person. It can, however, be embodied in natural events like blowing wind and creaking floorboards.[120]

Sartre then asserts that someone can be experienced as absent only on the ground of a more primordial presence of the Other-as-subject. One is only absent from places one is expected to be, but this expectation indicates this primordial presence.[121] It makes experienced absence possible. Similarly, in the example of F. and the diary, even if his sister were not outside the door, her absence would not eliminate the permeating gaze through which the Other-as-subject transforms F. This primordial presence is not always in the foreground, but it constitutes part of everyone's situation. Each person is located with respect to the presence of all Others of all types, and this presence may at any moment become explicit in the experience of the social self. Thus Sartre takes the certainty of the Other's existence to derive not from his appearance in person, but from the *basic transformation* his subjectivity effects. This transformation makes possible the perception of another human body infused with subjectivity.[122]

Sartre actually has to alter his thesis to successfully reply to this objection. The obvious questions are whether the transcendent and non-imaginary status of the Other has been compromised and whether its intelligibility and its coherence with other phenomena have been retained. Essentially, Sartre's reply to the objection is that the Other-as-subject *is present*, even though the Other's body (or objectivity) is absent. He holds that the experience of Others' absence presupposes the experience of the presence of the Other-as-subject. Hence the objection fails. A reexamination of Sartre's assertions about the Other-as-subject now seems necessary.

Further clarification of the Other-as-subject

Sartre's position on the Other-as-subject is torn by three tensions; the two sides of each tension seem contradictory; yet Sartre wishes to maintain both. Whether this is possible needs investigation.

In the first tension, Sartre oscillates between the claims that the Other-as-subject is identical to the social self and that he is distinct. On the side of identity, Sartre offers assertions like: the Other is the very being of the social self,[123] its milieu and environment;[124] the upsurge of the Other and self's experience of social self are one unity; they cannot even be conceived of separately;[125] plus his constantly reiterated view that the certainty which guarantees the social self can be translated into certainty of the Other-as-subject.[126] On the side of difference, Sartre claims that the Other is the *transcending condition* of the social self[127] and that the relation between the two is analogous to that of motivating moment of consciousness to a motivated one.[128]

In the second tension, Sartre oscillates between the claim that the Other-as-subject is absolutely present to self and the claim that he wholly transcends one's world. By 'transcendent' here Sartre does not mean 'spatially separate' or 'beyond the phenomena,' but 'capable of limiting the organization of one's world, one's freedom, and one's existence.'[129] Yet if the Other is absolutely present, this would seem to make him a part of one's world even though he lacks distance or intermediary.[130]

In the third tension, Sartre oscillates between conceiving the Other as abstract and as concrete. On the one hand, claiming the Other to be pre-numerical, and thus unindividuatable, makes him into something generalized rather than specific and situated.[131] Also, the claim that his presence pervades and is presupposed by both lived presence and lived absence also suggests an abstract, general condition or function rather than a concrete, specific entity.[132] Yet, on the other hand, Sartre insists that he reaches a concrete Other, not the abstract synthesis of all Others that would be God,[133] and thus he is able to avoid his own criticism of Heidegger — being unable to reconnect the Other to whom one is essentially related to the concrete Other before one. But concreteness seems only to apply to the Other-as-object; what has happened to the concreteness of the *Other-as-subject*? And what is their relationship?

These are the tensions that must be resolved; in the course of the discussion some additional implications of Sartre's view will be elucidated.

Sartre resolves the first tension — between the identity and difference of the social self and the Other-as-subject — by indicating the ways in which one's social self is a co-production of oneself and the Other and by clarifying the relationship between identity and difference as it applies here.

The social self is the ontological result of an encounter between subjectivities; it depends on each, emanates from each, but is not wholly identical with either. In so far as the Other is a subject, he uses me for his purposes, and my social self emerges necessarily as a result;

it is me-as-an-object-for-him. But I must exist and encounter him in order for him to use me, and the particular manner in which I live conditions the uses to which he puts me. My projects thus bear indirectly on my social self. The social self requires the existence of both of us and is our co-production; it genuinely qualifies me even if I cannot intuit its content, and it is 'made to exist' by the Other simply because he pursues his purposes. It depends on no particular intention of either of us; it is the *necessary* result of our interaction.

Yet the social self is identical to neither of us; indeed, it is the bond which prevents us from falling into an identity with one another. Each retains his distinctness through a *negation*; the Other negates me directly by making me an object; I negate the Other indirectly by refusing to be identical with the object he creates. My refusal acknowledges the relatedness of the social self to me — accepts responsibility for it — even though I cannot know it lucidly and cannot compare it to my experience of myself. These negations are *internal*; they bond me to the Other essentially; part of my identity exists only because of the Other. The social self thus defines me even though I am distinct from it, and it emanates from the Other yet is no more identical with him than any other object he confronts.

The second tension in Sartre's conception of the Other-as-subject, between transcendence and absolute presence, can be resolved through clarifying the social self. The tension results from taking 'transcendence' to mean beyondness and 'presence' to mean withinness. However, Sartre wishes to claim that precisely *because* the Other is absolutely present, he transcends self's world.[134] By transcend, Sartre means *limit, encompass, circumscribe*. In so far as the Other's subjectivity displaces one, he does not occupy and cannot be given a place within the spatial organization of one's world. Precisely because the Other is absolutely present, he transforms one's own presence to the world and thus transcends one in so far as he undermines one's relation to one's own projects. One's world contracts within the limits the Other has constituted. The Other-as-subject occupies no place *in* one's world because he is the one who makes a *place* happen to oneself; one occupies a place amidst other instruments for his purposes.[135] The transcendent character of the Other does not mean he is inaccessible, but it does mean that he is not an object for one like other objects.

Thus, the social self — the border between Other and self — is not just a limit or a bond, but it is also like an enclosing sphere.[136] While one is aware of it, this sphere undermines one's ability to posit purposes. The Other, on Sartre's view, does not produce the *being* of consciousness or subjectivity as it is for itself; there is still an interior to the sphere that is inaccessible to the Other. Hence each subject exists independently of Others; yet each has a nature only because of Others. The Other is present to one's nature, but there is still an aspect of self to which he is not present. He never becomes identical with one in the sense that he knows or has one's experiences, but he is never wholly distinct from one (merely externally related) because he constitutes one's nature or identity across time. The sphere metaphor makes clear how his simultaneous presence and transcendence are not only possible, but necessary.

The third tension, between the concreteness and the abstractness of the Other-as-subject, can be resolved only by cutting a path between the two alternatives. Let us begin with the dichotomy itself. The clearest example of concreteness is a material object, e.g., another's body; the Other-as-subject is not concrete in this sense because he is precisely that which cannot become object. On the other side is the abstract ideal totalization that would unify all the other subjects into a single, monolithic, always-present Observer (God); Sartre thinks this unification of subjectivities cannot be achieved; one can attain no experience of it. So the Other-as-subject is not exactly a generalized Other that integrates all possible subjects. This is an abstraction that lacks experiential reality; it can only be thought or at best imagined. The Other-as-subject Sartre describes is livingly experienced.

The most problematic aspect of the Other-as-subject is its *pre-numericality*; this feature makes individuating it impossible and gives it the kind of generality one usually attributes to universals. Sartre seems to deny that one can experience *plural looks*;[137] yet he does not assert that every instance of the look instantiates the *same* subject; this would be to give the Other-as-subject oneness, which is a number, and Sartre's Other is allegedly prior to all numbering.

Sartre may want to say that the social self is a never-quite-attained synthesis of all the perspectives one has experienced through Others and that the look of this particular gazing Other stands out from the synthesis like a figure on a ground. Indeed one does sometimes experience the social self in this fashion. Yet if the Other-as-subject is given some *determinacy*, then the experience of *that* Other's look may not be confirmed; *that* Other may not be looking. Sartre might, however, reply that the ground is there even if the figure is wrong, and the certainty of the Other-as-subject is not affected.[138] The pre-numerical Other would thus be present even if this particular person is not now embodying it. Although this claim sacrifices the Other's determinacy, Sartre could still maintain that because the pre-numerical Other is *livingly* experienced it cannot be merely abstract.

If Sartre's theory were correct, it would provide an explanation of why the individuality of other people is extraordinarily difficult to apprehend (I take this to be the case); for whenever experienced as an object, the Other would only be a *type* or an *instrument*, and when experienced as subject, the Other would be experienced amidst a synthesis of subjects, instead of being individuated as such. When one experiences something as a type, one rarely grasps its individuality; it is one among many. When one experiences the instrumentality of something, it is intersubstitutable with any number of other entities that could serve the same function. If, when one experiences another as subject, one grasps only a quasi-totality of other subjects, then the specificity of *this* subject is missed. Thus in no mode of experiencing the Other can his individuality easily become manifest.

Yet I think that Sartre's conception of the Other-as-subject is troubled — on both experiential and theoretical grounds. One does not always experience a generalized subjectivity through the looks of concrete Others. Although the Other one experiences is not always as differentiated as the number of looks one experiences, it nevertheless becomes relatively determinate through the looks of different Others. There are specifications of the Other-as-subject even if one restricts oneself to Sartre's descriptions. To make the Other pre-numerical renders its status ethereal and ghostlike.

In addition, from the standpoint of theory, Sartre must clarify how Others-as-subject experienced by different persons are related to one another, and Sartre's theory lacks the capacity to answer such questions.[139] The Other's pre-numericality renders him mysterious; it allows almost any answer to any question. The theory loses contact with experience and with the possibility of confirmation. Although Sartre sought to create a sophisticated conception of the Other-as-subject, he seems guilty of the charge with which he berated Heidegger — an inability to relate the Other-as-subject to concrete other subjects.

An evaluation of Sartre's position

My assessment of Sartre's approach is partially favorable. If one interprets his position cautiously, one can show that he has discovered a useful way to explore the nature of Others. Nevertheless, his argument and methodology have real problems, and I shall examine these first.

The strategy of the argument: mystical experience

Sartre's first problem lies with his general strategy. One might wonder whether it is *too strong* since it may sanction the existence not only of the Other-as-subject, but also of creatures like God and/or evil demons. The crucial premise in Sartre's argument is that the Other is a necessary condition for a certain experience. Mystics and some other theists might claim that special states of mind, e.g., union with the cosmos, complete grace and absolution, or living in 'light' rather than 'darkness,' can be achieved by anyone and also *could not* exist if a God did not exist to make them possible. They might also argue that God's existence is not an inference from the experience, but is a necessary condition (ontological or causal) for it. Indeed they might even claim that God has a special, internal relation to each human being (or each entity), such that, by clearly understanding one's experience, one can see that its crucial aspects presuppose God. Naturally, some theory of blindness would be needed to show why some people fail to apprehend their experience correctly, but even here theists may use a strategy similar to Sartre's, viz., asserting that all past ways of thinking about God have mistakenly addressed only *one* of His modes and that a *different mode* reveals His more basic reality and is more clearly manifest in these special experiences.

The mystic can thus develop a remarkably parallel argument which might force the atheist Sartre to accept theism. There is at least some burden on Sartre to establish significant disanalogies. Moreover, the form of argument might allow one to establish much more than God's existence: experiencing oneself as evil might entail the existence of demons; experiencing oneself transfixed by aesthetic objects might entail the transcendent existence of Beauty, etc.

Sartre's first reply to this objection would be that not everyone has mystic experiences but that everyone does have the experiences he elucidates, shame or fear. Even if this were true, Sartre does not make his own view dependent on the universality of the experience he explicates; he seems content to show that the conclusion can be established on the basis of the explication of the experience of a single consciousness. Moreover, as I shall show below, Sartre's experience is *not* universal; indeed there are significant types of exceptions to it. This, however, demonstrates only that Sartre's conclusion has *limited* application; only those who have experienced the social self will assent to his argument.

Similar considerations apply to the theist; those who have not had the experience to which he calls attention will be unmoved by whatever explication he provides for it. Even if there is a difference in the universality of these basic experiences, this would only show a difference in the degree to which their explications would gain assent. Sartre would not have shown a deep enough disanalogy to differentiate his form of argument from the theist's. Thus Sartre's initial reply seems to lack the necessary force.

Sartre might continue his replies by claiming that no one who does not antecedently believe in the existence of God could have the relevant experiences; thus, the theist only develops a *self-reinforcing* position. He uses an experience that presupposes a prior belief to further buttress that belief; he would thus be begging the question in some sense. This is quite different from claiming that the theist only infers the existence of God on the basis of the characteristic experience; the claim is rather that *no such experience would be possible* if one did not already believe in God's existence. Sartre would be claiming that such a belief functions as a foundation for the constitution of the experience in the way Husserl believes that the experience of one's own mental states is constitutionally prior to perceiving mental states of Others.

The theist here has three sorts of replies. First, he might try to show Sartre's claim is simply false. There have been many cases of atheists who underwent conversions and whose experiences seemed unintelligible without God's existence. The apostle Paul is one of these. If Sartre shifts to some notion of unconscious belief in responding to such cases, then he will have to face similar objections to his own theory. For the experience of the Other-as-subject might also presuppose some sort of *unconscious* belief in the existence of Others.

The theist's second reply might indicate that Sartre's argument could have similar difficulties. He might point out, for example, that shame seems to presuppose the acceptance of an institutionalized set of evaluations.[140] Could one experience shame if one did not acknowledge the value in terms of which the Other accuses one? If F. did not accept a person's right to privacy or believed that promises are made to be broken, *could* he experience shame under the accusing eye of his sister? But such valuations are socially conditioned; thus, shame seems to have an additional necessary condition which requires *a previous commitment to the existence of Others.* If that is true, perhaps Sartre's argument begs the question in a way similar to the theist's — supposing that his does. Hence the theist could still maintain the position that if Sartre accepts his own argument he must also accept the theist's.

The theist's third reply might be to claim that a prior commitment to the existence of God does not undermine the force of the argument, if indeed God is a genuine necessary condition for the existence of the experience. In short, he might deny the claim that he begs the question. What needs demonstration is that the prior commitment undermines the claim that God *is necessary* for the occurrence of the experience. Alternatively, he might argue that the only prior necessity is that one possess the *concept* of God, and this is quite distinct from having a belief in God. Mystic experience would thus show that the concept *has application* or refers to something; this is what the explication of the experience would demonstrate.

Since Sartre would have to admit that the lack of explicitness of the alleged belief in God would imply that no belief is present or necessary (belief is an explicit state, for Sartre), and since he cannot deny that instances of religious experience do seem to *befall* people, catching them unawares (thus arising without any prior cognitive commitment), he would have to accept the theist's position here. So Sartre's second reply is equally unsuccessful.

This leaves Sartre two other possible replies. He could try to show that in religious experience no genuine modification of one's being occurs, and/or he could try to show that the existence of a transcendent God is not really a necessary condition for having such experiences —

that they can be explained in other ways. Moreover, if the theist posits an internal relation between God and persons, Sartre might claim that this assertion lacks experiential confirmation. Sartre might claim that he is not engaging in fancy philosophical footwork but is trying to develop a theoretical framework that adequately captures the tensions of interpersonal experience, while the theist is doing fancy philosophy that lacks any connection to experience.

Whether Sartre could show that the transformation that happens to a person in religious experience does not alter his being is a difficult question; much depends on how one conceives *the being* of a person; I rather doubt that this strategy could succeed. Within the framework of Sartre's ontology, the theist might claim that religious experience provides consciousness with a positive content, that the nothingness which Sartre believes defines consciousness is really only a regional attribute, applicable only to those who do not yet "know" God. Certainly this would be a significant challenge; moreover, most of the transformations described by theists seem radical and qualitative; the altered person exists differently, far more fruitfully and expressively, than he did before. Whatever disputes might arise between Sartre and the theist on this issue would probably be verbal.

This leaves Sartre one final strategy: to deny that mystical experiences require the existence of God as a necessary condition. Here Sartre seems on far firmer ground than in his previous replies, for everything that *God* is alleged to be requisite for is something that can occur through the intercession of *other people*. Forgiveness, for example, is something people can offer each other, and the modification of being involved still occurs. It perhaps occurs more completely if the Other who forgives is institutionally or culturally sanctioned, but this is not always the case, nor does this alter the basic point. The forgiveness *can occur* through persons, and God cannot thus be claimed as a necessary condition for it.

Similarly, harmony with the cosmos can be achieved collectively through chant, orgy, or festival. The union of persons with each other can create a sense of complete unification with everything – a transcendence of separateness and individuality. Living in light rather than darkness involves either being understood or existing with a vision of goodness which seems by itself sufficient to motivate one to achieve it; both of these experiences can be achieved through persons. Persons can act as embodiments of virtue which move one naturally yet dramatically, and they can be the agents of understanding and comprehension. Indeed, those emerging from treatment with a skillful psychoanalyst might describe the fruits of their treatment in that fashion.

Thus, all these instances of religious experience seem achievable without the existence of God. The theist might think that other persons have these capacities only because God grants them to them, but this is an inference, and a contention that would not be easy to defend. Hence, there does seem to be a crucial difference between Sartre's argument and the theist's: Sartre can more readily demonstrate that God is not a necessary condition for the occurrence of religious experience.

Some important conclusions follow from this discussion. First, the crucial contention in Sartre's argument is the necessary condition claim; if that is problematic, his argument not only becomes unacceptable, but parallel with the theist's, and rehabilitating *it* may rehabilitate the theist's position as well. My critique will therefore focus on this claim.

Second, this reply to the theist works only if Sartre admits that other persons really do have the capacities I have claimed they have and thus that these capacities are not ruled out on theoretical grounds. If Sartre *denies* that Others can make such experiences possible, then the theist's argument will again appear in a more promising light. Thus, I can use the theist's argument as a lever to force Sartre to accept the emendations and additions to his concept of the Other-as-subject which I will later propose to improve his general theory of interpersonal experience.[141]

Third, one should now have a clearer understanding of the kind of position Sartre is taking and the pitfalls he is trying to avoid. Also, one can see how Sartre's intuition of the structural similarity in deliberations about God and other persons can be used to clarify both types of argument. I agree with Sartre, however, that God is an abstraction and generalization from the experiences of Others that lacks intuitive foundation. Although the theist's argument raises questions about Sartre's argument and suggests important critical issues, it does not establish that Sartre's position is unsound; it only necessitates a modification of some of his particular claims.

Lived solipsism

My second main criticism is not a conclusive objection, but it does limit the applicability of Sartre's position. The basic experience of the Other-as-subject that Sartre explicates is not an experience everyone has. There is a level of experience on which some persons do live, and most people sometimes live, which lies wholly beneath (lacks all awareness of) Sartre's Other-as-subject. I term this level of experience "lived solipsism," and it is a very real phenomenon quite distinct from egoism or the desire to dominate.[142] The present focus of this critique is the major argument; the premise being questioned is the major experience explicated. This experience is held to be *universal*,[143] for the explication is intelligible only for those who have had the experience.

This may be one reason why Sartre does not think he is giving a *proof*: his position is wholly contingent on the reader's having had the experience he explicates. Sartre does grant the possibility that a conscious being might exist who had never experienced the social self. He says that such a conscious being would not be a "man." At best, this is a verbal maneuver that will not circumvent any real issues or objections; at worst, it makes his theory definitionally true but leaves open the question whether "there are men."

Let us briefly examine the nature of lived solipsism. I give the phenomenon this name because a person who lives it *acts as if* he is a solipsist whether or not be believes the thesis that Others do or do not exist. It involves a fundamental obliviousness to the existence of Others, an unconscious indifference which is not reactive but which simply fails in any way to acknowledge the existence of Others. Lived solipsists never experience the Other-as-subject in Sartre's sense; indeed the paradigmatic Sartrean experience is perhaps the most powerful way to be awakened from lived solipsism. In general, because other centers of consciousness are not experienced, the lived solipsist experiences only his own purposes; he lacks any awareness that other purposes are possible or might conflict with his. Moreover, he takes no external viewpoint on his actions, nor does he label them; in effect, he is a man without qualities in the sense that he lives without any experience of public definition.

There are two main varieties of lived solipsism. A person who exhibits the first type lives wholly immersed in his own projects; he does not pursue them in contrast to or against the projects of Others. Others are simply additional bodies in the vicinity, no different from other physical objects. For him, the world is an expanse that exists between his present and his future self; he has no explicit awareness that he is self-absorbed; no other possibility presents itself to him. There are only his purposes and projects; everything else is ignored.

A person who exhibits the second type of lived solipsism lives no specific project of his own and does not experience himself in any significant sense either. He has been allocated a way of life, a set of tasks to perform, and he sets about them mechanically, automatically. He is as oblivious to his own feelings, wants, and potential choices as he is to those of Others. He lives his life as if he were a cog in a well-oiled machine. The machine may have been planned, but he has no awareness of or belief in the planners. Although he may have a dim awareness that other cogs must exist to make the machine perform, he has no explicit awareness of those cogs or of their importance to him.

Neither of these ways of life involves *choosing* isolation; indeed, lived solipsists may *believe* that Others exist and live amidst them, but they are not *touched* by them, and they remain wholly unconscious of any effect they may be having on Others. I make no claim that this frame of mind is primordial. I claim only that it lacks the paradigmatic Sartrean experience and, indeed, lacks all experience of the Other-as-subject in any sense. Lived solipsism is a level of existence, a dimension of personal and interpersonal comportment that remains perpetually open to everyone. It is rarely chosen; one slips into it. The Other's subjectivity can be forgotten and simply fails to register for significant periods of time.

In addition, lived solipsism is not a *reactive* phenomenon; all reactive ways of life retain consciousness of what they are reacting against, if only in order to sustain the reaction. For the lived solipsist, Others have either vanished or failed to emerge as subjects, and for such people the Sartrean subject would "lack reality, intuitive certainty, and acknowledgment." Lived solipsism may not be a common mode of approach to the world, but it does exist. For any theorist of interpersonal experience, it functions as the "zero degree" of that experience. Indicating its existence by no means overturns Sartre's position, but it does confine its range of applicability.

Sartre misses the phenomenon because he thinks all indifference is a *reaction*;[144] this view results from his inattention to the possibilities of experience. Moreover, if the Sartrean subject has never been experienced, I can explain why the perception of Others' bodies motivates no apprehension of their consciousness. Sartre insists that the Other-as-object appears to be human (creates a quaking in one's ordering of the world) *only because* it refers to the Other-as-subject. Without such a reference, no suggestion that bodies have subjectivity would arise, and one can thus understand how the lived solipsist can apprehend other bodies while maintaining his basic obliviousness to them. He grasps human bodies like any other physical object and integrates them into his world as he would any other instrument.

Were one to develop a full-blown theory of concrete relationships as Sartre does, the significance of this objection would be greater, for an entire level of experience — and thus a whole different set of relationships — would need to be clarified. Also the fact that this level is one to which anyone can regress has great importance for understanding the dynamics *and* structure of personal relationships.

Problems with Premise 3

I shall now provide objections that raise doubts about whether Sartre's argument establishes its conclusion. Specifically I shall question the truth of Premises 3 and 4. Premise 3 asserts that a physical object or event cannot make the transformation of oneself from subject to object possible. Two very different hypothetical examples cast some doubt on this position. In order to avoid begging the question against Sartre by presupposing the Other-as-subject, the most effective examples would be *empirical* cases of humans who had *never* had contact with any other humans (or animals); one would then need to determine whether the social self could arise for them. I know very little about what such people would be like, and I certainly do not have any examples to run experiments on — assuming that this were possible and ethical. So I must try to envision hypothetical situations in which the humans involved had no experience with Others, and I must imagine what they would be like and try to see whether the social self *could* emerge even though they have no experience with other subjects. The hypothetical quality of the examples may reduce their effectiveness, but philosophy often must do the best it can with imaginary cases.

Imagine a baby born on earth, immediately put to sleep, and sky-rocketed to a distant space station. The ship runs entirely automatically, monitored by computers. They ensure the child's nourishment and instruct his mind when he awakens. The baby matures alone, without human contact, yet he acquires language and all the normal cognitive capacities possessed by typical contemporary humans. He matures without awareness that there are other humans; the planners have decided that space station monitors, who must live their entire lives alone, are better left without awareness of the existence of Others like themselves. The child does communicate with the computers; together they run the ship and eventually the space station.

One day, the child undergoes a particularly vehement display of emotion; this emotion can be identified and named by the computer; it informs the young man that he is "excitable." Suddenly the space-adolescent experiences his social self; he realizes that he can be seen, classified, and totalized by the machine with which he works. If Sartre objects that mere trait-description is not sufficient for the experience of the social self, one can image a situation in which boy and computer disagree over the appropriate course of action. The computer, it turns out, is right and overrides the boy's orders. Here the boy not only experiences his nature, he also experiences his purposes limited and transgressed; he experiences himself as a mere instrument for the computer. This *will* be sufficient for the experience of the social self, and it has been made possible by the "actions" of the computer, presumably a "physical" object.

Sartre's reply to this case may appear obvious. The computer *is* the Other-as-subject; he may argue that the computer is a subject. The problem here is that computers are not typically taken to be conscious, which is the crucial requirement for Sartre. Admittedly, this computer has some extraordinary capacities, but they may be no greater than those of the actual computers that are currently used on manned space flights. Certainly, Sartre *cannot* say that some *other human* subjectivity is being apprehended across the behavior of the computer. Sartre *has to* attribute subjectivity to the computer itself to save his position.

Phyllis Morris offers a number of replies to this kind of objection that seem beside the point.[145] That the computer was constructed and programmed by other people is nowhere in the experience or understanding of such a boy, and hence it does not bear on this objection. She also suggests that the boy could not possess all the normal social predicates of our language; this is probably correct but has no force since what matters is whether the computer can make the boy experience his social self — not whether the boy is in all other respects like people are on earth. The issue is not whether the computer has another mind in the classical sense, but whether it can perform the function of Sartre's Other-as-subject. My example demonstrates the plausibility of this hypothesis.

Someone might wonder why Sartre need be bothered by this objection. He can either grant subjectivity to computers, or he can grant that computers can embody the Other-as-subject just like the wind and creaking floorboards. The first move is probably unavailable to Sartre because it implies that computers can have their own intentionality, transcendence, and privileged access, and Sartre would be unlikely to grant these capacities even to very sophisticated computers. The second move is a possible one for Sartre, but in my example the boy *never* has experienced another subjectivity before. So if Sartre takes this option, he must grant that computers can be the *founding* or *primordial* motivation for the boy's social self. Sartre's willingness to accept manifold embodiments of the Other-as-subject seems plausible only if one supposes that the initial transformation of one's existence must come at the hands of a person. Without this amendment, the ontological import of his position becomes suspect. Specifically one must wonder whether Sartre's Other is truly transcendent; it may become another way of talking about a transformation of oneself.

Consider another case. Suppose a young shipwrecked Robinson Crusoe lands on a deserted island and suffers total amnesia. He forgets his former self, the functions of objects, his past, his language, etc. He awakens with the simplest form of consciousness imaginable — sentience and goal-directedness. Somehow he learns to fend for himself and to survive; fortunately, the island is plentiful in natural fruits and other sustenance. No other animals exist there. What sort of awareness would this person have?

Let us suppose his recollection of experiences from the moment he awoke is retained. He then would have all the normal structures of pre-reflective consciousness: he would organize a world, realize projects (even though he does not name them), and experience a temporally unified stream of events. Presumably, he would be capable of determining the success and failure of various efforts to achieve ends; so he can improve. On the island he perceives only natural phenomena, flora and fauna, weather changes, etc., but no signs of civilization. He forms no self-concept and lives a day-to-day existence, sometimes exploring, other times resting or building.

Suppose, in addition, he has been struggling to achieve something but cannot do it (e.g., reach a particular mountain plateau). In the course of his efforts, it begins to rain, but he remains oblivious. He makes one more effort and fails again; he collapses in discouragement. Suddenly a startling rumble of thunder explodes above, and at that moment he suddenly experiences his social self; the thunder has reinforced his own discouragement. The thunderclap is experienced as a summary judgment on his efforts. The crucial fact here is that I have presupposed no reflective ability on his part. The judgment is not communicated in language; he himself comprehends it only vaguely and implicitly. But now he can experience his actions from an external viewpoint.

Sartre may again try to reply that the mere sense of an external dimension is insufficient to constitute the social self. I might then suppose that lightning strikes the place where he was engaged in his efforts and makes his climb impossible. Should he persevere, the thunder repeats a number of times. He may now experience a set of purposes outside himself conflicting with his own, making it impossible for him to live his own purposes. This will certainly be sufficient to constitute an experience of the social self.

Yet Sartre does have another reply at this point; he believes that natural phenomena cannot be experienced in the way I claim. They can only be seen as adverse, and therefore can only motivate alternative, or substitute, behavior; they cannot present a set of *conflicting* purposes.[146] One should note here that the *fact* of the matter — i.e., whether nature does have its own purposes in this case — is *irrelevant*; what counts is whether the man *can experience* nature in this way. (This is why Morris's way of reconstructing Premise 3 is incorrect: the issue is not whether physical objects inherently lack the capacity to objectify, but whether they can ever be experienced as having this capacity.) I see no reason why nature cannot be so experienced; indeed many theorists have thought one could project one's own subjectivity into such events. I criticized such a view while discussing Husserl, but this example suggests one way in which natural events can be experienced as more than merely adverse. Most people today have some concept of *fate* — something which affects their own purposes without their being able to ultimately affect it. The process by which this concept develops in us (it need not derive from Others) might be analogous to that involved in the Crusoe case.

The central element in this example is that no other conscious being is ever experienced; no language is used to communicate the judgment or the limitation of one's purposes. Yet a *physical event* seems to have made the experience of the social self possible. If Sartre is to save his argument, he must now make the highly implausible statement that nature is a subject, but nature is precisely what Sartre wishes to contrast with subjectivity.

In both examples, I have tried to forestall the potential reply that a *previous experience* of subjectivity made possible these experiences of the social self; so Sartre cannot use this reply. Perhaps the Other-as-subject is a single, real, transcendent being that *can be instantiated* by such events, but that view makes the Other function like a universal or a concept. Moreover, this kind of reply renders the nature of the Other-as-subject difficult to understand; more and more it seems to be an *hypostatization* to account for an event that Sartre cannot explain in other ways. Taken together these two examples cast some doubt on Premise 3, and whatever replies Sartre has available seem to lead from the frying pan into the fire.

Problems with Premise 4

I can now examine Premise 4, which asserts that one cannot by oneself make the transformation of oneself into an object possible. I shall begin this discussion with counter-examples and then investigate the supporting arguments Sartre uses to buttress Premise 4. I shall explore two sorts of related counter-examples: guilt and hyper-consciousness.

Let us assume that G. has articulated a coherent system of values of his own but that he continually fails to live up to them. Because his ideals are self-chosen, G.'s guilt is especially intense. He feels incapable of anything. These are not reflective judgments but pre-reflective intuitions; one might see them as internal radicalizations of the kind of discouragement Crusoe experienced in the example above. Guilt, like shame, can be a shudder that runs through one's being. Guilt can also be as debilitating as shame; it can neutralize G.'s purposes as effectively as an external Other, often more effectively. Moreover, it can create a devastating, inescapable totalization. G. cannot see himself as anything but a person who has transgressed or cannot attain his ideals.

Thus, the basic effects that Sartre associates with the social self can occur in guilt. One sees oneself as an object but only for oneself, and one can become mesmerized by this object. No other person is required to experience guilt; the case I have offered does not involve an internalization of the Other's look. There thus may be a case of self-induced transformation of oneself into an object.

Sartre might retort that guilt presupposes a prior experience of shame, or judgment by Others. Guilt would then be shame in which the self takes the role of the Other, and without the initial experience of the Other, adopting that role would not be possible. Here again, Sartre's reply is not easy to evaluate.

If it could be shown that the Crusoe-figure described previously could experience guilt, that would be a definitive reply. Almost certainly some story of how guilt might arise in him could be told, but its plausibility would be more difficult to determine. At least three steps would be required: the formation of judgments, the application of judgments to his own actions, and the radicalization of this application. Although judgment exceeds perception, it does not seem to require the existence of Others; it may not even have to be formulated in a language. Moreover, the phenomenon of discouragement indicates that a pre-reflective judgment can be made on one's own actions; this judgment would seem to be independent of Others. Finally, the severity of judgment seems to depend only on the degree and repetition of failure, and this is independent of Others. Hence it would seem that the constitution of guilt could occur without the presence, or even assumed existence, of Others. The main question is whether the formation of an internal standard that could not be satisfied, or principle that could be transgressed, is possible in the absence of all Others.

The other experience from which the social self may arise without the intervention of Others is hyper-consciousness. In hyper-consciousness one gains an explicit objectified sense of one's own lack of being anything; one literally experiences oneself as nothing because one dissociates from all one's actions and qualities.[147] One does not just experience oneself as not-this and not-that; one eventually experiences oneself as being incapable of having any nature or quality. And one comes to experience this formlessness as self-definitional; this is how the experience of being-nothing gets objectified.

Here the Other is not the source of the transformation. Although he *may* motivate the original dissociation through rejection, his intervention is by no means necessary. The complete withdrawal of one's "own" viewpoint to an observational position can occur solely through one's own reflection. Here, too, one experiences an objectified self – *a self which can never be anything*, a perpetual void – and the purposes of the astral-observer self are wholly exhausted in the dissociation. The difference between this experience and guilt is that in guilt one has specific content over which one despairs while in hyper-consciousness one's lack of content is the very objectivization one experiences. Both cases seem to indicate ways in which one's objectivity might be induced solely by oneself.

Sartre does have some replies. He can say that if one experiences guilt or one's own nothingness, the being he calls the Other-as-subject now exists *within* oneself or at least can be instantiated by some aspect of oneself. This is less inconsistent than it might sound, for the aspect of self that is the center of judgment in guilt is *not* the acting subject, and the astral self that experiences the nothingness is distinct from the acting, everyday self; both observe from a removed standpoint. Hence Sartre, even in this case, may be able to distinguish the Other-as-subject from the self-as-object.

However this reply does begin to bleed the Other-as-subject of content; it seems more and more to be a universal function that can be instantiated by computers, nature, and oneself, rather than a concrete being that can be clearly delineated or made determinate. In short, in these replies Sartre is moving toward a more and more abstract Other-as-subject, and thus he will become more susceptible to the objections he made to Heidegger.

Sartre's other reply is that these cases depend on types of reflective self-evaluation, which he claims cannot exist without the prior experience of other people. Once again, one must consider whether the Crusoe-figure could experience himself in this fashion. If he failed often enough, he might be reduced to a sense of his own incapacity to do or be anything. His ability to experience a sense of general vacuity would depend on his ability to synthesize the various instances of failure into a single evaluation. One imagines a character in one of Beckett's short plays reduced to mute inaction, unwilling to respond to any stimulus. Thus, this experience may be possible without the intervention of other people.

If these examples have any persuasiveness, then something must be wrong with the considerations Sartre adduces to support Premise 4. Recall that I distinguished three kinds of reasons used to defend this premise: empirical ones, a *reductio* argument, and a priori ones.

Empirical considerations

The empirical consideration is that since the transformation *appears* to derive from a source other than oneself, that source must *actually* be distinct. Four problems can be raised about this point.

First, in some cases, notably the ones previously indicated, the assertion does not seem true. The source of the transformation appears to be *within* oneself rather than outside oneself. Consciousness seems to be splitting, turning back on itself, and successfully providing itself with a nature. Although these examples are not common, they do occur frequently enough to render this empirical consideration problematic.

Second, if the *underlying premise* of this consideration (i.e., things are what they seem) is accurate, then the first point would lead one to assert that in fact the source of the transformation *is oneself*, not merely that it so appears. Hence if Sartre's underlying view is convincing, it renders the conclusion he seeks problematic because of my counter-examples.

Third, the underlying premise is not generally reliable in this area, for what appears to be the case often is not the case, as the phenomena of projection and introjection attest. Sometimes one is angry, but one apprehends the Other as angry instead; one fails to correctly locate the source of anger. Also, the Other may be depressed, and instead of locating it in him, one suddenly finds oneself depressed. These cases occur frequently; confusion about the owner or locus of mental states is far more common than Cartesians and incorrigibilists believe. They suggest that, at least in the area of interpersonal experience, things are not always what they seem.

Fourth, empirical considerations alone can never vindicate a premise asserting the *impossibility* of something; at best they can *only* lend support; here they fail to do even that.

The reductio *argument*

In the second kind of consideration, the *reductio* argument, Sartre assumes that the source of the transformation *could be* within oneself and derives the apparently false conclusion that the Other-as-subject would be functioning either like a Kantian concept or an object in one's own world. Since this is precisely how the Other-as-subject is not experienced, the original assumption is taken to be wrong.

As an argument against an opponent, this consideration is not very strong, for it seems to use the correctness of the view it seeks to establish in the course of the argument; it implicitly begs the question. The issue is how the experience of the Other is to be comprehended; to conceive the Other as a concept may provide the best account; it cannot be excluded solely on the basis of how the experience appears.

However, the stronger point against this argument is that although an experience of something can be produced by or through oneself, this need not entail that the existence of the entity is dependent on, or a function of, oneself and thus lacks transcendence. Many concepts, for example, emerge through complex abstraction and comparison between previously learned concepts. One comes to experience and understand such concepts on one's own; yet on at least one view of concepts, their existence is not dependent on oneself nor reducible to the consciousness one has of them. The experience is one of insight into something beyond oneself; one is *initiated*; one discovers something that had been accessible to Others but not yet to oneself.

Moreover, the objects of dream experience, while wholly originating with oneself, do not function either like Kantian concepts or like ordinary objects of perception. Dreams can be lived vividly; one's own body even moves in response to the imagined creatures and events in the dreams. One can dream of an Other-as-subject and experience a relevant transformation and then retain this experience while awake. The dreamed Other is not a filter or rule that organizes one's experience, nor is he an ordinary object.

These examples show that self-constituted entities need not function like Kantian concepts (dreams), and need not even be dependent on oneself for their existence (concepts). Thus the main assumption in the *reductio* argument is problematic, and the counter-examples previously presented against Premise 4 do not seem affected by it.

The a priori considerations

This leaves the a priori considerations, viz., that consciousness cannot objectify and cannot limit itself. Although consciousness has the capacity to reflect, this process allegedly cannot generate the sense of limit and objectification that the Other-as-subject does. One reason Sartre thinks reflection lacks this capacity is that he sees it as primarily retrospective; consciousness retains awareness of its open future, and hence of its transcendence and unlimitedness, even if its past is wholly totalized by the reflective act.

However, the reflective state of mind can often overflow its temporal boundaries and be experienced as determining the entire future. This is especially true in illness, but also in many emotional states; in such cases the transcendence of consciousness seems qualified, if not limited.[148] There are also cases in which careful reflection over one's past exhibits a pattern so clear and a "disposition" so ingrained that one can see no way beyond it. It has a fatalistic aura around it, and one expects it to be operative in future situations as much as in past ones. Here the sense of limitation is much stronger.

Moreover, reflection can operate like guilt. The judgment involved can be severe enough to provide an intense shock: one experiences oneself objectified and frozen by the assessment. This can happen when one's ordinary behavior is given a new interpretation, and this conclusion corroborates a pattern one is trying to avoid. One wonders if one will ever succeed in freeing oneself from it.

Sartre might try to differentiate these experiences from that of the social self by claiming that one eventually *emerges* from the assessments of reflection; however, this is also true of the social self. One eventually recovers from the Other's look.

He might argue, further, that one *must* emerge from the reflective state; one cannot exist in it indefinitely. However, Sartre's own novels suggest the improbability of this view. Mathieu Delarue, in the *Age of Reason*, seems to be a man lost in reflection, unable to return to the pre-reflective level. Everything he does is inhabited by his self-image, by his states and dispositions, his past commitments; he thinks they must of themselves carry over into the future. Even though he embarks on new projects, he cannot experience them pre-reflectively. One could live one's entire life in this fashion. Although I agree that there is some difference in degree between the typical case of social self-consciousness and reflective self-consciousness, the self that emerges in reflection can seem just as limiting and just as objective as the social self.

Sartre's last objection to this sort of case would be that reflection cannot arise without previously experiencing social self-consciousness. Here I think Sartre is on weak ground. If a person retains memories, then he has the capacity to organize them into a narrative, and this is the basic task of reflection. It is an activity which synthesizes previous acts into totalities that extend beyond their sources. If *any* perception of patterns is possible without social self-consciousness, I see no reason why this capacity could not be applied to memories, and this, in essence, is reflection in Sartre's sense.

Sartre might still wonder how one's sense that there could be a pattern to one's acts of consciousness and behavior arises. If there were other sentient beings or even other persons in the vicinity, one could learn this by objectifying their actions, and even if one had not experienced the Other-as-*subject*, one could apply such processes of objectification to oneself on the basis of perceived similarities between one's memories of their acts and of one's own acts. In short, Sartre forgets that even if one assumes that one's experience of one's own consciousness is qualitatively distinct from the experience of the Other-as-object, one's *memories* of Others and those of self do not differ in this way, and on the basis of these retrospective memories, reflection in Sartre's sense could be built.

Pure introspection also seems capable of emerging on its own without the necessity of social self-consciousness. Any startling experience is bound to produce amazement and may motivate an effort on the part of consciousness to grasp itself. Thus, there are plausible ways in which reflection could emerge without requiring an antecedent experience of the Other-as-subject.

These replies taken collectively weaken the force of Sartre's considerations supporting Premise 4. Whether the counter-examples plus these replies are sufficient to overthrow those considerations is difficult to determine. Sartre's a priori considerations are the strongest ones, but such considerations often do not carry much weight in the face of examples; here, however, the examples are only imaginary possibilities. On balance, they do seem convincing enough to force Sartre into an undesirable analysis of the Other-as-subject.

Problems in Sartre's replies to objections

I initially attempted to reconstruct Sartre's argument as persuasively as possible; in doing so I presented his replies to two important objections. However, the force of the first reply, that the Other is a necessary condition of − not an inference from − the experience of the social self, wholly depended on the correctness of the premises which have now drawn important criticism. Moreover, his reply there depended on the claim that inference and belief are explicit processes.

There are, however, important instances where inference, judgment, and belief are subliminal, and additional arguments would be needed to show that these cases can be more effectively analyzed in another fashion. I happen to have sympathy with Sartre's position, but the difference between inference, interpretation, judgment and pure perception (if it exists) can be virtually non-existent. One can think one is hearing someone's words, but one may have already made an inference from them. So one must acknowledge that the phenomenological considerations concerning standard cases of belief and inference may not be conclusive. Hence Sartre's reply to the first objection stands in need of greater defense, at minimum.

Also, the reply to the second objection, that the absence of the Other assumes a more primordial presence of the Other-as-subject, though initially convincing, may need further support. Key questions are: *which* Other's presence is presupposed? what is the concrete content of this more basic presence? can one verify or determine the presence of the Other-as-subject in any way other than through the experience of the social self?

In a sense Sartre is noting that one lives amidst Others even when they are distant, and one certainly does retain some sort of awareness of them. But one's grasp of their relation to oneself is often mistaken; one may believe they remain in love, but in fact they may have long forgotten. Yet the absent Other's presence is not just one's own imagination. The texture and flavor of his life suffuse the world one experiences; he can function as the target to whom one addresses one's acts. But is he more than this address and that experience? What justifies the assertion that this experienced presence means that there is a real being of some sort corresponding to it? There are many presences which fail to have corresponding existent objects, e.g., after-images. They seem to inhabit the twilight zone between imagination and perception; that may also be the residence of the Other-as-subject.

Although I have already shown that Sartre must make this Other-as-subject a more abstract, universal function that can be instantiated by many different kinds of events if he is to save his argument, a number of additional problems with his conception can be raised. They are of two sorts: metaphysical and phenomenological. Although Sartre might reject the metaphysical standpoint, certain questions raised by his conception require some discussion. One question is: from the viewpoint of the whole, how many Others-as-subject are there? Is there a pre-numerical subjectivity *for each person*, and are these all distinct? Would then the 'number' of these beings be the same as the number of persons experiencing them? Another question arises in a situation where two different people experience the look of a single third: are there two Others-as-subject in such situations, or just one? Suppose the third sees each person very differently (or very similarly); does this affect the answer? Answers to these questions would help clarify the status of the Other-as-subject.

Sartre rejects such questions because they are offered from a point of view different from that of phenomenological ontology. This is true. Yet the concerns raised by these questions cannot be swept aside with the assertion that the Other is pre-numerical. Experience does bear on the questions even if the point of view that corresponds to them (i.e., the absolute spectator) cannot itself be experienced by anyone.

One might perhaps rephrase the same questions within the phenomenological perspective: to what extent is the Other-as-subject whom I see objectifying L. (who also experiences him) identical to the same Other seeking to, and partially succeeding in, objectifying me? Can I not experience differential effects from two different centers of subjectivity at once (e.g., one approving, another critical)? Does this mean that the Other-as-subject is divisible? This is how one experiences it on occasion, and the clarity of these divisions suggests that conceiving the Other as a pre-numerical quasi-totality does not accurately capture one's entire experience of the Other-as-subject.

If, as Sartre believes, all comprehension of the Other's concrete vision were hidden from us, Sartre's view of the Other-as-subject would be more plausible, for such divisions could not be experienced as such. The fact that they are experienced only adds additional reasons against his claim that the Other's assessment is not in any way apprehended.

A second phenomenological consideration is that we do experience the Other as subject as *particular* on occasion: *this* Other sees this side of me; *that* Other sees another, and the effect of the Other on us differs when different bodies instantiate the Other-as-subject. Yet this suggests that the Other-as-subject himself differs.

Here I am only echoing Sartre's earlier objection against Heidegger: that he does not account for the particularity of the Other's subjectivity. If the Other is pre-numerical, he *cannot* be made particular, and this suggests some inadequacy in Sartre's conception.

The bond between self and Other: the social self

Sartre now turns to a fuller elucidation of the ontological relation between two persons and the ontological status of the structure that binds them together: the social self.[149] In this section Sartre's discussion remains technical and philosophical, but he returns to an elucidation of the essential structures of interpersonal experience. Hence, my criticisms will again seek a broader perspective: I shall explore alternatives and press various kinds of problem cases, as well as engage in direct refutation.

In this part of his theory, Sartre offers much less in the way of argument and justification for his conclusions; some of his assertions have been defended in earlier sections of *Being and Nothingness*, and he probably believes that some simply follow from his earlier claims. Since the supporting evidence is sparser, this exposition can be more condensed. Where his analysis depends on discussions that appear earlier in the text, I shall offer synopses but omit the details.

The second series of claims

Two irreducible dimensions

Sartre begins by noting that one's social self cannot be reduced to or derived from one's own consciousness;[150] this is the force of his claim that the Other-as-subject is a necessary condition for its existence. Neither can consciousness be derived from the social self.[151] The mode of existence of each is different, for the social self exists *without* having to be sustained by consciousness, while consciousness must continually sustain and rechoose itself. The social self is imposed on consciousness by Others; even if one sought to abandon it, one could not do so. Thus, in a world of Others, a person always exists in two dimensions: for-himself and for-Others.[152] There is no necessity to this two-dimensional existence: it exists only because Others exist, and their existence is a contingent fact.[153]

Although Sartre acknowledges the experience of lived time, the inner flow of conscious states, he thinks that the experience of time necessary for experiencing oneself as an *historical* being arises because of the Other-as-subject. When one experiences the social self, one is placed amidst 'objective' spatio-temporal coordinates. To understand one's life as a narrative with respect to those coordinates is only possible if one adopts the viewpoint of Others. Since Others make this experience of historicity possible, the emergence of the Other-as-subject *cannot be dated*; it is the origin of the experience of datability.[154] This experience of time also permits one to grasp oneself as identical through time. One cannot experience the self as the sort of thing that *could be* identical through time except under the gaze of Others.

Internal negation

Consciousness exists in the same relation to Others as to any other entity: internal negation.[155] This simply means that consciousness *makes itself not-be*, and hence *is not*, that object. This relation is *internal* because it constitutes the essence of consciousness. For Sartre, the being of consciousness is wholly parasitic: *it exists only in so far as it is not its object*. The being of consciousness is only the peripheral awareness of *not-being* the object which it reveals. The plenitude of the object threatens the existence of consciousness; it escapes this threat by distinguishing itself from (making itself not-be) that plenitude.[156] Yet consciousness *cannot exist* without an object to not-be; an object-less consciousness is impossible. So too is a consciousness that is *identical* to its object; but this potential *fall* into identity and consequent loss of itself is a perpetual threat to consciousness.

In what ways does consciousness have a relation of internal negation to the Other? First, in any encounter with the Other, consciousness must make itself not-be the Other; in this process a peripheral awareness of itself as being distinct from the Other arises and, consequently, the Other's distinctness is experienced.[157] In this implicit awareness (of not-being the Other) lies the origin of the possibility of being aware of oneself as identical through time.[158] The pre-numerical Other-as-subject always appears as the same, and one's own sense of continuity arises from the continual necessity to negate (make oneself not-be) this Other.[159]

There are two ways in which consciousness can make itself not-be the Other: *direct negation*, in which the Other is made into an object, and *indirect negation*, in which one differentiates oneself from the social self.[160] The mode of being in which one exists depends on which type of negation is operating: if one negates the Other directly, one retains one's subjectivity; if one experiences one's social self, one can negate the Other only indirectly by negating (and thereby assuming) it.

A continuous choice to not-be the Other is necessary if the differentiation of self and Other is to exist in the subject's experience — rather than being merely established from the theoretical perspective of a third witness.[161] The monad view of self has become so predominant because many philosophers have conceptualized the self-Other relation only from the third-person, observer's viewpoint. If one adopts the first-person, actor's viewpoint, the only way this distinction can be established is through an internal negation.

Reciprocal internal negation

But this story is still incomplete, for the difference between other people and ordinary material objects is that Others are conscious and must thus also internally negate oneself.[162] Thus, two *opposed* negations interact in any encounter. Sartre asserts, without much argument, that *only one* of these negations can predominate.[163]

The dominant, direct negation makes there be a social self for the Other. The subordinate person distinguishes himself from the social self by indirectly negating it.[164] The indirect negation operates on *the social self* that has been imposed on one, but in the process one also accepts that structure as *part* of what one is, for the need to negate it establishes that it has some existential status and some relation to oneself.[165] One does not differentiate oneself from just *any* social self but from the one that qualifies oneself. This indirect negation could potentially become a direct negation of the Other himself. The self-differentiation it provides threatens to become explicit and thereby to objectify the Other.

Moreover, as can be seen from the description, the social self arises *through* one negation (the direct one) and *motivates* another (the indirect one). The social self is neither wholly identical nor wholly distinct from either consciousness; it is their bond and their separation, the limit produced by one and implicitly assumed — yet indirectly negated — by the other.[166] The social self is an ontological membrane constituted by both *in so far as they must both negate each other.*

Asymmetry

The social self must arise in any encounter between two subjects, and one person becomes dominant by imposing the social self on the other: one is subject and the other becomes object. Two consciousnesses can *never* both be subjects for each other or objects to one another; I shall call this the "asymmetry claim." Whenever self is *object*, Other is *subject*; whenever Other is *object*, self is *subject.*[167] This is the first truly relational claim in Sartre's theory; it asserts a relation *between two entities* rather than between different modes of one's own experience.

Sartre also infers that, since the social self arises in any encounter, the experiences of the Other-as-subject and the Other-as-object *exhaust all possibilities*; they are the *only* two modes of experience of the Other.[168] The asymmetry claim and the exhaustivity claim are central to Sartre's theory of concrete relationships. Social life, for Sartre, consists in the perpetual oscillation of these modalities. Despite this alternation, Sartre asserts that the *fundamental* mode of the Other is his subjectivity; to make the Other into an object is only a defense against the totalization of oneself he creates by constituting one's social self.[169]

The transformations between modes are emotional.[170] Sartre describes three of them, one of which has already been clarified: shame, fear, and pride. His descriptions of fear and pride are not sufficiently interesting to discuss in detail. His point in all cases is that one only escapes the experience of the social self by *making* the Other into an object, making his social self appear.[171] Although one may still retain awareness of his designs on one, one overcomes them by incorporating them into one's own designs: the Other becomes an objectified-subject.[172]

The Other-as-object

Sartre's central point is that the objectivity of the Other is not simply something that exists; it is something one *makes happen* to him. In this sense one is responsible for the modality in which the Other exists even though one need not have any specific intention toward him; if one simply pursues one's own ends and utilizes the Other when his paths intersect with one's own, one thereby constitutes his object state.[173] There remains an ever-present threat that he will become the Other-as-subject. Sartre concludes that most relationships with Others are designed to maintain the Other as an object so that one can avoid experiencing the displacement of one's own projects that arises when one experiences the Other-as-subject.[174]

The object state is the only mode in which the Other can be *known*, but, in principle, he can be known *exhaustively* by comprehending all the instrumental relations by which his world is organized.[175] Using this method, one can understand his basic purposes and their hierarchical relationships. These are as accessible to the observer as they are to the actor. Precisely because he is so immersed in them, the actor often has difficulty cognizing them. Thus one does not comprehend the Other by referring his qualities and aims in the object state to a subjectivity behind them; they refer only to other instrumental relations with the world.[176] Although one can be mistaken about the Other's aim, so can he, and both self and Other discover their errors by learning future developments in self's relation to the world.[177] Although this theory shares with behaviorism the effort to comprehend the Other by studying his observable actions, it differs in so far as it strives to see the Other as a goal-directed being rather than one who responds mechanically to antecedent conditions.

The Other-as-subject can never be *known* as such, and he has no relation to the organization of projects that characterize the Other-as-object. The ideal of *self-knowledge* demands an exhaustive elucidation of one's instrumental relations with the world.[178] In short, *knowledge* of oneself is possible, but *only* from the *viewpoint* of the Other; although one has additional access to oneself, this only provides an intuitive certainty that is very difficult to articulate into *knowledge.*

The two modes of the Other are simply distinct; they have no relationship to one another, except exclusion.[179] Neither mode of the Other is beyond one's experience, but each is experienced in a wholly distinct, and mutually exclusive, fashion. One learns nothing more about one dimension of the Other by referring it to or comparing it with the other dimension; they have no common measure. Each mode of the Other conceals the other mode, and at any moment a transformation of modes can occur; the disappearance of one evokes the other.[180]

In Sartre's system, the two dimensions or modes of a person seem to diverge even *more widely* than the classical conceptions of body and mind, but he overcomes the alleged hiddenness of the Other, first, by elucidating the *phenomenal* presence of *both* dimensions; second, by establishing internal relations among persons; and, third, by providing a different method of access to each dimension of a person.

Synopsis

One can distill this movement of Sartre's theory into five additional claims:

Claim 6   The basic relation between self and Other is internal negation, direct or indirect.

Claim 7   Between conscious beings the internal negations are reciprocal and, consequently, one undermines the other; only asymmetrical (subject-object; object-subject) interpersonal relations are possible.

Claim 8   The Other-as-subject is the *primordial* modality; the effort to make the Other into an object is a defensive measure against the Other-as-subject. Thus, all relationships strive to maintain the Other in his objectivity.

Claim 9   Each mode of the Other is self-sufficient and self-contained; only the Other-as-object can be known.

Claim 10 The Other-as-subject and the Other-as-object are *exhaustive* modalities.

Discussion and evaluation

Sartre's claims have problems of inconsistency, of limited application, and of inaccuracy. I shall present objections to each claim separately, concentrating only on the most important issues.

Claim 6

Claim 6 asserts that the basic relation between self and Other is internal negation, direct or indirect. In this section, I wish to explore the ways Sartre was overly captivated by his own theory and thus remained blind to the phenomena. I respect Sartre's efforts to elucidate an internal relationship between self and Other and agree that the monad view of the self — the view that self-Other relationships can only be external — has hindered the development of an adequate theory of Others. Still, in believing that the internal relation *had to be* a negation, Sartre was mesmerized by his own conception of the nothingness of consciousness and by his seemingly innocuous definition: the Other is the one who is *not-oneself.*

At least three other types of internal relation can exist between self and Other: (1) they can find themselves in a *primordial* unity; (2) they can establish an ontological bond with each other through *explicit affirmation* rather than negation; (3) there can be a *non-active* negation among people who are part of the same emotional or normative system. In the third case, alternations in any individual subliminally alter the states of all the Others, but no explicit negation is involved. A loose bond threads the group together but yet does not unite it into a real totality.

The *first* alternative internal relation between self and Other is antecedent primordial unity — to exist without any self-differentiation.

The child may not differentiate himself from the family; the family's feelings, thoughts, attitudes, expectations, and ideals can be his own. Other groups can assume a similar role later in life. The unification they effect may vary in depth, but the bonds are more evident than the separations. In this case, there are *not* wholly separate selves functioning as independent centers, but rather a common set of experiences is instantiated in many particular people. Instead of internal *negation*, there is implicit internal *identification*; no *explicit* process of unification is required. Once the experience of a stranger or an out-group arises, this identification begins to become explicit; it must then be *affirmed* if it is to be maintained.

A *second* alternative is the affirmation of self and Other that comes from most responsive encounters with Others. Here one discovers oneself through receptiveness to the Other — not through any definition he imposes — but through who he is and the manner in which he approaches one. For example, one sits alone depressed; the telephone rings. A friend cheerfully solicits a game of tennis. Depression disappears; one's spirit quickens in response to his cheerfulness, and a new self emerges in response — one that is capable of friendship. The Other elicits a response which is part of one's potential but which would not emerge without him. Here what appears is the reality of the *dyad* over and above one's momentary experiences; it forges new possibilities. Yet no definition of the Other as not-self will accurately capture the reciprocity, the mutual completion, that these dyads create. No negation exists here, only affirmation; one rediscovers one's relatedness to that person, *that dyad*, and the self existing *in* that dyad *emerges* to meet the Other who calls one out of one's isolation and self-enclosedness. One exists outside oneself with the Other; all that is needed to bring this self to realization is his presence, his call.

The *third* alternative consists of individuals who acknowledge their separation, yet exist in proximity to one another, e.g., spectators at a play, a film, or a lecture. No awareness of antecedent unity exists, and there is insufficient knowledge of one another to respond in reciprocally affirmative ways. Yet no social self forms among them. They have only *ancillary* awareness of each other. They are *neither subjects nor objects* for each other. They all exist in the midst of the event, and even their *co-subjectivity* does not explicitly register in their awareness. Nevertheless, they are not isolated; each affects all the Others. The excitement of one magically spreads to Others — as if they all exist in an implicit system whose alterations are felt by all of them. They do not lose their separateness; yet their underlying mood is transmitted to one another, and this unites them in subtle ways. Although there is a separation, it is not either explicit or implicit in Sartre's sense; awareness of the Other *as such* is not explicit here. The persons are ontologically bound to one another, but the bond is not negation, direct or indirect. No *explicit* awareness of this bond exists; yet it underlies their experience.

These are just a few of the alternatives to which Sartre's position remains oblivious. Although Sartre might try to deny the possibility of these experiences or argue that they are evanescent psychological states without ontological import, both replies would be weak. Everyone has had these experiences. One does *not* always negate Others; yet one may nevertheless have an internal relation to them in that what one is (how one exists) depends on what they are (how they exist).

One cannot rely on simple formulas when one elucidates lived experience. One must *look*: investigate the *whole range* of the area one is seeking to clarify. The theorist's task, however, only begins with thorough phenomenological investigation. It may yield a typology, but one must go on to create a way of organizing the types into a system and to grasp the connections among its terms.

Claim 7

Claim 7 asserts that between conscious beings the internal negations that operate are reciprocal; one of the negations predominates; the other can only be indirect. This means that only asymmetrical self-Other relations are possible. This latter claim is probably the most important proposition in Sartre's theory of concrete relations; hence it will be treated in some detail.

The reciprocity claim

The first part of the claim has two deep problems: (1) Sartre has not demonstrated that the Other-as-subject (or object) has the capacity to negate us, to differentiate himself from us as we do from him, for he has not demonstrated that the Other-as-subject has consciousness in the sense that we have it; (2) Sartre *cannot*, within the parameters laid down by his theory, demonstrate this claim because to grasp its truth directly would be to *know* the Other-as-subject, which is impossible, and to grasp it indirectly would require that one adopt the standpoint of an *external observer*, which Sartre claims to be invalid. There is no path within the boundaries of his theory by which Sartre can legitimately defend this claim.

Let us examine these two problems more closely. When Sartre asserts that the internal negation is reciprocal because the Other is a being who is a for-itself, and thus makes-himself-be by differentiating himself from his object, he is claiming something far more than he has shown in his previous discussion. Moreover, some of his explicit assertions raise doubts about this claim. Sartre seems to forget that the Other-as-subject is not a correlate of that particular person's body over there, but is, instead, a pre-numerical, semi-universal quasi-totality that gets instantiated by many different events.

Sartre may safely assert that the Other-as-subject has purposes and has the capacity for judgment since these are the aspects of the Other which are experienced when the social self emerges: one's purposes are qualified and circumscribed by his, and one's definitionless nature suddenly acquires qualities as a result of his look. Nevertheless, this does not demonstrate that the Other-as-subject is conscious in the way that people are conscious, for, as was shown above, computers can perfectly well have those capacities, and they do not seem to be conscious in the way people are.

Sartre must demonstrate that the Other-as-subject has a *simultaneous*, *non-thetic* awareness of his purposes, and show that he exists perpetually *in question* as people do. This he has not known, and, indeed, one's experience of the Other-as-subject in so far as it is a quasi-totality *does not confirm* this view. The Other-as-subject seems impervious to one's resistance, always capable of emerging, regardless of one's efforts to prevent this. He exhibits a unity and continuity that one lacks. Thus, on experiential grounds, the Other does not appear to be similar to ourselves.

There are, however, even stronger theoretical grounds for doubt. *Can* a pre-numerical, quasi-totality *be conscious* of itself? On the basis of Sartre's discussion of we-subject fusion, the closest analogue to a quasi-totality, the answer would seem to be no, even within Sartre's framework. The *we-subject*, he holds, *is not* a *genuine unity of consciousness*, only an ancillary, evanescent, psychic construction.[181] Moreover, the semi-abstractness or universality of the Other-as-subject suggests that he does not exist *in question* as we do, for he has manifold incarnations in a way that we do not.

Sartre errs here in thinking he has established the existence of another being wholly like oneself; the differences seem more impressive than the similarities. Moreover, Sartre does not demonstrate that the Other has the capacity to negate in the way that his reciprocal negation claim requires, nor has he shown that the Other-as-object differentiates itself from our look by negating the social self we constitute for it. Sartre has simply *transferred our viewpoint on ourselves into the Other-as-subject*, but he has not shown that this Other can have these characteristics.

There is a more serious difficulty. Not only is it the case that Sartre *has not shown* the Other reciprocally negates oneself, but he *cannot* show this without denying one of the assertions that establish the parameters of his theory. Sartre believes that if one were to intuit the conscious states of the Other as they are for-himself, one would *be* the Other since the only one who can intuit a person's conscious states is himself. Yet to apprehend that the Other-as-subject is conscious as one is and exists as one does would require that one intuit his conscious states. Although one can grasp his transcendence, his purposes, and his judgments, one cannot grasp the consciousness that posits those purposes, nor his specific process of arriving at those judgments. As long as one remains within the first-person standpoint, one cannot know what Sartre requires one to know in Claim 7, viz., that the Other is like oneself. In addition, Sartre asserts that adopting a third-person, external-observer viewpoint will only allow one to apprehend the Other-as-object; one will be able to grasp nothing at all about the Other-as-subject from this standpoint.

Hence from neither viewpoint, first- or third-person, can the consciousness of the Other be known, intuited, apprehended, or grasped. These are the limits of Sartre's theory. Although he needs to be able to speak of Others who are conscious like oneself, he *cannot* do so: his theory prevents him from doing so.

The asymmetry claim

As a transition to a concrete discussion of the asymmetry claim, consider some ways in which the negations that can occur between two conscious beings may exist without having the basic effect that Sartre takes to be their necessary consequence. Sartre thinks that one negation must predominate; it creates the social self of the Other.

There are at least three ways in which an internal *negation* can be present and not yield the basic effect that Sartre describes: (1) the negation can be one-directional *without any reciprocation*; (2) there can be reciprocal negations which do not cancel each other; both may predominate *to a similar degree*, and both may be explicit; and (3) there can be reciprocal negations which *do not affect each* other; they pass over each other but do not touch. I shall explore each of these possibilities; they demonstrate that even if one accepts negation as the basic relation between self and Other one must acknowledge greater complexity than Sartre grants.

The first kind of alternative exists when a person's entire existence is conditioned by the Other's negation or when he explicitly affirms that negation. In the first instance, one's entire life is provided organization, direction, and coherence by the requirements, ascriptions, and purposes of the Other. One has *no other* life but what one is for the Other. No self exists *for-itself* here. In such cases the dominating negation is *not reciprocated* since no self-differentiation occurs. This is the 'slave' whose entire existence is encompassed by his slave-role; his 'self' becomes literally an appendage of the master's purposes. In the second instance, the social self is explicitly affirmed. One *makes oneself* be co-extensive with the social self; one chooses not to differentiate oneself from it. One may accept one's social self either because it is impressive or because it agrees with how one sees (or wants to see) oneself.

Sartre would reply that one cannot *be* identical with the social self; one can only *make oneself be* identical with it — thus acknowledging that one *is not* actually identical with it. Hence, one is implicitly 'negating' the social self in so far as one is striving to retain it. The response to this is that one can become so fascinated and immersed in the social self that one fails to realize one is *not* identical with it. Although one may be deceiving oneself in this state, it still can occur. One may thus implicitly affirm, and later implicitly accept, absorption by the social self. Sartre's account of his own youth in *The Words* suggests that this was the way he existed for some time.

The second alternative possibility exists when reciprocal negations interlace, but neither predominates; both operate to the same degree. In this case, both persons experience the social self, and both retain their own differentiation from it by maintaining their purposes. This, I would suggest, is the *normal case* in interpersonal life, even when Sartre's structures do apply. Both persons simultaneously maintain their own projects, yet *are also aware* of the Other's impositions. Each may counter the Other's efforts to the same degree, or each may integrate the Other's judgments into his purposes; the interaction can then be acceptable to all. This happens when purposes are not in conflict, and there is no necessity that they must be. Both persons can even become paralyzed by the look of the Other; in a vicious fight between lovers, quite often things are said by each that so devastate the other that both are equally debilitated. *Neither negation dominates*; both are overcome by their social self. No one really wins. Hence, there are numerous ways in which reciprocal negations can occur without either becoming dominant.

The third possible alternative exists when the negations between people are reciprocal but neither *touches* the Other; each negates the Other, but neither responds to the Other's negation. Such is the lot of those who *agree to disagree*; both opponents differentiate themselves from each other actively; both see each other as limited, circumscribed, even deluded; yet each remains oblivious to the judgment of the Other. The legitimacy of the Other's judgment has been so undermined that its effect is neutralized; it need not be negated because it is not experienced, or it has been negated before it occurs. In either case the Sartrean claim that one negation must predominate is inaccurate.

Each of these three alternatives exhibit ways in which Sartre misses the empirical possibilities within his own framework. Each demonstrates that there is greater separation between self and Other than Sartre is willing to see.

Sartre may object that many of these examples have been described from the third-person viewpoint, but this is the only viewpoint one can adopt if one is to grasp *two concrete persons* in interaction with one another. I shall examine more concrete counter-examples from within the first-person viewpoint below. I am not trying to show that the asymmetry claim *never* holds, only that it fails to hold in a very large class of cases.

To directly demonstrate the inadequacy of the asymmetry claim, one must provide examples in which the persons involved not only experience themselves as subjects (or, alternatively, as objects), but also examples in which self experiences self *and* Other *both* as subjects (or *both* as objects). This is required to prevent Sartre from revising the scope of his claim. Instead of addressing the *actual* modality in which the Other exists, Sartre may seek to address the modality *in which he is experienced.* Although this strategy seems to save the empirical import of the claim, it is counter-productive because the asymmetry claim is meant to relate ontologically distinct entities, rather than elements within one's own experience. My counter-examples will challenge both ways of interpreting the asymmetry claim.

Let us first examine some cases in which self and Other are both objects (or are both experienced as such). The obvious case arises when one person objectifies another but is in turn objectified by a third. The initially objectified Other experiences himself defined, but he can also simultaneously apprehend the Other's objectification by the third. This may not eliminate his own objectified state. The bandit, the hostage, and the hero constitute the typical case.

The third is not necessary to this example, for each person can be (and/or can experience himself to be) manipulated by the Other, and each can thus be an object for the Other; each can even experience himself as objectified. In a discussion, the participants can see each other as mere information dispensers and as nothing more than that, and each can *be* merely an intellectual instrument for the edification of the Other. Both can thus exist in the object mode, and each can experience both self and Other in that mode.

Another case arises when two shy people meet: neither can escape the sense of being overwhelmed by the Other. Often each perceives the Other's shyness as well; each falters for words, and their helplessness and uncertainty is manifest to both. Yet the Other's apparent shyness is not enough to break the spell of the Other-as-subject; both remain objects to one another (and experience each other as such) throughout the evening.

A final example consists of persons who relate through roles (e.g., student-teacher). A moment opens in which genuine personal expression might for once occur; both see it, and both wish to transcend the restrictions of the role. Yet both are trapped by its demands, and both submit to what each thinks the Other expects; the opening closes. Here both remain role-objects for each other, and both experience each other in this fashion. Mutual objectivity is a common event, not the exception.

The same is true for the mutual experience of subjectivity; many cases occur in which both are subjects, and both experience themselves as such. In social dancing when two partners move together, neither experiences the Other as leading; each adjusts to the movements of the partner. Each lets the music be expressed through him/her, and each responds automatically to the Other's expressions. The sense of oneself as an object almost never arises. Here one experiences both oneself and the Other as subjects; two persons seem to mesh and interlock to form one subject in the dance. Another example occurs in social ritual in which each person performs his role perfectly; the subjectivity of self and Other are simultaneously grasped. The ritual seems to function as a medium uniting the individuals; it neutralizes the effect of the asymmetry claim.

A different kind of example occurs when each experiences himself as transcending the Other: the Other's responses and suspicions have been anticipated and accounted for; each experiences both the Other and himself as a subject. This can also occur when one experiences the Other as transcending oneself and yet experiences oneself as transcending the Other in a *different* fashion: one person is being sacrificed to the cause in being tortured by another; yet he overcomes the torturer by keeping the secrets to himself. Both self and Other are experienced as subjects at once, and indeed both are subjects.

These examples demonstrate that self and Other do not always exist asymmetrically, as Sartre believes. One's own modality does not always evoke the complementary modality in the Other; social life is more complex than Sartre's general principles suggest.

Claim 8

Claim 8 asserts that the Other-as-subject is the primordial mode of the Other and that all one's social actions are directed toward maintaining the Other as an object so that his subjectivity cannot appear. One is thus responsible for the Other's objectivity. This claim asserts that the Other-as-subject forms the background of all social life; its threat is always present.

This claim requires the Other-as-subject to be generally present, explicitly or implicitly, but this requirement conflicts with both the exclusivity claim — which requires the Other's subjectivity to be excluded when he is experienced as an object — and with the assertion that interpersonal life consists in perpetual oscillations between the two modes. If the latter assertion is correct, neither modality can be primordial; they simply swing back and forth like movements of a pendulum. Although there are passages in which Sartre suggests that the Other-as-subject is omnipresent, he cannot preserve both this view and the exclusivity claim. If the Other-as-object excludes the Other-as-subject, the latter cannot always be present.

Sartre has two replies here: first, he may say that the Other-as-object is perceived only by negating the Other-as-subject, thus presupposing his primary presence. Second, he may say that the Other-as-object conceals the Other's subjectivity without eliminating it. Indeed, the figure-ground, explicit-implicit distinction seems to be the only instrument that could rescue Sartre here.[182] The problem is that the Other-as-subject must then conceal the Other's object-mode in the background; so this reply will not establish the primordiality of the Other-as-subject.

To answer the other reply, I must locate the deeper problems in Sartre's account. Here Sartre momentarily forgets what he elsewhere remembers, viz., that one's own objectivity can be desired and that one can thus negate the Other-as-object in order to elicit his subjectivity. This means that one's underlying attitude to the social self can be very different than Sartre presupposes. A number of reasons cast suspicion on the primordiality of the Other-as-subject.

First, the Other-as-object is experienced before his subjectivity ever emerges. For periods of time, the Other conforms to the child's world; the initial upsurge of the Other-as-subject is a shock and surprise; it alters one's existence, but this emergence is so stark only because the child has been incorporating the Other with his own projects.

Even *after* the Other-as-subject emerges, one does not always retain a subliminal awareness of it; indeed, most human bodies – those that one passes by in streets each day – are not even experienced as having *the capability* of embodying the Other-as-subject. The Other-as-subject suddenly reemerges, and one is surprised that one had forgotten it.

Moreover, for different people the Other-as-subject has different degrees of salience. The social self is not always predominant; often it becomes irrelevant; one loses concern about it. Then only a serious alteration in the Other's perceived deportment or judgment will affect one. These examples demonstrate that the empirical adequacy of this claim is limited.

Claim 9

Claim 9 asserts that each mode of the Other is self-sufficient – the only relation between them is mutual exclusion. Neither illuminates the other; each refers only to itself, and only the Other-as-object can be known. This assertion is baffling because Sartre has striven to establish an internal relation between self and Other in order to overcome the monad view of persons. Yet with this claim, *external* relatedness – the radical separation characteristic of the monad view – reinstates itself between the two dimensions of the Other. One's relation to one's own social self becomes *external*, and the Other-as-subject's relation to his objectivity becomes external. Hence, the separation that previously existed between self and Other now splits the *modalities* of self *and* Other. Little theoretical gain is achieved if old divisions emerge in new places. In addition, this claim seems to conflict with the theory of indirect internal negation offered in Claim 7.

One can also ask whether this view is really true. One allegedly knows the Other-as-object. This knowledge affects how one experiences oneself vis-à-vis *this* Other-as-subject. Perhaps the real reason that Sartre does not want to address the problem of relating the two modalities is that his Other-as-subject is a semi-universal, quasi-totality; he may not be able to relate the concrete Other-as-object to a *concrete* Other-as-subject because there is no place for that concreteness in his theory. Yet *we do experience concrete subjectivities*. Not every look is the same, and not every use Others make of one is part of a single coherent whole. Others have disparate views and purposes, and one has some comprehension of this. To this extent one can apprehend the determinateness of another-as-subject. It is not simply pre-numerical and undifferentiated.

There are problems with the access to Others that Sartre allows as well. He claims that one knows only the Other-as-object, and one does this by comprehending the organization of his projects. Two problems arise here: first, when one grasps the Other as an object, he is integrated into one's own purposes, the instrumental relations with which the world is furrowed are *one's own*. How then can one reach an adequate understanding of the *Other as such* if the relevant instrumental relations one perceives are *not his*? In the only modality in which one supposedly *can* know another, precisely what one needs to know *cannot* appear. Second, even if one assumes one's own instrumental organization of the world does not distort one's view of his ordering, *how* does one determine what his projects are? By the hierarchy of instrumental organizations he establishes? But how does one apprehend these? They do not just *appear* on the face of the world. What is the role of interpretation, of drawing analogies, and of background social comprehension in this process? All one sees is the Other's behavior, which is radically ambiguous. It can be seen as a means to hundreds of ends, and it can be given any number of submeanings depending on how one sees the larger meaning of his life. What justifies these large-scale interpretations?

Does a reference to *this* Other-as-subject, in so far as his projects intersect and/or cut across one's own, play some role here? Does one not refer to the Other's self-understanding to verify one's hypothesis? But this means that one achieves comprehension of the Other, if at all, only through relating his subjectivity to his objectivity? Then the two modes are not self-sufficient and independent; they require each other in order for either to be fully understood. The same dialectical interplay applies to modalities of oneself: never does one restrict oneself to

Cartesian intuition about oneself. One also refers this to what one learns from the Other's standpoint, and one supplements each viewpoint with the other. The task is to understand how the two viewpoints can be interwoven to produce this deeper comprehension.

Claim 10

Claim 10 is the exhaustivity claim; it asserts that the two modes of the Other (and self) exhaust all possibilities; there are no other ways in which to experience Others. I have already addressed this claim in depth and will thus do no more than summarize previous points.

In so far as I have established the existence of intermediate states between Sartrean subjectivity and objectivity, Sartre's exhaustivity claim fails. Moreover, every additional dimension of the Other-as-subject (and object) that is ontologically significant and is not reducible to Sartre's types also establishes alternative modes of the Other. I shall examine three of these in the next section. In addition, the various extreme comportments discussed earlier — lived solipsism and living in Others — establish wholly distinct levels on which relations take place. Although these extremes may represent degenerate experiences of Other and self respectively (the zero degree of such experiences), they are useful for understanding the basic parameters within which all other modalities can be located.

Sartre's two modalities actually exist; no theory that excluded them could be adequate, but his effort to reduce all other modes to his own does not succeed.

An extension of Sartre's theory

Despite these difficulties with his general claims, Sartre does successfully clarify a powerful dimension of the Other's subjectivity. I will now use his method to reveal some of its additional dimensions. Although these dimensions were sketched earlier,[183] here I shall explicate them more fully and demonstrate both that they are distinct from Sartre's look and that they satisfy all the conditions for philosophical importance that Sartre's Other-as-subject fulfills.

Sartre does not simply describe intersubjective phenomena at random; he concentrates on the look because it essentially alters one's "pre-social" nature and creates an emergent structure (the social self) which is uniquely related to the existence of Others. Only phenomena which satisfy these criteria will have sufficient philosophical interest to merit phenomenological explication. I will show that at least three additional intersubjective phenomena satisfy these conditions: inspiration, pure recognition, and de-individuation. The implications of each are very different from those of Sartre's look.

Inspiration

The virtues Others embody and the intensity with which they live are often inspiring. Others challenge one's way of life and call one to something greater; some theorists term this capacity "charisma." Inspiration is a broader phenomenon than the mutual facilitation that bonds Heidegger's authentic persons, but it functions in a similar fashion. An inspiring Other typically addresses the ethical quality of one's existence; he may enliven old ideals, engender new ethical possibilities, or introduce one to new kinds of ethical comportments. For example, another's courage in the face of dangerous circumstances may elicit a similar capacity in oneself, or another's sensitivity to and compassion for people may alter the meaning of serious ethical living for oneself, or another's capacity to fine-tune his ethical responses to specific situations may loosen one's excessive reliance on principles. In each case, the Other inspires simply by living his virtues; he does not consciously intend to influence other people, but the quality of his life is inherently attractive and transformative.

Inspiration has a very different effect than Sartre's look. The social self is a limit imposed by Others which displaces one's own practical engagements with the world, but inspiration enables one to transcend previous limits — to achieve what might not have been possible alone — and encourages one to actualize one's ideals. Someone might argue that inspiration can be reduced to feeling obligated to conform to an ideal image of oneself projected by the Other and thus is only an instance of Sartre's look. No doubt this kind of imperativistic expectation exists, but the inspiration which I am elucidating operates differently.[184] The inspiring Other typically is unaware of his impact on Others; radiant virtue acts through its inherent attractiveness, not through evoking an ideal image of oneself. Just as beautiful art compels devotion, radiant virtue impels one to change by exemplifying serious ethical existence. One retains one's subjectivity, and one feels drawn by magnet-like forces which radiate from Others but are unrelated to their expectations. Inspiring Others reinforce what is best in oneself and provide a source of strength; none of this is compatible with Sartre's transformation.

Inspiration enlivens one's attachment to virtue. Just as Sartre's look establishes a new dimension of oneself, the inspiring Other evokes a new level and intensity of existence. He may introduce the very possibility of living ethically, or he may simply stimulate a greater attunement to value qualities. The transformation that inspiration achieves is no less dramatic, pervasive, or penetrating than the emergence of Sartre's social self. Often one becomes numb to value qualities, and inspiration strips away this insularity and allows the force of values to be felt again. Inspiration is the milieu of extraordinary ethical achievement just as the Other-as-subject is the milieu of the social self. Some may argue that inspiration is a marginal phenomenon, but it operates implicitly − positively or negatively − in many social circumstances. Others can corrupt through their evil as well as enliven through their nobility; moreover, the impact of inspiration can be decisive in one's development. Without it one may well have not become what one is.

Some may doubt whether the Other is a necessary condition for inspiration. Fictional characters and the ideals themselves can be powerfully moving. But one's ability to experience fictional characters as inspiring is probably dependent on already having experienced other people. Although one may not have had to experience another person *as inspiring*, without some experience with people one could not apprehend fictional characters as beings like oneself and thus as embodying states to which one could aspire. An isolated Crusoe would probably be unable to experience fictional characters in the appropriate fashion. Moreover, a fictional character is able to inspire because one regards him as equivalent to a real person; he functions as a stand-in for the person one has not yet been fortunate enough to meet.

The second objection registers an important fact: Others are the vehicles of inspiration, not its source. The value qualities themselves are the source, but they all too easily remain abstract and irrelevant to one's everyday life unless embodied by other people. Value qualities can inspire independently of persons, but persons are their privileged embodiments. Just as Sartre's Other could only be shown to be the *privileged* carrier of the look, so too actual Others are only the most *effective* agents of inspiration.[185] Inspiration is a special capacity of the Other's subjectivity; a full comprehension of interpersonal life cannot ignore it.

The ontological implications of inspiration are quite different from those of Sartre's look. First, instead of establishing a new structure, an appendage to one's pre-reflective awareness, inspiration attunes one more completely to a particular dimension of human life. Just as the lived solipsist loses touch with the reality of Others (including Sartre's look), the amoralist can live within an ethical vacuum and remain deaf to any aspiration. Inspiration shatters that ethical numbness like Sartre's Other penetrates social obliviousness. Second, inspiration can be mutual and symmetrical: two people may be differently inspired by one another. This does not always occur, but it can occur. Finally, persons provide values with an ontological home. Values transmit themselves through persons who embody them, and values influence one another through social interaction. Inspiration plays a central role in this process. Just as Sartre's Other sustains the social self, other people also sustain the realm of ideals and aspirations.

Pure recognition[186]

Pure recognition is the reciprocal acknowledgment of social legitimacy which establishes a bond of community. One abandons one's claim to uniqueness, and one achieves a new sense of social reality which completes and transforms one's primitive sense of individual reality. A social 'place' is established for oneself and maintained by Others as long as they continue to recognize one. Too easily this social embeddedness is forgotten. Only when recognition is lost and the bonds severed does one realize the extent of the loss — part of oneself withers.

Pure recognition establishes a mutual bond and a kind of social being that some might regard as a subtype of Sartre's social self. But the kind of selfness that emerges is both different from and logically independent of Sartre's phenomenon. One can be defined, judged, and limited by another without being recognized by him, and one can be recognized by another without being defined, judged, or limited in Sartre's sense. The master dominates the slave but does not recognize him. Soldiers who are strangers may recognize one another without imposing any judgments. Moreover, the kind of social being that emerges from recognition is more integrative and liberating than Sartre's social self. A third element that binds persons together into a cohesive whole emerges; it establishes a sense of unity rather than one of isolation and antagonism. This social being is more subliminal than the social self, but it is no less important. When it is threatened, one quickly moves to restore one's legitimacy. Sartre would not have argued so forcefully against Hegel if he had not recognized a radical alternative to his own vision of interpersonal life.

The essential transformation created by pure recognition is the establishment of the social totality which unites individuals. The totality is produced through mutual recognition and is sustained by it, but the totality transforms the individuals who become its members. Each becomes socially real, more than what he was; each has a stake in maintaining the totality and his membership in it. The totality now pulses through his actions just as they keep reproducing the totality. This social being radically alters the consciousness and life of a "pre-social" creature; it creates an interworld. Social being becomes as essential to one — as much of one's second nature — as one's habitual way of dealing with the environment.

The existence of other conscious beings does seem to be a necessary condition for the existence of pure recognition, but young children reared by animals or a person in the midst of a culture of androids whose non-humanness remains concealed from him might experience it. The other conscious beings do not have to look like oneself in order for pure recognition to occur because recognition defines those with whom one can identify. In order to establish a functioning social totality, the androids would have to respond like human beings, and thus would probably be conscious, at least in the sense that animals are. Once again, actual other people are the *privileged* vehicles for pure recognition:

Others in some form are necessary because they create both the problem of recognition and its solution. In a world without Others, the issue of recognition would not arise, and social totalities would not exist. In a world with other conscious beings, the issue of recognition will necessarily arise; social being exists even among social animals.

The central ontological implication of pure recognition is the simultaneous emergence and mutual reinforcement both of social being within recognized individuals and the social totality itself that exists through them. Unlike Sartre's social self, Hegel's social being joins people together and is mutually, symmetrically produced by them. Each loses his particularity in merging with the group, but each gains a universality through the process, and individuality need not be wholly sacrificed. The kind of relatedness pure recognition achieves lies between the very general structures which exist because of socialization and condition all encounters between people and Sartre's social self, which emerges directly out of concrete encounter and is renegotiated in every meeting. Hegelian social being emerges at the moment one enters a group (or creates one) and is sustained by a tacit acceptance which never becomes wholly habitual but also need not be perpetually reasserted. It is a condition one can lose, but to be unrecognized is no less a fact of one's social being.

De-individuation

A third essentially social phenomenon is the ecstatic loss of individuated selfhood that occurs in emotional infection and/or mass participation. While pure recognition allows the agents to retain a sense of their own distinctness, this is lost completely in de-individuation; the individual fuses with and becomes submerged in the group. He becomes an organic extension of it — adopting its feelings, attitudes, and intentions. Examples of this phenomenon can be found in active team sports, in religious rites, in orgiastic festivals, and in crowd violence.

Sartre explicitly denies that this kind of group fusion is possible.[187] The kind of self-loss it produces is the opposite of the self-creation that results from the Other's look. Not only do Others have the power to establish one's sense of continuant self-identity, they can also dissolve one's self-enclosedness and take over the functions of one's consciousness. Distinct individuality is not a necessary condition of being human, but only one modality in which humans can exist — one form of relatedness to Others. Scheler suggests that de-individuation is the earliest stage of development in children and in primitive cultures, an archaic stage which can reemerge at any moment.

De-individuation is one of the most drastic transformations one can undergo, for it eliminates what many regard as a central face of life — separateness. Heidegger's impersonal mode of existence is a modern vision of this absolute immersion in the group. De-individuation is the opposite pole from lived solipsism; it is the most complete form of social cohesion. The ontological significance of this phenomenon is central; it demonstrates that persons do not individuate like human bodies and thus that an entirely different conception of human relatedness is needed. Lived solipsism and living-in-Others are best conceived as extreme ends of a continuum of social permeability; everyone falls somewhere on this spectrum in any particular situation, and the kind of selfness and relatedness one experiences will be a function of that *locus*.

De-individuation seems to require Others because the larger mass which absorbs one is composed of persons, and their ecstatic states draw one out of one's own isolation. No doubt there are other ways to induce the loss of self (alcohol, drugs, meditation) and other entities into which one can be absorbed (the cosmos, nature), but these states do not engender the social organicism to which I am drawing attention. Moreover, there is an intentional element in these forms of self-loss that is lacking in group fusion. In the latter one is literally swept away; one returns to a more primitive way of being with and amidst Others; one becomes an instantiation of the group. Others who are capable of similar self-loss and who are open to this complete immersion are necessary partners in the process.

In this era extreme de-individuation is an isolated phenomenon. Since contemporary people experience it only occasionally, they can too easily dismiss its ontological significance. Yet most people do undergo some form of this experience, and there is evidence that this state of being was more common and pervasive in other cultures and historical eras. Individuated, isolated selfness is only one mode in which humans exist; the current conception of social relationships is restricted to a mode of experience that is most pronounced in our era. Persons can be related to groups in much the same way they can be related to diseases; just as the disease literally reproduces itself in every host, so too the Crowd can literally reproduce itself in every infectible being.

A synopsis

All of these phenomena (including Sartre's look) are avoidable; the lived solipsist simply remains blind and immune to the forces of interpersonal life. He lives the most asocial form of life possible. Most people, however, are not (very often) lived solipsists; they remain accessible to all the transformations discussed: inspiration, pure recognition, de-individuation, and the social self. Sartre sought to show that people are far more pervasively bound to one another than the monad view of persons suggests. I have offered three additional reasons for this conclusion. One's attunement to higher ideals, one's social recognition, and one's mode of selfness (individuated or not) are all essentially related to Others.

Interpersonal life is a complex network of threads, bonds, forces, relays, transformations, and impulses. These elements do not simply supplement an already constituted consciousness and substantial self; rather they condition the core of selfness and alter the structures of experience. These factors are not always explicit, especially when one adopts a philosophical-reflective stance to lived experience. Nevertheless they can be uncovered and clarified. Sartre has offered one powerful procedure for unearthing these structures; the ontology of persons and personal relations must be reconceived in accordance with these insights.

Implications for Sartre's theory of concrete relations with Others

In order to understand the implications of these criticisms for Sartre's analysis of concrete relationships, I must show how he derives that theory from his views on the Other-as-subject and the social self.

Sartre's theory

Sartre develops a *functional* theory of concrete relationships. It allows him to reduce the variety of relations to two basic types and to provide incisive and coherent interpretations of each. This function can now be easily explained, but one technical point must be clarified at the outset. Sartre's theory is not about relationships *per se*, i.e., the two-sided reciprocal interaction between two people. Indeed, because he assumes one cannot reach the Other's experience as it is for himself and because one cannot reach the perspective of the totality (the dyad or relationship *per se*) itself, at best all he *can provide* is a theory of one's responses, approaches, or orientations to the Other-as-subject and to the social self.[188] Hence one might better term his theory: "concrete orientations to the Other-as-subject."

As I have shown above, the experience of the Other is, for Sartre, highly disorienting; one is stripped of one's contact with the world and provided with an essence – a fixed identity. Sartre thinks *the basic function* of responding to the Other-as-subject is to *recover full control over the social self.* One can do this in either of two ways: confrontation or assimilation. In confrontation modes one tries to be the foundation of the disappearance of the social self by insuring that the Other remains objectified (indifference, sexual desire, and sadism exemplify this approach). In assimilation modes one tries to seduce the Other into constituting the social self one seeks (love and masochism exemplify this approach). Thus one attempts either to eliminate the social self entirely or to be the source of its content; in either case one dominates the Other-as-subject.[189]

If one could succeed via either approach, one would have achieved what Sartre thinks is everyone's fundamental aim: to attain both the solidity and self-sufficiency of a material object and the freedom of a conscious being – to be god-like.[190] The social self is amenable to this project because it is the dimension of oneself that is most thing-like; if one could control it, one would be the foundation of one's thing-like nature. One seeks to use the Other's freedom to provide what would be impossible for oneself alone.[191]

Unfortunately, both strategies are futile; Sartre's stunning conclusion is that all orientations toward Others fail.[192] The Other's subjectivity cannot be completely eliminated by any effort to objectify him, and one cannot mesmerize him forever. His actual subjectivity inevitably remains beyond one's reach.[193] The ultimate source of the social self is always the Other himself; one can never recover control of it; this is what makes it *distinct* from oneself. This is the first sense in which all orientations to Others must fail.

Beyond this, every interpersonal strategy is an effort in self-deception; invariably it must break down.[194] One cannot actively inflict oneself with *passivity*, nor can one *forget* a threat which must be constantly *confronted* to be kept at bay. These contradictory efforts can temporarily succeed by shifting from one moment to the other, but eventually the contradictions will explode the tenuous equilibrium that has been achieved.

Yet a third sense in which these approaches to Others fail is that each contains an internal dynamic that generates its own dissolution and frees the Other from one's efforts to control him. Some of the failures Sartre describes are external, resulting from contingent facts, but for most of these orientations, he is able to demonstrate that the full completion or realization of the orientation will lead to its own destruction.

Sartre's theory of "orientations to Others" thus is Hegelian in at least two respects: in its functional or teleological character (depicting all comportments as seeking *one* aim) and in its emphasis on internal mechanisms that generate the disintegration of the orientation – contradictions between its ultimate aim and the mode of action or experience that must be adopted to achieve it.

The difficulties with Sartre's theory

What problems can be discerned in this theory on the basis of this discussion? First, one can better locate the inner tensions of Sartre's theory, and second, one can better identify the limits of its applicability.

Let us begin by noting that Sartre's theory can only be about one's orientations to Others because he *cannot* provide a theory of relationships *per se* since he does not think that the perspective of the relationship *per se* can be achieved by either participant and since the actual response of Others to a relationship, the response as it is for them, is forever hidden from one. Because the third-person viewpoint falsifies the experience of relationships[195] and since the first-person viewpoint cannot capture the relationship *per se*, Sartre's ability to offer a phenomenology of personal *relations* is severely limited.

Moreover, the entity to which one is responding, according to Sartre's theory, is *not* the individual Other with whom one is in love or for whom one has sexual desire, but is the generalized, pre-numerical Other which Sartre terms the Other-as-subject. All of one's intercourse with individuals, on his view, actually addresses this generalized Other through them. Although not *all* concrete relations are dominated by such concerns, Sartre's perspective may have genuine usefulness. The trouble here, as before, is that only some aspects of one's relationships to Others can be explicated in this fashion.

Also, the tension between the certainty and transcendence of the Other threatens to further confine Sartre's theory to the relationship between one's consciousness and a quasi-imaginary satellite that exists at the periphery of one's awareness without being distinct from it. If he insists on the certainty of the Other, his theory becomes a theory about the relation of one mode of oneself to another; in that case he loses all connection to a transcendent Other.

There are deeper objections to his theory, however. Sartre posits *one* dominant functional response to a *single* specific nature. But the thrust of my discussion is that there are *many* salient structures of oneself which exists because of Others, that there are *many* levels which must be distinguished in any theory of interpersonal orientations, that *many* structures *mediate* and alter the outcome of any encounter, and that there are *many alternative responses* even if one examines a paradigmatic Sartrean situation. Each of these factors influence the kind of functional response that is appropriate.

I showed that there are many alternative, equally-potent experiences of the Other's subjectivity; thus, if one seeks to provide a Sartrean theory of encounter, one will have to determine basic functional responses to *each* of these phenomena and carefully clarify their relationships to one another. Hegel's position suggests that functional theories must be relativized to the level of personhood that members of a relationship have achieved (e.g., pure versus impure recognition). Depending on that level, the functional orientation persons will have to one another will differ. The operation of Heideggerean mediating structures (e.g., the impersonal self; being-with) will alter the results of one's encounters and will thus affect the functional orientation people will have in them. Finally, all the criticisms that indicated restrictions on the applicability of Sartre's theory demonstrate that his analysis, *even when restricted to his level of interaction*, will have powerful restrictions.

Each of these lines of criticism reinforces the basic intuition one has on first considering Sartre's theory: that *any* effort to theorize about relationships by viewing them all as efforts to achieve one basic goal will be hopelessly inadequate. There are *too many functions*, too many *relevant structures*, too many different *types* of people and *types* of relationships to introduce illuminating theoretical order in this fashion. Hence not only are the particular functions Sartre identifies problematic, the value of the general strategy he uses is also questionable.

Sartre's conclusion is that all interpersonal orientations fail both to achieve their aim and to remain stable. Had he only been able to extend his vision, even within the confines of his theory of interpersonal experience, to the *reciprocal response* of the Other in the relationship, he would have had to alter this conclusion. For the Other can adopt *complementary* strategies. On Sartre's view, the masochist and the sadist would form a perfect pair, each solving the problems of the other. The masochist accepts his objectivity and controls the Other through the sadist's continual effort to make him an object; the sadist forces the Other into perpetual objectivity, and the masochist will continually experience his objectified state. Thus, if the right orientations are paired, the futility that Sartre envisions might be overcome.

In addition, my efforts to demonstrate the real possibility of pure recognition and to indicate additional ways in which the two dimensions of self (and Other) can be internally related suggest that Sartre's gloomy conclusion and the premises from which he argues for it are mistaken.

Hence, my criticisms raise serious doubts about Sartre's theory at every point: in its *basic design* (its functional structure; its claim to be *inter*personal); in its *general plausibility* (single function; single structure); in the general field of its *applicability* (the look, the social self; the Other-as-subject); and in its *conclusions* (necessary failure).

Although I am sympathetic with Sartre's efforts to find an underlying logic or pattern to relationships, I do not believe he has discovered the way to articulate it. I was equally critical of this functional approach in Hegel. In the face of the manifold complexity of social life demonstrated throughout this essay, the serious question becomes: how can an illuminating theory of interpersonal relationships be constructed? My positive suggestions for such a theory are presented in the next chapter.

Chapter 5

Some conclusions

I have examined the theories of intersubjectivity of Husserl, Hegel, Heidegger, and Sartre. Each explores new approaches and offers suggestive insights. My criticisms have uncovered important restrictions, qualifications, and supplements to their positions, have discerned problems left unaddressed, and have challenged some of their methodological strategies. Here I shall suggest a synthesis of their contributions and offer some recommendations which may advance the richer understanding of Others they have initiated.

Three central revisions of the Cartesian picture[1] define this new understanding of the relations of self and Other: (1) instead of measuring knowledge of Others by knowledge of oneself or seeking to justify (rationally reconstruct) one's knowledge of Others, one should elucidate and organize the many ways in which Others transform and constitute one and the various kinds of relations that interlace self and Other; (2) where the Cartesian sees distinct, isolated, self-sufficient monads, one should see permeable, interdependent, mutually constituting creatures who often function as relays in larger social systems; (3) rather than portray the mind as a private, inner sanctum that "contains" experiences, one should picture it as realizing itself through its expressions; typically it is as accessible to Others' understanding as to one's own. These three innovations integrate the contributions of these philosophers and establish a new paradigm for thinking about Others.

From certification to elucidation

Hegel, Heidegger, and Sartre jettison the Cartesian obsession with certifying one's knowledge of Others. They suggest ways in which the Other is more powerfully revealed and more deeply interwoven into the texture of one's experience. The Cartesian skeptic assumes a self-sufficiency and independence from Others that does not exist, and the attitude he adopts toward Others when he seeks to certify knowledge conceals these deeper bonds. Only by abandoning the Cartesian point of view can one discover the deeper relations to Others that render it unnecessary. These philosophers do not wholly dispense with questions

259

about knowing Others, but they suggest both that there are other sources of knowledge than theoretical contemplation and other aspects of Others to be known than the particular states of mind of individuals.

Although Husserl remains thoroughly Cartesian, he does initiate a search for alternative questions and approaches. He seeks to explicate a structure (the sense 'Others') that all knowledge of Others presupposes.[2] If no other entity could be experienced as a conscious being like oneself, then the question of whether such entities are known to exist simply would not arise. Husserl might even assert that the obsession with knowledge has concealed the importance of his constitutional questions, but he would acknowledge the relevance of the epistemological task and admit that his position provides a foundation for that higher-order inquiry. He would not challenge the value or plausibility of the Cartesian quest; his own theory is one culmination of it.[3]

Hegel abandons the epistemological enterprise, but his position suggests some good reasons for doing so. He studies interpersonal interaction − its structures, aims, and dynamics. He elucidates interaction from an engaged-participant standpoint, rather than a withdrawn disinterested standpoint. To study Others only from the third-person viewpoint and apart from any social interaction is to miss most of the ways people depend on and constitute one another in the course of interaction. Hegel thinks that the central issue in one's interaction with Others is acknowledgment, not knowledge; each person seeks recognition and is transformed when he receives it.[4] Hegel elucidates the ways people enrich each other's self-consciousness and make possible the achievement of personhood. Only the barest forms of consciousness and desire can exist without interaction with Others. Interaction makes us human; in so far as conscious beings have become persons (rather than human organisms), the existence of Others is interwoven with their existence. Hegel also suggests that the withdrawn, isolated self-consciousness that is necessary for skepticism can only emerge after interaction sufficiently develops one's self-consciousness and after one has failed to satisfactorily resolve the struggle for recognition.[5] Skepticism arises out of the failure of interaction; if pure recognition is achieved, one transcends the viewpoint and issues of skepticism.

Heidegger thinks that the presuppositions guiding the Cartesian approach to Others are false; they are belied by central features of everyday life which the Cartesian orientation conceals. A more lucid comprehension of one's experience suggests that Others are implicated in the deepest structures of one's existence. All of one's projects are oriented to Others, and one's everyday mode of selfness is an expression of the Crowd that dominates one's inauthentic existence.[6] Even if the Cartesian inquiry is theoretical and contemplative, it is nevertheless a way of being-in-the-world and thus presupposes both being-with and the impersonal mode of selfness. It cannot disprove, challenge, or undermine these deep, pervasive structures because it embodies or instantiates them. The Cartesian inquiry also presupposes and is guided by the traditional assumptions that Heidegger questions. Others cannot be conceived on the model of things; presence does not define their fundamental mode of existence, and they do not consist of thing-like egos inside mechanical bodies. Others are engaged in worldly affairs, and they stand most revealed in those projects.[7] One comes to know them most intimately by sharing their tasks and by relying on the "sight" that guides this mutual contact. Heidegger thus challenges the Cartesian quest and substitutes a deeper kind of access to Others; in addition, he points the way toward more fundamental orientations to Others than knowledge.

Sartre demonstrates that the frame of mind implicit in knowing Others conceals their subjectivity, and he uncovers one pervasive structure that they impose on one — the social self. The Other's subjectivity is not a hidden ghost inside another's body but an all too explicit power to limit, define, and disorient one's life.[8] This dimension of Others cannot be known because it cannot be objectified and knowledge objectifies what it knows. But it can be experienced and elucidated; this project uncovers deep ontological bonds between self and Others. The epistemological orientation conceals the real relations that render it superfluous. In addition, Sartre argues that the reflective standpoint characteristic of the epistemological approach presupposes the existence of Others.[9] It is only an internalization of the experience of the Other's subjectivity, and it does not typically emerge if Others do not impose it. Thus the Cartesian standpoint presupposes the entities on which it casts doubt. In addition, Sartre contributes to the clarification of everyday knowledge of Others by conceiving them as totalities that express themselves completely in every act. This implies that one can achieve a deeper understanding of Others by comparing their various actions and discerning the hierarchy of projects implicit in them; in principle, everything about a person can be comprehended in this way.

The combined impact of these challenges is devastating for the Cartesian enterprise of certifying knowledge. In various different ways, Hegel, Heidegger, and Sartre show that the effort to know Others conceals the fundamental relations we have to them, suggest that it presupposes the existence of Others and specific kinds of interaction with them, and note that deeper kinds of knowledge can be discovered by further exploring these deeper structures. Though they substitute entirely different enterprises and questions, they seriously question the value of the Cartesian quest.

This is not to say that they solve Cartesian problems on Cartesian terms. They try to substitute new questions and fields of inquiry.

Some conclusions

Sartre, Hegel, and Heidegger reveal distinctive kinds of internal relations to Others — relations that irrevocably alter and/or constitute human nature. Some epistemological issues may remain, but these remain tractable, solvable problems. They also demonstrate that the Cartesian approach is extremely limited. Even if it were to succeed, it would only clarify the behavior of particular individuals when they are present to a disinterested and disengaged point of view. These philosophers suggest that one must also examine the generalized Other, Others engaged in practical pursuits, and relations to absent Others. Most importantly, one must elucidate Others from an engaged, first-person, interaction-oriented point of view; this will reveal an important field of relations which interlace self and Other.

From monads to interlacings

To reconceive the nature of personal relations is the second task of this new position. In the Cartesian picture, a person has a self which individuates him from Others and which owns or possesses all his experiences. The self is born with the person and constitutes his humanity; the continuity of this self accounts for personal identity over time. The suppressed metaphor underlying this conception is a midget-homunculus; one's "self" is a little person hidden within. Each person becomes a world within himself and exists independently of Others. Throughout this essay, I have referred to this position as "the monad view of self": the phrase suggests independence, self-sufficiency, and completeness. Personal relations, on this view, may introduce new particular experiences, but these are confined to the periphery of the person; his inner core, his self, is wholly independent of these relations.

The new position challenges every element of the monad view: There is no prior, monadic self. The conceptual problems that the homunculus is introduced to resolve all recur at the level of the homunculus itself; hence, the Cartesian view simply relocates the problems. To the extent that any self exists, it develops through relations to Others and emerges only because of them. Each person's self is integrally related to Others. Similarly, the self is not metaphysically primary; often the person functions merely as a relay in a larger social totality. The totality is as real as the person, and he can sometimes be only a moment of its functioning. Groups are not reducible to their individual members. Finally, experience itself is impregnated by Others; they constitute much of its structure, coloring, and cadence. There is no sacrosanct realm that escapes the penetration of Others.

Because Husserl remains loyal to the Cartesian ideal, he asserts the primacy of one's own independent, self-sufficient sphere of ownness. He is committed to the monad view of persons.[10] However, Husserl initiates the process of transcending this view, for he realizes that some features of experience — the experience of objectivity and reciprocal social acts — involve essential modifications of the primordial stream of experience in the sphere of ownness.[11] Only one additional step is needed to regard this "primordial stream" as an abstract construction and the life-world as primary. Moreover, one need only investigate the impact of unbracketed *existent* Others in everyday life, rather than the constitution of the sense 'Others,' to move in the direction of Hegel, Heidegger, and Sartre. In different ways, they challenge the monad view of persons by attacking three distinct assumptions.

The first assumption is the existence of an independent, impermeable self. These thinkers show that the self does not exist without Others; each establishes an internal relationship between persons. Internal relationships establish relatively permanent structures for those who they relate; the ones I clarify in this essay are social. When they function, they transform the nature of their relatees by establishing new dimensions or modes of existence. The basic result of the emergence of an internal relation is the creation of a larger, semi-organic system of which the relatees become functioning parts; they lose their isolated, self-contained identity and become moments of the larger whole.[12]

The internal relations I have elucidated in this essay are not necessary features of being a human organism; they require a sustaining social milieu and/or specific interpersonal experiences to emerge. They typically develop as a result of normal social intercourse. They establish stable structures of selfness and experience. The self is sometimes depicted as an onion; internal relations create many different layers of this onion. The structures they establish can flower and atrophy, and they can become more or less significant to particular individuals at particular times. They do not always operate, but rarely do they ever disappear entirely. Most people who are reared in a familial milieu will experience them. Internal relations do not need a special effort to be created or sustained; they typically function whenever one undergoes certain types of experiences. Their influence may be subject to some degree of control once an individual becomes conscious of them. These internal relations establish different kinds of structures.

Hegel shows that recognition is required in order to become a person and to develop full self-consciousness. The self is actualized through recognition; through *mutual* recognition, living beings come to experience a larger unifying totality: species-being.[13] The social totality becomes their fullest expression; they are expressed in its action, and they are incorporated into it as it acts through them. Recognition transforms persons by integrating them into a larger social whole. The recognized self cannot be a monad. Hegel shows that the fortress-like isolated self arises through the *failure* of the recognition process. But this combative self exists only in opposition to Others.

Others constitute the background against which it defines itself and the resistance with which it struggles. Thus even the "isolated" self exists only in relation to Others. In either type of recognition, the self is defined through its relation to Others, and the kind of self that emerges depends on the kind of relation one has to Others.

Heidegger shows that individuated selfness arises only on the basis of a more characteristic condition in which one lives impersonally. The Crowd speaks and acts through one's words and deeds. Even if one does attain a provisional authenticity, one lives a variation on a theme that originates with and is made possible by Others. Others establish the forms, patterns, and rhythms by which one lives. Persons are best characterized as modifications of a hidden, amorphous totality which pulses through all its members.[14] I stressed that the Crowd *arises* through long-term interaction. Through the mediation of the generalized Other, each constitutes the impersonal mode of selfness of all the Others. Each is internally related to those who have forged his impersonal self. The self is not a monad but a modification of a larger social reality — a dialect of a common language.

Sartre shows that the fixed, stable self which provides one with a sense of continuity and substantiality exists only because of the Other's look.[15] As soon as one experiences one's objectivity, one inhabits a world in which one dimension of one's identity is constituted by Others. One's own sense of oneself is a pale reflection of the stark reality in their eyes. Without Others, there would only be an onward flow of events that would lack synthetic meaning; this flow is frozen and named by Others. One's identity exists only if Others impose it on one. One may struggle to refashion or alter this social self, but it remains part of one's life as long as one is open to the subjectivity of Others.

Hegel, Heidegger, and Sartre examine different dimensions of the self, and each shows that his dimension is essentially related to Others; Others produce and sustain it. Heidegger shows that typically the *core* of the self — its volitional, cognitive, and evaluative functions — simply is the will, thought, and desire of the Crowd. Sartre shows that the *shell* or outer casing of the self — its public definition, nature, and social possibilities — is constituted by Others. Finally, Hegel shows that the *kind* of self one has — combative or harmonious, isolated or integrated — depends on the kinds of relations one has with Others. These structures can all exist at once; together they exhaust much of the traditional conception of the self. The self exists and has the shape it has only because of one's relations to Others. The monad view of the self cannot be maintained.

A second assumption under attack is the metaphysical primacy of the self. Though groups require the existence of individuals, they are not reducible to them. On the Cartesian view, social wholes are created by antecedent individual atoms who remain their basic units. Only

264

when such units voluntarily combine via contract or consent does a larger social unit emerge. On the alternative position, social totalities are as actual as individual persons; indeed, they govern persons even if they are also created through them. Persons often exist as mere moments of or relays in larger social wholes even though they may modify them. Both the species-being that Hegel describes and the functioning of the Crowd in Heidegger support this view. Persons and groups are reciprocally constitutive. At best, individuality is a *mode* of existence for persons; it may even be a special type of social existence unique to the modern age. Even the most isolated or the most self-determined individual is still related to and parasitic on social wholes. The proper ontological analysis of these totalities still needs to be provided. Sartre has offered the most recent attempt at this in his *Critique of Dialectical Reason.*[16]

The third assumption that is challenged is the monad character of *experience.* The advocate of the Cartesian picture may try to save the monad analysis of persons by insisting that experience is impermeable to Others, but Hegel, Heidegger, and Scheler demonstrate that Others penetrate *the texture of one's experience* itself. The connections they establish are deeper than external, causal relations or the stimulation of new experience. Different persons' experiences are more directly related than the monad view allows; the "influence" of Others extends to the tone, coloring, and even the structure of one's experience. The contours of experience do not adequately conform to the boundaries between persons; they transcend the limits of individual bodies.

My treatment of inspiration[17] suggested that one person's ethical tenor could be transmitted to Others without effort or intent; it functions like a colored beam of light that alters the corresponding color in the Other; in the presence of another's red, one's own blue becomes purple. This bond functions beneath one's conscious awareness; one only need be open to this radiating beacon while in the Other's presence. Emotions can be transmitted to Others in similar ways; Scheler isolates the phenomenon of emotional infection in which one becomes suddenly filled by the passion of another or even by a feeling that is "in the air."[18] Emotions can also be literally shared, and they can propagate themselves like waves in a river which overflows the boundaries between persons.

In addition, thoughts are more literally shared by persons in conversation than the monad picture (which dominates much of communication theory) suggests. One often is literally drawn through the arc of another's thought when conversing; one sometimes sees its developments more clearly than the Other. As he speaks, one echoes and responds to his words as he does, and one's answers arise as much from the internal demands of that train of ideas as from one's own reservoir of opinions. Sometimes the loss of self in the Other's thoughts can be so extreme that one must isolate oneself to recover any sense that one's thoughts are one's own. Even this drastic maneuver is not always effective.

Different kinds of experience interweave persons in different ways, but the examples of inspiration, emotion, and thought should demonstrate that the interlacings of experience can transcend the apparent separation of persons.

Not only particular types of experience, but the current of the entire stream unites one with one's neighbors. Élan, the liveliness that permeates one's actions and approach to the world, is deeply related to the élan of Others. Others' blazing effusion sparks one to life just as Others' cooling embers transform one's flame into glowing ash. Élan is one of the many intersubjective fields of energy which are produced and often sustained without any conscious intention or effort. One meaning of "sensitivity" is an openness to these energies emanating from Others, but one can be more or less sensitive. One can remain closed to Others, but then one lives in a tomb. Rarely does one remain absolutely closed to them; such closure is a kind of spiritual "shock." This intertwining of élan demonstrates an internal relatedness of the currents of different persons' streams of experience.

In addition, the *structure* of one's experience is deeply related to one's social existence. Heidegger elucidates the social structure of the instrumental significations that constitute the map of one's world.[19] The map orients one's life and defines one's possible projects. The achievements of one's tradition condition and suggest the next steps that will both challenge and sustain it. Moreover, some important tenets of structuralism substantiate the view that social categories furrow individual experience. Persons inhabit socially-constituted symbolic and structural systems which function as the rails along which their experience runs.[20] The codes establish the seams of experience. Finally, Hegel's *Phenomenology* suggests that certain shapes of Consciousness, Self-consciousness, and Reason cohere with distinct types of social organization (Spirit).[21] Specific kinds of social relations engender parallel structures in the other spheres of experience. Undoubtedly each of these positions has limits, but together they provide some evidence for a deeper connection between the social milieu and the structure of experience than is conceivable on the monad view.

Hence, whether one examines special types of experience that interlace persons, or the intersubjective energy fields that color the background of experience, or the social basis of the structure of experience, one discovers social bonds interlocking many aspects of persons' *experience*. The monad view can find no site to which to retreat. The central assertion of this essay is that the nature and status of persons must be reconceived because of the reality of the internal relations binding both their selves and their experience.

At minimum, this new position implies that relations are as ontologically primary as their terms. A person's identity is defined by his internal relatedness to Others; he also participates in the modes of existence and experience of his neighbors. At maximum, it implies that any particular person is ontologically derivative from his internal relation to Others. On this extreme view, there are only occupiers of roles, place-holders for sets of qualities created by Others, contextually elicited general forms of deportment, and phases in the functioning of larger machines; and a person is the interfacing site of all these relations. Some contemporary experiences support this extreme view; e.g., the fact that one acts in radically different ways in different fields of interaction; one's lack of personal coherence across time.

But the extreme view is as one-sided as the monad view; persons are neither worlds unto themselves nor wholly absorbed by their internal relations. *External* relations demonstrate this; people do intentionally influence one another as distinct agents. There is separation *and* integration, distinction *and* deep connection; internal bonds cannot completely overcome the distances, but the slack never fully severs the threads. Persons are nodes in a network, nodes and network mutually constitute one another. The Cartesian view obliterates the network. This essay seeks a restoration; simultaneously it reveals many hidden dimensions of one's existence and the concrete reality of Others.

Of course, the overall critical effect of this essay has been to indicate the numerous limits, restrictions, mediations, and slack in these internal relations. But these restrictions are often socially constituted, and they typically only qualify (not undermine) the reality of the interlacings. The new position implies that persons are essentially social beings in the strong sense that the core and key dimensions of their selves *and* the structure, currents, and quality of their experience are internally related to Others.

Someone might wonder about the relation between these interlacings and the zero degree of sociality that has played an important critical role throughout this essay: lived solipsism.[22] Does the person who lives the solipsist form of life still have internal relations to Others? If that orientation remains a state of being to which anyone can regress, how stable and how powerful are these internal relations?

One answer is that the lived solipsist is an experiential concretization of the monad view of persons. None of his actions recognize the reality of Others; he never experiences their subjectivity. As soon as one grasps the poverty of this comportment, one begins to understand the practical implications of three centuries of the monad view. If one deludes oneself about the reality of internal relations long enough, they *will* begin to atrophy, but so will much of the richness of life.

Still the question remains. Another answer is that in lived solipsism internal relations to Others are reduced to a minimum, but not eliminated. The taproot of the phenomenon is a deadness or closedness to the social realm as a special region of deportment and as a source of the Other's subjectivity. Every structure of selfness that requires the sustenance of Others withers. Although the lived solipsist loses awareness of larger social totalities that are functioning through him, these relations continue to operate without his explicit awareness. Moreover, the socially derived structure of the solipsist's experience continues to exist even if his responsiveness to concrete Others atrophies. Thus, although some of the threads that typically do intertwine self and Other can and do unravel, some remain and continue to function even in lived solipsism; it is the *minimum degree of sociality*.

In addition, lived solipsism is not an inevitable condition, nor is it immutable. The Other's subjectivity can break through the hermetic solipsist's membrane in many different ways. When this happens, he sees with different eyes and lives in a newly constituted world. Accretions of new selfness develop; experience becomes richer and more complex. To the extent that he experiences the reality of Others, he will begin to participate in new internal relations.

I should also note that there is a highest degree of sociality which one might call *immersion in Others* in which one's life becomes nothing but these internal relations. Individuality is reduced to a minimum. One is no longer a node but a wholly parallel thread. Although some may be frightened by this possibility, at least some cultures that have emphasized interpersonal unity have been refined, noble, and erudite; to exist in such a culture may represent an unusual realization of human potential. The lived solipsist represents a lowest limit of internal relatedness; immersion in Others represents a highest limit. Between these two poles, most of us find a typical site — only occasionally oscillating to one of the two extremes.

From asymmetrical to parallel access

The third element in this new position replaces the Cartesian view that mental states are necessarily private and immediately apprehended. On this view, one's access to one's own states is transparent and unmediated, but one's access to Others' mental states is always mediated through behavioral expressions that are only contingently related to them and at best are mere signs of them. This view implies that one's access to one's own states is always richer, more complete, and more adequate than one's access to Others' states because one is, in effect, never in contact with Others' actual states of mind at all.

The new position suggests that one's access to one's own states is often inadequate and nearly always mediated in some fashion and that one's access to Others' states is sometimes direct and often as penetrating as their own access to them. In short, there is a *parallelism* in one's access to one's own and to Others' states of mind. If there is a difference, it is one of degree, and, at least for an extended class of states, the difference may favor one's access to *Others*. I do not claim one's access to Others is *always* adequate — only that it is very often *as adequate as* one's access to one's own. Moreover, I do not think Others can have adequate access to *all* one's states, but they can grasp a great many of them, and, in certain circumstances (by no means atypical), their grasp can be superior to one's own.

Two main strategies will buttress the new position: the first shows that one's access to one's own states is typically mediated and fraught with difficulties analogous to those in one's access to Others; the second shows that one's access to Others' states is more direct and adequate than it is usually taken to be. At the outset I must note the breadth of the topic and caution that not all the details of this discussion can be developed.

The four theorists are more deeply divided on this thesis than on the others. Husserl, for example, remains thoroughly Cartesian; he simply assumes that one's access to Other's mental states is always appresentational (less than adequate) and that one's access to one's own is typically pellucid.[23] For this I criticized him severely.

More importantly, on this issue Sartre represents only minimal improvement over Husserl. To be sure, he discovers a dimension of one's self that is primarily accessible to Others, but it defines one's nature from an *external* standpoint that is incomparable with one's own viewpoint. The Other's viewpoint is inaccessible to oneself just as one's own viewpoint is inaccessible to him.[24] Although in one sense Sartre places the Other on an equal footing with oneself in that he has access to a set of one's properties to which one has no access (just as one has access to a set of one's properties to which he has no access), in another sense Sartre leaves each in his old position, for each retains a *private* access to one set of properties and *no* access to the other set.

Sartre also leaves little doubt about the primordial character of one's own viewpoint; although neither viewpoint is the measure of truth of the other, one's own viewpoint yields certainty while the Other's offers mere knowledge.[25] There remain two sets of properties which are only contingently related to one another even if they both "apply" to oneself. The exclusivity of these two sets of properties was challenged in my criticisms of Sartre as was his insistence on a privileged access for both self and Other.[26] Thus in so far as Husserl and Sartre were unable to transcend the Cartesian picture, I sought to discredit their conclusions.

In Hegel's theory, the broad outlines of the new position unfold. Hegel supplies two major supports for it. As a preliminary step, he construes persons as hierarchies of gradually developing capacities, each level of which emerges from the previous ones. This hierarchy provides a more complex delineation of "the mental." Hegel's crucial contention is that interaction with Others is a necessary condition for the development of some of these capacities, and that through certain forms of interaction some capacities develop together in both persons.[27] In such cases, because one participates in the development of the Other and because this development occurs simultaneously in oneself, one achieves adequate access to the transformations of the Other. For example, one can experience the actualization of the Other's self-consciousness that occurs in one's recognition of him because one participates in that recognition and because one experiences the same event in oneself.

This preliminary step has three important implications. First, one's access to the moral, social, self-expressive properties of Others can be as intimate as his because one participates in the formation of those properties. Second, since one's own development requires interaction with Others, one cannot have access to these emergent qualities until they are produced by the interaction. Neither one's own nor the Other's species-being is accessible until it emerges in interaction. Third, one's abilities to comprehend oneself and Others develop symmetrically. As one becomes capable of understanding a higher-level property in Others, one becomes capable to similar understanding of oneself. One's ability to understand oneself and one's capacity to understand Others mutually facilitate one another.

Hegel's second main support for the new position is his insistence that the mind understands itself only through its expressions; without these mediations (many of which are also accessible to Others, e.g., spoken and written words, actions, gestures, tones, styles, and unintentional expressions and deportments), a person's self-apprehension is empty.[28] Hegel thinks that one's own mind is the most difficult object to which to gain adequate access; although another person may be equally difficult to comprehend, the process of and requirements for comprehension in each case are parallel.

Thought, for example, comes to realization through language; a not-yet-articulated thought is a pure intention, an empty thought. Similarly, morality is realized only in desire and action; passion in gestures and styles of expression and action. On this view, the "expressions" are not merely the external clothing of antecedently existent mental states; they specify and concretize those states; the states are completed in their expressions. Thus until such states of mind are expressed, they do not fully exist and can only be emptily intuited, and, once they are expressed, Others' access to them is parallel to one's own.

Of course, not *every* state of mind requires such expression (e.g., imagination) and not every form of expression is publicly accessible: sentences can be spoken to oneself silently, and thinking can take place in that medium. But one's access to silently spoken monologue is fraught with all the difficulties of interpretation that plague Other's access to one's spoken or written words. One does not always immediately understand one's own train of thought, and one can misinterpret oneself. Although one may often be able to tell when one's silent assertions fail to precisely capture one's intent (even if the unarticulated thought is *bare* direction, it is still a *direction*), Others are nearly as often able to discern this property in one's spoken words.

The crucial implication of this "expressivist theory of mind" is that when one apprehends the Other's expression, one is apprehending the actualization of the state itself. One is not grasping the causal result of the antecedent state; the expression constitutes the state as much as anything that precedes it. The inner *becomes defined* through the outer. Instead of merely grasping signs which are contingently related to the realities, one perceives the only constituent by which anyone can achieve full clarity about the state itself. The Other comprehends many of his states through their expression in just the way one learns them oneself.

Heidegger makes three contributions to the defense of parallel access to oneself and Others. First, he questions the translucency and immediacy of one's access to oneself; this access is befogged by mistaken philosophical presuppositions, inadequate attention to lived experience, and inauthentic ways of life.[29] One's own existence is *least evident* to one; only a patient uncovering, recalling, and resurrecting of lived experience can supply the necessary clarity. Any misunderstanding of one's own way of life replicates itself in (or may derive from) basic misunderstanding of Others. Heidegger stresses that clarity also requires a transformation of existence that simultaneously alters one's comprehension of Others and of oneself; if understanding is achieved at all, it illuminates both Others and oneself with equal intensity.[30]

Second, one can extend Heidegger's theory and suggest that one has a more penetrating access to Others than is typically assumed. The impersonal mode of selfness provides a universal medium through which persons have as direct an understanding of one another as they have of themselves. For to understand oneself in this mode *is* to understand Others *and* vice versa. There is no essential difference in the object of understanding; each is interchangeable; none is differentiated.[31] In this impersonal mode, one comprehends factors like "how things are done," "bounds which cannot be transgressed," and "what things mean." Moreover, the mode of selfness of Others becomes apparent through their influence on oneself. When Others exist authentically, one is momentarily thrust toward the possibility of authenticity oneself; in this way one comprehends something of their existence. The symmetries in modes of existence yield symmetries of access, and these symmetries allow one to transcend the apparent separation between self and Other.[32]

271

Third, Heidegger transcends the Cartesian analysis of mind by reconceptualizing the nature of persons. A person is most fully revealed in his cares, and these can be grasped in the way he relates to his surrounding instrumental and interpersonal milieu.[33] Heidegger transcends the mind/body distinction by describing the unified structure of cares that precedes it and by demonstrating that the merely mental or the merely physical are abstractions which are rarely experienced. When one perceives a person, either attentively or in passing, one apprehends his cares. For any phenomenon that might be divided into mental and physical components, Heidegger locates a more basic phenomenon in which the two are synthesized and which is also accessible to Others as well as to oneself. Care unites and is prior to inner intention and outer behavior. A person's cares have a characteristic pattern that is accessible. Cares are embodied in actions, and actions are accessible (not only because behavior is accessible, but also because the purposes that animate actions in particular contexts are also accessible to those who live in the same culture and surroundings). Sometimes one's own cares are more easily seen and understood by Others than by oneself.

Both Hegel and Heidegger take large strides toward rendering the doctrine of parallel access between self and Other plausible. Perhaps some additional observations will help support this new position. The character of a person becomes manifest in all his actions; one can grasp this character directly. A brief encounter is surprisingly sufficient to illuminate a person; one can formulate much that is accurate after but twenty minutes' conversation. Sometimes one's grasp of the person's nature will never be clearer, even after many years of companionship. A person's nature is manifest to Others, but the person himself may be virtually unable to discern it. He sees *too much* and *too often*; nothing stands out in relief; everything is always familiar. This fact functions as a reply to those who think that a person's private memories will always give him an advantage in self-understanding. One reply is that co-participants also remember, but the stronger point is that one's memories offer as disparate and ambiguous a picture as one's present self-apprehensions. Too many data conceal the basic shape of one's nature.

In addition, exactly what one is doing or saying simply fails to be accessible until the action is performed or words are spoken. To see one's action through another's eyes can be immensely informative; one sees one's action more completely. Of course, there are insensitive or inarticulate Others, but sometimes their actual assessment is less crucial than their invitation to consider another viewpoint. When one is planning an action, one of its aspects easily absorbs one's attention; one misses the rest of the relevant aspects. Once performed, all its aspects become more accessible, and often one only then learns what one was doing. One's grasp of one's own action is incomplete and insufficient until one sees the Other's viewpoint.

One is often wrong about oneself. One may deceive oneself; one can mislead oneself not only about what one is experiencing but also about its motivation and its genuineness. Most people are prone to see themselves either in too favorable or too unfavorable a light; they have the same motivation for doing so as Others do. My point is not that Others are seers while self is blind, but that Others can often see as well as oneself.

Perhaps the most definitive testimony of one's access to Others is the skill with which one can hurt them: sometimes love seems only a way of discovering a person's weaknesses. When no holds are barred, the knife is twisted with uncanny accuracy. One is often able to get Others to act as one wishes, and this usually requires access to their nature and motivations. Someone will say that this knowledge can only be gleaned with the Other's cooperation, and to some extent this is true. But the Other need not *tell* one what will most hurt him; some familiarity with him will reveal his vulnerable spots as long as he is not striving to convey a false persona. And even personas can be unmasked.

Some ramifications

I have now sketched and defended the outlines of a new position on the relation between self and Other which draws upon and integrates the results of my critical discussions. I have also presented a new approach and indicated some of the payoffs of a phenomenological elucidation of intersubjectivity. In conclusion, I shall briefly mention some ramifications that might be pursued by a proponent of this new position.

These efforts to reconceive mind, self, and personhood imply that the person is open to his milieu. The openness is two-directional: the person acts in the environment and is vulnerable and accessible to it. He functions as part *of it* rather than as a world unto himself. He is necessarily immersed in a public world — nature, culture, ethical and aesthetic qualities. The mind is neither a self-enclosed nor a self-enclosing membrane; quite the contrary, it is that which takes shape according to its milieu and leaves one vulnerable to it.

So far I have stressed the many ways in which one's self is constituted by Others. Yet one must also attend to the other side — the contribution one makes to concrete Others, to one's social milieu, and ultimately to the historically developing world. The monad view is wrong on *two* counts; not only does it suggest a static and self-enclosed self, it implies a complete and fully constituted world. Even though a person is a modification of larger totalities, he participates in creating, sustaining, and transforming those totalities — natural, cultural, perceptual, and ideational. He is not only a reporter; he is also an effector. This is the *first* ramification. Just as individuals are syntheses of all the institutions which have been important to them, so institutions are ongoing syntheses of all the salient actions people within them have performed. The social totality can act on itself through individuals, but individuals can act on themselves through totalities.

In order to fully comprehend oneself, one must comprehend all the systems that function through one and integrate the results of all the relationships that have constituted one. The *second* ramification is a new path to self-knowledge. The self is not inside in a special place which, if one could only find it, one could then simply see; the self is everywhere — in all the environments in which one dwells, created by all the interactions that fashion one's life.

One's openness to the world entails one's accessibility to Others; the only way one can remain hidden is by concealing oneself — twisting one's expression and offering false masks to Others. To do this one must benumb oneself to one's expressions. Something chatters on and offers a show, but one is elsewhere. In this concealment, two dangers lurk: the costumes one tailors for oneself may become one's permanent uniform, and the truth one is hiding can become lost to oneself. One can say that the more accessible one is to Others (the more "straight" one's expressions), the easier it is to know oneself, although the feat is still considerable. One can also say that Others are no less difficult to know fully and adequately than oneself, and this may prevent the temptation to regard their expressions simply at face value; there is always more to be found and hence more to be known. This 'more' exists in additional expressions, not in deeper layers — for both oneself and Others.

The *third* ramification is that individualism is very problematic. Its primary support was the monad view of persons, which now has been superseded. Persons are not necessarily individuals; to become an individual is a task, one which may or may not have high value. Many aspects of many people's lives remain impersonal or pre-personal; few individuate themselves, and many that try do it reactively — by defining themselves against the dominant norm — and this hardly produces an identity of one's own. The basic errors of individualism are that it posits a personal identity that is independent of social totalities and that it tries to reduce those totalities to individuals. Although one can *achieve* a personal identity, one must *accept* the culture of which one is a modification to do it; one cannot create a unique identity *ex nihilo. My* theoretical task is to understand how genuine personal identity can develop out of an already-functioning social totality.

The need to explore the importance of the public media of expression — social and cultural forms — for the development of subtle, rich personal experience is the *fourth* ramification. If the expression actualizes and defines the experience, experience will remain thin if the media of expression are few. Only if the means of expression are not gross, worn, or deadened can experience become vibrant. Within rich rituals, individual variations, emphases, and modulations can be immensely expressive. Within hackneyed forms, even the most extreme innovation will seem empty. Many who seek unique personal expression snub the common forms (e.g., language) and seek to create alternatives; but a more viable approach is to revitalize those forms by using them with uncharacteristic power and insight. One cannot invent languages on one's own; even less can one single-handedly create social rituals through which to express one's experiences. To develop, complexify, intensify, and transform existing forms is well within an individual's capacities, but the dream of starting from scratch would make one mute and leave one blank.

A final ramification is the need to scrutinize personal responsibility. If a person is internally related to many social networks and to many concrete Others, then rarely is he the sole or primary source of his actions. Too often one punishes an individual because he is palpable and present; the forces and larger totalities operating through him are more difficult to reprimand and restrain. One invents the fantasy of a self-moving, isolated, captain-at-the-wheel in order to vindicate one's policies of punishment. This essay demonstrates just how illusory that picture is, and I would encourage tempering any effort to punish with the realization that rarely are persons the sole sufficient conditions of their actions, and rarely does the claim that they could have done otherwise (even if true) justify the intensity of the punishment. In most cases, social policy must seriously struggle to influence the larger totalities if it is to have any significant impact and if it is to have some claim to justice.

Notes

Preface

1 This claim about the current status of interpersonal relationships could be supported from many sources: social science statistics; informal interviews; recent narrative literature and film, e.g., the novels of Updike, Robbe-Grillet, Beckett, Heller, the films of Bergman, Antonioni, Godard, and Altman; and recent cultural criticism, e.g., Lasch, Lefebvre.

2 This relationship between philosophical conceptions and practical interpersonal life is assumed rather than defended in this essay. A separate work would be necessary to provide a complete defense. Nevertheless, the affinities between the Cartesian picture and the sensibility I describe will become more evident in the Introduction.

3 Here I assume that phenomenology can reveal essential structures of interpersonal experience, structures that continue across vast historical and societal transformations. However, even if the basic structures of experience change in the course of history, a phenomenology of current interpersonal structures will still be necessary, and political theory will have to renew and modify itself accordingly.

4 Though I explicitly criticize "theory" in this section, I do not mean to dismiss theory altogether. The richer comprehension of everyday experience that I seek is resisted by *traditional* theory; I seek to develop *more adequate* theories on the basis of this more lucid understanding of everyday life.

Introduction

1 This point is similar to an objection Sartre makes to what he calls "realism" in Jean-Paul Sartre, *Being and Nothingness: An Essay on Phenomenological Ontology*, trans. and with an introduction by Hazel E. Barnes, New York, Philosophical Library, 1956, p. 223.

2 Ibid., pp. 159–62. This is one of Sartre's few explicit discussions of purifying reflection. Presumably, the results of Sartre's book issue from this source.

3 Ludwig Wittgenstein, *Philosophical Investigations*, 3rd edn, trans. G.E.M. Anscombe, New York, Macmillan, 1958, paras 20, 23, and 43.

4 Ibid., paras 122 and 131.

5 Ibid., para. 182.
6 Ludwig Wittgenstein, *On Certainty*, ed. G.E.M. Anscombe and G.H. von Wright, trans. Denis Paul and G.E.M. Anscombe, New York, Harper & Row, Harper Torchbooks, 1972, paras 105, 115, and 243.
7 Ibid., paras 191 and 192.
8 Wittgenstein, *Philosophical Investigations*, para. 303.
9 Ibid., para. 287.
10 Ibid., para. 302.
11 Ibid., para. 272.
12 Ibid., para. 288.
13 Ibid., para. 258.
14 Ibid., para. 257.
15 Ibid., paras 260—3.
16 Ibid., para. 268.
17 Ibid., paras 280, 404.
18 Ibid., paras 305, 308.
19 Ibid., paras 402- 9.
20 Gilbert Ryle, *The Concept of Mind*, New York, Barnes & Noble, 1949, Chap. 1.
21 Ibid., Chap. 5.
22 Ibid., Chap. 1.
23 Ibid., p. 61.
24 Ibid., p. 184.
25 Ibid., pp. 155—6.
26 Ibid., p. 90.
27 Ibid., p. 171.
28 Ibid., pp. 205—10.
29 Ibid., pp. 186—98.
30 Ibid., pp. 195—6.
31 In J.L. Austin, *Philosophical Papers*, 2d edn, ed. J.O. Urmson and G.J. Warnock, Oxford, Oxford University Press, 1961; Escondido, Calif., Galaxy Books, 1970, pp. 76—116.
32 Ibid., pp. 84—7.
33 Ibid., p. 98.
34 Ibid., p. 99.
35 Ibid., pp. 91—3.
36 Ibid., p. 94.
37 Ibid., pp. 103—4.
38 Ibid., pp. 108—9.
39 Ibid., pp. 104—5.
40 Ibid., pp. 112—14.
41 Husserl is an exception to most of these generalizations about the "European tradition"; for the most part I ignore him in these comparisons. There are analogs to Husserl in the Anglo-American tradition, e.g., Ayer and Chisholm.
42 These include H. Pitkin, P. Winch, and S. Toulmin.
43 In both traditions this kind of methodological strategy is now under attack; Quine questions the value of the analysis of meaning

and uses, and Foucault and Derrida question the efficacy of the appeal to lived experience.

44 Not only is the borderline between philosophy and the social sciences fading, e.g., in the work of Harré and Giddens, but, more compellingly, the borderlines between philosophy, linguistics, neurosciences, and computer science are fading in the work of philosophers like Dennett, Dreyfus, and the Churchlands.

Chapter 1 Husserl

1 Edmund Husserl, *Cartesian Meditations: An Introduction to Phenomenology*, trans. Dorion Cairns, The Hague, Netherlands, Martinus Nijhoff, 1960. (All emphasis and interpolations appear in the texts.)
2 Ibid., pp. 11, 18.
3 Ibid., pp. 11, 12, 13.
4 Ibid., p. 15.
5 Ibid., pp. 15–16.
6 Ibid., pp. 18–19, 89.
7 Ibid., pp. 19–20.
8 Ibid., pp. 20–1.
9 Ibid., p. 21.
10 In this interpretation I am following Dagfinn Føllesdal, "Husserl's Notion of Noema," in Robert Solomon, ed., *Phenomenology and Existentialism*, New York, Harper & Row, 1972, pp. 241–50 and Robert Sokolowski, *Husserlian Meditations*, Northwestern University Studies in Phenomenology and Existential Philosophy, Evanston, Ill., Northwestern University Press, 1974.
11 See Husserl, op. cit., Section 17.
12 Ibid., Section 34.
13 Ibid., Sections 23 and 26.
14 Ibid., Sections 37 and 38.
15 Ibid., pp. 96, 100, 106.
16 Ibid., pp. 106–7.
17 Ibid., p. 121.
18 See pp. 1–4 above.
19 Husserl, op. cit., pp. 108–9.
20 Imperturbably I must hold fast to the insight that every sense that any existent whatever has or can have for me — in respect of its 'what' and its 'it exists and actually is' — is a sense *in* and *arising from* my intentional life, becoming clarified and uncovered for me in consequences of my life's constitutive syntheses, in systems of harmonious verification. (Ibid., p. 91.)
21 Ibid.
22 The second ego, however, is not simply there and strictly presented; rather is he constituted as 'alter ego' — the ego indicated as one moment by this expression being I myself in my ownness. The 'Other', according to his own constituted

sense, points to me myself; the other is a 'mirroring' of my own self and yet not a mirroring proper, and analogue of my own self and yet again not an analogue in the usual sense. (Ibid., p. 94.) See also pp. 91–2.

23 This unitary stratum, furthermore, is distinguished by being essentially the *founding* stratum — that is to say: I obviously cannot have the 'alien' or 'other' as experience, and therefore cannot have the sense 'Objective world' as an experiential sense, without having this stratum in actual experience; whereas the reverse is not the case. (Ibid., p. 96.)

24 Ibid., pp. 90–1.

25 Ibid., p. 109.

26 Ibid., p. 89.

27 Husserl's exact stance toward metaphysical solipsism will be discussed below when I examine Sartre's objections, see pp. 38–40.

28 Husserl, op. cit., p. 92.

29 Ibid., p. 148.

30 Ibid., p. 93.

31 Husserl does attempt to delineate the boundaries of 'own' via the concept of 'not-alien', but this is not much help; they are interdependent ideas. He also suggests that what is 'own' is what appears as 'own', but this opens the way towards drawing the distinction anywhere. The various criteria he does offer presuppose some antecedent understanding of 'ownness'; hence they are not independent.

32 Husserl, op. cit., pp. 98–9.

33 Ibid., pp. 104–5.

34 Ibid.

35 Ibid., pp. 106–7.

36 the other is himself there before us 'in person'. On the other hand, this being there in person does not keep us from admitting forthwith that, properly speaking, neither the other Ego himself, nor his subjective processes or his appearances themselves, nor anything else belonging to his own essence, becomes given in our experience originally . . . . A *certain mediacy of intentionality* must be present here, going out from the substratum, 'primordial world', . . . and making present to consciousness a 'there too', which nevertheless is not itself there and can never become an 'itself-there'. We have here, accordingly, a kind of *making 'co-present'*, a kind of 'appresentation'. (Ibid. pp. 108–9.)

37 Ibid.

38 Ibid.

39 As we said once before, appresentation as such presupposes a core of presentation. It is a making present combined by associations with presentation, with perception proper, but a making present that is fused with the latter in the particular function of 'co-perception'. In other words, the two are so fused that they stand within the *functional community of one*

perception, which simultaneously presents and appresents, and yet furnishes for the total object a consciousness of its being itself there. (Ibid., p. 122.)

40   On the one hand, experiencing someone else cannot be a matter of just this kind of appresentation, which already plays a role in the constitution of primordial Nature: Appresentation of this sort involves the possibility of verification by a corresponding fulfilling presentation (the back becomes the front); whereas, in the case of that appresentation which would lead over into the other original sphere, such verification must be excluded a priori. (Ibid., p. 109.)

41   Ibid., p. 110.

42   Ibid., p. 111.

43   Ibid., p. 110.

44   "Closely connected with the first peculiarity is the circumstance that *ego* and *alter ego* are always and necessarily given *in an original 'pairing'*." (Ibid., p. 112.)
    pairing first comes about when the Other enters my field of perception. I, as the primordial psychophysical Ego, am always prominent in my primordial field of perception, regardless of whether I pay attention to myself and turn toward myself with some activity or other. (Ibid., p. 113.)

45   Pairing is a *primal form of that passive synthesis* which we designate as *'association'*, in contrast to passive synthesis of 'identification'. In a *pairing association* the characteristic feature is that, in the most primitive case, two data are given intuitionally, and with prominence, in the unity of a consciousness and that, on this basis — . . . — as data appearing with mutual distinctness, they *found phenomenologically a unity of similarity* and thus are always constituted precisely as a pair. (Ibid., p. 112.)

46   Ibid., p. 113.

47   "it *seems* clear without more ado that, with the transfer of sense, this body must forthwith appropriate from mine the sense: animate organism." (Ibid.)

48   The body that is a member of my primordial world (the body subsequently of the other ego) is for me a body in the mode There. Its manner of appearance does not become paired in a direct association with the manner of appearance actually belonging at the time to my animate organism (in the mode Here); rather it awakens reproductively *another*, an immediately similar appearance included in the system constitutive of my animate organism as a body in space. It brings to mind the way my body would look 'if I were there'. In this case too, although the awakening does not become a memory *intuition, pairing* takes place. (Ibid., pp. 117–18.)Cf. n. 44 above.

49   Every experience points to further experiences that would fulfill and verify the appresented horizons, which include, in

the form of non-intuitive anticipations, potentially verifiable syntheses of harmonious further experience. Regarding experience of someone else, it is clear that its fulfillingly verifying continuation can ensue *only by means of new appresentations that proceed in a synthetically harmonious fashion*, and only by virtue of the manner in which *these appresentations owe their existence-value to their motivational connexion with the* changing *presentations proper, within my ownness*, that continually appertain to them. (Ibid., p. 114.)

50 The experienced animate organism of another continues to prove itself as actually an animate organism, solely in its changing but incessantly *harmonious 'behaviour'*. . . . The organism becomes experienced as a pseudo-organism, precisely if there is something discordant about its behaviour. (Ibid.)

51 Ibid., p. 115.

52 It is clear that, with the other Ego, there is appresented, in an analogizing modification, everything that belongs to his concretion: first, *his* primordial world, and then his fully concrete ego. In other words, *another monad* becomes constituted appresentatively in mine. (Ibid.)

53 How can I speak at all of *the same* body, as appearing within my primordial sphere in the mode There and within his and to him in the mode Here? These two primordial spheres, mine which is for me as ego the original sphere, and his which is for me an appresented sphere — are they not *separated* by an abyss I cannot actually cross, since crossing it would mean, after all, that I acquired an original (rather than an appresenting) experience of someone else? (Ibid., p. 121.)

54 Therefore it is not as though the body over there, in my primordial sphere, remained separate from the animate bodily organism of the other Ego, as if that body were something like a signal for its analogue . . .; it is not as though consequently, with the spreading of the association and appresentation, my primordial Nature and the other's appresented primordial Nature — therefore my concrete ego and the other concrete ego — remained separate. . . . In so doing, it appresents first of all the other Ego's governing in this body, the body over there, and mediately his governing in the Nature that appears to him perceptually — identically the Nature to which the body over there belongs, identically the Nature that is my primordial Nature. It is the same Nature, but in the mode of appearance: 'as if I were standing over there, where the Other's body is'. The body is the same, given to me as the body there, and to him as the body here, the central body. Furthermore, 'my' whole Nature is the same as the Other's. (Ibid., pp. 122–3.)

55 See n. 39 above.

56 Husserl, op. cit., p. 123.

57 The experiential phenomenon, Objective Nature, has, besides

the primordially constituted stratum, a superimposed second, merely appresented stratum originating from my experiencing of someone else; and this fact concerns, first of all, *the Other's animate bodily organism*, which is, so to speak, *the intrinsically first Object*, just as *the other man is constitutionally the intrinsically first "Objective" man*. In the case of the primal phenomenon of Objectivity, the situation is already clear to us: if I screen off my experience of someone else, I have the lowest constitution, the one-layered presentive constitution of the other body within my primordial sphere; if I add that experience, I have appresentationally, and as coinciding synthetically with the presentational stratum, the same animate organism as it is given to the other Ego himself, and I have the further possible modes of givenness available to him. (Ibid., pp. 124–5.)

58   *every* natural Object experienced or experienceable by me in the lower stratum receives an appresentational stratum. . . , a stratum united in an identifying synthesis with the stratum given to me in the mode of primordial originality: the same natural Object in its possible modes of givenness to the other Ego. (Ibid., p. 125.)

59   Whatever, by virtue thereof, is experienced in that founded manner which characterizes a primordially unfulfillable experience — an experience that does not give something itself originally but that consistently verifies something indicated — is 'other'. It is therefore conceivable only as an analogue of something included in my peculiar ownness. Because of its sense-constitution it occurs necessarily as an *'intentional modification'* of that Ego of mine which is the first to be Objectivated. (Ibid., pp. 114–15.)

       See also n. 23 above.

60   Ibid., p. 125.

61   Ibid., p. 126.

62   there is implicit a *mutual being for one another*, which entails an *Objectivating equalization* of my existence with that of others — . . . just as his animate bodily organism lies in my field of perception, so my animate organism lies in his field of perception and that, in general, he experiences me forthwith as an Other for him, just as I experience him as *my* Other. (Ibid., pp. 129–30.)

63   Ibid., p. 140.

64   Ibid., pp. 130, 140.

65   Ibid., p. 132.

66   A deeper understanding, one that opens up the horizon of the past (which is co-determinant for an understanding of the present itself), is essentially possible to all members of that community, with a certain originality possible to them alone and barred to anyone from another community who enters into relation with theirs. (Ibid., p. 133.)

67 Ibid., pp. 134—5.
68 Jean-Paul Sartre, *Being and Nothingness: An Essay in Phenom-enological Ontology*, trans. and with an introduction by Hazel E. Barnes, New York, Philosophical Library, 1956, p. 233.
69 Ibid.
70 Ibid.
71 Ibid.
72 Husserl, op. cit., pp. 150—1.
73 Ibid., pp. 18—19, 91, 96.
74 Because the question of the real existence of the referents of constituted senses is wholly bracketed inside the phenomenological standpoint. See also the discussion below, pp. 55—7.
75 Sartre, op. cit., p. 233.
76   my affirmation of the Other demands and requires the existence beyond the world of a similar transcendental field. Consequently the only way to escape solipsism would be here again to prove that my transcendental consciousness is in its very being, affected by the extra-mundane existence of other consciousnesses of the same type. Because Husserl has reduced being to a series of meanings, the only connection which he has been able to establish between my being and that of the Other is a connection of *knowledge*. Therefore Husserl can not escape solipsism any more than Kant could. (Ibid., p. 235.)
77 Husserl, op. cit., pp. 98—9, 100.
78 Sartre, op. cit., p. 234.
79 Ibid.
80 Ibid.
81 See n. 52 above.
82 Sartre, op. cit., p. 234.
83 Ibid.
84 Husserl, op. cit., pp. 109, 114—15. See also nn. 36, 50 above.
85 Sartre, op. cit., p. 234.
86 See below, pp. 52—5.
87 Sartre, op. cit., p. 235.
88 See Husserl, op. cit., Section 43, pp. 90—2.
89 Ibid., Sections 44—8, pp. 92—106.
90   that reduced world is the intrinsically first, the *'primordial'* transcendency (or 'world'); and, regardless of its *ideality* as a synthetic unity belonging to an infinite system of my potentialities, it is *still a determining part of my own concrete being*, the being that belongs to me as a concrete ego. (Ibid., p. 106.)
91 See above, p. 29.
92 David Carr, in his stimulating article "The 'Fifth Meditation' and Husserl's Cartesianism," *Philosophy and Phenomenological Research*, 34, 1973—4, pp. 14—35, proposes the following criterion: the sphere of ownness contains whatever can be the object solely of one's own mental processes, actual and possible (p. 18). Does the self/Other (own/alien) distinction satisfy this

criterion? Does the Other have any perspectives on one's own body that are not available to one's actual or possible consciousness? Are the Other's sensations beyond the scope of one's *possible* consciousness? (Can one not envision odd cases in which one might be moved to include what is beyond the sphere of ownness as objects of possible acts of our consciousness?) Though there are some problems, Carr's is the most promising explication of Husserl's distinction.

93 Husserl, op. cit., pp. 111, 112.

94 Ibid., p. 113.

95 Ibid.

96 Could this peripheral self-awareness be what is apperceived with the Other's body via pairing? This seems improbable for two reasons: (1) often one has a more vivid grasp of Others' states of mind than one's own (e.g., their desires in a specific situation versus one's own), and a peripheral awareness could hardly function as the basis for this greater vividness; (2) one's peripheral awareness is directly related to one's present state of mind, but the Other's state of mind is typically different from one's own; so this peripheral awareness is an unlikely basis for one's grasp of the Other's states of consciousness.

97 This statement is acceptable for the purposes of this discussion, but it is ultimately too strong. In fact, the lived body and the objective body are integral parts of the whole: body-in-situation. This integrity of the two aspects of the body is learned and realized through observing and interacting with Others, however. They provide the basis for apprehending the unity of one's own body, rather than the reverse.

98 The objection has a textual basis; see Husserl, op. cit., Section 54, pp. 117—18. He seems to hold two different positions on this issue.

99 This position is defended by Jacques Lacan in his essay "The Mirror-Stage as Formative of the Function of the I," in *Ecrits: A Selection*, trans. Alan Sheridan, New York, W.W. Norton, 1977, pp. 1—7.

100 See Husserl, op. cit., p. 120.

101 The theorist who has contributed most to the elucidation of the lived body and its role in Other-perception is Merleau-Ponty in *Phenomenology of Perception*, trans. Colin Smith, International Library of Philosophy and Scientific Method, London, Routledge & Kegan Paul, 1962, especially pp. 346—67.

102 Husserl, op. cit., p. 114.

103 This point is made most effectively by Alfred Schutz in "The Problem of Transcendental Intersubjectivity in Husserl" in *Collected Papers*, Vol. III, The Hague, Martinus Nijhoff, 1970, p. 66.

104 Husserl, op. cit., pp. 110, 122. See also n. 22 above.

105 This overlaying can bring a total or a partial coincidence, which in any particular instance has its degree, the limiting

case being that of complete 'likeness'. As the result of this overlaying, there takes place in the paired data a mutual transfer of sense — that is to say: an apperception of each according to the sense of the other, so far as moments of sense actualized in what is experienced do not annul this transfer, with the consciousness of 'different'. (Ibid., p. 113.)

106 Ibid., pp. 122–5.

107 I owe this point to Prof. Holly Goldman.

108 Someone might object that the objectivity of Husserl's object is not simply limited to the profiles that could be presented to one's own actual *and possible* experience but also includes those which are presented to Other's actual and possible experience as well. But these are the very same profiles; the set of them is not enlarged by adding another potential percipient. The only real addition is the fact that the distinct profiles can now be seen as simultaneously presentable (to different conscious beings) in a way that is not true only for oneself. Still, one could imagine this possibility by oneself on the basis of memory. Perhaps the simultaneous presence of Others to an object *necessitates* the superaddition of this layer, but I see no reason why it could not be developed without the sense 'Others.'

109 Husserl, op. cit., pp. 130, 140. See also n. 62 above.

110 This possibility anticipates the discussion of Hegel's battle to the death in Chapter 2 below, pp. 71–2.

111 Husserl, op. cit., pp. 18–19.

112 It is possible, therefore, as these examples show, for the same experiences to be given both 'as our own' *and* 'as someone else's'; but there is also the case in which an experience is simply given, *without presenting itself either as our own or as another's*, as invariably happens, for example, where we are in doubt as to which of the two it is. (Max Scheler, *The Nature of Sympathy*, trans. Peter Heath, with a general introduction to Max Scheler's work by W. Stark, Hamden, Conn., Archon, 1970, paperback edn, 1973, p. 246.)

113 See Husserl, op. cit., Section 61, pp. 141–8.

114 Scheler, op. cit., pp. 246, 258.

115 It is not the case therefore, as these theories suppose, that we have to build up a picture of other people's experiences from the immediately given data furnished by our own, and then to impute these experiences, which have no intrinsic marks of 'foreignness' about them, to the physical semblances of other people. What occurs, rather, is an immediate flow of experiences, *undifferentiated as between mine and thine*, which actually contains both our own and others' experiences intermingled and without distinction from one another. Within this flow there is a gradual formation of ever more stable vortices, which slowly attract further elements of the stream into their orbits and thereby become successively and very gradually identified with distinct individuals. (Ibid., p. 246.)

116 But if there is a general human *tendency* to err in one of these two directions rather than the other, it is certainly not the error of empathy, so-called, whereby we impute our own experience to others, but the *opposite* tendency, in which we entertain the experiences of other people as if they were our own. In other words, a man tends, in the first instance, to live more in *others* than in himself; more in the community than in his own individual self. (Ibid., pp. 246–7.)

117 Ibid., pp. 245, 255, 258.

118 Ibid., pp. 260–1.

119 For we certainly believe ourselves to be directly acquainted with another person's joy in his laughter, with his sorrow and pain in his tears, with his shame in his blushing, with his entreaty in his outstretched hands, with his love in his look of affection, with his rage in the gnashing of his teeth, with his threats in the clenching of his fist, and with the tenor of his thoughts in the sound of his words. (Ibid., p. 260.)

See also ibid., pp. 252, 264.

120 Sartre, op. cit., p. 362.

121 Martin Heidegger, *Being and Time*, trans. John Macquarrie and Edward Robinson, New York, Harper & Row, 1962, p. 103.

122 In Jean-Paul Sartre, *Transcendence of the Ego: An Existentialist Theory of Consciousness*, trans. and annotated with an introduction by Forrest Williams and Robert Kirkpatrick, New York, Farrar, Straus & Giroux, Noonday Press, 1957, pp. 35–42 and 54–60.

123 See Husserl, Section 63, in which he suggests that his entire phenomenological precedure (which is a critique of the natural attitude) is in need of a deeper, second-order critique. The infinity of tasks this invitation suggests boggles the mind.

124 Near the end of his *Meditations* (Section 59), Husserl opens the possibility of this kind of enterprise, but he claims that these concrete life-world elucidations are not properly philosophically grounded unless they are related back to constitutional processes in the transcendental sphere. My arguments in this section seek to question this claim. Investigating the transcendental sphere provides no greater certainty and involves no fewer assumptions than examining the life-world. Husserl's whole enterprise is a labyrinth that leads away from a richer comprehension of Others their relationship to ourselves, and our access to them.

125 The most important example of this approach is Maurice Merleau-Ponty's *Phenomenology of Perception*, op. cit.

Chapter 2 Hegel

1 G.W.F. Hegel, *Phenomenology of Spirit*, trans. A.V. Miller, with Analysis of the Text and Foreword by J.N. Findlay, Oxford, Oxford University Press, 1977, pp. 104–19. (All emphasis and interpolations appear in the texts.)

2   Alexandre Kojève, *Introduction to the Reading of Hegel: Lectures on the "Phenomenology of Spirit"*, assembled by Raymond Queneau, ed. Allan Bloom, trans. James H. Nichols, Jr, New York, Basic, 1969. This is a partial translation of the original text.

3   Jean Hyppolite, *Genesis and Structure of Hegel's "Phenomenology of Spirit"*, trans. Samuel Cherniak and John Heckman, Northwestern University Studies in Phenomenology and Existential Philosophy, Evanston, I11., Northwestern University Press, 1974.

4   Hegel, op. cit., pp. 50, 51.

5   But the dissociation, or this semblance of dissociation and presupposition, is overcome by the nature of the object we are investigating. Consciousness provides its own criterion from within itself, so that the investigation becomes a comparison of consciousness with itself; for the distinction made falls within it. . . . But the essential point to bear in mind throughout the whole investigation is that these two moments, 'Notion' and 'object', 'being-for-another' and 'being-in-itself', both fall *within* that knowledge which we are investigating. Consequently, we do not need to import criteria, or to make use of our own bright ideas and thoughts during the course of the inquiry; it is precisely when we leave these aside that we succeed in contemplating the matter in hand as it is *in and for itself*. (Ibid., pp. 53–4.)

6   Ibid., p. 55.

7   Ibid., pp. 50–1, 55.

8   Ibid., p. 51.

9   I mean to be denying some influential standard views of Hegelian "necessity," viz., that it is purely retrospective or a function of interpretation or teleological or merely non-arbitrary. (See, for example, Walter Kaufmann's gloss of "necessary" in his *Hegel: Texts and Commentary*, New York, Anchor, 1965, p. 9, n. 6; John Findlay's unease with Hegel's efforts in his *The Philosophy of Hegel: An Introduction and Re-examination*, New York, Collier, 1962, p. 78; and Charles Taylor's *Hegel*, Cambridge University Press, 1975, pp. 214–21.) To demonstrate the inadequacy of these alternatives would require a full clarification of the logical structure of the entire book, too lengthy a task for this chapter. Thus here I shall have to state my position as a bald assertion; I may attempt to establish this thesis in a later work. One salient citation is:

        But it is just this necessity itself, or the *origination* of the new object, that presents itself to consciousness without its understanding how this happens, which proceeds for us, as it were, behind the back of consciousness. Thus in the movement of consciousness there occurs a moment of *being-in-itself* or *being-for-us* which is not present to the consciousness comprehended in the experience itself. The *content*, however, of what presents itself to us does exist *for it*; we comprehend

287

only the formal aspect of that content, or its pure origination.
For it, what has thus arisen exists only as an object; *for us*,
it appears at the same time as movement and a process of
becoming. (Hegel, op. cit., p. 56.)

10 Ibid., p. 54.

11 Ibid.

12 In pressing forward to its true existence, consciousness will
arrive at a point at which it gets rid of its semblance of being
burdened with something alien, with what is only for it, and
some sort of 'other', at a point where appearance becomes
identical with essence, so that its exposition will coincide
at just this point with the authentic Science of Spirit. (Ibid.,
pp. 56–7.)
Some of my comments on identity and life, below, will elucidate
this conception of identity more fully.

13 Ibid., p. 109.

14 Hegel suggests these symmetries late in the text because they are
not obvious from the linear progression of the stages. Each stage
consists of three major moments; Hegel suggests that the corresponding (e.g., the first or the third) major moments of each
stage are deeply interconnected and that the dynamic can be
reconceived as one sweep through the major moments of all
stages at once:
Thus while the previous single series in its advance marked the
retrogressive steps in it by nodes, but continued itself again
from them in a single line, it is now, as it were, broken at these
nodes, at these universal moments, and falls apart into many
lines which, gathered up into a single bundle, at the same time
combine symmetrically so that the similar differences in
which each particular moment took shape within itself meet
together. (Ibid., pp. 414–15.)

15 Ibid., p. 104.

16 Ibid., p. 101.

17 Ibid.

18 Ibid., p. 105.

19 Ibid.

20 Consciousness, as self-consciousness, henceforth has a double
object: one is the immediate object, that of sense-certainty
and perception, which however *for self-consciousness* has the
character of a *negative*; and second, viz. *itself*, which is the
true *essence*, and is present in the first instance only as
opposed to the first object. In this sphere, self-consciousness
exhibits itself as the movement in which the antithesis is
removed, and the identity of itself becomes explicit for it.
(Ibid.)

21 Ibid.

22 See n. 20 above.

23 the 'I' is the *content* of the connection and the connecting
itself. Opposed to an other, the 'I' is its own self, and at the

same time it overarches this other which, for the 'I', is
equally only the 'I' itself. (Hegel, op. cit., p. 104.)

24 Ibid., p. 106. The commentator most impressed with the importance of Hegel's discussion of Life, both in itself and for Self-
consciousness is Hyppolite, op. cit., pp. 160–2. Although his
view of what Hegel says about Life differs from mine, I acknowledge a debt to him for forcing me to think about the implications
of this apparent intervention seriously.

25 Ibid. Here Hegel indicates that the discussion of life is given from
the viewpoint that is *for-us*, the meta-viewpoint; hence the discussion is an intervention. Hegel indicates much that could
not yet be demonstrated at this point. Yet these passages also
suggest that Hegel is *deriving* the discussion of Life and thus that
it is part of the experience of the ideal-typical individual being
studied. My interpretation tries to capture this duality.

26 Ibid., p. 109.

27 A self-consciousness, in being an object, is just as much 'I' as
'object'. With this, we already have before us the Notion of
Spirit. What still lies ahead for consciousness is the experience
of what Spirit is — this absolute substance which is the unity
of the different independent self-consciousnesses which, in
their opposition, enjoy perfect freedom and independence:
'I' that is 'We' and 'We' that is 'I'. (Ibid., p. 110.)

28 Ibid., p. 106.

29 Ibid.

30 Ibid., p. 107.

31 Ibid., pp. 107, 108.

32 Ibid., p. 108.

33 It is the whole round of this activity that constitutes Life:
not what was expressed at the outset, the immediate
continuity and compactness of its essence, nor the enduring
form, the discrete moment existing for itself; nor the pure
process of these; nor yet the simple taking-together of these
moments. Life consists rather in being the self-developing
whole which dissolves its development and in this movement
simply preserves itself. (Ibid.)

34 Ibid., pp. 108–9.

35 The latter two are objects of Stoicism-Skepticism and the Unhappy
Consciousness respectively; they are not further discussed in this
essay.

36 See Taylor, op. cit., p. 155.

37 The observation originates with Hyppolite, op. cit., p. 158.

38 Hegel, op. cit., p. 109.

39 Ibid.

40 "In this satisfaction, however, experience makes it aware that the
object has its own independence." Ibid., p. 109.

41 "Desire and the self-certainty obtained in its gratification, are
conditioned by the object, for self-certainty comes from superseding this other: in order that this supersession can take place,

there must be this other." Ibid.

42 Ibid.

43 "On account of the independence of the object, therefore, it can achieve satisfaction only when the object itself effects the negation within itself; and it must carry out this negation of itself in itself. . . ." Ibid. Note the irony in this failure: the initial inadequacy of Self-consciousness is its distinguishing trait — the capacity to actively realize itself. This failure leads to the tendency to withdraw and retain an abstract self-identity which occurs in both impure recognition and in Stoicism.

44 *"Self-consciousness achieves its satisfaction only in another self-consciousness."* Ibid., p. 110.

45 "A self-consciousness exists *for a self-consciousness.* Only so is it in fact self-consciousness; for only in this way does the unity of itself in its otherness become explicit for it." Ibid.

46 Hegel's synopsis in Section 176 (p. 110) is the basis for this second interpretation. The final sentence sums up this development from abstract to living self-consciousness:

> The object of self-consciousness, however, is equally independent in this negativity of itself; and thus it is *for itself* a genus, a universal fluid element in the peculiarity of its own separate being; it is a living self-consciousness." (Ibid., p. 110.)

George Kelly, in "Notes on Hegel's 'Lordship and Bondage' " in Alasdair MacIntyre, ed., *Hegel: A Collection of Critical Essays*, Modern Studies in Philosophy, Garden City, NY, Doubleday, Anchor, 1972, pp. 189–217, suggests that the Master-Slave chapter can be read as a story about the split of self-consciousness within itself and its efforts to master itself, in addition to being a story about interpersonal encounter. Although internal division plays a role in the encounter between self-consciousnesses, I disagree with Kelly's basic point for three reasons: (1) his views would displace the import of the discussion of divided Self-consciousness in Unhappy-Consciousness. Hegel's main contention is that the disharmony between self and Other *precedes* and makes possible that disharmony of Self-consciousness against itself. The Master-Slave relation comes to be *internalized*; (2) in impure recognition each side tries to establish its independence of life by risking it, but if one side is thought to be living *consciousness* (as Kelly thinks), this effort of detachment is self-contradictory and inconceivable; both sides must be both abstractly self-conscious *and* livingly embodied if this effort to declare independence from life is to make sense; (3) Hegel's claims about the mutuality of recognition and necessity of reciprocity are intelligible only if two separate self-consciousnesses are assumed.

47 Since the object is in its own self negation, and in being so is at the same time independent, it is consciousness. . . . But this universal independent nature in which negation is present as absolute negation, is the genus as such, or the genus as *self-*

consciousness. (Ibid., pp. 109–10; see also n. 46 above.)

48 Here I agree with Kojève, op. cit., p. 40, even though I disagree with his interpretation that pure recognition is desire of another's desire.

49 Here Sartre's view that Hegel is primarily concerned with knowledge in the traditional sense is markedly unfair.

50 "We have now to see how the process of this pure Notion of recognition, of the duplicating of self-consciousness in its oneness, appears to self-consciousness." Hegel, op. cit., p. 112.

51 Ibid., p. 111.

52 Self-consciousness exists in and for itself when, and by the fact that, it so exists for another; that is, it exists only in being acknowledged. The Notion of this its unity in its duplication embraces many and varied meanings. (Ibid.)

53 There, at least, the criterion of *Self-consciousness* is satisfied; by then, however, the criterion itself has developed so that the dynamic of consciousness must continue. Not until the end of the *Phenomenology* does Self-consciousness become wholly realized.

54 Hegel, op. cit., pp. 111–12.

55 "Self-consciousness is faced by another self-consciousness; it has come *out of itself*. This has a twofold significance: first, it has lost itself, for it finds itself as an *other* being. . . ." Ibid., p. 111.

56 ". . . secondly, in doing so it has superseded the other, for it does not see the other as an essential being, but in the other sees its own self." Ibid.

57 Each is for the other the middle term, through which each mediates itself with itself and unites with itself; and each is for itself, and for the other, an immediate being on its own account, which at the same time is such only through this mediation. (Ibid., p. 112.)

58 "It must supersede this otherness of itself." Ibid., p. 111.

59 First, it must proceed to supersede the *other* independent being in order to thereby become certain of *itself* as the essential being; secondly, in so doing it proceeds to supersede its *own* self, for this other is itself. (Ibid.)

60 Ibid., p. 112.

61 "This ambiguous supersession of its ambiguous otherness is equally an ambiguous return *into itself*." Ibid., p. 111.

62 "For first, through the supersession, it receives back its own self, because, by superseding *its* otherness, it again becomes equal to itself. . . ." Ibid.

63 . . . but secondly, the other self-consciousness equally gives it back again to itself, for it saw itself in the other, but supersedes this being of itself in the other and thus lets the other again go free. (Ibid.)

64 Each sees the *other* do the same as it does; each does itself what it demands of the other, and therefore also does what it

does only in so far as the other does the same. Action by one side only would be useless because what is to happen can only be brought about by both. (Ibid., p. 112.)

65   Thus the action has a double significance not only because it is directed against itself as well as against the other, but also because it is indivisibly the action of one as well as of the other. (Ibid.)

66   "They *recognize* themselves as *mutually recognizing* one another." Ibid.

67   Although, as consciousness, it does indeed come *out of itself*, yet, though out of itself, it is at the same time kept back within itself, is *for itself*, and the self outside it, is for *it*. It is aware that it at once is, and is not, another consciousness, and equally that this other is *for itself* only when it supersedes itself as being for itself, and is for itself only in the being-for-itself of the other. (Ibid.)

68   The most important alternative reading of pure recognition is given by A. Kojève (op. cit., p. 6) and largely retained by J. Hyppolite (op. cit., p. 167). Kojève's key claim is that one realizes the other conscious being is also capable of desire; this is his similarity to oneself. One then desires to be desired by the Other; this kind of desire can be satisfied without destroying the Other. Desires that seek reciprocation by other desires are uniquely human; if they are satisfied, one is elevated beyond the processes of Life. Mutuality is expressed through reciprocal desires; each is desired by the Other. This reading incurs a number of problems: (1) Kojève does not clarify why desiring another is a kind of self-negation (the failure of desire demands an object that negates itself). In its initial form, desire is a type of self-realization, and its nature seems unchanged; (2) if pure recognition is to be at once the action of self and Other, then Kojève's reading implies that desiring the Other's desire and the Other's actual desire are equivalent. But this is false: to be desired by the Other is not always to desire that desire; they frequently exist without one another. Reciprocity of desire is more difficult to achieve than reciprocal acknowledgement of species-being; Kojève's view makes Hegel more vulnerable to Sartre's objections; (3) reciprocal desires create a unity like that of lovers which is often exclusive and which is not easily extended to many self-conscious beings. Hegel seems to be seeking a more realistic and more encompassing unity than love in his discussion of pure recognition.

69   Hegel, op. cit., pp. 111, 112.

70   A not wholly adequate version of pure recognition exists at the outset of the stage of Spirit, in "The Ethical World." The remaining sections of the book continue to be governed by the goal and standard of pure recognition. The final section of Spirit again approximates it without completely achieving it. Absolute knowledge achieves a kind of pure recognition, but the kind of social order in which absolute knowledge could be broadly embodied

remained an issue for Hegel throughout his philosophically active life.

71   Self-consciousness is, to begin with, simple being for self, self-equal through the exclusion from itself of everything else. For it, its essence and absolute object is 'I'; and in this immediacy, or in this [mere] being, of its being-for-self, it is an *individual*. What is 'other' for it is an unessential, negatively characterized object. But the 'other' is also a self-consciousness; one individual is confronted by another individual. (Hegel, p. 113.)

72   "Appearing thus immediately on the scene, but they are for one another like ordinary objects, *independent* shapes, individuals submerged in the being [or immediacy] of *Life*. . . ." Ibid.

73   "Each is indeed certain of its own self, but not of the other, and therefore its own self-certainty still has no truth." Ibid.

74   Ibid.

75   The presentation of itself, however, as the pure abstraction of self-consciousness consists in showing itself as the pure negation of its objective mode, or in showing that it is not attached to any specific *existence*, not to the individuality common to existence as such, that it is not attached to life. (Ibid.)

76   Ibid.

77   Ibid.

78   Ibid., pp. 113–14.

79   This trial by death, however, does away with the truth which was supposed to issue from it, and so, too, with the certainty of self generally . . . . death is the *natural* negation of consciousness, negation without independence, which thus remains without the required significance of recognition . . .; and the two do not reciprocally give and receive one another back from each other consciously, but leave each other free only indifferently, like things. (Ibid., p. 114.)

80   Their act is an abstract negation, not the negation coming from consciousness, which supersedes in such a way as to preserve and maintain what is superseded, and consequently survives its own supersession. In this experience, self-consciousness learns that life is as essential to it as pure self-consciousness. (Ibid., pp. 114–15.)

81   Although Hegel does not explicitly assert this, the point at which self-consciousness is left after the battle (an abstract sense of self facing the environment plus a dead body) suggests that it must be thrown back to the opening phase of Self-consciousness and must return to this phase again. Moreover, since this initial step of the second moment of Self-consciousness should parallel that of the second moment of Consciousness (Perception) and since such a return happens there, this view receives additional support.

82   Hegel, op. cit., p. 115.

83   Ibid., p. 116.

84   Ibid., p. 115.

85 Ibid., p. 116.
86   Here, therefore, is present this moment of recognition, viz.
        that the other consciousness sets aside its own being-for-self,
        and in so doing itself does what the first does to it. Similarly,
        the other moment too is present, that this action of the second
        is the first's own action; for what the bondsman does is really
        the action of the lord. The latter's essential nature is to exist
        only for himself; he is the sheer negative power for whom the
        thing is nothing. (Ibid.)
87   But for recognition proper the moment is lacking, that what
        the lord does to the other he also does to himself, and what the
        bondsman does to himself he should also do to the other.
        The outcome is a recognition that is one-sided and unequal. . . .
        In this recognition the unessential consciousness is for the lord
        the object, which constitutes the *truth* of his certainty of
        himself. (Ibid.)
88   the object in which the lord has achieved his lordship has in
        reality turned out to be something quite different from an
        independent consciousness. What now really confronts him
        is not an independent consciousness, but a dependent one.
        He is, therefore, not certain of *being-for-self* as the truth
        of himself. On the contrary, his truth is in reality the
        unessential consciousness and its unessential action. (Ibid.,
        pp. 116–17.)
    I am again forced to include this way of putting the aim of
    recognition because it is suggested by Hegel, perhaps here most
    strongly. Despite this, as indicated, one can still read the failure
    of mastery consistently with the overall interpretation offered
    herein. The failure is *not* that the master *depends on* the slave's
    labor or his recognition.
89 Ibid., p. 117.
90   For this consciousness has been fearful, not of this or that
        particular thing or just at odd moments, but its whole being
        has been seized with dread. . . . In that experience, it has been
        quite unmanned, has trembled in every fiber of its being, and
        everything solid and stable has been shaken to its foundations.
        But this pure universal movement, the absolute melting-away
        of everything stable, is the simple, essential nature of self-
        consciousness, absolute negativity, *pure being-for-self*, which
        consequently is *implicit* in this consciousness. (Ibid.)
91 Ibid.
92 Ibid., p. 118.
93   It is in this way, therefore, that consciousness, *qua* worker,
        comes to see in the independent being [of the object] its *own*
        independence. . . . Through this rediscovery of himself by
        himself, the bondsman realizes that it is precisely in his work
        wherein he seemed to have only an alienated existence that he
        acquires a mind of his own. (Ibid., pp. 118–19.)
94 Of course, one knows oneself better as one *becomes more*, but

Hegel's main focus is the development needed to make this addition to self-knowledge possible.

95 Hegel treats his version of solipsism in the section entitled "The Spiritual Animal Kingdom," pp. 237–50.

96 Alternatively, one could read the passage as an internal division within self-consciousness into two aspects that must enter the recognition process: living, embodied self-consciousness and abstract self-consciousness.

97 The basic possibilities are pure and impure recognition, but as Self-consciousness develops, new forms become possible, e.g., see "Reason" and "Spirit."

98 Two attempts can be found in the section on "The Law of the Heart," pp. 221–8, and "The Beautiful Soul," pp. 395–402.

99 This point also applies to the individual's relation to the larger society and culture.

100 This is the spirit in which I try to read Hegel when I discuss the problems of regarding pure recognition as an ideal. See below, pp. 116–19.

101 The three parts run respectively from pp. 235 (bottom) – 238 (top); pp. 238 (top) – 240 (top); pp. 240 (top) – 244 (middle) in Sartre, *Being and Nothingness: An Essay on Phenomenological Ontology*, trans. and with an introduction by Hazel E. Barnes, New York, Philosophical Library, 1956.

102   To begin with, this 'I am I,' a pure, universal form of identity, has nothing in common with the concrete consciousness which we have attempted to describe in our Introduction. There we established that the being of self-consciousness could not be defined in terms of knowledge. . . . If it is true that this description is the only one which allows us to understand the original fact of consciousness, then we must judge that Hegel has not succeeded in accounting for this abstract doubling of the Me which he gives as equivalent to self-consciousness. (Ibid., pp. 238–9.)

103 Ibid., pp. 235–36, 235–6, 236–7, 238.

104 See ibid., n. 5, p. 237; n. 7, p. 238; and n. 8, p. 240.

105 Ibid., p. 238.

106 Ibid., p. 235.

107 Ibid., p. 239.

108 Ibid., p. 236.

109 "Thus Hegel's brilliant intuition is to make me depend on the Other *in my being*. I am, he said, a being for-itself which is for-itself only through another." Ibid., p. 237.

110 Ibid., pp. 237–8.

111   Therefore the Other penetrates me to the heart . . . . first the negation which constitutes the Other is direct, internal, and reciprocal; second, it calls each consciousness to account and pierces it to the deepest part of its being; the problem is posited on the level of inner being, of the universal and transcendental 'I' . . . . (Ibid.)

112 Ibid., p. 236.
113 See pp. 73—4 above.
114 See pp. 65—6 above.
115 I owe this observation about transcendental arguments to Prof. Frithjof Bergmann.
116 Sartre, op. cit., p. 238.
117 This is demonstrated in Chapter 4 of this essay.
118 This study immediately follows the Master-Slave section of the Self-Consciousness chapter: "Stoicism, Skepticism, and the Unhappy Consciousness."
119 See Hegel, op. cit., pp. 237—50.
120 Sartre, op. cit., p. 236.
121 Ibid.
122 See pp. 67—71 above.
123 See n. 71 above.
124 See pp. 61—2 above.
125 Sartre, op. cit., pp. 236—7.
126 See nn. 55 and 71 above.
127 Sartre, op. cit., p. 236.
128 See pp. 59—60 above.
129 Sartre, op. cit., p. 238.
130 See n. 102 above.
131 Sartre, op. cit., p. 238.
132 Ibid.
133 Ibid.
134 See p. 61 above.
135 See pp. 61—2 above.
136 See n. 27 above.
137 See n. 57 above.
138 See pp. 62—5 above. The clearest textual support for this view appears in the notes to those pages.
139 See pp. 89—96 below.
140 Sartre, op. cit., p. 239.
141 Ibid. By 'transform' I mean undergo alteration or development of structure. Sartre grants that encountering Others may change the mode in which one experiences oneself, but this change leaves the structure of the original mode of self untouched; one may return to it just as it was despite the encounter with Others.
142 Ibid.
143 Here I provisionally adopt a linear reading of the stages of the *Phenomenology*; in actual fact matters may be more complex, but a book on Hegel would be needed to articulate how and why. See n. 14.
144 Sartre, op. cit., p. 243.
145 Ibid., p. 240.
146 Ibid., pp. 241—2.
147 Ibid., p. 242.
148 Ibid., pp. 240, 243.
149 Ibid., p. 242.

150 Ibid., p. 244.
151 Sartre seems to waffle in presenting Hegel's view on this issue, for compare pp. 236 and 244. Sartre holds both that Hegel obliterates plurality and that he founds it properly.
152 Ibid., p. 243.
153 Ibid., pp. 243–4.
154 One can see this reply emerging in ibid., pp. 241–2.
155 Ibid., p. 243.
156 Hegel, op. cit., p. 109.
157 Ibid.
158 Ibid., pp. 237–50.
159 Ibid., p. 113.
160 Ibid., p. 114.
161 Ibid., pp. 115–16.
162 Ibid., pp. 116–17.
163 Ibid., p. 117.
164 This point can be derived from Prof. Frithjof Bergmann's discussion in *On Being Free*, Notre Dame, Ind., University of Notre Dame Press, 1977, Chap. 3.
165 This empty universal self-consciousness is the direct antecedent of Sartre's "nothingness" of consciousness. For Hegel, it is only one moment of Self-consciousness, not its defining characteristic.
166 Hegel, op. cit., pp. 118–19.
167 See pp. 67–71 above.
168 Hegel never explicitly claims that pure recognition is an ideal, but he does believe it is the telos or aim of most interpersonal encounters. Since it plays so central a role in the development of the *Phenomenology*, I think I can safely assume Hegel valorized it.
169 See, for example, the discussion of the relations of the family to the society as a whole in "The Ethical World," in Hegel, op. cit., pp. 267–79.

Chapter 3 Heidegger

1 Martin Heidegger, *Being and Time*, trans. John Macquarrie and Edward Robinson, New York, Harper & Row, 1962, p. 19. (All emphasis and interpolations appear in the texts.)
2 Yet that which remains *hidden* in an egregious sense, or which relapses and gets *covered up* again, or which shows itself only 'in disguise', is not just this entity or that, but rather the *Being* of entities, as our previous observations have shown. This Being can be covered up so extensively that it becomes forgotten and no question arises about it or about its meaning. Thus that which demands that it becomes a phenomenon, and which demands this in a distinctive sense and in terms of its ownmost content as a thing, is what phenomenology has taken into its grasp thematically as its object. (Ibid., p. 59.)
3 Ibid., pp. 25–6, 29, 61.
4 Ibid., p. 26.

5   Looking at something, understanding and conceiving it,
     choosing, access to it — all these ways of behaving are
     constitutive for our inquiry, and therefore are modes of Being
     for those particular entities which we, the inquirers, are
     ourselves. Thus to work out the question of Being adequately,
     we must make an entity — the inquirer — transparent in his
     own Being. The very asking of this question is an entity's
     mode of *Being*; and as such it gets its essential character from
     what is inquired about — namely, Being. (Ibid., pp. 26–7.)
6   Ibid., pp. 27–8, 33.
7   If to interpret the meaning of Being becomes our task, Dasein
     is not only the primary entity to be interrogated; it is also that
     entity which already comports itself, in its Being, towards
     what we are asking about when we ask this question. But in
     that case the question of Being is nothing other than the
     radicalization of an essential tendency-of-Being which belongs
     to Dasein itself — the pre-ontological understanding of Being.
     (Ibid., p. 35.)
8   Ibid., pp. 41, 42, 43.
9   Ibid., p. 44.
10   Ibid., p. 26.
11   Ibid., pp. 36–7, 150.
12   Ibid., pp. 85, 149.
13   Not only, however, does an understanding of Being belong to
     Dasein, but this understanding develops or decays along with
     whatever kind of Being Dasein may possess at the time;
     accordingly there are many ways in which it has been
     interpreted, and these are all at Dasein's disposal. (Ibid.,
     p. 37; see also pp. 33, 34.)
14   Ibid., pp. 47, 48.
15   Ibid., pp. 85–6.
16   Ibid., p. 31.
17   Ibid., pp. 30–1.
18   Ibid., p. 32.
19   Ibid., p. 34.
20   But in that case, this is a constitutive state of Dasein's Being,
     and this implies that Dasein, in its Being, has a relationship
     towards that Being — a relationship which itself is one of
     Being. And this means further that there is some way in which
     Dasein understands itself in its Being, and that to some degree
     it does so explicitly. It is peculiar to this entity that with and
     through its Being, this Being is disclosed to it. *Understanding
     of Being is itself a definite characteristic of Dasein's Being.*
     Dasein is ontically distinctive in that it *is* ontological. (Ibid.,
     p. 32.)
21   Ibid., p. 33.
22   Ibid., p. 34.
23   Ibid.
24   Michael Gelven, for example, in his book *A Commentary on*

Heidegger's "Being and Time," New York, Harper & Row, 1970, stresses the meta-level of Heidegger's inquiry. Gelven does not see sufficiently clearly that Heidegger is trying to clarify human being *per se*; in doing so he also elucidates the meta-level of the inquiry. Although Kant plays a prominent role in Heidegger's book, Heidegger is not simply trying to rework Kant's investigation. Richard Schmitt, in his book *Martin Heidegger On Being Human*, New York, Ransom House, 1969, stresses the object-level aspect of the inquiry, and further interprets that as an essentially conceptual inquiry. Although Heidegger does refashion a number of concepts, that is not the primary intent of his inquiry; he is trying to get us to apprehend our being and Being itself better, and ultimately to *live* differently, not simply to revise our philosophical concepts.

25   The question of Being aims therefore at ascertaining the *a priori* conditions not only for the possibility of the sciences which examine entities as entities of such and such a type, and, in so doing, already operate with an understanding of Being, but also for the possibility of those ontologies themselves which are prior to the ontical sciences and which provide their foundations. (Heidegger, op. cit., p. 31.)

26 For example, he does not pursue the meta-level aspects of Being-in-the-world, worldhood, Being-with, They-self, and Being-in, as much as their implications for understanding man.

27   In our introduction we have already intimated that in the existential analytic of Dasein we also make headway with a task which is hardly less pressing than that of the question of Being itself — the task of laying bare that *a priori* basis which must be visible before the question of 'what man is' can be discussed philosophically. (Heidegger, op. cit., p. 71.)

28 Ibid., p. 70.

29 Ibid., p. 78.

30 Ibid., pp. 17, 71.

31 Ibid., p. 67.

32 I offer this condition because Heidegger justifies his existential claims by showing that every apparent exception is really, when understood correctly, only a form or variant of the existential.

33 Ibid., pp. 67, 84.

34   Heidegger calls the necessary ways of viewing the self existentials (see chart, p. 19). Like categories, the existentials are *a priori*, and further, like categories, the existentials are necessary ways in which the mind operates. Categories are necessary ways in which the mind imposes order on things *other* than the mind itself. (Michael Gelven, op. cit., p. 50.)

35 Ibid., pp. 77, 99, 105.

36   'Worldhood' is an ontological concept, and stands for the structure of one of the constitutive items of Being-in-the-world. But we know Being-in-the-world as a way in which Dasein's character is defined existentially. Thus worldhood itself is an

existentiale. . . . Ontologically, 'world' is not a way of
characterizing those entities which Dasein essentially is *not*; it
is rather a characteristic of Dasein itself. (Ibid., p. 92.)

37   Since I am only using worldhood to illustrate what an existential
is, I will not present Heidegger's arguments and considerations in
defense of these views.

38   Heidegger, op. cit., p. 87.

39   Ibid., pp. 88, 107.

40   Ibid., pp. 88–9, 107.

41   In this kind of '*dwelling*' as a holding-oneself-back from any
manipulation or utilization, the *perception* of the present-at-
hand is consummated. Perception is consummated when one
addresses oneself to something as something and *discusses* it as
such. (Ibid., p. 89.)

"The presence-at-hand of entities is thrust to the fore by the
possible breaks in that referential totality in which circumspection 'operates' . . . . " Ibid., p. 107.

42   Ibid., p. 78.

43   And because Dasein is in each case essentially its own
possibility, it *can*, in its very Being, 'choose' itself and win
itself; it can also lose itself and never win itself; or only 'seem'
to do so. But only in so far as it is essentially something which
can be *authentic* — that is, something of its own — can it have
lost itself and not yet won itself. As modes of Being,
authenticity and *inauthenticity* (these expressions have been
chosen terminologically in a strict sense) are both grounded
in the fact that any Dasein whatsoever is characterized by
mineness. But the inauthenticity of Dasein does not signify
any 'less' Being or any 'lower' degree of Being. Rather it
is the case that even in its fullest concretion Dasein can be
characterized by inauthenticity — when busy, when excited,
when interested, when ready for enjoyment. (Ibid., p. 68.
See also Sections 35, 37, and 38.)

44   By 'difference' here I mean qualitative not numerical difference.

45   The phenomenological assertion that 'Dasein is essentially
Being-with' has an existential-ontological meaning. It does
not seek to establish ontically that factically I am not present-
at-hand alone, and that Others of my kind occur. If this were
what is meant by the proposition that Dasein's Being-in-the-
world is essentially constituted by Being-with, then Being-
with would not be an existential attribute which Dasein, of its
own accord, has coming to it from its own kind of Being.
It would rather be something which turns up in every case
by reason of the occurrence of Others. (Heidegger, op. cit.,
p. 156.)

46   With their Being-with, their disclosedness has been constituted
before-hand; accordingly, this disclosedness also goes to make
up significance — that is to say, worldhood. . . . The structure
of the world's worldhood is such that Others are not

proximally present-at-hand as free-floating subjects along with other Things, but show themselves in the world in their special environmental Being, and do so in terms of what is ready-to-hand in that world. (Ibid., p. 160.)

47 In clarifying Being-in-the-world we have shown that a bare subject without a world never 'is' proximally, nor is it ever given. And so in the end an isolated 'I' without Others is just as far from being proximally given. (Ibid., p. 152.)

48 By 'Others' we do not mean everyone else but me — those over against whom the 'I' stands out. They are rather those from whom, for the most part, one does *not* distinguish oneself — those among whom one is too. This Being-there-too [Auch-da-sein] with them does not have the ontological character of a Being-present-at-hand-along- 'with' them within a world. This 'with' is something of the character of Dasein; the 'too' means a sameness of Being as circumspectively concernful Being-in-the-world. (Ibid., p. 154.)

49 "By reason of this *with-like* [mithaften] Being-in-the-world, the world is always the one that I share with Others. The world of Dasein is a *with-world* [Mitwelt]. Being-in is *Being-with* Others." Ibid., p. 155.

50 *The 'they' is an existentiale; and as a primordial phenomenon, it belongs to Dasein's positive constitution.* . . . . If Dasein is familiar with itself as they-self, this means at the same time that the "they" itself prescribes that way of interpreting the world and Being-in-the-world which lies closest. Dasein is for the sake of the 'they' in an everyday manner, and the 'they' itself Articulates the referential context of significance. . . . *Proximally*, it is not 'I', in the sense of my own Self, that 'am', but rather the Others, whose way is that of the "they". In terms of the "they", and as the "they", I am 'given' proximally to 'myself' [mir "selbst"]. (Ibid., p. 167.)

51 Ibid., p. 165.

52 From the kind of Being which belongs to the "they" — the kind which is closest — everyday Dasein draws its pre-ontological way of interpreting its Being. . . . Thus by exhibiting the positive phenomenon of the closest everyday Being-in-the-world, we have made it possible to get an insight into the reason why an ontological Interpretation of this state of Being has been missing. *This very state of Being, in its everyday kind of Being, is what proximally misses itself and covers itself up.* (Ibid., p. 168.)

"Knowing oneself [Sichkennen] is grounded in Being-with, which understands primordially." Ibid., p. 161.

53 In these characters of Being which we have exhibited — everyday Being-among-one-another, distantiality, averageness, levelling down, publicness, the disburdening of one's Being, and accommodation — lies that 'constancy' of Dasein which is closest to us. This 'constancy' pertains not to the enduring

Being-present-at-hand of something, but rather to Dasein's kind of Being as Being-with. Neither the Self of one's own Dasein nor the Self of the Other has as yet found itself or lost itself as long as it is [seiend] in the modes we have mentioned. In these modes one's way of Being is that of inauthenticity and failure to stand by one's Self. (Heidegger, op. cit., p. 166.)

54   The Self of everyday Dasein is the *they-self*, which we distinguish from the *authentic Self* — that is, from the Self which has been taken hold of in its own way [eigens ergriffenen]. As they-self, the particular Dasein has been *dispersed* into the 'they', and must first find itself. (Ibid., p. 167.)

55   Ibid., Section 35 and 37.

56   Ibid., p. 151.

57   Ibid., p. 150.

58   Ibid., p. 155.

59   But even if Others become themes for study, as it were, in their own Dasein, they are not encountered as person-Things present-at-hand: we meet them 'at work', that is, primarily in their Being-in-the-world. (Ibid., p. 156.)

60   Even if we see the Other 'just standing around', he is never apprehended as a human-Thing present-at-hand, but his 'standing-around' is an existential mode of Being — an unconcerned, uncircumspective tarrying alongside everything and nothing [Verveilen bei Allem und keinem]. The Other is encountered in his Dasein-with in the world. (Ibid.)

61   "Being-with is an existential characteristic of Dasein even when factically no Other is present-at-hand or perceived." Ibid. "Even if the particular factical Dasein does *not* turn to Others, and supposes that it has no need of them or manages to get along without them, it *is* in the way of Being-with." Ibid., p. 160.

62   Ibid., pp. 153–4.

63   This Dasein-with of the Others is disclosed within-the-world for a Dasein, and so too for those who are Daseins with us [die Mitdaseienden], only because Dasein in itself is essentially Being-with. . . . Only so far as one's own Dasein has the essential structure of Being-with, is it Dasein-with as encounterable for Others. (Ibid., pp. 156–7.)

64   According to the analysis which we have now completed, Being with Others belongs to the Being of Dasein, which is an issue for Dasein in its very Being. Thus a Being-with, Dasein 'is' essentially for the sake of Others. This must be understood as an existential statement as to its essence. (Ibid., p. 160.)

65   Ibid., p. 157.

66   Even in our Being 'among them' they are *there with* us; their Dasein-with is encountered in a mode in which they are indifferent and alien. Being missing and 'Being away' [Das Fehlen und "Fortsein"] are modes of Dasein-with,

and are possible only because Dasein as Being-with lets the Dasein of Others be encountered in its world. (Ibid.)

Being for, against, or without one another, passing one another by, not 'mattering' to one another — these are possible ways of solicitude. And it is precisely these last-named deficient and Indifferent modes that characterize everyday, average Being-with-one-another. (Ibid., p. 158.)

67   Even Dasein's Being alone is Being-with in the world. The Other can *be missing* only *in* and *for* a Being-with. Being-alone is a deficient mode of Being-with; its very possibility is the proof of this. (Ibid., pp. 156–7.)

68   But just as opening oneself up [Sichoffenbaren] or closing oneself off is grounded in one's having Being-with-one-another as one's kind of Being at the time, and indeed *is* nothing else but this, even the explicit disclosure of the Other in solicitude grows only out of one's primarily Being with him in each case. (Ibid., p. 161.)

69 Ibid., p. 158.

70   It can, as it were, take away 'care' from the Other and put itself in his position in concern: it can *leap in* for him. This kind of solicitude takes over for the Other that with which he is to concern himself. The Other is thus thrown out of his own position. . . . In such solicitude the Other can become one who is dominated and dependent, even if this domination is a tacit one and remains hidden from him. (Ibid.)

71   In contrast to this, there is also the possibility of a kind of solicitude which does not so much leap in for the Other as *leap ahead* of him [ihm *vorausspringt*] in his existentiell potentiality-for-Being, not in order to take away his 'care' but rather to give it back to him authentically as such for the first time. This kind of solicitude pertains essentially to authentic care — that is, to the existence of the Other, not to a '*what*' with which he is concerned; it helps the Other to become transparent to himself *in* his care and to become *free for it.* (Ibid., pp. 158–9.)

72 Another exception to my reading of the basic thrust of Heidegger's theory is the fact that authentic group existence is possible; cf., On the other hand, when they devote themselves to the same affair in common, their doing so is determined by the manner in which their Dasein, each in its own way, has been taken hold of. They thus become *authentically* bound together, and this makes possible the right kind of objectivity [die richte Sachlichkeit] , which frees the Other in his freedom for himself. (Ibid., p. 159.)

73 Sartre's theory of the essential assymmetry of modes of existence in self and Other will be explicated in Chapter 4. Sartre's "modalities" (subject-object) of course differ from Heidegger's (authentic-inauthentic).

74   This Being-with-one-another dissolves one's own Dasein

completely into the kind of Being of 'the Others', in such a way, indeed, that the Others, as distinguishable and explicit, vanish more and more. In this inconspicuousness and unascertainability, the real dictatorship of the 'they' is unfolded. (Heidegger, op. cit., p. 164.)

75 Ibid.
76 Ibid., p. 165.
77 Ibid.
78 Dasein's everyday possibilities of Being are for the Others to dispose of as they please. These Others, moreover, are not *definite* Others. On the contrary, any Other can represent them. . . . The 'they', which is nothing definite, and which all are, though not as the sum, prescribes the kind of Being of everydayness. (Ibid., p. 164.)
79 Ibid., pp. 164—5.
80 Furthermore, the 'they' is not something like a 'universal subject' which a plurality of subjects have hovering above them. . . The 'they' is not the genus to which the individual Dasein belongs, nor can we come across it in such entities as an abiding characteristic. That even the traditional logic fails us when confronted with these phenomena, is not surprising if we bear in mind that it has its foundation in an ontology of the present-at-hand — an ontology which, moreover, is still a rough one. (Ibid., pp. 166—7.)
81 Ibid., pp. 163—4.
82 "The 'who' is not this one, not that one, not oneself [man selbst], not some people [einige], and not the sum of them all. The 'who' is the neuter, *the 'they'* [*das Man*]." Ibid., p. 164.
83 Ibid., pp. 150, 152, 153.
84 See nn. 50 and 54.
85 *Authentic Being-one's-Self* does not rest upon an exceptional condition of the subject, a condition that has been detached from the 'they'; *it is rather an existentiell modification of the 'they' — of the 'they' as an essential existentiale.* (Heidegger, op. cit., p. 168.)
86 See n. 50.
87 What is decisive is just that inconspicuous domination by Others which has already been taken over unawares from Dasein as Being-with. One belongs to the Others oneself and enhances their power. 'The Others' whom one thus designates in order to cover up the fact of one's belonging to them essentially oneself, are those who proximally and for the most part *'are there'* in everyday Being-with-one-another. (Heidegger, op. cit., p. 164, See also n. 47.)
88 Of course it is indisputable that a lively mutual acquaintance-ship on the basis of Being-with often depends upon how far one's own Dasein has understood itself at the time; but this means that it depends only upon how far one's essential Being with Others has made itself transparent and has not

disguised itself. (Ibid., p. 162. See also n. 52.)
89   Ibid., p. 168.
90   Ibid.
91   If Dasein discovers the world in its own way [eigens] and brings it close, if it discloses to itself its own authentic Being, then this discovery of the 'world' and this disclosure of Dasein are always accomplished as a clearing-away of concealments and obscurities, as a breaking up of the disguises with which Dasein bars its own way. (Ibid., p. 167.)
92   Ibid., p. 158.
93   Jean-Paul Sartre, *Being and Nothingness: An Essay on Phenomenological Ontology*, trans. and with an introduction by Hazel E. Barnes, New York, Philosophical Library, 1953, p. 245.
94   Ibid., pp. 244–5.
95   Ibid.
96   Thus the relation of the *Mit-Sein* can be of absolutely no use to us in resolving the psychological, concrete problem of the recognition of the Other. There are two incommunicable levels and two problems which demand separate solutions. (Ibid., p. 248.)
97   Ibid., p. 249.
98   Ibid., pp. 244, 247.
99   Ibid., p. 245.
100 Ibid., p. 246.
101 Ibid.
102 Ibid.
103 Ibid., pp. 246–7.
104 Ibid., p. 246.
105 Ibid.
106 My being-with, apprehended from the standpoint of 'my' being, can be considered only as a pure exigency founded in *my* being; it does not constitute the slightest proof of the Other's existence, not the slightest bridge between me and the Other. (Ibid., pp. 248–9.)
107 Ibid., p. 249.
108 Ibid., pp. 245, 246. See also n. 96.
109 Ibid., pp. 244, 247.
110 Ibid., p. 247.
111 Ibid., p. 248. See also n. 106.
112 Ibid., p. 247.
113 Ibid., p. 248.
114 Ibid., pp. 247, 248.
115 Ibid., p. 250.
116 Ibid.
117 See n. 66.
118 See nn. 63, 66, and 68.
119 Heidegger, op. cit., p. 157.
120 See n. 61.
121 Sartre, op. cit., p. 249.

122 See n. 106.

123 One can derive this reply from n. 63.

124 Heidegger might try to claim that the a priori status of the existentials is restricted to the meta-level of his inquiry; that is, he might claim that the existentials are prior to and condition all possible *philosophical inquiry*, but not all possible forms of life. The existentials would then express the essential features of these forms of life because of general facts like living in a culture. Their "necessity" would result from the typical features of human development. On this view, ontic structures would be particular specifications of these general structures, and the ontological structures would express very general empirical facts of the human world as we know it, but facts which might not apply in all possible worlds in which human organisms might exist.

125 This analogy was suggested to me by Prof. Frithjof Bergmann.

126 See nn. 66 and 67.

127 Heidegger, op. cit., pp. 153–4.

128 See n. 48.

129 Even if authenticity is a modification of the impersonal mode of selfness, it does engender a distinctive sense of self, a sense of directing one's own life.

130 Heidegger, op. cit., pp. 88–9, 107.

131   The relationship-of-Being which one has towards Others would then become a Projection of one's own Being-towards-oneself 'into something else' . . . . The presupposition which this argument demands — that Dasein's Being towards itself is Being towards an Other — fails to hold . . . . Not only is Being towards Others an autonomous, irreducible relationship of Being: this relationship, as Being-with, is one which, with Dasein's Being, already is. (Ibid., p. 162.)

132   But it is essential to Dasein that along with the disclosedness of its world it has been disclosed to itself, so that it always *understands itself*. The call reaches Dasein in this under-standing of itself which it always has, and which is concernful in an everyday, average manner. The call reaches the they-self of concernful Being with Others. (Ibid., p. 317.)
        The tendency of the call is not such as to put up for 'trial' the Self to which the appeal is made. but it calls Dasein forth (and 'forward') into its ownmost possibilities, as a summons to its ownmost *potentiality*-for-Being-its-Self. (Ibid., p. 318.)
The first of these quotes suggests that Dasein's relation to itself is not unlike its relation to its world (including Others); the second indicates one similarity between conscience (a relation to oneself) and the relation of *authentic* Others to oneself.

133 See n. 54.

306

Chapter 4   Sartre

1 Sartre's discussion of purified reflection appears on pp. 159–62 in *Being and Nothingness: An Essay on Phenomenological Ontology*, trans. and with an introduction by Hazel Barnes, New York, Philosophical Library, 1956. (All emphasis appears in the texts.)

2 The differences between transcendental and existential phenomenology were explored in Chap. 1, pp. 55–7 above.

3 This distinction is clarified in Sartre's Introduction, "The Pursult of Being," pp. xlv–lxvii.

4 See ibid., especially pp. l–lxii.

5 The non-directed component of conscious acts is clarified in ibid., pp. li–lvi.

6 See ibid., pp. li–lvi (perception), pp. 150–70 (reflection), and pp. 47–70 (bad faith).

7 See ibid., pp. 3–45.

8 See ibid., pp. 73–105 and pp. 171–219.

9 See ibid., pp. 107–49.

10 I owe this way of formulating the matter to Prof. Frithjof Bergmann.

11 See Sartre, pp. lxii–lxvi.

12 This theme is developed in ibid., pp. 34–45, 55–67, and 432–555.

13 See, for example, ibid., pp. 361–4.

14 See, for example, ibid., pp. 564–8.

15 Sartre explores the relations between those aspects in his chapters on "The Body" (pp. 303–59) and "Freedom" (pp. 433–556).

16 These strategies are explored in ibid., pp. 47–71.

17 "Such a theory can not offer a new *proof* of the existence of others, or an argument better than any other against solipsism." Ibid., p. 250;

> A theory of the Other's existence must therefore simply question me in my being, must make clear and precise the meaning of that affirmation; in particular, far from inventing a proof, it must make explicit the very foundation of that certainty. (Ibid., p. 251.)

18
> Thus this relation which I call 'being-seen-by-another,' far from being merely one of the relations signified by the word *man*, represents an irreducible fact which can not be deduced either from the essence of the Other-as-object, or from my being-as-subject. (Ibid., p. 257.)

19 See n. 17.

20
> The Other must appear to the *cogito* as *not being* me. This negation can be conceived in two ways: either it is a pure, external negation, and it will separate the Other from myself as one substance from another substance — and in this case all apprehension of the Other is by definition impossible; or else it will be an internal negation, which means a synthetic,

active connection of the two terms, each one of which constitutes itself by denying that it is the other. This negative relation will therefore be reciprocal. (Ibid., p. 252.)

21   What the *cogito* must reveal to us is not the-Other-as-object.... Since the Other is neither a representation nor a system of representations nor a necessary unity of our representations, he can not be probable: he can not *at first* be an object . . . but as one who 'interests' our being, and that not as he contributes *a priori* to constitute our being but as he interests it concretely and 'ontically' in the empirical circumstances of our facticity. (Ibid., pp. 251–2.)

22   On the other hand, Hegel's failure has shown us that the only point of departure possible is the Cartesian *cogito*. Moreover the *cogito* alone establishes us on the ground of that factual necessity which is the necessity of the Other's existence.... Thus we must ask the For-itself to deliver to us the For-others; we must ask absolute immanence to throw us into absolute transcendence. (Ibid., p. 251.)

23   See ibid., pp. 252–69.

24   Now at last we can make precise the meaning of this upsurge of the Other in and through his look. The Other is in no way given to us as an object. The objectivation of the Other would be the collapse of his being-as-a-look. Furthermore as we have seen, the Other's look is the disappearance of the Other's *eyes* as objects which manifest the look. (Ibid., p. 268.) See also p. 257.

25   Ibid., pp. 269–82.

26   Ibid., pp. 282–97.

27   "These considerations do not exclude the possibility of an ethics of deliverance and salvation. But this can be achieved only after a radical conversion which we can not discuss here." Ibid., p. 412, footnote.

28   "Thus the appearance among the objects of *my* universe of an element of disintegration in that universe is what I mean by the appearance of a man in my universe." Ibid., p. 255. See also p. 254.

29   Ibid.

30   Ibid., p. 256.

31   Ibid.

32   "It is in and through the revelation of my being-as-object for the Other that I must be able to apprehend the presence of his being-as-subject." Ibid.

33   I am alone and on the level of a non-thetic self-consciousness. This means first of all that there is no self to inhabit my consciousness, nothing therefore to which I can refer my acts in order to qualify them. They are in no way *known*; I *am my acts* and hence they carry in themselves their whole justification. (Ibid., p. 259.)

34   Ibid., p. 260.

35 Ibid.

36 Ibid.

37 Ibid., p. 266.

38 Ibid., p. 265.

39   First of all, I now exist as myself for my unreflective
       consciousness. . . . But here the self comes to haunt the
       unreflective consciousness . . . the person is presented to
       consciousness *in so far as the person is an object for the
       Other*. This means that all of a sudden I am conscious of
       myself as escaping myself. . . . I am for myself only as I am a
       pure reference to the Other. (Ibid., p. 260.)

40   Nevertheless I *am that Ego*; I do not reject it as a strange
       image, but it is present to me as a self which I *am* without
       knowing it; for I discover it in shame and, in other instances,
       in pride. (Ibid., p. 261.)

41   It is given to me as a burden which I carry without ever
       being able to turn back to know it, without even being able
       to realize its weight. If it is comparable to my shadow, it is
       like a shadow which is projected on a moving and unpredict-
       able material such that no table of reference can be provided
       for calculating the distortions resulting from these movements.
       Yet we still have to do with *my* being and not with an image
       of my being. We are dealing with my being as it is written in
       and by the Other's freedom. (Ibid., p. 262.)

42 Ibid., p. 263.

43   I should willingly say here: we can not perceive the world and
       at the same time apprehend a look fastened upon us; it must
       either be one or the other. This is because to perceive is to
       look at, and to apprehend a look is not to apprehend a look-as-
       object in the world. . .; it is to be conscious of *being looked
       at*." (Ibid., p. 258.)
       See also n. 24.

44   "My original fall is the existence of the Other . . . but my nature
       is − over there, outside my lived freedom − as a given attribute of
       this being which I am for the Other." Ibid., p. 263; "To be looked
       at is to apprehend oneself as the unknown object of unknowable
       appraisals − in particular, of value judgments." Ibid., p. 267.

45 See n. 43 above and n. 57 below.

46   But to be exact, in so far as the other temporalizes *himself*, he
       temporalizes *me* with him; in so far as he launches out toward
       his own time, I appear to him in universal time. . . . I am
       thrown into the universal present in so far as the Other makes
       himself be a presence to me. But the universal present in which
       I come to take my place is a pure alienation of my universal
       present. (Sartre, op. cit., p. 267.)

47   I am a slave to the degree that my being is dependent at the
       center of a freedom which is not mine and which is the very
       condition of my being. In so far as I am the object of values
       which come to qualify me without my being able to act on

this qualification or even to know it, I am enslaved. (Ibid.)
48 See n. 17 above.
49 Sartre, op. cit., p. 268.
50 The Other's existence will always be subject to doubt, at least if one doubts the Other only in words and abstractly, in the same way that without really being able to conceive of it, I can write, 'I doubt my own existence.' (Ibid., p. 250.)
51 The difference of principle between the Other-as-object and the Other-as-subject stems solely from this fact: that the Other-as-subject can in no way be known or even conceived as such. There is no problem of the knowledge of the Other-as-subject, and the objects of the world do not refer to his subjectivity; they refer only to his object-state in the world as the meaning . . . of the intramundane flow. (Ibid., p. 293.)
52 Everything takes place as if I had a dimension of being from which I was separated by a radical nothingness; and this nothingness is the Other's freedom. The Other has to make my being-for-him *be* in so far as he has to be his being. (Ibid., p. 262.)
53 Ibid., pp. 361—412.
54 Ibid., p. 256.
55 Ibid., p. 253.
56 Ibid., pp. 261—8. See nn. 39—47 above.
57 There is produced here something analogous to what I attempted to show elsewhere in connection with the subject of the imagination. We can not, I said then, perceive and imagine simultaneously; it must be either one or the other. I should willingly say here: we can not perceive the world and at the same time apprehend a look fastened upon us; it must be either one or the other. (Ibid., p. 258.) See also p. 266 and n. 43 above.
58 "Beyond any knowledge which I can have, I am this self which another knows." Ibid., p. 261. See also pp. 263, 265.
59 I am not here asserting that a gap between experience and reality necessarily exists, only that it sometime does. I discuss Sartre's efforts to bridge the gap below, see pp. 210—13.
60 Sartre does this explicitly in his theory of relationships.
61 Sartre considers the strategy I am discussing here in his analysis of love. This point is one of many reasons for love's failure.
62 One must also show that the transformation cannot occur without the existence of Others. This second requirement provides the phenomenon with ontological import. Sartre shows that the social self fulfills this condition in the second movement of his theory, the transcendental argument. In further analysis, pp. 249—54 below, I shall review each of the modes of subjectivity investigated here in order to establish that they fulfill this second condition at least as adequately as Sartre's social self does.
63 Since Hegelian recognition was thoroughly discussed in Chapter 2, I shall recall only the bare essentials here. Although Sartre

would reply that Hegelian recognition is impossible, my arguments against his position in Chapter 2 forestall this line of attack.

64 See below, pp. 249–54.
65 See below, pp. 210–13 and n. 117 below.
66 Of course what *most often* manifests a look is the convergence of two ocular globes in my direction. But the look will be given just as well on occasion when there is a rustling of branches, or the sound of a footstep followed by silence, or the slight opening of a shutter, or a light movement of a curtain. (Sartre, op. cit., p. 257.)
67 See especially *Interaction Ritual: Essays on Face to Face Behavior*, Garden City, New York, Anchor, 1967.
68 In so far as I am the object of values which come to qualify me without my being able to act on this qualification or even to know it, I am enslaved. . . . This danger is not an accident but the permanent structure of my being-for-others. (Sartre, op. cit., pp. 267–8.)
69 Ibid., p. 263; see also n. 43 above.
70 See n. 57 above.
71 It is rather in itself a solidification and an abrupt stratification of myself which leaves intact my possibilities and my structures 'for-myself,' but which suddenly pushes me into a new dimension of existence – the dimension of the *unrevealed*. (Sartre, op. cit., p. 268.)
72 There is other evidence of Sartre's uncertainty about the exclusivity claim; he claims that each mode remains in the background while the other lies in the foreground. See Sartre, op. cit., pp. 283–97.
73 On p. 264 Sartre discusses a similar example; there he asserts that all possibilities one might have become dead – made into objective probabilities by the Other-as-subject. I am disputing his view.
74 Sartre's analysis of sexual intercourse suggests that each is a quasi-object for the Other and for himself; in accepting one's embodiment, one abandons one's subjectivity. But one still experiences one's own aims and registers the intentions of the Other; these reciprocate and stimulate one another. One experiences oneself neither as dominating nor as submitting to the Other. This fact is what I seek to capture by saying that one exists *between* Sartre's two modes.
75 For a fuller discussion, see below, pp. 253–4.
76 See n. 40, above.
77 However *that other* consciousness and *that other* freedom are never *given* to me; for if they were, they would be *known* and would therefore be an object, which would cause me to cease being an object. (Sartre, op. cit., p. 271.)
78 Such a theory can not offer a new *proof* of the existence of others, or an argument better than any other against

solipsism. Actually if solipsism is to be rejected, this can
not be because it is impossible or, if you prefer, because
nobody is truly solipsistic. (Ibid., p. 250.)
See also p. 251.

79 See n. 19 above.
80 See n. 40 above.
81   The proof of my condition **as man**, as an object for *all* other
living men, as thrown in **the arena** beneath millions of looks
and escaping myself **millions of** times — this proof I realize
concretely on the **occasion** of the upsurge of an object into *my*
universe if this object indicates to me that I am probably
an object at present functioning as a *differentiated this* for a
consciousness. This proof is the ensemble of the phenomenon
which we call the *look*. (Sartre, op. cit., p. 281.)
82 Ibid., p. 269.
83 Ibid., p. 271.
84   If someone looks at me, I am conscious *of being* an object.
But this consciousness can be produced only in and through
the existence of the Other. In this respect Hegel was right.
However *that other* consciousness and *that other* freedom
are never given to me; for if they were, they would be *known*
and would therefore be an object, which would cause me to
cease being an object. (Ibid., p. 271.)
85 "The Other is, to be sure, the condition of my being-unrevealed.
But he is the concrete, particular condition of it." Ibid., p. 269;
"First, the *Other's look* as the necessary condition of my objectivity is the destruction of all objectivity for me." Ibid.
86 Arthur C. Danto, *Jean-Paul Sartre*, Modern Masters, New York,
Viking, paperback edn, 1975, pp. 111–12.
87 Ibid., p. 111.
88 "The presence to me of the Other-as-a-look is therefore neither a
knowledge nor a projection of my being nor a form of unification
nor a category. It *is* and I cannot derive it from me." Sartre, op.
cit., p. 272.
89 Marjorie Grene, *Sartre*, New Viewpoints, New York, Franklin
Watts, paperback edn, 1975, p. 145.
90 Ibid., pp. 146–7.
91 See n. 84 above.
92   The escape of the world and of my self from me when it is
absolute and when it is effected towards a freedom which is
not mine, is a dissolution of my knowledge. The world
disintegrates . . .; but this disintegration is not given to me; I
can not know it nor even think it. (Sartre, op. cit., p. 272.)
93 Ibid., p. 269.
94 "It is as fact — as a primary and perpetual fact — not as an
essential necessity that we shall study being-for-others." Ibid.,
p. 283.
95   It would perhaps not be impossible to conceive of a For-
itself which would be wholly free from all For-others and

which would exist without even suspecting the possibility of being an object. But this For-itself simply would not be 'man.' (Ibid, p. 282.)

96   "If someone looks at me, I am conscious *of being* an object. But this consciousness can be produced only in and through the existence of the Other." Ibid., p. 271. This brief statement of the argument leaves the conclusion implicit. See also Sartre, p. 268, and n. 85 above.

97   Ibid., p. 276. See also nn. 81 and 84 above.

98   Thus I am referred from transfiguration to degradation and from degradation to transfiguration without ever being able either to get a total view of the ensemble of these two modes of being on the part of the Other — for each of them is self-sufficient and refers only to itself. (Ibid., p. 297.) See also n. 51 above.

99   Ibid., p. 271.

100   It is for and by means of a freedom and only for and by means of it that my possibles can be limited and fixed. A material obstacle can not fix my possibilities; it is only the occasion for my projecting myself toward other possibles and can not confer upon them an *outside*. (Ibid., pp. 270–1.)

101   Ibid., p. 271.

102   See Phyllis Sutton Morris, *Sartre's Concept of a Person: An Analytic Approach*, Amherst, Mass., University of Massachusetts Press, 1975, pp. 132 and 137. Morris's book is one of the better expositions in English; nevertheless, there are problems with it. Some of these will be discussed below.

103   Sartre, op. cit., p. 270.

104   Ibid., p. 273.

105   "But this limit can neither come from me nor be thought by me, for I can not limit myself; otherwise I should be a finite totality." Ibid., p. 286.

106   Ibid., p. 268.

107   Ibid., p. 270.

108   "But it follows that even in reflection I assume the Other's point of view on my body; I try to apprehend it as if I were the Other in relation to it." Ibid., p. 355.

109   Morris, op. cit., pp. 139–40.

110   Sartre, op. cit., p. 268.

111   Ibid., p. 270.

112   Ibid., p. 273.

113   Ibid., p. 274, 275. See also n. 85 above.

114   Ibid., p. 274.

115   Ibid., pp. 274–5.

116   Ibid., p. 275.

117   I apprehend in myself a certain 'being-looked-at' with its own structures which refer me to the Other's real existence. But it is possible that I am mistaken; perhaps the objects of the world which I took for eyes were not eyes; perhaps it was

only the wind which shook the bush behind me. . . . (Ibid., p. 276.)

118 Ibid., p. 277.

119 "It is the Other's *facticity*; that is, the contingent connection between the Other and an object-being in *my* world. Thus what is doubtful is not the Other himself. It is the Other's *being-there*." Ibid.

120 Each look makes us prove concretely . . . that we exist for all living men; that is, that there are (some) consciousnesses for whom I exist. We put 'some' between parentheses to indicate that the Other-as-subject present to me in this look is not given in the form of plurality any more than as unity. . . . Being-looked-at, by causing (some) subjects to arise for us, puts us in the presence of an unnumbered reality. (Ibid., p. 281.)

121 Ibid., pp. 278–9.

122 For the appearance of a man as an object in the field of my experience is not what informs me that *there are* men. My certainty of the Other's existence is independent of these experiences and is, on the contrary, that which makes them possible. (Ibid., p. 280.)

123 Ibid., p. 272.

124 Ibid., p. 269.

125 Ibid.

126 See n. 22 above.

127 Sartre, op. cit., pp. 269, 270–1, 275.

128 Ibid., pp. 272–3.

129 Ibid., pp. 270, 271, 277.

130 Ibid., pp. 269–70.

131 Ibid., p. 281.

132 Ibid., pp. 278–9, 282.

133 Ibid., p. 281.

134 Ibid., p. 277.

135 Ibid., p. 269.

136 Ibid., p. 286.

137 In fact we are not conscious of a concrete and individualized being with a collective consciousness; these are images which will be able to serve after the event to translate our experience and which will more than half betray it. But neither do we apprehend a plural look. It is a matter rather of an intangible reality, fleeting and omnipresent, which realizes the unrevealed Me confronting us and which collaborates with us in the production of this Me which escapes us. (Ibid., pp. 281–2.)

138 This 'being-looked-at' is presented as the pure probability that I am at present this concrete *this* — a probability which can derive its meaning and its very nature as probable, only from a fundamental certainty that the Other is always present to me inasmuch as I am always *for-others*. (Ibid., p. 281.)

139 Sartre would claim that no one could achieve the viewpoint necessary to provide this answer. See below, pp. 233–4.

140   Arthur Danto, op. cit., makes a similar point against Sartre on p. 122.

141   See below, pp. 249–54.

142   Reviewing my earlier discussion of this phenomenon in Chap. 3, pp. 161–5, may prove useful.

143   This view is even made explicit:

> Let each one refer to his own experience. There is no one who has not at some time been surprised in an attitude which was guilty or simply ridiculous. The abrupt modification then experienced was in no way provoked by the irruption of knowledge. It is rather in itself a solidification and an abrupt stratification of myself. (Sartre, op. cit., p. 268.)

144   It is this attitude which we shall call *indifference toward others*. Then we are dealing with a kind of *blindness* with respect to others. But the term 'blindness' must not lead us astray. I do not suffer this blindness as a state. I *am* my own blindness with regard to others, and this blindness includes an implicit comprehension of being-for-others, that is, of the Other's transcendence as a look. This comprehension is simply what I myself determine to hide from myself. (Ibid., p. 380.)

My contention here is that in some indifference there is genuine blindness to the consciousness of Others; there is no implicit comprehension of the social self which one is hiding from oneself; the indifference is *not* a *project* of the person in any explicit sense.

145   See Morris, op. cit., pp. 141–3.

146   See n. 100 above.

147   This point is amplified in Frithjof Bergmann, *On Being Free*, Notre Dame, Ind., Notre Dame University Press, 1977, Chap. 3.

148   Sartre elsewhere recognizes this, cf., Sartre, *Transcendence of the Ego*, New York, Farrar, Straus, & Giroux, 1957, pp. 61–8.

149   Sartre, *Being and Nothingness*, p. 282.

150   "This is the fact that being-for-others is not an ontological structure of the For-itself. We can not think of deriving being-for-others from a being-for-itself as one would derive a consequence from a principle." Ibid.

151   ". . . nor conversely can we think of deriving being-for-itself from being-for-others." Ibid.

152   "Of course our human-reality must of necessity be simultaneously for-itself and for-others." Ibid.

153   "What the *cogito* reveals to us here is just factual necessity: it is found — and this is indisputable — that our being along with its being-for-itself is also for-others." Ibid.

154   Ibid., pp. 282–3.

155   Ibid., p. 283.

156   Ibid.

157   If in general there is an Other, it is necessary above all that I be the one who is not the Other, and it is in this very negation effected by me upon myself that I make myself be and that

315

the Other arises as the Other. (Ibid.)

158 "This negation which constitutes my being and which, as Hegel said, makes me appear as the Same confronting the Other, constitutes me on the ground of a non-thetic selfness as 'Myself'." Ibid.

159 ". . . that selfness is reinforced by arising as a negation of another selfness and that this reinforcement is positively apprehended as the continuous choice of selfness by itself as *the same* selfness and as *this very selfness*." Ibid.

160 Ibid., p. 287.

161 Ibid., p. 283.

162 Ibid., pp. 284–5.

163 This double negation, however, is in a sense self-destructive. One of two things happens: Either I make myself not-be a certain being, and then he is an object for me and I lose my object-ness for him; in this case the Other ceases to be the Other-Me — that is, the subject who makes me be an object by refusing to be me. Or else this being is indeed the Other and makes himself not-be me, in which case I become an object for him and he loses his own object-ness. (Ibid., p. 285.)

164 Ibid.

165 Ibid.

166 Yet this Me, produced by the one and assumed by the other, derives its absolute reality from the fact that it is the only separation possible between two beings fundamentally identical as regards their mode of being and immediately present one to the other; for since consciousness alone can limit consciousness, no other mean is conceivable between them. (Ibid., pp. 286–7.)

167 "Since I can not realize both negations at once, the new negation, although it has the other negation for its motivation, in turn disguises it." Ibid., p. 287;

Thus by one and the same stroke I have regained my being-for-itself through my consciousness (of) myself as a perpetual center of infinite possibilities, and I have transformed the Other's possibilities into dead-possibilities by affecting them all with the character of *'not-lived-by me'* — that is as *simply given*. (Ibid., p. 288.)

"In this way I *recover* myself, for I can not be an *object for an object*." Ibid., p. 289. See also n. 163 above.

168 "This original presence can have meaning only as a being-looked-at or as a being-looking-at; that is, according to whether the Other is an object for me or whether I myself am an object-for-the-other." Ibid., pp. 279–80.

169 Ibid., p. 287.

170 Ibid., p. 288.

171 Ibid., pp. 288, 289.

172 Ibid., p. 289.

173 Ibid., pp. 287, 291, 292.

174   Ibid., p. 297.
175   Ibid., p. 293.
176   Ibid.
177   Ibid., pp. 293. 294.
178   Ibid., p. 293.
179   Ibid., pp. 296—7.
180   Ibid., p. 297.
181   Ibid., pp. 423—9.
182   Ibid., p. 287.
183   See above, pp. 189—90.
184   One might think that the Other is acting on one through his social self, through the self one sees in him, but even this is inaccurate. When one *looks at* another, one transforms him; when one is inspired by another, one is transformed by him.
185   For the sake of argument I am setting aside the fact that cultures may be necessary for the emergence of any value qualities at all.
186   This phenomenon has also been discussed in Chap. 2, pp. 67—71.
187   Sartre, op. cit., pp. 413—33. Even in the *Critique of Dialectical Reason*, where he modifies his position significantly, Sartre still refuses to admit that groups are emergent totalities; individuals remain the fundamental realities.
188   Ibid., pp. 362—3.
189   Ibid., p. 363.
190   Ibid., p. 365.
191   Ibid., p. 363.
192   Ibid., pp. 365, 408.
193   Ibid., p. 408.
194   Ibid.
195   Ibid., pp. 243, 244.

Chapter 5   Some conclusions

1   The Cartesian picture is explicated in the Introduction above, pp. 1—4.
2   See pp. 24—6 and 27—8 above.
3   See p. 26 above.
4   See pp. 67—71, 77—8, and 90—1 above.
5   See pp. 64, 73—4, and 113 above.
6   See pp. 133—6 above.
7   See pp. 132—3 above.
8   See pp. 183—6 above.
9   See pp. 209—10 above.
10 See pp. 26, 28—31 above.
11 See pp. 32—4 above.
12 See pp. 67—71, 78—80, 98—100, 185—6 above.
13 See pp. 67—71 above.
14 See 134—6 above.
15 See pp. 185—6 above.
16 Jean-Paul Sartre, *Critique of Dialectical Reason*, trans. Alan Sheridan-

Smith, London, NLB, 1976, especially pp. 45—7, 374—82, 445—79, and 664—77.

17 See pp. 249—54 above.
18 See pp. 51—5 above.
19 See pp. 126—9 above.
20 One influential text which supports this view is Claude Lévi-Strauss, *The Savage Mind*, Chicago, University of Chicago Press, 1966.
21 See pp. 59—60 above.
22 See pp. 78, 161—5, and 221—3 above.
23 See pp. 23—6 above.
24 See pp. 199—201 and 235 above.
25 See pp. 202—6 and 237—8 above.
26 See pp. 194—9 and 247—9 above.
27 See pp. 67—71 above.
28 See pp. 62, 73—4 and 96—8 above.
29 See pp. 123—6 above.
30 See p. 136 above.
31 See pp. 134—6 above.
32 See p. 137 above.
33 See pp. 127—30 above.

List of texts cited

Primary sources

Major sources

Hegel, G.W.F. (1977), *Hegel's Phenomenology of Spirit*, translated by A.V. Miller, Oxford, Oxford University Press.

Heidegger, Martin (1962), *Being and Time*, translated by John Macquarrie and Edward Robinson, New York, Harper & Row.

Husserl, Edmund (1960), *Cartesian Meditations: An Introduction to Phenomenology*, translated by Dorion Cairns, The Hague, Martinus Nijhoff.

Sartre, Jean-Paul (1956), *Being and Nothingness: An Essay on Phenomenological Ontology*, translated and introduced by Hazel E. Barnes, New York, Philosophical Library.

Sartre, Jean-Paul (1957), *Transcendence of the Ego: An Existentialist Theory of Consciousness*, translated, annotated, and introduced by Forrest Williams and Robert Kirkpatrick, New York, Farrar, Straus & Giroux, Noonday Press.

Sartre, Jean-Paul (1976), *Critique of Dialectical Reason*, translated by Alan Sheridan-Smith, London, NLB.

Scheler, Max (1970), *The Nature of Sympathy*, translated by Peter Heath, Hamden, Archon.

Minor sources

Austin, J.L. (1970), *Philosophical Papers*, 2nd edn, edited by J.O. Urmson and G.J. Warnock, Oxford, Oxford University Press.

Ryle, Gilbert (1949), *The Concept of Mind*, New York, Barnes & Noble.

Wittgenstein, Ludwig (1958), *Philosophical Investigations*, translated by G.E.M. Anscombe, n.p., Macmillan.

Wittgenstein, Ludwig (1972), *On Certainty*, edited by G.E.M. Anscombe and G.H. von Wright, translated by Denis Paul and G.E.M. Anscombe, New York, Harper & Row, Harper Torchbooks.

Secondary sources

Bergmann, Frithjof (1977), *On Being Free*, Notre Dame, University of Notre Dame Press.

Danto, Arthur C. (1975), *Jean-Paul Sartre*, Modern Masters, New York, Viking Press.

de Beauvoir, Simone (1953), *The Second Sex*, New York, Knopf.

Findlay, John (1962), *Hegel: An Introduction and Re-examination*, New York, Collier.

Føllesdal, Fagfinn (1972), 'Husserl's notion of noema,' in *Phenomenology and Existentialism*, pp. 241–50, edited by Robert Solomon, New York, Harper & Row.

Gelven, Michael (1970), *A Commentary on Heidegger's "Being and Time"*, New York, Harper & Row.

Grene, Marjorie (1973), *Sartre*, New Viewpoints, New York, Franklin Watts.

Hyppolite, Jean (1974), *Genesis and Structure of Hegel's "Phenomenology of Spirit"*, Northwestern University Studies in Phenomenology and Existential Philosophy, translated by Samuel Cherniak and John Heckman, Evanston, Northwestern University Press.

Kojève, Alexandre (1969), *Introduction to the Reading of Hegel: Lectures on the "Phenomenology of Spirit"*, assembled by Raymond Queneau, edited by Allan Bloom, translated by James H. Nichols, Jr, New York, Basic Books.

Kaufmann, Walter (1965), *Hegel: Texts and Commentary*, New York, Anchor.

Kelly, George (1972), 'Notes on Hegel's "Lordship and Bondage",' in *Hegel: A Collection of Critical Essays*, pp. 189–217, edited by Alasdair MacIntyre, Garden City, Doubleday & Co., Anchor.

Laing, Ronald (1969), *Self and Other*, New York, Pantheon.

Laing, Ronald (1970), *Knots*, New York, Pantheon.

Merleau-Ponty, Maurice (1962), *Phenomenology of Perception*, International Library of Philosophy and Scientific Method, translated by Colin Smith, London, Routledge & Kegan Paul.

Morris, Phyllis Sutton (1975), *Sartre's Concept of a Person: An Analytic Approach*, Amherst, University of Massachusetts Press.

Rosen, Stanley (1974), *G.W.F. Hegel: An Introduction to the Science of Wisdom*, New Haven, Yale University Press.

Sokolowski, Robert (1974), *Husserlian Meditations*, Northwestern University Studies in Phenomenology and Existential Philosophy, Evanston, Northwestern University Press.

Index